THE
POLITICAL
ECONOMY
OF BASIC
HUMAN NEEDS

THE POLITICAL ECONOMY OF BASIC HUMAN NEEDS

Bruce E. Moon

Cornell University Press Ithaca and London

To my father,
whose values and vision remain alive,
reflected in these pages

Contents

PART IV
Distal Influences on State, Society, Economy, and
Basic Needs

Acknowledgments

It is impossible to acknowledge individually my debt to the scores of scholars whose work is cited throughout this book. I can only hope that the volume itself will repay them in some small measure for their contributions to my understanding of the vital issues surrounding the plight of the poor.

I do want to personally acknowledge, however, the essential contribution made by my longtime friend and collaborator William Dixon. The project in which this work is grounded began as a joint effort which has produced several co-authored papers. Indeed, Chapter 6 is based on our 1985 article in the *American Journal of Political Science*, and Chapter 7 originated in our 1986 article in the *Journal of Conflict Resolution*. More than that, our thinking has been so intertwined that I can no longer distinguish which ideas were his and which were mine. I wish that he had been able to collaborate fully on this volume; it surely would have been improved by his involvement. As it is, his contributions have been substantial and I am grateful for them. Simply put, this volume would not have been possible without him.

I also acknowledge the support of my many friends and colleagues at Lehigh University. Their encouragement has been vital at many points. I owe special thanks to Rajan Menon, Michael Raposa, Richard Matthews, and Henri Barkey.

Most important, I thank my family for sharing all the pain of writing, but, alas, very little of the pleasure. In particular, Beverly Winters Moon has been a constant inspiration while enduring with good humor the demands this project has placed on her.

Bruce E. Moon

Bethlehem, Pennsylvania

PART I

The Study
of Basic
Human Needs

Chapter 1
Basic Human Needs

Basic Needs Attainment: The Mission

In some nations, the lives of the poor are like those in Hobbes's state of nature: "nasty, brutish, and short." By contrast, the poor fare dramatically better in other nations despite similar levels of aggregate wealth. It is a central mission of political economy scholarship and the goal of this study to understand the processes that produce these differences.

The welfare of individuals is often—though wrongly—assumed to be synonymous with development. Instead, development should be understood as a broad umbrella concept that denotes a complex set of interactive processes. The resultant structural, institutional, and behavioral changes offer different faces to the viewer depending on the perspective from which they are approached. In contrast to more frequently studied dimensions such as aggregate growth, this book singles out the welfare of the mass citizenry for special attention. More specifically, the focal point is a particular feature of this welfare face of development, namely the extent to which basic human needs have been attained by all members of a society.

The distinction between development and welfare is important because both are often thought of in terms of standard production measures such as GNP (Seers, 1973). But the assumption that development improves welfare is only approximately true and the counterexamples, some of which are sketched below, are dramatic and numerous enough to have spurred a serious challenge to development theory in the last couple of decades (Fishlow, 1972; Chenery et al., 1974; Adelman and

Morris, 1973; Seers, 1973; Griffin, 1978; Streeten, 1981; Morris, 1984). Moreover, welfare gains, even when they do occur, are shared very unequally among the population.

Although the uneven distribution of welfare within societies has long been acknowledged (Adam Smith, 1976; Marx and Engels, 1969), it was not as widely recognized until more recently that this unevenness is itself a highly variable property of nations (Pant, 1974; Singer, 1979). Thus, the belief that poverty could be attacked directly and that success could be achieved out of proportion to aggregate growth was later in developing (Lewis, 1955; Myrdal, 1968; Griffin, 1977). By the late 1970s, however, reducing absolute poverty as a central or even primary goal had become the new orthodoxy (Hoadley, 1981; Streeten, 1981).

Development approaches that emphasize basic needs attainment and absolute poverty reduction are the heirs to a history of efforts to rethink development goals dating from at least the late 1960s. While each of these approaches rejects GNP growth as the sole aim of development, both the targets chosen as companion goals and the relative emphasis placed on each have subtly shifted over time. The motivation underlying all these attempts to "dethrone GNP" is a concern about issues of distribution. The advance of these alternative theoretical views and planning principles was fueled through the 1960s and 1970s by widening evidence from field-workers that rapid economic growth and diminished standards of living were by no means incompatible outcomes. As the frequency of these experiences belied the interpretation that they were idiosyncratic, the conviction that development thinking had to incorporate these lessons spread among development agencies.

The International Labour Organization (ILO) was among the first to press for alternative development objectives. It emphasized employment creation on the grounds that GNP growth generated by capital-intensive production could not only worsen income distributions but, by increasing unemployment, actually produce growing poverty side by side with growing plenty. Although employment creation did not become the dominant priority of development planning as the ILO had hoped, the potential for perverse distributional consequences of aggregate growth did become an enduring theme of most subsequent development thinking.

A pivotal event was the poverty-oriented 1973 speech of Robert McNamara, then president of the World Bank, to the Board of Governors in Nairobi. In it he called for action to alleviate absolute poverty, which he defined as "a condition of life so degraded by disease, illiteracy, malnutrition, and squalor as to deny its victims basic human necessities" (McNamara, 1973: 6–7). Following the Nairobi address, the Bank spearheaded both the theoretical effort to construct a vision of economic development with poverty concerns in the foreground and the policy effort to seek means of channeling development in directions that would reduce poverty.

The resulting complementary family of approaches often referred to collectively by the surname "growth with equity" is by now well known. The "redistribution with growth" strategy, laid out in a 1974 World Bank volume of the same name, emphasized the shifting of investment into areas that would maximize benefits to poverty groups. If the output and productivity of the poor could be thus improved, incomes among those groups would be expected to rise and welfare gains to follow. "Human capital" approaches emphasize that the improvement of the skills and capabilities of the poor, especially via education and training, should be pursued as a capital investment with side benefits in the form of welfare gains for owners of "human capital." "Rural development" strategies focus on asset patterns in agriculture, advocating, for example, land reform to optimize production while leveling incomes and reducing absolute poverty. Basic human needs strategies fit comfortably within this family, yet go beyond it.

Basic Human Needs Defined

The goal of reducing absolute poverty is often expressed in terms of increasing the provision of basic human needs. In fact, these two goals are virtually interchangeable in concept and complementary in definition and measurement. Both are principally concerned with the quality of life of the poorest elements of society. The needs considered basic are those minimally required to sustain life at a decent material level. Conventionally, these are defined in terms of adequate food, water, health care, shelter, and minimum education. Adequacy is defined in a minimum way and measured in terms of observable outcomes rather than in relation to income or consumption of such basic "goods." Thus, the most common indicators of national achievement of basic needs are life expectancy, infant mortality, and literacy.

Identifying absolute poverty arrives at a similar destination via a slightly different path. The "absolute poor" are defined as those at risk of poverty-induced undernutrition because of incomes too low to afford a minimal caloric intake, usually 2,250 calories per person per day. Because that caloric requirement is controversial (Lipton, 1988: 8–15) and because both incomes and prices are difficult to specify, estimates of the number of absolute poor are often unreliable. Thus, outcome indicators like those just mentioned are often used instead. Employing them involves very little loss of meaning since, for example, the number of people at risk of undernutrition is surely reflected in mortality rates. More specific discussion of the indicators used to measure basic needs attainment appears in Chapter 2.

In this book, basic needs attainment is accepted as a development goal, but commitment to the meeting of basic needs does not entail commitment to any particular strategy for bringing it about. Indeed, this book has rather little to say about development strategies and even less about specific programs designed to alleviate poverty. Instead, it is an effort to fill an often-observed lacuna in basic needs studies: in what kinds of nations have basic needs standards—such as those in life expectancy, infant mortality, and literacy—been met and in which has basic needs attainment lagged? Nonetheless, in order to clarify the meaning of basic needs, it may be helpful to briefly sketch characteristic features of basic needs strategies.

Because these strategies narrowly identify and directly target a problem of basic needs attainment, they tend to be sectorally specific and often geographically limited. The underlying philosophy of achieving minimum effects on a maximum population is represented most clearly by "barefoot doctor" programs, which expressly provide relatively low-quality medical care to many poor people rather than higher-quality care to the much smaller number who can afford its greater cost (Streeten, 1979; Isenman, 1980). Precise targeting of particular groups (usually requiring rural bias) and an emphasis on short-term relief can achieve a highly cost-effective outcome by mimimizing the "leakages" that dominate "trickle-down" approaches. Lipton (1988: 49), for example, calculates that perfect targeting would permit the basic needs goal of eliminating caloric deficiency in the entire population to be accomplished with less than 2 percent of GNP, even in the desperately poor nation of Bangladesh.

Despite differences among them, most basic needs strategies contain quite radical and controversial components, especially land reform, which pits the rural poor against more politically powerful landowners. Such redistribution of existing resources entails a revolutionary—and unlikely—transformation of alliances among the state and various social groups. Employment generation schemes call for redirecting investment to human capital, labor-intensive production, infrastructure, and public facilities. State action to redistribute income or directly subsidize consumption through fiscal spending and tax policies is a common element.

The core of these efforts is an emphasis on short-term changes that dramatically better the material and nonmaterial living standards of the very poor. These changes are assumed to lay the groundwork for more rapid and desirable growth in the future, though it is unclear whether this approach requires a willingness to sacrifice some conventionally measured long-term growth in economic aggregates. The public case for such approaches typically denies the trade-off or emphasizes its short-term character. Moreover, as Ahluwalia and Chenery (1974) point out, aggregate growth rates are strongly weighted to growth in income of the richest elements of society. Regardless of actual outcomes, the paradigm's roots in equity ideals and redistributive politics guarantee strong opposition from those who prefer more liberal economic administration of policies more oriented toward output and external competition.

The Case for Emphasizing Basic Needs

The focus on the relative living standards of the poor is motivated by three considerations. First, the normative case for concern with the poor is unassailable, universal, and compelling. There is virtually no major strand of religious or, indeed, secular humanist philosophy which does not recognize the virtue, if not the moral imperative, of charity in the face of need. The challenge that "the measure of a society is the way it treats its poor" strikes a resonant chord even if those threatened by it stop short of subscribing to the "idea that the basic needs of all should be satisfied before the less essential needs of a few," as Streeten (1981: 8) so elegantly puts it. Indeed, Rawls (1971) elevates this idea to the status of a moral principle derivable from rational calculation under uncertainty as much as from inherited religious tradition. Anyone who has seen the blank stare of a hungry child need look no further for an incentive to cope better with the problem of abject poverty.

Second, a study of the processes that determine welfare outcomes can open a window that exposes other facets of national development, including some not visible from other angles. This exposure is particularly significant because aggregate economic growth has attracted so much inquiry that the growth-centric principles derived from its study have come to dominate both our vision of development and the manner in which we have sought to shape it. This book aims to complete the picture by offering a welfare-centric approach that directs attention to the processes that make individuals poor as well as those that make societies wealthy.

Third, the provision of basic human needs appears to require few compromises among alternative normative goals. Whatever one's notion of "the good life," it presupposes freedom from early death, for example. The key issue in this regard concerns the alleged trade-off between growth and equality which some have suggested is implied by the U-shaped curve between level of development and equality found in cross-national studies (Kuznets, 1963; Robinson, 1976; Ahluwalia, 1974; Chenery and Syrquin, 1975; Okun, 1975; Flammang, 1979). Analyses of shorter-term growth, however, find no such evidence (Adelman and Morris, 1973; Chenery et al., 1974), and most have concluded that just as growth does not eliminate poverty, egalitarianism does not slow material progress (Isenman, 1980; Hicks, 1980; Berry, 1984).

Indeed, there is good reason to suppose that, particularly at low levels of income and among poorer sectors, improvement in the provision of basic needs may be *necessary* for rapid growth. For sizable percentages of the population, no further growth in efficiency or productivity can occur until basic human needs are met. Narrowly, it is hideously true that decent nutrition is required to provide humans the raw energy levels to perform useful work, and to sustain brain function at levels necessary for intelligent action (Bliss and Stern, 1978). More broadly, basic literacy is necessary for the growth of production processes associated with classical industrial development, to say nothing of the high-technology processes that represent the future. In short, abject poverty constitutes inadequate investment in the human resources that are the only ones possessed in abundance by the poor (World Bank, 1980a). Thus, the presence of unmet basic needs is itself a barrier to development.

Finally, emphasis on basic needs measures like life expectancy may spur action by eliminating doubt about the appropriateness of income-related goals. First, arguments advanced by various conservatives concerning the incentive-dampening effects of income transfers do not apply to the end state of basic needs (Gilder, 1981). It cannot be argued that the poor are better off dead in the same way it can be argued that they may be better off with smaller short-run incomes. Second, the notion that the condition of the poor has been exaggerated or that it reflects primarily unwillingness to work is defeated by the extremity of the results captured by measures of basic needs. It cannot be seriously argued that the forty thousand children who die of malnutrition-related causes every day are not really poor nor that the 15 percent of all children who die before the age of one in tropical Africa are looking only for a handout. In this respect, the concept of "life chances" is the great lever on specious arguments of incentives or effort. A person is truly poor—no argument, no rhetorical trick, no intellectual sleight of hand can deny it—when his poverty kills him. In nations—or, indeed, in neighborhoods—where the life expectancy is low, poverty is a *real*

problem, most immediate to the children and to the poor, but as concrete in its reality to large segments of the population as the flies
around the faces of children too feeble to brush them away.

Thus the maintenance of minimal standards of living is a prerequisite
for economic growth, political development, social evolution, cultural
adaptation, and spiritual fulfillment. Basic human needs are, in short,
basic.

A word must be said about the reduction of income inequality, a
parallel goal pursued primarily because of the assumed link between
income and welfare (Chenery et al., 1974). Though the two cannot be
perfectly distinguished, this book is concerned with the absolute poverty of basic needs deprivation rather than the relative poverty associated with income inequality. Of course, definitions of the former must
always reflect a standard of reference that imbues judgments with a
certain amount of the latter (Marx, 1969). Witness, for example, Adam
Smith's (1976: 82) explanation that "by necessaries I understand not
only the commodities which are indispensably necessary for the support of life, but whatever the custom of the country renders it indecent
for creditable people, even of the lowest order, to be without."

Nonetheless, the measurement approach taken here minimizes this
subjective, contextual element for several reasons. First, it is desirable
that goals be realistically achievable, and social stratification is historically more persistent than abject privation. As Streeten (1981: 20)
points out, defining poverty in terms of inequalities "would make poverty eradication rather like the electric hare used to spur on grey-
hounds at dog races." Second, equality is not so primary a normative
imperative as survival, which is made possible only by the provision of
basic human needs (Rawls, 1971; Beckerman, 1979). Third, it is easier
to compare actual provision of basic needs to concrete standards than
to evaluate interpersonal utilities that include perceptions of inequality.

The Role of Political Economy Scholarship

The focus of this book is on the broad-scale social, political, and economic processes that yield basic needs outcomes. It does not evaluate
the effects of particular policies nor counsel on their future implementation. These valuable pieces of the puzzle have been pursued by policy analysts and development administrators (Hofferbert, 1985; Lappé
and Collins, 1977; World Bank, 1980a, 1980b). But the perspective offered by political economy argues that this approach does not go far
enough.

The problems cannot be understood or solved within the narrow confines of program analysis because they are the product of interactions among countless social, political, and economic processes. Some of these are strongly influenced by government programs, but policy actions are far from simply related to the solution. The consequences of even a single government program are too complex to be isolated, and the list of actions potentially related to basic needs levels is long indeed. It would certainly include exchange rate arrangements, credit policies, tax levels and distributions, food price subsidies, education programs, and multinational corporation controls—and probably dozens of others. In fact, many of the policies with the greatest impact on basic needs levels are not even designed to have implications for absolute poverty. Where complex dynamics make even the relationship between economic growth and welfare improvements equivocal, the diagnostic role of micro analysis is necessarily limited.

Of course, government is itself a relatively small part of the problem since most of the determinants of basic needs levels are beyond the immediate control of policy makers. Moreover, even if state policy is critical, the greatest barrier to alleviating absolute poverty seldom lies in the lack of technical knowledge or administrative skill. Political will is usually more important than improved technique. Interestingly enough, the point is granted even by those who have devoted their energies to the narrower task of policy design. The paradigmatic *Redistribution with Growth*, for example, observes that "the key factor is the emergence of a coalition of interests able to grasp power that sees some advantage in implementing a redistributive strategy" (Chenery et al., 1974: 72). Unfortunately, in most policy planning this key reformist coalition "appears to emerge as a deus ex machina" (Ayers, 1984: 80).

Of course, these approaches are complementary despite their differences. For example, health care analysts have attempted to model the determinants of health levels for both individuals and societies. The former are surprisingly resistant to intrasocietal differences (Boardman and Inman, 1983; Edwards and Grossman, 1983) while the latter emphasize a "technical production function" (Newman, 1983) typified by the formulation of Grosse and Perry (1983: 244–45):

> The problem of determining what "explains" mortality and changes in mortality is similar in concept to determining the production function of an industrial or agricultural product. That is, many inputs, resources, and environmental conditions are necessary. At any given level of output, all the factors of production make contributions. The question of whether to increase the use of some or decrease the use of others is answered by testing the effects on changes in output of small changes in one or another of the inputs.

This view *assumes* the existence of a central "producer" with a single-minded commitment to cost-minimized production of the "good" in question. This formulation of the problem is fully appropriate only in the mythical case of a state that affords the highest priority to citizen welfare and is unconstrained in its resource allocation. Rather than assuming that such a state exists, however, this book is oriented toward discovering the circumstances under which a more or less close approximation to it may arise.

Basic Needs Attainment: The Puzzle

Thus, this book seeks an explanation for basic needs performance at the broad level of political economic structure, with an emphasis on the orientation and strength of key actors. Of course, the value of the approach itself is an empirical question. If basic needs determination occurs primarily at the micro levels of policy decision and program implementation, correlates of basic needs performance at the system level should be elusive. If, by contrast, levels of basic needs can be predicted from such structural elements, one might conclude that government policies are either ineffectual or themselves entailed by the structures that predict outcomes.

The centerpiece of the analysis is a cross-national statistical study of 120 nations designed to answer the deceptively simple question, "In what kinds of economies, societies, and polities are basic needs most effectively met?" The dependent variable is the Physical Quality of Life Index (PQLI) created by M. D. Morris (1979) for the Overseas Development Council. Its components—infant mortality, life expectancy, and literacy—are discussed in more detail in Chapter 2. The central cross-sectional analysis is supported by a panel design and a lagged design when appropriate. The interested reader is directed to the elaborate discussion of research design found in that chapter.

There is good reason to suppose that an analysis of political economic structure can shed light on the problem. The World Bank has surely expressed interest in learning from "country experience" (Streeten, 1981; Ayers, 1983; Stewart, 1985), and a number of analyses have been undertaken. For example, previous studies have generated a list of nations whose basic needs performance is surprisingly strong and identified a group which have attained lower levels of welfare than would be expected on the basis of overall societal wealth. Preliminary analyses have attempted to tie these lists to attributes that would explain these outcomes.

This study thus begins where the others have ended: with the puzzles that these patterns generate. The goal of the book is threefold: to confirm in a more detailed and controlled study the patterns themselves, to explain theoretically why they should appear, and to piece together an integrated picture of the dynamics that yield basic needs performance.

The book is motivated as much by the absence of expected patterns as by the appearance of mysterious ones. Among the former, the most striking fact is the great variation in basic needs performance found even among nations at similar levels of development. Only about half of the variance in basic needs measures can be accounted for by development measures like GNP per capita. Further, some individual nations stand as stark exceptions. The most widely noted case is that of Sri Lanka, whose PQLI of 82—achieved with a GNP per capita of $179—compares with Singapore's 83 ($2,111), Venezuela's 79 ($2,171), and Portugal's 80 ($1,535). Burma is also a frequently cited success story with a GNP per capita of $105 which supports a PQLI of 52. Countries with similar levels of aggregate wealth include Upper Volta (16), Chad (18), and Rwanda (27). Dramatic underperformers include Ivory Coast, whose GNP of $506 yields a PQLI of 28, while the poor in nations of similar wealth fare dramatically better: Ecuador (68), Albania (75), and South Korea (82). Clearly there is much more involved in the welfare of the poor than aggregate wealth.[1]

This conclusion does not mean, however, that the factors responsible are clear. Indeed, some seemingly obvious explanations fail. Government spending levels on health and education do not seem to matter. Nor is there an association with overall levels of public spending. Military expenditures show no regular pattern. Numbers of medical personnel have no consistent effect. Studies indicate that neither the percentage of population with access to potable water nor the aggregate caloric intake account for the differences. In particular, a major priority of previous analyses has been the stipulation of the political characteristics of the most and least successful nations in basic needs provision. Rather than finding a single archetype, however, "a glance at the good' performers shows that they are a very disparate lot, from any point of view. All three continents are represented; large countries and small; countries of every political persuasion are on the list; and countries which have pursued very different economic strategies" (Stewart, 1985: 70).

1. Nor are these cases statistical flukes. These same contrasts emerge when alternative basic needs indicators are used, in various studies with different data sources, and, most significantly, at widely separated points in time. Indeed, even differential economic growth rates between nations account for less variation than enduring dispositions to better basic needs performance in some nations than others. Whatever factors produce these differences in basic needs attainment are long-lived and consistent in their effects.

Against this backdrop, this book attempts a more theoretically grounded and more methodologically rigorous search for patterns by employing an approach more attentive to the insights of the schools of thought in political economy. At its conclusion, we will see that patterns do emerge, that these patterns are consistent with theoretical explanations, and that they can be integrated into a model of basic needs attainment which accounts for nearly 95 percent of the variance in basic needs levels. Indeed, the striking cases identified above are not exceptions to the rules, but rather precise manifestations of rules not previously recognized. For example, the success stories of Sri Lanka and Burma are not out of line with the patterns revealed in the final model of this study—in reality, Burma's basic needs performance is actually significantly *lower* than predicted. Nor is Ivory Coast—cited above as an underperformer—an exceptional case. In fact, among the seven nations that appear to be underperformers in the comparisons above, six are subsequently seen to provide *higher* levels of welfare than expected on the basis of a proper model of basic needs attainment. Further, three of the five apparent overperformers actually achieve *lower* basic needs levels than predicted when the patterns are properly specified.

These seeming contradictions thus become part of the puzzle this study is designed to solve: why do some countries achieve basic needs levels so far out of line with expectations derived from their aggregate wealth? And what are the alternative patterns that *should* form our expectations concerning basic needs provision? The answers can be revealed only by a systematic, theoretically grounded, methodologically rigorous study of the political economy of basic human needs.

While no single theory is being espoused or tested in these analyses, the eclectic theoretical elements are compatible with the framework formed by the political economy perspectives of world systems and dependency theory. Effects traced across levels of analysis and over substantial periods of time form a system of complex causal dynamics rather than a collection of simple, elegant, and isolated propositions. This complexity is introduced gradually, however, following Chapter 2's introduction to the technical details of the analysis, a discussion the reader is invited to skim. The major themes are discussed in the following three sections, which parallel the organization of the substantive analyses of the book itself into three interrelated parts. Part II considers the most proximate economic influences on the welfare of the poor—the level of development and the structure of the economy—in artificial isolation. Part III takes up the character of the political and social systems that are partially a consequence of economic structure and partially autonomous from it. Part IV describes more distal influences including linkages between the nation and the global political economy and the historical residue of precolonial and colonial systems. These

more distal influences tend to be channeled through the more proximate mechanisms, as they shape the evolution of the domestic economy and polity and thereby influence basic needs levels.

Proximate Economic Determinants

The basic structure of the economy is the single largest determinant of
basic needs provision and certainly the most immediate. Although one
might assume that basic needs levels are a function of GNP per capita,
political economies with different structural arrangements produce
characteristic resource distributions. In fact, even though the empirical
analysis of Chapter 3 begins by considering each nation's basic needs
level relative to GNP per capita, aggregate national wealth explains
only about half of the cross-national variance in PQLI (Morris, 1979;
Sheehan and Hopkins, 1979; McGranahan et al., 1985). Thus, Chapter
4's analysis of basic needs propensities of economic systems highlights
several processes that tend to lower the PQLI relative to the levels that
would be expected on the basis of aggregate national wealth. Some of
these are constants in *all* systems, more are characteristic of certain
paths of development, and still others are a consequence of a given *level*
of development.

We consider, for example, (1) conditions that affect patterns in the
return to capital, land, and labor referred to as the "functional distribution of income," (2) implications of the size distribution of income attributable to unequal endowments of key productive factors, (3) inefficiencies engendered by the absence of institutions with the resources
to provide collective goods, (4) sectoral and geographical inequalities
attributed to backwash effects and market dynamics, especially in response to external articulation, (5) resource loss through direct external
flows or various forms of unequal exchange, and (6) "unproductive"
consumption.[2]

---

2. Inequality is surely a significant hallmark of nations whose basic needs performance
is likely to lag national wealth because any increment of income shifted from the poor to
the more well-to-do is less likely to be targeted to basic needs fulfillment. Since most of
the processes that generate inequalities also tend to lower relative basic needs levels, the
literature on income inequality is a key source of theoretical explanations for processes
that carry implications for basic needs provision, though it must be emphasized that
inequality is only one predictor of underperformance in the provision of basic needs. The
limits of the inequality–basic needs relationship are most starkly illustrated by the fact
that the most egalitarian societies—those centered around an economy of subsistence
agriculture—are also the worst providers of basic needs. Moreover, inequality must be
conceived in much broader terms than income. To rely only on income risks dubious
assumptions concerning the stability and comparability of prices, the identity of house-

A consideration of these factors leads to Chapter 3's specification of the functional form of the relationship between national income and basic needs which is logarithmic.[3] Chapter 3 also identifies those stages of development within which basic needs progress is most rapid as well as those in which basic needs levels are most sensitive to structural differences *among* systems of similar aggregate wealth. The resulting analyses of Chapters 4, 8, and 9 pay particular attention to the input and product composition of production, the distribution of the labor force across sectors, and the size and character of the foreign sector.[4] Although the bulk of the study concerns development within a market economy, the differences among capitalist, precapitalist, and state socialist systems are considered.

To foreshadow that analysis, alternative modes of production provide starkly contrasting levels of basic needs. State socialist systems are vastly superior providers of basic needs, in part because they disable several key market mechanisms that generate inequalities in capitalist systems. The ideological commitment of the state to programs that directly affect basic needs levels is also a key factor. By the same token, systems dominated by the "precapitalist" subsistence agricultural sector engender basic needs levels strikingly below those of even equally poor political economies with more modern production and exchange systems. The inability of nonmonetized systems to generate a fungible surplus available for investment in collective goods is probably largely responsible.

Among capitalist systems, dependency theory's insights on immiserizing growth and peripheralization of the poor within dependent development enhance the study of economic structure. Industrialization and balanced growth paths that minimize external linkages generate superior basic needs levels relative to economies marked by export growth derived from multinational corporation investment or specialization in mining and capital-intensive sectors. In particular, basic needs levels track the percentage of the labor force in agriculture much more closely than GNP per capita, even when the latter is corrected for known international variations in purchasing power due to incommen-

---

holds as consumption units, and consumption as the determinant of welfare. The emphasis on income also ignores the importance of the public/private and monetized/nonmonetized distribution of consumption.

3. That is, basic needs levels increase as GDP increases, but at a progressively shrinking marginal rate.

4. These structural elements are later shown to assume special importance because they affect other visible processes—including political development and state growth, government spending priorities, urbanization, and fertility behavior—as well as processes that are more difficult to measure directly, such as class formation.

surable price structures. Agricultural production typically yields a lower level of basic needs provision than industrial processes, although some differentiation is required.[5]

Domestic Political and Social Determinants

A second major source of differential basic needs performance is found among the social and political correlates of development. Chapter 5 examines two sets of these. The first encompasses the mediating effect of urbanization dynamics as well as the role of the demographic transition. The second lies in the nexus of social relations and the role of the state. The analysis of the distribution of economic and political power among various groups bridges the discussion of the economy and the polity.

Chapter 6 reports that the size and strength of the state, its foundation in democratic or authoritarian processes of state-societal relations, the ideological orientation of the ruling regime, and the impact of the classlike status of state personnel are all significant determinants of basic needs levels. To again foreshadow the theoretical and empirical analysis, the interests of the poor can be protected in two very different ways. First, as implied by democratic theory, political systems that emphasize mass representation through the electoral mechanism and maintain institutions that protect civil liberties perform very well with respect to basic needs. Of course, such institutional structures cannot arise in all contexts and the actual impact of the democratic processes themselves is not easily distinguished from the effects of the political economy that spawns them. Nonetheless, even controlling for these determinants, democracy is positively associated with superior basic needs achievement. In short, democracy works.

A second path to basic needs achievement concerns regime ideology. In addition to the above-mentioned positive effect of state socialist systems, regimes on the right of the political spectrum significantly underperform those of the center and left. Even excluding state socialist nations, there is another intriguing complexity in this relationship, however. The effect of ideological differences is magnified by an interaction with the size of the state. If the fiscal size measure is interpreted

5. As noted, subsistence agriculture underperforms even relative to its characteristically low income levels while plantation economies, by contrast, perform very well in the provision of basic needs. Through an intricate series of causal connections rooted in the colonial past, plantation systems overcome the propensity of political economies with a strong external orientation and highly unequal land distributions to yield relatively low PQLIs.

as an indicator of the capacity of the state to achieve goals defined by an ideological disposition, it is not surprising that the worst basic needs performances are turned in by countries with a large state headed by a rightist regime.

The success of these general factors in predicting basic needs levels also eliminates any significant explanatory power for more specific policy programs. Naturally, this finding should not be interpreted to mean that governmental programs concerning health and education, taxation, social security, and social welfare have no effect on the welfare of the poor. Rather, the analysis suggests that a considerable degree of commitment to such programs can be predicted from the more general model of economic and political effects (e.g., democratic governments engage in more welfare spending than nondemocratic rightist ones). Moreover, there are a variety of alternative program arrangements that achieve similar welfare levels.

One exception concerns military spending, which does retain a marked impact on basic needs levels even after controlling for the character of the ruling regime. The analysis of Chapter 7 indicates that that role is quite complex, however. The widespread socialization afforded by military service produces a modernization effect that can benefit the poor, while military expenditures may either progressively distribute income or harm the poor by diverting scarce resources and foreign exchange to weaponry. The capital intensity and the pay scale of the military seem to be the decisive factors in determining the net impact of the military budget.

Chapter 7 also focuses on the controversial role of the military in policy determination. In particular, military regimes are linked to basic needs propensities through four intermediate mechanisms, some of which appear to spur basic needs provision and others to constrain it. Since military regimes cannot be sharply distinguished from civilian regimes in many key respects—including spending priorities and the size of the military itself—the absence of a generalized and unequivocal impact on basic needs levels is not so surprising. However, even though the rightist orientation and antidemocratic norms characteristic of military regimes guarantee that they underperform the average nation, they appear to do no worse—perhaps even somewhat better— than most comparably nondemocratic, rightist civilian governments.

Distal (Historical and External) Determinants

The last part of the book seeks to link the pieces of the model into a more comprehensive structure by focusing on two types of more distal influences which are channeled through the more proximate ones discussed up to now. First, Chapter 8 considers the "spatially distal" arguments of world system and dependency theories. The domestic political economies of nations are shaped by their incorporation into the global economic and political system. Foreign investment and trade influence basic needs performance directly as well as indirectly by affecting most other domestic processes. The more abstract concepts of structural position within the global division of labor are also considered, but they are found wanting on both conceptual and empirical grounds. The core-periphery imagery serves some heuristic purpose, but it does not help much in directly predicting levels of basic needs, in part because the concrete features of national economies to which it applies are also accessible from other theoretical viewpoints.

Nonetheless, external economic relations *are* a factor in basic needs levels. When structural position is used as an umbrella to summarize and incorporate several relatively minor causal linkages, peripheral status is seen to produce the hypothesized effect on basic needs. More interesting, it is shown that the effects of trade fit the pattern expected by dependency and world systems theory. Among peripheral nations, a large trade sector appears to *harm* basic needs provision, while trade *improves* the welfare of the poor elsewhere.

Second, Chapter 9 treats the "temporally distal" effects of colonial history on the proximate determinants as well as basic needs levels themselves. Such influential contemporary features as plantation economies and extractive mining sectors—together with ethnic cleavages in the population—are a product of colonial decisions with lingering impact on the overall political economy. The length and character of the colonial experience and the identity of the colonial master are also shown to have impact on key political characteristics such as democratic practices and state ideologies over lags of several decades. Most notably, former British colonies have evolved more democratic and centrist states than former French colonies, which are also marked by a greater incidence of military regimes. Nations enjoying a relatively long period of postcolonial independence have significantly higher basic needs levels than those experiencing independence more recently.

Finally, Chapter 9 introduces some additional elements that are more effective from the standpoint of predicting basic needs levels than in explaining them. These factors—especially religion and regional variations—are introduced as puzzles for future research to probe in greater detail.

In sum, the political economy of basic human needs is an intriguing window on development processes. Eschewing the emphasis on economic growth opens a wider range of phenomena to investigation and permits a broader-scale treatment of the influences that determine the way poor people live. In the process, the analysis accounts for well over 90 percent of the cross-national variance in PQLI while weaving together explanations that span social, political, and economic factors within a framework that highlights rather than deemphasizes the causal complexity of the interactions.

Chapter 2
Research Design

Measuring Basic Human Needs Attainment

The welfare-centric perspective on development which has introduced innovative conceptual and theoretical thinking has also given rise to new approaches to the measurement of economic development. Of course, the mounting evidence that national economic growth is often accompanied by both relative and absolute declines in living standards of the poor has obvious implications for both policy and theory (Fishlow, 1972; Adelman and Morris, 1973; Chenery et al., 1974; Morawetz, 1977; Streeten, 1981; Griffin, 1981). Just as clearly, it suggests that neither standard indicators of aggregate production nor distributional measures based on income are adequate gauges of the extent to which basic human needs have been provided universally.

First, GNP is a measure of neither consumption nor personal income, both of which are conceptually one step closer to welfare than is production (Nordhaus and Tobin, 1973). Even the standard economic concept of consumption is not entirely adequate because it implies monetized purchase while "consumption" as an input to welfare or needs satisfaction implies no such step.[1] Further, what many consider

---

1. This difference is substantial in economies with large nonmonetized sectors, as is well known, but the extent of the nonmonetized sector is not always adequately appreciated. Usually identifed with the subsistence agriculture sector in poor countries, it also includes a substantial number of services that in all nations are used without being paid for (personal and family labor, for example). Whether or not such consumption enters

"unnecessary" consumption that does not contribute to welfare (e.g., defense spending) varies across nations and over time (Best and Connolly, 1982; O'Connor, 1973).[2] Thus, there is widespread agreement that GNP is an inadequate measure of even aggregate welfare (Kuznets, 1953; Seers, 1976; Denison, 1971; Okun, 1971; Abramovitz, 1959).

Second, the distributional considerations that are invisible to GNP measures are only partially addressed by income inequality data. Both aggregate and distributional measures expressed in the metric of currency rely on assumptions about the stability and universality of prices which are always violated by comparisons between nations and frequently by those within nations as well. The internation variation in prices is by now a well-known consequence of segmented markets for nontraded goods but more unified markets for tradables (Clark, 1951; Beckerman, 1966; Barlow, 1977). The tendency of official exchange rates to reflect the latter better than the former—and political pressures better than either of them—produces the need for a purchasing power parity method of comparison. Indeed, a major project to correct for this distortion has estimated the error to be as high as 350 percent for some poor but relatively closed nations (Kravis et al., 1975, 1978a). The extent of the error in intranation comparisons—especially between urban and rural areas—has not been measured with similar rigor, but it is also known to be relatively large (Kuznets, 1972; Lipton, 1977).[3] In sum, the same income buys very different levels of basic needs fulfillment, even within a single country.

Third, differences in accounting units can obscure individual level

---

national account statistics will vary from nation to nation according to the method of payment. Surely a measure of welfare should not make this distinction. The most familiar case in wealthy nations is that of the household member who joins the formal workforce and whose unpaid domestic labor is replaced by a combination of labor hired directly (e.g., a housekeeper) and changed consumption patterns, the greater cost of which is indirectly hired labor (e.g., prepared foods). The increase in monetized transactions suggests a larger increase in consumption than in fact occurs. Cross-national as well as cross-time differences occur in these patterns, but it has been estimated that as much as 25 percent of *American* product derives from the unreported activities of housewives (U.S. Dept. of State, 1974: 7).

2. That portion of GNP which originates in services designed to allocate rather than produce goods is another interesting example. Arrangements for police protection, penal expenses, insurance, legal services, brokerage fees, etc. vary considerably across nations and comprise quite different percentages of GNP. Yet they make only a small contribution to welfare.

3. Moreover, even these adjustments are necessarily inadequate because they sum price differences that vary markedly across goods; because the consumption baskets of different groups vary widely—especially between rich and poor and between urban and rural groups—there is no single weighting equally relevant to all. The most obvious example is the differential role of food prices, which dominate the budget of the poor while only marginally affecting the real incomes of the more well-to-do.

consumption. On the one hand, household level data hide the actual distribution of consumption within households, especially that of adult men versus women and children.[4] Cross-national differences in these distributions may be large enough to be significant for basic needs provision. On the other hand, much consumption occurs not out of personal income but from public spending. Thus, in systems with high levels of public provision of infrastructure necessities such as water and education, inequality in private incomes may overstate the inequality experienced in welfare. Since services provided in common are often markedly cheaper than if purchased individually—consider that community water supplies are bargains from the metropolis to the village common well—marked cross-national welfare differences can occur at similar income levels.

Finally, the cost of goods is not a measure of their welfare-enhancing value. For example, a personal auto and a public bus may have a very similar economic value (i.e., sale price) but a very different use value (and thus welfare impact). It also must be recognized that actual consumption choices may vary considerably even among those of similar income.[5] Moreover, prices are not the only barrier to consumption; "goods" required to meet basic needs (e.g., food, education, potable water, medical treatment) may simply be unavailable at any feasible price.

All of these issues suggest reasons why economic growth may not generate enhanced citizen welfare. GNP may rise for artifactual reasons involving price movements or sector shifts without any real change in production levels. More broadly, any given change in GNP is consistent with several alternative "consumption" pattern changes that carry very different consequences for welfare. In response, some have attempted to measure welfare on the basis of adjustments to GNP (Nordhaus and Tobin, 1973; Kravis et al., 1975, 1978b), while others have used income approaches to focus on the poor (Sen, 1976, 1981; Chen-

4. Worse, most compilations of income inequality data contain a mixture of measures derived from individual surveys and household surveys. These are obviously not comparable. Moreover, even the laudable effort to correct for the difference between them by introducing a dummy variable (Russett et al., 1981) must fail, since the intrahousehold distribution is far from a constant across nations. In sum, "there does not now exist an adequate conceptual and technical basis for common international measurement of income distribution and cross-national comparisons of it" (McGranahan, 1979).

5. For example, the relationship between maternal literacy and infant mortality has been attributed precisely to the different contents found in the consumption basket of an educated family even if its monetary value does not differ from that of an uneducated family (Kasarda et al., 1986; Meegama, 1986). This same pattern underlies the concern with the distorting effect of multinational corporations on consumption patterns (e.g., breast-feeding vs. infant formula) (Biersteker, 1978).

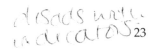
ery et al., 1974; Pyatt and Round, 1977). Fortunately, such problematic inferences are not necessary; instead, welfare can be measured more directly and with greater sensitivity to distribution by social indicators that focus on outcomes.[6]

To be useful, social indicators must be readily available for a large number of nations and comparable across the cases. Some promising indices have failed due to demands on data availability which are impractical for all but the richest countries, within which the incidence of absolute poverty is relatively small anyway (Stone, 1975; Seers, 1977; Drewnowski and Scott, 1966). Others introduce ethnocentric bias or deny the contextual differences among nations. The use of government expenditure on health or education as an indicator, for example, assumes wrongly that the proportion of these expenses borne by governments is constant across nations while ignoring the tendency of cross-national differences in medical technology to be more divergent in cost than in effects on mass welfare.

Outcome indicators such as life expectancy tend to be more tractable than measures of their presumed inputs. A common measuring stick for nutrition, for example, is difficult to find because needs vary with climate, body size, and activity level while the diets characteristic of nations differ in proportions of animal and vegetable protein and other nutritional necessities. Similarly, housing *needs* and the *type* of housing stocks available, which are determined in part by climate and other variable factors, both vary cross-nationally more than the *adequacy* of housing. Thus, the consumption of goods that are thought to meet basic needs is more difficult to measure than is the evidence that needs have, in fact, been met.

Such technical concerns, of course, are not the only considerations in choosing a measure of welfare for the poor which reflects "basic human needs." The definition of what needs are basic must always be a prior question, despite its uncomfortable roots in ethics, aesthetics, and metaphysics. Given the desire to avoid ethnocentrisms and value biases, a general measure should concentrate as much as possible on least common denominators, needs that are widely if not universally shared and needs that are instrumental toward a wide variety of other values rather than desirable in and of themselves. Such a choice can never be wholly unassailable nor defended outside of a given normative frame of reference, of course.

Nevertheless, the efforts of development planners have tended to

6. Due to inherent ceiling effects implicit in some (e.g., life expectancy) and the equal weighting of individuals in others (e.g., literacy rates or infant mortality), social indicators are surely less skewed than income or wealth.

coalesce around a very small set of measures that reflect one common principle—that life chances are the great adjudicator of alternative claims to value priority. That which kills is bad, that which prolongs life is good. Length of life seems to correlate fairly highly with physical quality of life simply because whatever kills in high doses tends to produce illness and misery in lower doses.[7]

The available measures are thus widely known and though researchers with particular interests may choose among them in idiosyncratic ways, the options are both limited and well agreed upon. The five "basic needs" and the indicators conventionally used to assess their leverage on life chances are health (life expectancy, health expenditures, doctors per thousand population, hospital beds), education (literacy, primary school enrollment, education expenditures), nutrition (caloric and protein intake), water supply and sanitation (percent with potable water, access to sanitation facilities, infant mortality), and housing (no good indicator available) (Hicks and Streeten, 1979). Nearly all efforts to compile a list of core elements of welfare—especially one weighted to the attainment of basic needs by the poor—have included these elements and very few others (McGranahan et al., 1972, 1985; OECD, 1973; U.N. ECOSOC, 1975; Morawetz, 1977; USAID, 1977; UNESCO, 1976; Sheehan and Hopkins, 1979; Sivard, 1979; Morris, 1979).

The choice among these indicators is less difficult than it might appear for two reasons. First, many of these indicators violate principles noted above, especially the desire to measure results rather than inputs. Second, the validity of each of these as measures of overall well-being among the poor is sufficiently great that the intercorrelations among items are quite high. Such correlations have been found in numerous studies with different indicators, samples, and time frames and are confirmed for the sample in this study below (McGranahan et al., 1972, 1985; Streeten, 1981; Silber, 1983; Moon and Dixon, 1985). This pattern suggests the option of combining the best of the indicators into a single composite index, the procedure I use here, following M. D. Morris's (1979) creation of the Physical Quality of Life Index (PQLI) from infant mortality, life expectancy, and literacy.

7. The correlation is not perfect, of course, since one can live in misery for a long time or live happily though briefly. Such occurrences are more the exception than the rule, however, and, in any case, usually appear at levels of welfare above that which is of greatest concern to us. Millionaires in developed countries can have miserable lives extended to lengths more commonly associated with the healthy and happy, but the correlation between health and life chances is less attenuated by such artificialities in the poorer strata that attract our focus.

The Physical Quality of Life Index (PQLI)

The advantages and disadvantages of an index approach have been hotly debated (Morris, 1979; Hicks and Streeten, 1979; Silber, 1983; Ram, 1982). Few disagree on the relevant considerations, though the balance of the argument has been assessed differently by various researchers. Opponents argue that a loss of information results from creating an index of indicators that measure slightly different components of basic needs results. If these components respond differently to government programs, for example, use of a broad index might obscure changes that would be visible if the more narrow individual components were used. Thus, sectoral policy implications might be missed. Operationally, the combination of measures also requires a weighting and scaling scheme that is essentially arbitrary. Opponents of indices sum up their case: "It is not possible to prove that the PQLI gives a 'correct' index of progress on human needs, as opposed to some alternative index having different weights or a different selection of component indices. It is not clear what is gained by combining the component indices with a weighting system that cannot be defended" (Hicks and Streeten, 1979: 576).

These arguments are, of course, well-known considerations in measurement theory and are not unique to this particular index construction. Thus, the responses are equally well known. Indeed, the rules of thumb for choosing between the two sets of arguments are also relatively well established. First, the use of an index rather than a series of colinear items greatly eases the burden of analysis. In the case of the PQLI, using the items rather than the index would multiply by three the time and cost of analysis and the space of presentation of results. Such a burden should not be taken on lightly, certainly not in the absence of evidence that it matters significantly. In fact, quite to the contrary, there is evidence that it does not matter much, simply because of the extremely high colinearity among all the plausible alternatives (Moon and Dixon, 1985; Moon, 1987a; Morris, 1979; Silber, 1983; Ram, 1982). Most important, analyses reported in Appendix 4 confirm that the substantive conclusions of this study—as reflected in the parameter estimates of the final model—are not significantly affected by the decision to use the index rather than the components.

Second, if one assumes that the individual items are different manifestations of a single theoretical construct, then the construct should be represented by a single index rather than by multiple measures. An index is particularly appropriate if the underlying construct has synergistic components, as many have suggested (Isenman, 1980; World Bank, 1980a, 1981) and some quantitative analyses have confirmed

(Grosse and Perry, 1983; Sheehan and Hopkins, 1979). Streeten (1981: 22), oddly enough a critic of the PQLI, makes this case best when he refers to "problems that are apparently separate, but, on inspection, prove to be related." Moreover, as Streeten also warns, using single indicators may lead to an overly narrow interpretation of the problem and a policy response that fails to recognize that the measure is a proxy for a concept, not the concept itself. Thus, one might devise policies that lead to improvements in an indicator while not really attacking— or at least not attacking efficiently—the inadequate provision of basic human needs.

Third, combining the items will also reduce the impact of the idio-syncrasies of any one item. This is an important consideration because there may well be cases in which one of the indicators is more an arti-factual consequence of a developmental peculiarity than an accurate indicator of a more general construct.[8] Moreover, in light of concern with data quality, an index, which attenuates a problem in any one variable, is to be preferred.[9] In sum, an index should yield more accu-rate measurement of the underlying concept than any individual com-ponent and thus a more accurate model of its determinants.

Of course, the choice between an index and its components also de-pends very much on the purpose for which they are to be used. In that sense, it is no surprise that development administrators and econo-mists with sector level interests in policy evaluation would opt for the concrete, though narrow, indicator, while the political economy gener-alist would opt for the proxy of a broader concept. The former is no doubt superior for the purposes of sector level evaluation. If, for exam-ple, one wished to evaluate a policy of rural health care, the presence of literacy in an output index would only introduce extraneous error. However, for a political economist concerned with structural transfor-mations not well represented by any single measure, the specificity and concreteness of the individual indicator are neither necessary nor desirable. Of course, the more highly correlated the individual items, the less consequential the choice becomes.

This study uses the most widely known of the available composite indicators, the Physical Quality of Life Index (PQLI), originally con-

8. McGranahan et al. (1985) present a detailed analysis showing the developmental peculiarities of nations. Many of these are probably due to measurement error, but many others are quite real.

9. McGranahan et al. (1985) use a conceptually similar approach. They correct indi-vidual data items by comparing actual scores to scores expected on the basis of regres-sions involving closely related items. In essence, they use an implicit notion of an index to reconstruct individual items rather than combining individual items into a composite index.

structed by Morris (1979) for the Overseas Development Council and
subsequently featured in annual editions of the Council's publications.
It is calculated as the simple arithmetic mean of measures of infant
mortality, life expectancy at age one, and basic literacy rate. The items
are summed after being individually scaled from 0 to 100. The 0 point
represents the worst performance by any nation since 1950, and the
highest feasible performance in this century is set equal to 100. In practice, infant mortality ranges from 229 per thousand to 7, life expectancy
at age one from 38 to 77; literacy is represented by the raw percentage
(from 5 to 100).

The implicit weighting obtained by simply adding the individual
scales does not appear to have much influence. Reweighting the individual components in various plausible ways produces measures with
a Spearman rank order correlation always above .98 (Morris, 1979: 48).
This is so simply because the individual items are themselves so highly
correlated—in all cases above .93 in a 116-nation sample (Moon and
Dixon, 1985); above .897 for 150 nations (Morris, 1979: 54); above .87 in
Silber's (1983) sample of 19. These figures are all well above the levels
of intercorrelation usually thought sufficient to make a composite index
fruitful. The figures would have to be higher to justify Streeten's flip-
pant remark that an index is not necessary since any individual component would do just as well. They would also have to be considerably
lower to justify concern that the items are not alternative indicators of a
single underlying concept.[10]

Of course, alternatives to the PQLI exist.[11] From a theoretical view,
there is very little to choose among these alternatives since they employ basically the same indicators in only slightly different combinations and with marginally different weightings. Empirically, neither direct replication (Moon and Dixon, 1985, and Appendix 4 below) nor

10. For this reason, more elaborate latent variable approaches (such as LISREL) are
unnecessary. They seek to limit the effect of measurement error by constructing "latent
variables" from observed ones. However, as noted above and demonstrated in Appendix
4, the model is very robust across different plausible constructions of the dependent
variable.

11. Silber (1983) proposes an elaborate weighting of morbidity data to correct for the
distribution-insensitive quality of life expectancy. His approach requires (1) data on the
age distribution of deaths, (2) the normatively based choice of a utility function involving
preferences for the optimal age at death and a weighting of the value of a one-year life
extension for those who die at each age, and (3) a multistage exponential calculation. For
the loss of generality, the smaller sample of nations and time periods which can be
included, the ambiguity of six different alternative measures of life expectancy, the noncomparability of results obtained from other choices among the alternatives, and the far
greater complexity of the calculation, one gets measures all of which are correlated with
PQLI above .95. Other alternative indices are those of McGranahan et al. (1972, 1985),
Ram (1982), and Stone (1975).

divergent conclusions from different indicators and indices have shown the choice to be consequential (Sheehan and Hopkins, 1979; Ram, 1982; McGranahan et al., 1972, 1985; Morris, 1979; Russett et al., 1981; Fulop and Reinke, 1983; Grosse and Perry, 1983). The selection of the PQLI is based simply on its ease, its very well known construction, and thus the comparability gained by using a measure widely reported in other studies.

The Reliability of PQLI Data

No one involved in studies of social indicators is under any illusion about the quality of the data. Indeed, users are better placed to know the limitations than are critics and no less candid. Morris (1979: 126) simply observes that "registration systems [for births and deaths] in most countries—certainly in most developing countries—are inadequate if they exist at all. Birth and death data often are the products of heroic estimation and/or periodic surveys."[12] Inadvertent errors occur due to inadequacies in the data collection process and the inherent difficulty of surveying relatively rare events like deaths in a relatively small sample (Morris, 1979; McGranahan et al., 1985).[13] These problems combine to limit reliability because estimates based on such fieldwork will tend to be unstable. The result is that data reported in successive years—or even for the same year by different agencies—will occasionally manifest uncomfortably wide deviations (McGranahan et al., 1985). Of course, deliberate manipulation of data by government officials cannot be ruled out either. Fortunately, there are three reasons for believing that these difficulties will have a limited impact on the conclusions of a study such as this.

First, cross-national statistical analyses make far fewer data demands than descriptive studies of a particular case. Indeed, so long as the errors are relatively small and randomly distributed, they need not be viewed with great alarm. Errors in individual data points do not seri-

12. While it would be foolish to deny that data problems exist, it would be equally foolish to dwell too much upon them. It is by no means evident that these problems are worse than in most data regularly utilized by social scientists. For example, social indicators do not require the use of the error-prone metric of official exchange rates, which have been shown to yield huge error (a factor of 3.5) for even that most respectable of indicators, Gross National Product (Kravis et al., 1975, 1978b).

13. Consider, for example, the frequency of infant death likely to be found in any feasible sample. With an average birthrate (about 40 per thousand population) and an average infant mortality rate (about 100 per thousand live births), a sample of 1000 would contain only 4 infant deaths. Huge samples would be required to produce a very narrow confidence interval around any estimate of such a rare event.

ously bias the parameter estimates in a study with such a large sample unless the error is quite systematic.[14]

Second, data points inaccurate enough to affect general relationships among variables are usually relatively easy to recognize. Some diagnostic and remedial work has already been undertaken at the original source on the data used in this book. Though the primary data are often generated elsewhere, compiling agencies such as the World Bank and branches of the United Nations routinely correct obvious cases of noncomparability. The most rigorous efforts to correct inaccurate measures have taken place at the United Nations Research Institute for Social Development (UNRISD, 1976, 1977; McGranahan et al., 1985), but the general procedure for recognizing suspect data points is both well known and frequently practiced at the major data compilation centers. Unusual data points can be immediately recognized because the major social indicators have been subjected to hundreds of empirical analyses and the usual patterns are well established. Fortunately, the most damaging error—the large and systematic variety resulting from manipulation—is also the most detectable. The comparison of data points over time as well as across cases is especially key to the identification of this source of error. The attempts of a regime to misrepresent its basic needs performance, for example, are constrained by the known resistance of PQLI measures to large short-term change. Thus, rapid fluctuations over time are easily recognized and regarded as suspect. The PQLI data used in this study have been further processed by Morris (1979).

Third, the current study attempts to minimize initial data problems, to diagnose those that remain, and to indemnify the conclusions against the biases they may introduce. Inevitably, however, a frequently faced dilemma must be acknowledged. One can allow important questions to remain unanswered due to poor data, or elect to go forward, do what one can to check data reliability, and acknowledge that results must be considered provisional until better data are available. Meyer and Hannan (1979: 7) represent poetically the position taken by this study: "We approached the task with the view that rational angels will acquire more reasonable fears about where to tread only if fools experiment. It also seemed clear that the retreat to more trustworthy data and safer analyses which characterizes much compar-

---

14. There is, of course, the strong suspicion that data error is likely to be largest and most frequent among relatively poor countries. This is not to say that measures are systematically inflated or deflated in such countries. It is the variance in the error term—not the error term itself—which is likely to be correlated negatively with level of development. This speculative pattern thus may diminish the efficiency of the estimates but it would not bias them.

ative research is often also a retreat from some of the most obvious and important intellectual issues of the field." Thus, the approach of this study to data reliability is cautious, but not disabling. It involves steps at each point in the study from data gathering to final model estimation.

The data gathering was carefully designed to limit problems of reliability and comparability. With very few exceptions, all of the values for any given variable come from the same source and thus avoid the problems of comparability which inevitably arise from combining sources. In nearly all cases, the data come from conventional sources frequently used in previously published research. Whenever possible, variables are measured over a range of years and the values averaged to minimize the impact of both conventional measurement error and fleeting conditions unrepresentative of a longer-term equilibrium.

To minimize the effect of idiosyncrasies in any one data source, alternative sources of the same or similar data were employed whenever possible. These multiple sources were used in two ways. As the model is presented chapter by chapter, the robustness of the interim results is confirmed by alternative parameter estimates reported throughout the text in footnotes. These alternative sources were also used at the conclusion of the analysis to test the final model in the more elaborate procedure described briefly below and documented in full in the appendixes.

Appendix 1 first establishes the overall reliability of the Morris data by comparing them with data from two alternative sources and then identifies particular cases in which the sources significantly disagree. This appendix also flags suspect data by noting the discrepant cases identified in previous studies, including those that document the usual patterns between health inputs and basic needs outcomes. Appendix 2 then augments the cross-source and cross-national pattern-checking with a cross-time analysis designed to identify errors exposed by too rapid (or too slow) change in indicators. The "alert lists" from these various diagnostics are then compared to pinpoint a smaller number of data points which warrant particular skepticism.

Of course, we are concerned not with the data error itself, but with the flawed conclusions it might produce. Moreover, it is surely inappropriate to regard any deviation from either a cross-national or a time-series pattern as a case of data error. Most of these deviations are accurate representations of real differences in national performance; to eliminate them from the analysis would strip the matrix of much of the variance that we want to explain. A study that omitted the most spectacular basic needs successes and the most distressing failures would surely limit our understanding of the processes involved and deny us the lessons that would enable us to duplicate the former and avoid the latter. Thus, the fourth step, reported in Appendix 3, involves the attempt to replicate the final model estimates on which the conclusions of the study are based, but over a sample of nations which omits these suspect cases.

Thus, one answer to the challenge of those who decry data flaws is found in the results of the Appendixes: the problems appear to be within the bounds of standard usage in cross-national aggregate data analysis. Further, the final model does not change significantly regardless of the sample over which it is estimated. The more relevant response, however, is the book itself. If the analysis contributes to the understanding of and future research in the political economy of basic human needs, the gamble on the data will have been worthwhile. If not, data limitations will not have been the principal weakness.

Explanatory Styles, Causal Structures, and Research Design

The choice among alternative approaches to exploring the determinants of success in basic needs provision must be made on the basis of both the special strengths and weaknesses of each approach and the skills of the individual analyst. The case for the choice made by this study—systematic quantitative examination of a broad cross-sectional sample—is sufficiently well known as to require no elaboration here.[15] Of course, other fruitful approaches have already been applied to the problem—such as the scrutiny of nations with exceptional success in welfare provision (Isenman, 1980; Streeten, 1981; Chenery et al., 1974)—and their insights are reflected in much of this analysis.[16] Of course, the case study method and quantitative analysis are necessarily

15. Measurement approaches that rely on quantitative indicators achieve greater precision and allow the presentation of a model with greater specificity which can be tested across a much wider range of cases. The necessity of making theoretical claims reducible to specified observables enforces a discipline and rigor on arguments that are otherwise prone to drift toward an ambiguity often not recognized until one attempts to apply them to another actual case.

16. The characteristic strengths and weaknesses of the case study approach are equally well known. These studies have been limited by their emphasis on a single case, their focus on success and inattention to failure, their reliance on a historical and contextual method that cannot sort out collinearity or identify variance, and the imprecision of their observations and conclusions. Of course, these analysts can treat in depth the particular details of an actual case and trace concrete causes and consequences in a thoroughly understood context. Still, even though the contextual richness of a historical case study can never be equalled by a broad-scale, aggregative study, the advantages of systematic quantitative analysis justify sacrificing the strengths of a case study approach.

complementary, and this study is appropriately seen in the context of a continuing conversation among analysts of different theoretical, methodological, and disciplinary orientations.[17]

In constructing and estimating a comprehensive model of basic human needs provision, this book walks a thin line between generality and specificity. Like Chenery and Syrquin (1975), the present study seeks what they call "stylized facts," a set of generalizations about the sequencing of structural changes that occur in most or all nations at similar stages in economic development. "Stylization" requires that many rare or idiosyncratic elements be ignored. Yet contemporary political economy theory emphasizes that development cannot be characterized as a linear process that unfolds everywhere in a similar pattern (Wilber and Jameson, 1979). Indeed, it is the variance in national experiences—from laudably high relative levels of welfare among the poor to drastically low ones—which motivates the study.

Between insisting on a single uniform process and admitting a hundred unique ones is the middle ground of recognizing the existence of several characteristic developmental paths. Chenery and Syrquin specify three such paths, distinguished by the size and economic resources of the nations that follow each, whereas this study seeks to identify empirically those paths that yield higher levels of welfare for the poor. The guiding theory of world systems and *dependencia*, for example, directs our attention to the influence of external factors in setting nations on paths that either accelerate or slow the economic transformation, political evolution, and social change that yield differential provision of basic human needs.

Unfortunately, there are no pat answers to the dilemmas in choosing among model approaches.[18] Particularly troubling is the complexity in-

---

17. The claims that seem reasonable on the basis of a single case must be checked against broader experience before they can be held to be valid even in the individual case, let alone true as a general pattern. Such comparisons are done informally in the above studies but can be done better with a larger sample, more systematic evidence, and a formal set of criteria. Similarly, claims that seem reasonable on the basis of an aggregate study must be applied to particular cases so that we can see if they shed light on the way these causal factors are actually played out in the individual case. Some of this application is done here, though it can be done better by the area specialist who knows the case more intimately.

18. Structural theories present particular challenges because the ordinary language formulations of theory seldom express a precise structure of causal interactions. Indeed, the picture offered of the causal structure often varies with the theorist and circumstance. The attempt to render statistically the causal logic of the world system argument that structural position affects the relative welfare of the poor is especially illuminating (Moon, 1987a). It was common in the early literature examining dependency effects on inequality to regress inequality on measures of structural position in an attempt to determine their "total effect." Of course, this approach fails to include control variables which

troduced by independent variables, which may be related to one another in complex ways. This issue should not be neglected because, for example, theoretical and empirical studies have established dependency—one of the factors thought to affect basic needs provision—as a partial determinant of many dimensions of the domestic political economy, including level of economic development (Bornschier et al., 1978; Weede and Tiefenbach, 1981b; Delacroix, 1977; Jackman, 1982), level of democracy (Bollen, 1983; Jackson et al., 1978; O'Donnell, 1979), state strength (Delacroix and Ragin, 1981; Rubinson, 1977), and ideological orientation of the ruling regime (Jackson et al., 1978; O'Donnell, 1979).

For this study I chose a hierarchical design meant to highlight rather than deemphasize this causal complexity. Zero-order correlations are frequently reported to assist in sorting out causal dynamics, but no important interpretations are made on that basis. Instead, the main analysis builds a comprehensive model by sequentially adding explanatory factors while taking note of the intercorrelations among predictor variables. Where appropriate, the results of a path analysis are reported.

With few exceptions, the analyses reported throughout the book are variants of a cross-national design. While the limitations of cross-sectional designs are well known, equally serious problems exist in the application of time-series or panel designs to the type of causal structure found in the determination of levels of basic human needs attainment. Because the linkage between the anticipated causal structure and the choice of research design is not widely understood, it is appropriate to treat in some detail the considerations that should guide a choice between cross-sectional designs and those that take account of time in various ways.

Cross-sectional designs are typically dogged by two related problems. First, the customary interpretation is that cross-sectional results reflect long-term adjustment of the dependent variable to the exogenous variables (Chenery and Syrquin, 1975: 134; Intrilligator, 1978: 64). The assumption that the measured relationship between variables represents an equilibrium condition is undermined if the dependent variable has not yet completely absorbed the effects of the independent variable because of lags in the causal mechanism. These concerns are

---

reduce misspecification and clarify causal mechanisms (Bornschier et al., 1978). For example, the actual effect of multinational corporations could not be distinguished from the effect of the conditions—such as level of development, state ideology, and mineral resources—that accounted for the presence of MNCs (Bornschier and Chase-Dunn, 1985). However, an analysis in which controls are introduced and the predictive power of structural position is then assessed through marginal gains in r^2 will tend to understate world system effects that operate *indirectly* through the control factors.

typically alleviated by the introduction of a measurement lag equal to the assumed causal lag in order to capture the delay in effect of one upon the other. The seriousness of the problem and the length of measurement lag necessary to compensate for it obviously vary with the particular application, but empirical analyses can help to establish both.

Second, cross-sectional designs cannot themselves establish the causal direction of the relationship. In fact, estimates of the causal effect of X on Y suffer "simultaneity bias" because a cross-sectional model cannot exclude the reciprocal causal effect—of Y on X—from the estimate. The first problem can nearly always be simply diagnosed and frequently alleviated, but the latter admits of only complex solutions that apply only under particular conditions. Moreover, there is a real trade-off in solving these two problems, as we see in considering alternative designs.

Both estimation problems spring from the fact that most relationships in the social sciences exhibit "a time structure of response in the gradual reaction of the dependent variable to a change in the explanatory variable." Thus, "it becomes necessary to take explicit account of lagged variables when the lag between the change in the explanatory variable and that in the dependent variable exceeds the period of observation of the variables" (Intrilligator, 1978: 176–77). In principle, how one "takes account" of the lag depends on whether one's research priority is understanding structures or forecasting change.

> In general, cross-section and time-series data yield different estimates of a model. These data and their resulting estimates are generally not comparable. . . . Time series data usually reflect short-run behavior while cross-section data reflect long-run behavior, in particular a greater adjustment to long-run equilibrium. . . . Neither estimate is 'wrong,' and which one to use depends on the purpose. For structural analysis, in studying certain long-run elasticities it might be appropriate to use cross-section data, while for purposes of short-run forecasting time-series data might be more appropriate. (Intrilligator, 1978: 63–64)

Thus the time-series designs, which strip the estimates of simultaneity bias, must also exclude the long-run adjustment process. Similarly, the in-between approaches of a panel or cross-lagged correlational design represent a trade-off that better incorporates a measurement lag but also provides a less satisfactory check against mistaking causal direction. Proponents of a panel design argue that it

> provides estimates of the existence of causal effects that are under most conditions more dependable than those produced by either cross-sectional or time-series analysis. It is not that there is any 'free lunch' associ-

ated with the use of panel analysis in the sense that strong causal inferences are produced without strong assumptions. Rather the assumptions
required for valid inference concerning the existence of causal effects in a
panel model are more realistic and plausible in this research context than
are those required for the same inference in either a cross-sectional or
time-series design. (Meyer and Hannan 1979: 5–6)

Quite obviously, this judgment must vary with the type of causal
structure assumed to exist in the particular case—most obviously, the
speed of the adjustment process, the speed of change in the exogenous
variable, and the divergence between short-run and long-run effects—
as well as one's confidence in those assumptions about the causal
structure. How these factors affect the choice of design in this study is
described more thoroughly below.

In practice, however, the choice depends at least as much on a number of more mundane factors concerning the resources available to
solve the research problem, especially the availability and reliability of
data and the range of values on relevant variables represented in the
sample. The latter consideration is an especially relevant factor in the
choice of cross-sectional over more time-sensitive designs (time series
or panels) for this study.

> A large part of the discrepancy between the two types of estimates is
> due to the fact that some factors omitted from the model vary system-
> atically across countries . . . , while other omitted factors vary system-
> atically over time. . . . Since the variation . . . is much greater among
> countries than in available time series, it is possible to get an idea of the
> nature of structural relations over a wide range of income and prices only
> from cross-country data. (Chenery and Syrquin, 1975: 117)

In summary, there are reasonably clear criteria for choosing among
the various approaches to time modeling. These approaches, in order
of increasing attention to cross-time and decreasing attention to cross-
national variance, are: (1) cross-sectional, (2) pooled cross-sections, (3)
panel designs, and (4) continuous time series. The criteria are as follows.

First, the greater confidence one has in the causal structure—particularly the direction of causation—the less necessary are the more elaborate time-modeling approaches designed to avoid false inference
based on reciprocal causation. This criterion highlights the adequacy of
the theory on which the model is built because the only alternative to
empirically ruling out certain causal paths is the willingness to discard
them on theoretical grounds. For most of the relationships discussed in
this study, the latter is easy. The history of colonial relations is temporally prior to current basic needs levels, for example, and economic

structure can be ascribed causal precedence to the welfare of the poor with reasonable confidence. Relationships such as that between democracy and inequality are more problematic, however, and suggest that an empirical check of causal direction would be welcome if it were possible (Rubinson and Quinlan, 1977). Fortunately, such causal ambiguity is rare; as we see below, the conditions for sorting out causal priority on the basis of statistical findings do not generally obtain.

Second, when the presumed causal lag is relatively long, more time-oriented approaches become less satisfactory. If, for example, the causal lag is twenty years, a time-series analysis using one year as the measurement interval will yield no reliable results, and even a panel design of less than twenty years will not fully pick up systematic effects (Meyer and Hannan, 1979). If a longer panel lag is not feasible due to data limitations or the absence of independent cases beyond that period, a cross-sectional design is necessary. Both are constraints for this study because the number of nations falls dramatically prior to 1960 and reliable data for even a handful of cases are absent prior to 1950. Further, it is widely believed that economic development processes do exhibit very long lags that exceed the range of accurate measurement. Investments in health care facilities, for example, may not be fully reflected in life expectancy for quite a long time. Certain of the empirical analyses reported throughout the book also suggest the existence of long lags; colonial histories, for instance, seem not to have exhausted their causal effects even yet.

Panel designs must also avoid a measurement lag greater than the causal lag, since such a design will also yield inaccurate estimates (Heise, 1970). Of course, shorter-acting effects can then be picked up by adding change measures on the independent variables (so-called delta predictors) to the panel, but only at the cost of reintroducing the simultaneity bias that panel designs are utilized to eliminate (Meyer and Hannan, 1979: 20).

A third and closely related consideration concerns the speed of change in the exogenous variables. The more rapid the change in the independent variable, the more necessary are continuous time-series designs, but if the variables change slowly, then the length of the lag becomes less critical because serial correlation will erode the differences between the results of models estimated with differing lags. By and large, the structural variables used as predictors in this analysis are relatively slow-changing.

Thus, while the limitations of cross-sectional designs for inferring direction of causality are well known, when the causal lag is long and change in both dependent and predictor variables is slow, no completely satisfactory approach to sorting out causal effects exists (Intrilligator, 1978). Panel designs are then less useful both because arbitrarily short measurement lags may misrepresent the time structure of causal response and because measurement error may be large relative to actual change in the dependent variable (Meyer and Hannan, 1979; Pelz and Andrews, 1964). Pelz and Lew (1970) and Heise (1970) demonstrate with simulated data that panel results are unusually sensitive to measurement error, sample error, measurement lag, and the stability of the variables. Indeed, under certain conditions, "when measurement lag departed substantially from the true causal interval, the cross-correlation and path coefficient could be opposite in sign to the actual causal influence" (Pelz and Lew, 1970: 36). In such cases, cross-sectional designs that "reflect long-term adjustment" are appropriate (Chenery and Syrquin, 1975: 134; Intrilligator, 1978).

Moreover, the more similar the effects of levels and changes (i.e., long-term and short-term effects), the less the need to disaggregate them through more advanced treatments of time. Finally, analyses of change assume that relatively short-run change is substantial. Because PQLI levels at 1960 and 1980—the longest available interval—are correlated above $+.95$, a panel design that analyzes change would little advance understanding of current levels. This high serial correlation does not mean that PQLI change has not occurred; rather, it has been proportional to "initial" levels. The correlation reflects great stability in the dependent variable which originates in part from measurement approaches and in part from very long causal lags. Consider, for example, that investment in education produces an increase in literacy rate which will continue until those educated pass from the populace, a period ranging around fifty years. Investments in infrastructure which produce potable water will benefit health conditions for the youngest members of society, but the benefit cannot be fully reflected in overall life expectancy for more than a generation. Thus, it can hardly be surprising that relatively short-term influences have only a marginal impact in the short term.

This causal lag not only produces change proportional to earlier levels, it also means that measures of change will suffer an abnormally high component of measurement error. For this reason, change in basic needs levels is known to be resistant to short-term explanation (Sheehan and Hopkins, 1979; Preston, 1976; World Bank, 1980b; Shin, 1975). In fact, panel designs yield such small increments of interpretable change that even the effect of increasing income has not been found a universal positive influence on some basic needs conditions (Grosse and Perry, 1983). The result is that cross-sectional designs have become the standard in examining basic needs issues. Indeed, change is more often examined with comparative cross-sections than with time-explicit designs (World Bank, 1980b).

For the current study, the case for a cross-sectional design is especially compelling. PQLI change manifests a strong auto-correlation coefficient, because the time lag of causation is very great and change in the independent variables is slow. Thus, short-term changes in the independent variables are neither large enough, fast enough, nor causally significant enough to measure through a time-series design or a delta regressor panel design. In fact, even relatively long panel designs will exaggerate the auto-correlation and underestimate the effects of other independent variables (Pelz and Lew, 1970). When the direction of causation is relatively clear—and in this study it is usually guaranteed by temporal priority—the cross-sectional design is fully adequate. Of course, the finding of a cross-sectional correlation, even if spuriousness can be ruled out, leaves open the question of whether the effect took place long ago or recently. Because there is some reason to believe that short-term and long-term effects may differ and that era effects may exist, that is a weakness that panel designs would help to correct.[19] Consequently, the study is based mostly on cross-sectional analyses, supplemented by panel analyses only when the issue of income change directly raises the question of differences in long-term and short-term impacts.

Data and Analysis

The unit of analysis in this study is the nation, though that does not imply that the values of the relevant variables are uniform throughout the unit. Indeed, this study is motivated precisely by the need to recognize distributional variation of welfare within a nation. Neither does the focus on nations imply that the causal system is coextensive with national boundaries. Although some key processes are surely national, others are not. A compromise is required which recognizes that the nation is overwhelmingly the measurement unit in available data sources even if it is not the causal unit in all the theories that inform the study. World systems and dependency theorists, for example, ar-

19. Bornschier (1985) argues that the predictability of national economic development success changes according to the system's location in the A or B phase of cycles of growth and contraction. Ragin and Bradshaw (1985) find that the determinants of deprivation change somewhat according to period. Meyer and Hannan's (1979) null panel but positive cross-sectional findings also suggest something of this sort.

gue that the appropriate unit is the global system (Chase-Dunn, 1981). This systemic focus implies two forms of analysis. One examines cross-time variation in the global system as it evolves, for example, through the growth of an *A* phase to the retraction of a *B* phase (Bergesen and Schoenberg, 1980). With three available time points—1960, 1970, and 1980—the present analysis can follow in only a limited way the suggestion of Bornschier (1985) that cross-time differences in significant systemic processes be sought in comparative cross-sections. The other form of analysis is implied by dependency theorists, who locate many significant processes in the interactions among blocks of nations with similar attributes (e.g., the core and the periphery). This cross-national analysis follows the essentially equivalent procedure of representing these groups of nations with dummy variables.[20]

Given the nation as the main unit of analysis, another issue concerns the sample of nations included. In order to preserve the general character of the analysis, all nations for which data are generally available are included. With few exceptions, the included nations are those commonly found in World Bank data sets.[21] Two objections to this choice may be raised. First, the inclusion of state socialist nations requires a translation of some key economic measures from the "material product system" of socialist countries into the "system of national accounts" accepted by capitalist nations. Because the differences between the systems are deeply conceptual and at base ideological, the translation is at best a hazardous enterprise.[22] Nonetheless, if we want to include the nature of the political economy or the ideology of the ruling regime among the explanatory variables, we must provide the variance on these variables necessary to allow such conclusions. Thus, there is no choice but to make the best of a difficult translation, though because the measurement error may be correspondingly greater for those nations, we must be alert to the distortion in the more general analysis caused by the inclusion of this group.

The second objection to the use of this large sample is that it includes nations at very different levels of development. Comparisons between similar variables in rich and poor nations can be misleading, because,

20. The reverse claim—that the real causal units are beneath the nation level—presents a more difficult problem for which the analysis must be less direct.

21. For reasons of data availability from other sources, some World Bank nations are omitted. Most often these are relatively recent nations for which even early 1970s data are problematic, due to change in the status of the nation—Angola and Viet Nam, for example.

22. Indeed, the source of the translation used here—the U.S. Arms Control and Disarmament Agency—no longer publishes such estimates, presumably because of the difficulty.

as Seers (1976) points out, the economic structure and the accounting methods of poor nations are no better represented by the national system of accounts (NSA) than are those of state socialist nations.[23]

It is also possible that key relationships differ across levels because of different social dynamics. This is the position of those who study only OECD countries and argue that the social, political, and economic dynamics of other nations, even Japan, are too different for a theory to have applicability beyond this homogeneous group. These arguments may well be correct, but once again the inclusion is necessary if the results are to have wide application. Further, at several points in the analysis, the robustness of the general findings is tested over key subsamples of nations.[24]

Most of the analyses, however, are conducted over the whole sample of 120 nations to maintain comparability. An exception occurs for a number of analyses that use data of considerable theoretical interest from the influential studies of Adelman and Morris (1967, 1973). Their sample of seventy-six nations excludes developed nations, socialist nations, and those for which data were not available for their time period of the late 1950s.

The core analysis is cross-sectional at the early 1970s, a time period that maximizes data availability from a variety of sources. To check for time shifts of the sort found in previous studies, the main analysis is augmented with an examination of 1960 and 1980 cross-sections (Chenery and Syrquin, 1975; Meyer and Hannan, 1979; Bornschier, 1985; Ragin and Bradshaw, 1985).[25] A panel analysis from 1960 to 1980 is employed in Chapter 3 to examine the impact of economic growth and in Appendix 3 to identify potential data problems.

All regression routines are those of SPSS-X. While many analyses using various combinations of hierarchical and stepwise designs were run to capture the interaction among the independent variables and the structure of the causal mechanisms, the reported results are all or-

---

23. Because the NSA originated in Britain in the interwar years, it reflects the theoretical and practical concerns of Cambridge economists who faced problems of unemployment and recovery; economic categories central to many Third World nations, especially nonmarketed production, are excluded or poorly represented in NSA.

24. Because some theorists have also suggested that the impact of some key processes like dependency is clearly visible only within middle-income nations, there is particular incentive to examine this group closely in isolation from others (Ragin and Bradshaw, 1985; Ragin and Delacroix, 1979; Delacroix and Ragin, 1981; Bornschier et al., 1978).

25. The former is the first really stable period for which data are widely available; 1970 is often thought of as the end of the post–World War II expansionary phase of the global economy, and 1980 reflects both the most recent year for which substantial data are available and a period well into a global downturn.

dinary least squares (OLS).[26] Most are presented both in the full form with the coefficients of all variables estimated and in the restricted form with only the significant variables retained in the analysis. The latter approach avoids misspecification due to inclusion of irrelevant variables, which can be just as disruptive as the exclusion of relevant variables.[27]

26. Where examination of residuals suggests a possible problem of heteroscedasticity, I use weighted least squares (WLS) estimation to confirm the stability of the model.

27. The inclusionary criteria are designed to reject those variables whose true parameter cannot be distinguished from zero. Retention requires a t value greater than 1 and a beta estimate larger than its standard error with a probability of significance greater than .10.

PART II

Before the State: Allocations by Market and Nonmarket Economic Processes

Chapter 3
Economic Development and Basic Needs

Wealth without Welfare

The goals of this chapter are both empirical and theoretical. Empirically, the basic relationship between GNP per capita and the PQLI must be documented as the starting point for a model of basic needs provision. Theoretically, I introduce some principles that underlie that relationship as preparation for the remainder of the analysis.

What relationship should we expect between PQLI and GNP per capita? Of course, the expectation of a smooth linear relationship rests on a simplistic view increasingly discredited—that poverty reduction in proportion to economic development is a natural and automatic developmental process. Basic needs advocates observe that wealth need not lead to welfare and that welfare—even if achieved—need not be evenly distributed. As Mahbub ul Haq (1971: 7) summarizes the controversy: "We were taught to take care of our GNP as this will take care of poverty. Let us reverse this and take care of poverty as this will take care of the GNP." An economic system that targeted all societal resources on the achievement of basic needs would no doubt yield a much higher PQLI than any contemporary system at a similar overall level of development. Basic needs levels lag the productive potential of the economy for many reasons.

First, capitalist economies contain sectors that have few positive welfare consequences and none at all for the life chances of the very poor. Consumption considered "unproductive" by this standard comes in a variety of forms.[1] In the public sector, for example, maintenance of civil order, protection of property rights, and expenditures on the military seem to consume an increasing share of societal resources. Among the many examples of similar expenditures in the private sector are insurance, advertising, and financial services. Of course, "wasted" consumption need not be unnecessary; these expenditures do perform functions. Indeed, some—such as certain welfare programs and state transfer payments—even directly benefit the poor. Yet, they may also be regarded as "waste" necessitated by the very structure of advanced capitalist political economies; the functions they perform would be either unnecessary or much cheaper in less advanced systems or noncapitalist ones (O'Connor, 1973; Best and Connolly, 1982).

Because the dynamic of a modern capitalist economy generates a structural necessity for spending on these functions, we may anticipate that capitalism underperforms in basic needs provision relative to socialist systems—an idea I explore in greater detail in Chapter 4. This consideration also provides our first hint concerning the relationship between GNP and PQLI: the marginal return of increasing national product for the provision of basic needs may decline as each increment is less likely to be targeted to basic needs and more likely to be targeted to system upkeep made necessary by development itself.[2]

Class Inequalities in Capitalist Development

A more frequent explanation for lagging basic needs levels concerns the effect of income inequality.[3] This effect is especially significant for the present purpose of stipulating the PQLI—GNP relationship because both class and sectoral inequalities, though endemic to capitalist development, are said to be more pronounced at certain stages of development. I remain somewhat skeptical, however, because both forms of inequality may depend much more on the *path* of economic develop-

1. Though often thought of in these terms, luxury consumption in personal goods is merely a reflection of income inequalities and represents presumed real increments to welfare, even though they may be proportionately small and not relevant to the interests of the poor.

2. This declining marginal return also follows from Lenski's (1966) thesis that changes in the relative strength of political, social, and economic actors—especially class representatives—result from structural change in the economy. Consequently, control of the surplus—and with it the level of equality—shifts with level of development.

3. Indeed, greater equality is generally assumed to increase overall societal welfare given almost any reasonable set of weightings of individual preferences. The special emphasis the PQLI affords the poor is not required to sustain the argument (Little, 1957; Meade, 1964; Lipton, 1968).

ment taken by a nation than on how far down the path it may have proceeded. Further, many of the social and political processes that target resources do not seem to vary principally by levels of development.

The sources of inequality in the size distribution of income are many and varied, but a substantial portion of it can be understood in relation to two patterns involving the factor share distribution of income. First, where wages represent the return to labor, interest the return to capital, and rents the return to land, the share of national product flowing to each factor of production varies cross-nationally. Second, the ownership of these factors by individuals is greatly unequal. Cross-national variance in the magnitude of the resulting income inequalities results from both differences in the return to a unit of each factor and differences in ownership patterns of those factors. Within agricultural systems, for example, not only are landholdings—the key factor of production—highly unequal (though this varies markedly cross-nationally), wages and other labor compensation are typically very low relative to rents.[4] When a high percentage of total output returns to a small number of landowners, the resulting skewed income distribution is accompanied by relatively poor basic needs performance.[5]

Contemporary inequalities in asset holdings arise from both the long-term legacy of initial patterns and shorter-term processes related to factor share imbalances. Although we might imagine that the initial distribution of assets is frequently obliterated either by periodic redistribution or by the continuous erosion of ongoing processes, to the contrary, these patterns are exceptionally enduring. For example, the initial colonial land grants in Latin America remain visible centuries later in today's "latifundio-minifundio" pattern of land ownership (Furtado, 1970).

These patterns continue because substantial asset redistribution is far from a routine political process. Indeed, it can be expected only with the major turnover in state control represented by foreign domination

4. Perfect equality in asset holding is not unequivocally good for basic needs provision if it prevents efficient allocation of factor inputs. In some Asian countries, for example, inheritance customs and rising populations have produced minuscule plots that can neither sustain their owners nor generate a surplus for public spending on infrastructure. Of course, the level of asset inequality in most nations is far greater than this functional requirement.

5. The short-term and long-term effects of inequality on basic needs provision may diverge if the theoretical "growth vs. equity" trade-off comes into play (Galenson and Liebenstein, 1955; Myrdal, 1973; Todaro, 1981: 154–56). Specifically, it is argued that inequality is required to yield the savings (and, therefore, investment) necessary to sustain growth and progress in basic needs. This trade-off surely exists, but the optimal level of inequality is probably very far below actual contemporary levels (Adelman and Morris, 1973; Hicks, 1980). See the last section of this chapter for some limited evidence.

or social revolution, as with the land reforms of South Korea (under Japanese colonialism and American occupation) and Cuba (after the socialist revolution). Thus, Part IV of the book traces the roots of contemporary basic needs performance to the character of colonial rule and even the type of political economy predating the colonial experience.

Initial asset distributions are also ultra-stable because the more contemporary processes that affect asset distributions interact in self-reinforcing ways with the processes that generate returns to factors. For example, initially unequal landholdings place small farmers in constant danger of production shortfalls that force the sell-off of land to less vulnerable producers (i.e., large landowners). Low wages paid to tenants or high rents charged to sharecroppers also prevent them from accumulating savings sufficient to purchase land and thus reverse the trend toward increasing centralization of assets. Further, the low wages and modest asset holdings that interact to limit investments in human capital thereby reproduce relative poverty across generations.

Of course, the processes that determine relative returns to factors of production are themselves strongly influenced by asset holdings that convey power to their owners. Bargaining power in negotiations over wage rates or land rents, for example, originates not only in narrow market conditions such as the supply and marginal productivity of labor. It is also strongly influenced by the structural and institutional context, which reflects the relative wealth and/or political power of claimants on the surplus (e.g., legislation governing labor union organization or tenant-landlord relations).

What do these considerations of factor returns imply about the form of the relationship between basic needs and level of development? In general, the distribution of factor holdings seems to imply that as wage rates rise relative to interest and rents, we can expect basic needs attainment to increase. This pattern is greatly attenuated, however, because wage rates—particularly in the urban formal sector—do not translate neatly into income for the poor. In many nations, an increase in urban wage rates tends to benefit middle-income groups at the expense of the share of national income earned by those in the agrarian and urban informal sectors who suffer the gravest basic needs problems. This is especially true in capital-intensive industrial production in which relatively high wage rates are often accompanied by falling employment levels as capital and technology are substituted for unskilled labor.[6] Segmented labor markets produce a multi-tiered wage rate in

_____

6. Because the functional share of income affects the actual employment of factors of

which the gap between sectoral wages begins to approximate the gap between incomes derived from different productive factors. Thus, capital-intensive industrialization probably signals sufficiently great inequality—largely sectoral—to predict a lower level of basic needs provision than would otherwise be expected.

Even without these complications, it is not clear how relative wage rates move with GNP growth. While capital accumulation and technological progress seem to diminish the demand for labor relative to that for capital, at the same time specialized skills become more significant and thus the "reserve army of the unemployed" is a less immediate drag on wage levels. Moreover, the institutional elements that greatly influence the returns on factors of production—the strength of labor unions and the class bias of the state, for example—are among the most highly variable of all the correlates of rising GNP. In fact, my examination of these social and political dimensions in later chapters suggests that the character of economic development is probably more important than its level in predicting these elements. In short, the contrary claims concerning the factor distribution of income must surely be adjudicated by empirical rather than theoretical evidence.

Uneven Sectoral and Geographical Development

Of course, inequalities arise from a number of sources besides the factor distribution of income, especially uneven sectoral and geographic development. Some argue that the gap between income levels in different sectors or geographical areas is as fundamental to capitalist development as the functional distribution of income. Lewis (1976: 26) puts it simply: "Development must be inegalitarian because it does not start in every part of an economy at the same time." Most believe that cross-national variance in the size of such gaps reflects particular types of capitalist evolution as well as particular stages of growth. Although Lewis is correct that in all economies growth is initiated in some sectors before others, the inequality resulting from change within one enclave varies markedly across economies. In particular, the impact of this initial perturbation on other sectors and regions of the country will vary with the nature of the economy and its internal sectoral linkages.[7]

In the classical model of a well-articulated economy, which is rea-

production, it is also possible for wage bargaining or state policy to achieve a factor share for labor that is detrimental to the size distribution of income by increasing unemployment of the overpriced factor (i.e., labor).

7. Spread effects will also differ depending on the type of triggering event (e.g., an infusion of capital or a technological innovation that lowers production costs).

sonably approximated by developed economies at near-full employment, multiplier effects quickly extend outside the initial enclave
through backward and forward linkages to other input and complementary products, through employment generation and the spread of
income effects, through tax revenues, and through infrastructural development (Lewis, 1976).[8] In this type of economy, trends in sectoral
inequality may be attributable to stages of development. In fact, the
changing distribution of the labor force across sectors may be a principal source of cross-national differences in the size distribution of income, which can be summarized by a curvilinear relationship in which
inequality grows through moderate income levels and then falls at upper levels. Shifts of the labor force from sectors of lower productivity
and wage rates to more advanced and remunerative sectors at first
bring about lower equality, which gradually increases as the process
nears completion (Robinson, 1976). The hypothesized effect on the relationship between PQLI and GNP per capita is a curvilinearity consisting of a dip in PQLI at moderate levels of development which corre-
sponds to the U-shaped curve between GNP per capita and income
inequality frequently confirmed by empirical analyses (Kuznets, 1963;
Ahluwalia, 1974; Weede and Tiefenbach, 1981a).

Economies that lack well-articulated sectors, however, may experience growth limited only to the initial enclave; worse, growth in one
enclave may actually come at the expense of lowered growth or even
retrogression in others. More important, there is no guarantee that the
net effect on basic needs will be positive, even if the initial growth
spurt is quite sizable. The processes involved are discussed in detail in
Chapter 4; for the moment we need only note that because sectoral
articulation is thought to be more a function of the type of economy
than level of development, there is reason to be skeptical whether sectoral inequality should predict to any particular form of the relationship
between GNP and PQLI.

Wealth and PQLI: The Functional Form

Before we can consider factors that yield individual variation in national basic needs provision, we must establish the functional form of
the relationship between the PQLI and GNP per capita. Even though
the assumption of a universal and automatic relationship has been increasingly challenged by political economists and development

---

8. Occasionally these mechanisms are referred to as "trickle-down" effects, but more
often that term is reserved for growth effects that spread (downward) across classes,
rather than (sideways) across sectors.

scholars, the logic of economic growth remains compelling enough that the existence of a positive cross-sectional relationship between GNP and PQLI has not been called into question.

There are, however, numerous candidates for a universal functional form of the GNP-PQLI curve, each suggested by the presumed timing of important transitional processes. The most obvious but least theoretically compelling possibility is a simple linear relationship in which basic needs attainment grows proportionally to GNP per capita. Such a relationship would require that changing income levels produce no differences in distribution of income across function, individual recipient, or expenditure categories, and that basic needs performance can be bought at a constant rate. Neither seems likely. In fact, the "stylized facts" analyses of Chenery and his associates make it clear that economic development involves a number of procésses, few of which are linear and many of which are not even monotonic. Insofar as the level of basic needs fulfillment is a reflection of many of those processes, it is reasonable to think that it too will be significantly curvilinear.

In particular, there are at least two reasons to suppose that the relationship may be essentially logarithmic; that is, the curve flattens at higher income levels, reflecting the diminishing marginal returns of aggregate income for basic needs levels.[9] First, ceiling effects suggest that further progress may be especially expensive to obtain at high levels and virtually impossible beyond the point already achieved in certain advanced areas. Literacy, for example, cannot rise above 100 percent under any circumstances, and improvements of life expectancy past age seventy-five and infant mortality rates below about seven per thousand are limited more by natural barriers and medical technology than by social, political, or economic processes. Second, the elasticities of Engels curves suggest that at higher income levels a smaller share of income is spent on the wage goods necessary for minimal satisfaction of basic needs.

A competing thesis emphasizing the role of income inequality suggests a more elaborate statistical form. As noted above, most theoretical and empirical work suggests a U-shaped curve in which middle-income nations manifest less equality than either rich or poor nations. Thus, as nations grow from low to middle income levels, a lower percentage of aggregate income accrues to the poorer strata whose living standards dominate a nation's basic needs performance statistics. Over that range, this fact would seem to imply a flattening of the PQLI-GNP

---

9. The family of logarithmic curves includes the logged squared, whose shape is slightly steeper than, but otherwise very similar to, the much more familiar log curve. Choosing between the two on empirical grounds is typically very difficult because their correlation is above $+.95$; the standard approach is to utilize the simple log.

curve similar to that anticipated by the diminishing marginal returns argument.[10] However, after the bottom of the U—that is, for nations at middle and upper income levels—equality tends to improve; thus we might anticipate that basic needs levels would not flatten out at higher income levels as markedly as suggested by marginal returns arguments.

There may also be a curvilinearity at low levels. Slow progress in basic needs among the poorest countries is anticipated by an argument considered in Chapter 4 concerning the subsistence sector. Until production rises to the point at which surplus can be extracted and monetized, it cannot be transferred to collective goods, investment in infrastructure, or distributional and planning ends, which are necessary to certain critical basic needs functions. Neither savings rates nor taxation rates can be positive fractions, let alone significantly large, when incomes are below subsistence levels. This expectation translates into a curve that shows slow PQLI progress until a "take-off point"—probably represented by a point of inflection—is reached. Until then, a variant of the "low level equilibrium trap" exists in which productivity gains—and, more important, gains in extracted surplus—do not grow sufficiently to provide for the collective goods necessary to improve basic needs provision, including education, water and sewage systems, and elementary medical care. Ironically, given the central emphasis of basic needs programs on reducing inequality, such subsistence sectors are poor providers of basic needs precisely because of their extraordinarily egalitarian nature (Lenski and Lenski, 1974). There are limits to the benefits of egalitarianism, at least at these very low income levels.

Linear and logarithmic relationships are easily modeled, but the implication of the inequality arguments for the GNP-PQLI relationship is not so easily represented. The usual form of the relationship between the income share of the poorest groups (usually the lowest 40 percent) and overall GNP per capita is conventionally expressed in a "semilog" form of the following type:[11]

10. Of course, the expectation of slow initial progress is also supported by the argument concerning the limited surplus produced by the subsistence sectors, which presumably dominate the economies of the poorest nations.

11. Alternative specifications are discussed in the Technical Appendix to Chenery and Syrquin, 1975. Generally, the fits do not improve significantly but the nonlinearities (beyond those embodied in the log formulation) greatly complicate estimation. For that reason, the text specification is nearly universal. Another option, explored below, is to split the sample and estimate the relationship separately for different samples. This move handles most of the nonlinearity difficulties because most of those effects are sizable only over relatively large variance, but it restricts the sample more than is desirable and greatly constrains the formulation of an overall model. The latter consideration is especially important for the present purpose, since the analysis in subsequent chapters will show that much of the nonlinearity can be accounted for by other factors. Thus, the

$$(1) \quad \text{INCOME-OF-POOR} \ / \ Y = a + b_1(\ln Y) + b_2(\ln Y)^2$$

$$\text{where } Y = \text{GNP per capita}$$

$$\text{and } \ln = \text{natural logarithm}$$

The Chenery and Syrquin (1975) estimates ($a = .466$, $b_1 = -.119$, $b_2 = .010$) are of the same relative magnitude as those of Weede and Tiefenbach (1981a), though the latter are presented only in the presence of other independent variables, a fact that prohibits direct comparison.[12] The ratio of b_1 to b_2 in both cases is about -12 to 1, however, indicating that each is modeling a curve of the same general shape. The scatterplots of Chenery and Syrquin support the prediction equation in showing the income share of the poorest 40 percent of the population beginning around 16 percent of national income below $100 per capita (1964 U.S. dollars), declining to a low of under 13 percent at about $300, then rising to about 15 percent above $1,000.

Clearly, however, an equation predicting PQLI could not be expected to have the same form as a prediction of an income share for two reasons. First, the latter case normalizes the dependent variable by income whereas the former does not. Second, the effect of income level on inequality is relatively modest with a variance over the entire income range less than 25 percent of the mean value. By contrast, the PQLI values for upper-income nations frequently double those of the poorest nations. Thus, it would seem that the best approximation of a prediction equation for PQLI informed by the U-shaped inequality argument would have to begin with a linear or log function of income and then introduce the deviation of income of the poor from overall income as a second factor.

The simplest of these forms would begin with equation 1, which predicts income of the poor as a percentage of GNP. Multiplying both sides of the equation by GNP (Y) would leave the left side equal to the absolute income level of the poorest 40 percent, a plausible correlate of PQLI.[13]

$$(2) \quad \text{INCOME-OF-POOR} = [a + b_1(\ln Y) + b_2(\ln Y)^2] \times Y$$

---

purpose here is to introduce a baseline estimate of economic effects to guide further analysis rather than to achieve the best possible univariate fit.

12. The parameter estimates from Chenery and Syrquin (1975) refer to 1964 U.S. dollars at factor cost. The translation to 1970 U.S. dollars at market prices—the metric used in the remainder of the empirical analysis—requires multiplying by a factor of roughly 1.5.

13. Of course, PQLI is conceptually, theoretically, and empirically different from the income level of the poor for all the reasons enumerated in Chapter 1. The point is that PQLI can be expected to vary more closely with the income *level* of the poor than with the income *share*.

For the purpose of maximizing the fit in a bivariate analysis, two alternative specifications that involve the nonlinear transformation of the PQLI rather than the GNP term are found in the literature. Goldstein (1985) insists that the "plateau curve" of infant mortality rates (IMR) is best modeled by a reciprocal specification—i.e., IMR = b(1/GNPCAP)—which, unlike the log function, has a true asymptote.

Another variant of the log specification is the logit function, which produces a faintly S-shaped curve familiar in constrained growth models and approximated by the findings of Chenery and Syrquin (1975) for many developmental processes. That function features a lower asymptote perfectly symmetrical with the upper one. To fit the relationship of GNP per capita to PQLI under this specification requires the transformation of PQLI according to the equation PQLI' = LN[PQLI/(100 − PQLI)] followed by the estimation of the relationship between logged GNP and PQLI'.

In sum, although the general shape of the curve is more or less agreed upon, the precise statistical expression of it is not entailed unequivocally by the theoretical arguments. The choice among the alternatives involves three considerations. First, the theoretical rationale must be clear and compelling. This consideration involves more than merely specifying the bivariate relationship, of course, especially when transformation of the dependent variable is required. Because additional independent variables will enter the analysis, any transformation of the dependent variable must avoid misspecification of these relationships as well. Second, preference should be given to formulations that maximize the comparability with existing literature and ease of estimation. Third, most obviously, the specification must fit the data. Thus I show here the empirical evidence for alternative functional forms.

The Empirical Evidence

The scatterplot of Figure 3-1, which displays the relationship between GNP per capita and PQLI, reveals a curve shaped much the way the diminishing marginal returns argument would suggest. The PQLI rises—though at a declining rate—over most of the income range, but progress virtually stops when GNP per capita reaches $3,000. Indeed, Figure 3-1 appears to be a textbook example of a log function, but, because a number of functional forms produce curves of similar shape, a statistical analysis must accompany the visual inspection. Figure 3-2 illustrates how similar are the shapes of curves produced by estimating five plausible specifications: (1) the simple log form, (2) equation 2 above, informed by inequality arguments, (3) the polynomial form, (4)

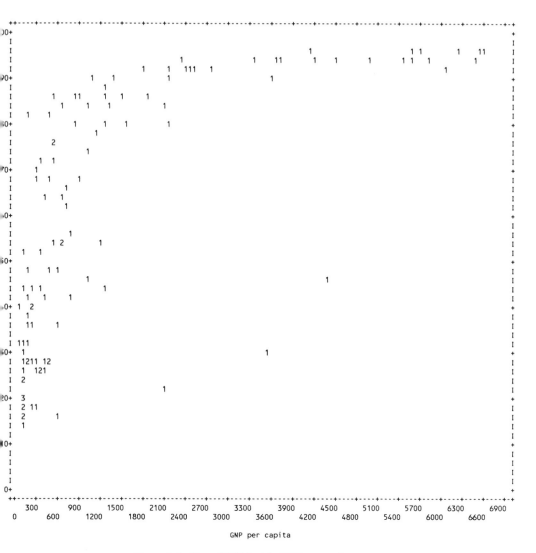

Figure 3-1. Plot of PQLI with GNP per capita

the logit transformation, with logged GNP, and (5) the inverse GNP "plateau curve."

Table 3-1 reports the estimations for each of these specifications as well as several variants. The simple log form is the preferred model at this juncture. It is evident that most of the more elaborate specifications offer little improvement over the logarithmic form confirmed by many other researchers (Morris, 1979; Hicks and Streeten, 1979; Isen-

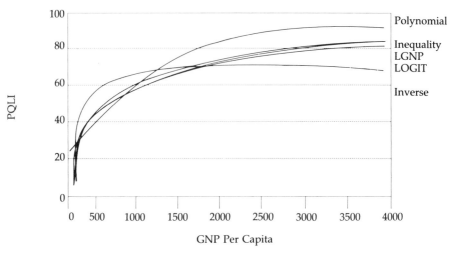

Figure 3-2. Alternative functional forms

man, 1980; Leipziger and Lewis, 1980; Preston, 1976; Grosse and Perry, 1983; McGranahan et al., 1972). Clearly, the simple linear and the inverse specifications are greatly inferior to the others. The variants of the log form are as similar in predictive power as they are in general shape; both the variables and the PQLI predictions they generate are very highly collinear. The very small increments of additional explained variance are purchased with statistical complexity not justified by theoretical clarity.

Table 3-1. Alternative specifications, PQLI and GNP per capita

Specification	Variables	Simple r	Adj. r^2	Beta	t	Sig.
Linear	GNP/cap	.660	.431	.009	9.6	.0001
Simple log	LN(GNP/cap)	.801	.638	17.094	14.5	.0001
Log + square log	LN(GNP/cap) +	.801		29.261	2.3	.02
	LN(GNP/cap)^2	.792	.638	− .911	− 1.0	.33
Log + linear	LN(GNP/cap) +	.801		19.901	8.4	.0001
	GNP/cap	.660	.641	− .002	− 1.4	.18
Polynomial	GNP/cap +	.660		3.299	8.3	.0000
	GNP/cap^2 +	.530		−5.021	− 5.6	.0000
	GNP/cap^3	.450	.647	2.447	4.3	.0000
Inequality	LN(GNP/cap) +	.801		19.471	9.3	.0000
	LN(GNP/cap)$^2 \times$ Y	.622	.647	− .000	− 1.4	.17
Inverse GNP	1/(GNP/cap)	− .693	.475	−5986	− 10.4	.0001
Logit w/GNP	GNP/cap	.747	.554	.001	12.2	.0001
Logit w/log	LN(GNP/cap)	.838	.699	.967	16.7	.0001

Only the logit specification offers discernible improvement and that is quite small. Further, to achieve it one must use logged GNP as the predictor. At this stage of the analysis, the simple log form is preferable to the logit specification for its theoretical clarity, its ease of estimation, and its comparability to other studies. The upper asymptote represents diminishing marginal returns and ceiling effects, but it is not clear what process or effect is being modeled by the logit transformation of the lowest PQLI levels. Moreover, the parameter estimates can no longer be interpreted in a straightforward fashion. Unlike the transformations of the GNP term, transformation of the dependent variable directly influences the analyses of all the other multivariate effects to be considered in later chapters. There is no reason to suppose that they too will follow the logit form. Indeed, these curvilinearities may well result from either random processes or the systematic ones discussed in subsequent analyses. In either case, it would not be fruitful to further pursue a theoretically arbitrary, marginally superior bivariate specification when our goal is a more comprehensive, theoretically coherent, multivariate explanation. It would be appropriate, however, to revisit this question at the conclusion of our study; thus, Appendix 4 reestimates these alternative specifications in the context of the final model.

Still, the curvilinearity indicates that the relationship is somewhat different at different points on the curve. The most obvious difference occurs as income reaches the $1,500 range. Above this level, basic needs progress slows considerably; the flatness of the curve witnesses that, as Chenery and Syrquin (1975) have established for many developmental processes, the transition is nearly complete and further structural changes are very incremental. Interestingly, the diminishing variance in the PQLI at this level suggests that basic needs attainment is either an automatic consequence of income levels this high or else the paths to basic needs success are so many that all nations have chanced upon one of them.[14]

Below this level, the relationship appears more linear, but also more erratic. Some of this variance is apparently due to the imprecision of GNP estimates for poor countries which is known to result from the peculiarities of price structures in very open economies.[15] Kravis et al. (1978a)

14. Statistically, the greater predictability of the dependent variable at some points along the curve than at others constitutes the condition known as heteroscedasticity. In such cases, the variance in the sampling distribution can introduce error in interpreting the significance of a relationship, though the parameter estimates themselves are unaffected. In this case, the great strength of the relationship precludes any possibility of false inference: the relationship is, beyond question, logarithmic. Further, a WLS estimation was undertaken to confirm both this bivariate relationship and the stability of the final model.

15. Because wage levels in poor nations are depressed by labor abundance, la-

have provided GNP reestimates normalized by purchasing power parity, thereby expressing each nation's GNP not in relation to its own unique price structure but rather to a uniform market basket of goods. The correlation of PQLI with Kravis GNP estimates is .807 as compared to .715 for conventional GNP over the sample of 101 nations for which both estimates are available. For the logged specification, the r using purchasing power estimates is .881 compared to .861 for conventional GNP. Two observations are interesting. First, the Kravis estimates are marginally better predictors of basic needs, as would be expected of any improvement in data quality. Second, the curvilinearity of the relationship is markedly reduced. It appears that at least some of the apparent curvilinearity is actually the result of measurement error.

Both trends are also apparent over the middle income range, from $300 to $2,300. Using purchasing power parity GNP estimates, the correlation for the linear specification is +.604, whereas using the logged term lowers that value to +.590. The comparable figures for unadjusted GNP (+.450 and +.488 when logged) illustrate both the superiority of the reestimates and the apparent impact of price distortions in making the relationship appear more curvilinear than it really is.[16]

In this income range, marked basic needs progress is quite obviously possible through growth in income, but the large deviations imply that other avenues to basic needs performance must be possible as well.[17] This conclusion supports the position of Leipziger and Lewis (1980) and Ahluwalia et al. (1979: 331), who declare that "in the typical middle-in-

---

sive goods, which form the bulk of Third World production, are undervalued in home prices relative to world prices. The result is that poor countries have purchasing power markedly greater than that indicated by their nominal GNP. Moreover, this understatement of the purchasing power implicit in market price expression of GNP varies across nations, though it is proportional to nominal GNP, since traded goods prices tend to equalize whereas purely domestically produced and consumed goods (i.e., "untraded goods") exhibit the greatest deviation in price. Relatively closed nations such as India have prices of labor-intensive goods especially depressed by labor market conditions without the upward pressure of international trade to equalize them. Kravis et al. (1975) estimate the understatement of Indian purchasing power, for example, at nearly 300 percent.

16. Of course, relationships within restricted ranges of the independent variable are almost always weaker and frequently of different apparent shape than those computed over the entire sample (McGranahan et al., 1985). Thus, though the r's are lower, the conclusion that major substantive differences exist in PQLI determination within this income range is unwarranted.

17. Once again, the greater deviations may be thought of as indicating heteroscedasticity, but it would be premature to consider this a problem. In fact, heteroscedastic models are usually the result of incomplete specification, and later analysis makes it very clear that this is indeed the case. As the model becomes better specified in later chapters, the heteroscedasticity declines to insignificance.

come countries, improved distribution is often more effective in reducing poverty than is accelerated growth."[18]

When the poorest nations are singled out for investigation, the picture is more murky. Below $300 GNP per capita, there is little evidence of the rapidly increasing PQLI at low income levels predicted by the marginal returns theory or the logarithmic specification. Indeed, the correlation between GNP per capita and PQLI is only .287 (.324 with the logged term and .381 with the Kravis reestimates).[19] The weakness of the relationship indicates that GNP growth is far from a guarantee of improved basic needs provision. It seems that the conclusion of Leipziger and Lewis (1980: 299)—"for low-income LDC's, growth is necessary to bring about welfare improvements"—is only partially correct. On the one hand, it is evident that the resources available at this income level cannot support the meeting of basic needs among the bulk of the poor, since the PQLI seldom reaches 50 for nations below $300 income levels. Yet, at the same time, the surprising internation variation indicates that growth is not a *sufficient* condition for substantial basic needs improvement.[20]

Basic Needs and Change

The cross-sectional picture offered above reflects the long-run adjustment process, but we are frequently interested in the trajectory of individual nation change over shorter time periods. Indeed, many of the controversies concerning basic needs development approaches center on trade-offs that are expected to be most visible in intranation, over-time change.

18. In fact, Ahluwalia et al. (1979) suggest that the determinants of basic needs performance may differ among groups of countries, with growth the key among the poorest, and government policies and other distributional elements the key in the middle income range. This analysis finds no evidence of such a difference.

19. It is probable that uninterpretable random variance rather than any systematic pattern accounts for the odd presence of two distinct groups of nations and the resultant better fit of the logit transformation over this range. The 15 nations below $160 show a positive linear relationship, though the r is only +.117, while the 14 nations between $200 and $300 show a statistically significant negative relationship (−.389).

20. It is interesting that the group of nations below $300 per capita GNP display less variance in basic needs performance than the middle income group. Their deviations from the predictions based on GNP are also smaller. When the model is completed, however, their deviation from the improved prediction is larger! That is, while the variation in basic needs performance among this group is small, it is less well explained than in the middle income group. Bartlett's test for heteroscedasticity is performed throughout the analysis to trace this changing pattern, and WLS estimations are undertaken to confirm the conclusions of the analysis. There is no evidence that the heteroscedasticity is significant nor that the estimates and conclusions are in any way damaged by its presence.

To fully capture these processes, we must recognize and disentangle three dimensions of change. First, there are known "time shifts" in relationships such that the basic needs levels associated with any given income level have increased over time. Because these level shifts are often associated with diminished variance and/or greater predictability of national scores, some explanations for this phenomenon center on such systemic processes as "contagion" effects and highlight the role of powerful international institutions. Other explanations center on national-level processes and consider time shifts a simple artifact of a second dimension of change, namely the incremental process through which most nations exhibit an improvement in basic needs roughly proportional to prior basic needs fulfillment. This pattern of change offers a particular challenge to over-time analysis techniques like panel designs, while suggesting some important principles of intranation PQLI determination. The third dimension is variation across individual nations in change scores. It is this variance that time-series designs seek to highlight in order to clarify causal determinants of change which should complement the lessons of cross-sectional analysis.

We begin with a test for time shifts by using data on the PQLI and GNP (in constant dollars corrected for purchasing power parity) of 103 nations for 1960 and 1980. By regressing the PQLI for each time point on the respective GNP measure, we can compare the level of basic needs provision predicted for each income level at the two time points. Not unexpectedly, a time shift does appear, but apparently one subject to the same ceiling effects observed previously in the cross-sectional analysis. It is evident from the parameter estimates displayed on the top of Table 3-2 that quite different models are required to predict the PQLI at the two time points. In particular, notice that the larger positive parameter estimate for GNP in 1960 is accompanied by a much larger negative intercept.

The markedly different shape of the curves is best illustrated, however, in the bottom half of Table 3-2 by the PQLI values predicted by each equation for several representative income levels. Generally speaking, the PQLI score associated with any given income level is higher in 1980 than in 1960, though the 1960 curve is quite evidently much steeper. In 1980, for example, income levels around $90 yielded PQLI levels around 25, whereas the same income in 1960 (even in constant dollars) produced a PQLI of less than 7. The gap decreases proportionately at higher income levels until rough equality is reached at about $2,500. This is the same point that our earlier analysis identified as the end of the rapid transition phase in PQLI growth and the beginning of a phase in which PQLI levels are both slower changing and more constant across nations.

Table 3-2. Time shifts in the relationship between PQLI and GNP per capita

	1960			1980		
Term	Simple r	Beta	t	Simple r	Beta	t
GNP/cap	.817	20.68	14.24	.829	15.11	14.89
Constant		−86.44	−8.76		−42.81	−5.73

Predicted values of PQLI at each income level

GNP per capita	1960	1980
$ 90	6.6	25.2
$ 150	17.2	32.9
$ 250	27.7	40.6
$ 450	39.9	49.5
$1,500	64.8	67.7
$2,300	73.6	74.2

Such a time shift is a common finding in studies of both basic needs (Preston, 1976; Grosse and Perry, 1983; Cochrane et al., 1980) and a variety of similar processes.[21] Chenery and Syrquin (1975) found time shifts in most developmental dimensions, the largest of which involved public sector shares and government spending on education. Meyer and Hannan (1979) find similar evidence of an increasing propensity for state growth and education spending and a consequent rise in educational enrollments.

Though the finding of time shifts is expected, it is far from satisfactorily explained. One interpretation in effect denies that these national experiences are independent of one another, instead attributing the national changes to systemic processes. The most frequently cited process is the change in development ideology toward more distribution-sensitive approaches. This change, which occurred initially in a few academic centers and development agencies, subsequently spread via the dominant role played in development planning (and funding) by international institutions and national aid programs influenced by them. Particularly in the last half of the 1970s, substantial biases toward basic needs and equity-centric development paths were introduced by both McNamara's World Bank and key national actors, especially the United States (Hoadley, 1981). By the end of the 1970s, development theory had undergone a striking revolution in which rural development and basic needs attain-

21. This finding is usual but not universal. Goldstein (1985), for example, expects to find such a time shift—and notes its presence in studies over the longer term—but does not uncover the pattern in his infant mortality data. The form of the change is also confirmed by Grosse and Perry (1983), whose curve of GNP with life expectancy is steeper in 1960 than in later periods.

ment had acquired much greater centrality in the development plans of nearly all nations (Hoadley, 1981; Weaver and Jameson, 1981; Wilber, 1979; Griffin and James, 1981). It would not be surprising if this theoretical revolution were manifested in development outcomes like basic needs provision since it has clearly affected development planning.

A related explanation emphasizes universal growth in the size and strength of the state. This phenomenon has been observed in a variety of settings (Hicks and Swank, 1984; Olson, 1985; Cameron, 1978), but its impact is nowhere more noticeable than in the increasing participation of government in economic development. Indeed, by the end of the 1970s the management of economic development had become accepted as the central mission of the state in poor nations, whereas two decades earlier the role of the state in this regard was considered much smaller.

Explanations that center on such universal changes also imply that variations in national experience should tend to decline. If patterns in resource allocation converge due to increasing similarity in development theory, then developmental outcomes should similarly converge. Models of basic needs levels should thus become more predictively powerful as deviant cases decline in number and degree. Yet, despite the large time shift, PQLI is only marginally more predictable from GNP levels in 1980 than in 1960. In fact, this slight difference is probably more than accounted for by the increased percentage of nations which had attained income levels above $1,500, the point at which predictability is much greater in both eras. Further, most previous studies show increasing—not decreasing—variance over time (Preston, 1976; Arriaga and Davis, 1969).

The meaning of the time shift is thus far from clear. In fact, until we have developed the full explanatory model of basic needs provision, we cannot be sure whether the time shift requires additional attention or not. Later additions to the model may eliminate these time shifts by associating them instead with widespread changes occurring in the independent variables that constitute the explanation for basic needs levels at both time points.

In addition, we must surely consider the possibility that the time shift is better seen as an artifact of a second form of change, namely incremental basic needs progress occurring simultaneously—but independently—in all nations. What does this conception suggest about the nature of PQLI determination and the strategy we ought to employ to study it? We begin by observing that the trend of increasing PQLI is practically universal across nations. Indeed, PQLI change is highly incremental; the correlation between PQLI levels in 1960 and 1980 is +.97. Moreover, contrary to the implication that a systemic process will tend to level the differences between nations, nations that perform relatively well—or relatively badly—in 1960 retain that basic needs orientation in 1980. To illustrate this point, the residuals from the 1960 and 1980 regressions reported in Table 3-2 are compared. The correlation between residuals (+ .89) suggests that internation differences remain, even while the trajectory of all nations' basic needs performance is upward.

The interpretation of this incrementalism is key to the argument advanced in Chapter 2 in support of the choice of a cross-sectional research design. In particular, most designs require an assumption about the origin of incremental change and thus the advisability and feasibility of partitioning this increment from the change induced by short-term factors. There are four possible sources of such incrementalism, each of which is relevant to design considerations. First, a times series can manifest high serial correlation simply because change is slow. This is probably not the principal explanation in this case since the mean PQLI level has grown from about 51 in 1960 to about 66 in 1980, with much more rapid growth among the poorer nations in the sample. Were the change between 1960 and 1980 not so proportional to initial levels, such a magnitude would yield much lower serial correlation than the levels reported above.

Second, correlated measurement error will yield greater serial correlation among indicators than among the "true" underlying variables. One major source of this form of measurement error is the use of longitudinal error detection or missing data estimation techniques that utilize one data point to estimate others. McGranahan et al. (1985) report that a considerable amount of such smoothing is performed by various data collectors on the basis of presumed stable time series. Though most of the measurement intervals are sufficiently short that this smoothing should not greatly compromise the independence of the 1960 and 1980 estimates, a small amount of "false incrementalism" (i.e., serially correlated error) nevertheless enters via this route.

Third, large incremental effects could result if the lags involved in PQLI determination were relatively long. If this is the principal source of the incremental pattern, attempts to sort out causality through panel or time-series designs will be futile. The effect of these lags on estimates derived from cross-sectional designs will depend on the presence of a fourth source of incremental change, however.

That fourth source is a constancy in causal forces. If PQLI levels are affected by causal variables that are themselves stable over time, incremental patterns in the dependent variable will result. Even if the effect is short-term, its continuous operation over a protracted period will yield an incremental pattern. If this is the source of incremental effects, panel designs are not only limited in value, but singularly misleading. They will tend to strip the dependent variable of this increment and thus ascribe variance actually caused by this continuously acting process to the initial conditions summarized by the incremental parameter for the lagged de-

pendent variable. By contrast, cross-sectional designs are especially appropriate in this case because the full effect of the independent variable is
"absorbed" in the dependent variable. Slowly changing independent variables also limit the specification error inherent in cross-sectional estimation when the causal lag is reasonably long, though there is obviously no
simple means of estimating a complex time-series response of the dependent variable to an independent variable.

What does the pattern of incremental change suggest about our analysis? It is not wholly clear whether the incremental pattern reflects the
long causal lags that are required for the dependent variable to "absorb"
the effect of the independent variables or a constancy in the presence and
operation of the causal mechanisms represented by the independent variables. We can establish clearly enough that the best single representation
of the causal lag between GNP and PQLI is zero since the correlation
declines with each additional yearly interval. If this fact leads us to accept
the fourth source of incremental pattern as the dominant one, then our
search for determinants should concentrate on relatively enduring characteristics of nations.

More immediate effects need not be wholly neglected, of course. Although much of the change between 1960 and 1980 can be ascribed to a
time shift and part to incremental processes capturable by stable structural conditions, some short-term change can be identified. In particular,
short-term economic growth affects basic needs propensities in a predictable way. For example, when the growth rate between 1960 and 1980 is
included in an equation with PQLI at 1960, the prediction of PQLI levels
at 1980 does improve significantly ($t = 3.7$). Given the limited role of
panel designs, however, the principal use of this finding is to enable us to
identify cases in which PQLI values seem out of line with a longitudinal
pattern. As part of the effort discussed in Chapter 1 to minimize the impact of unreliable data, Appendix 2 reports the results of analyses making
use of this strong serial correlation. I incorporate these results with the
results of Appendix 1 to identify particularly suspicious data points.

A Basic Needs Perspective on Growth versus Equity

Although these theoretical and measurement considerations dictate that
most of our analysis should be cross-sectional, one particular issue requires greater attention to short-term change—the alleged trade-off between growth and equity. This brief digression cannot do justice to either
the breadth or depth of the theoretical and empirical literature on this
question. The form and source of such a trade-off have been hotly debated for many years, yet its very existence is far from a settled question.

Much of the difficulty arises from differences in definition and measurement. Even in the relatively simple case of the so-called Brazilian miracle, for example—which involves only one nation over one decade—there is little agreement on the facts of change in citizen welfare (Fishlow, 1972, 1980; Fields, 1977, 1980; Beckerman and Coes, 1980). Attempts to assess the role of economic growth in that change—or to generalize from the particular case—are fraught with even graver difficulties.

Still, the data of this project do provide some evidence on two questions relevant to the controversy. Of course, neither is identical to its counterpart in the original controversy because, as we have seen, income inequality and basic needs attainment are conceptually and empirically distinct phenomena. Nonetheless, because many of the same causal influences are thought to affect both, evidence concerning parallel theoretical propositions is relevant. Thus, although a thorough treatment would carry the analysis very far afield, I briefly describe here cursory findings that may contribute to the growing body of empirical work on this important, if elusive, set of questions.

First, do nations marked by better than average provision of basic needs pay a price for that "equity" in the form of lower future growth? Most orthodox economists are inclined to answer in the affirmative on the grounds that the pattern of resource allocation and factor ownership which maximizes relative basic needs provision is likely to yield too little investment and too little efficiency to maximize economic growth. The linkages among the size distribution of income, the functional distribution of income, and the fulfillment of basic needs lie at the heart of this contention.

In particular, the reciprocal relationship between the marginal propensity to save and the income elasticities of demand for wage goods implies that equalization of income would predict both greater basic needs provision and reduced investment. One can think of rising inequality as an incremental process of shifting income from those below the income mean to those above it. Such an income shift—whether portrayed cross-sectionally or over time—has a characteristic impact on the pattern of demand, often represented in the form of Engels curves (i.e., the propensity to consume wage goods, especially food). Following Engels's law, as incomes rise, the proportion of income devoted to basic needs falls. The elasticity for food narrowly is around .8 for the poorest countries as a whole (Griffin and James, 1981: 16), while among the poorest strata it is nearly unity. More generally, some wage goods—particular forms of food, fuel, clothing, and housing, for example—are even "inferior" goods, that is, their consumption may even decline as incomes rise (Griffin and James, 1981). At the same time, saving rates are much lower—often negative—among the poor.

In sum, it is plausible to think that nations with favorable basic needs levels are relatively egalitarian and that the parallel with redistributive impacts would hold. That is, when money is taken from those who would spend it for basic needs and given to those who will save it, investment levels will rise as basic needs attainment will fall. Therefore, if growth follows from investment, basic needs fulfillment must come at the expense of economic growth. Moreover, most analysts feel that the policy actions usually required to benefit the poor also yield other outcomes that compromise future growth, because the leverage of policy on basic needs is frequently very poor. Thus, some "dead weight" loss is to be expected from policy inefficiency. The most frequently cited examples involve government corruption and/or incompetence in addition to the diminished incentive for growth-enhancing behavior implicit in redistributive taxation.

On the other hand, proponents of basic needs development strategies and human capital theorists are inclined to answer that systems providing superior basic needs have laid the groundwork for more rapid future growth in the form of investment in human capital and infrastructure. From this standpoint, relative success in basic needs provision is a proxy for a number of economic attributes in addition to relative egalitarianism. Recalling that basic needs levels also reflect efficiency of resource allocation, infrastructural "bargains," the absence of waste or leakage, and various other factors, it may be appropriate to treat relative PQLI levels as a dimension of economic performance which is positively correlated with other dimensions, perhaps including GNP growth.

The second question reverses the causal direction. Does rapid economic growth yield benefits for the poor which are reflected in enhanced fulfillment of basic human needs? The most radical position holds that the poor can actually be harmed by the distributional consequences of rapid growth, though immiserizing growth is usually thought to be restricted to particular forms of development. Most others contend that benefits do accrue to the poor, though they are not proportional to GNP growth.

To answer these questions, GNP data (corrected for purchasing power parity) and "semi-PQLI" data (on infant mortality and life expectancy) were compiled at half-decade intervals from 1960 to 1980. The "semi-PQLI" for each time point was regressed on the comparable GNP variable, and the residuals from each regression were calculated to form an index that measured the "basic needs efficiency" of every nation. A nation whose semi-PQLI was higher than predicted by its GNP received a positive Z score while an underperforming nation had a negative score. For each interval, both a GNP growth rate and a change in "basic needs efficiency" were computed. Correlations among these computed measures were then analyzed in the presence of two sets of controls. The first consisted of five dummy variables representing income ranges to correct for the propensity of change to be more rapid at some income levels than others. In particular, it is thought that change at both high and low income levels may be relatively difficult whereas more rapid change can be expected at middle levels. The five categories of 1960 GNP per capita were chosen to approximate equal numbers of nations in each. Second, the basic needs efficiency at 1960 is included to control for the possibility that improvements in basic needs are easiest for nations whose levels already lag expectations while most difficult for those that have already achieved the highest basic needs attainment possible at their income level.

The growth versus equity trade-off thesis received mixed support. First, it was evident that rapid growth produced a weaker "basic needs efficiency" than did more moderate growth. Over intervals ranging from five to twenty years, as the growth over the period increased, declines in relative basic needs provision were registered. Whether this was a short- to medium-term effect produced by a lag in trickle-down processes or whether the growth process produced allocations more resistant to eventual redistribution was unclear.

Two analyses will serve to illustrate the pattern of findings. The dependent variable in both cases is the change in basic needs orientation over the 1960 to 1980 period. The control variables did not operate precisely as expected. Relative improvements in basic needs were significantly smaller among the poorest nations, and significantly greatest among middle-income countries. Moreover, nations already overperforming in 1960 showed slightly greater subsequent relative gains. In the first analysis, whose findings are portrayed in Table 3-3, the independent variable is the GNP growth rate over the 1960 to 1980 period. The large negative estimate illustrates that GNP growth is very strongly negatively correlated with relative gain in PQLI. This is not to say that basic needs provision declined, but it is evident that the gains were far from proportional to GNP growth.

In order to trace the longevity of this dampening effect, a second analysis replaced the two-decade average growth rate with the rate for each of the four half-decades that comprise it. If the decline shown above was merely a reflection of the tendency for basic needs change to lag economic growth, the negative parameter estimate should be largest for the most recent half-decades and smallest for the most distant ones. As shown in Table 3-4, however, contrary to this expectation, growth in the 1960–65 period remains as large a damper on proportional PQLI change as more recent growth.

This finding suggests that the lag between growth and its full impact on basic needs improvements is very long indeed. It also raises a possi-

Table 3-3. Change in residual PQLI regressed on two-decade growth rate

Variables	Simple r	All variables				Significant variables		
		Beta	St. beta	t		Beta	St. beta	t
GNP $0–250	− .05	− .25	− .13	− 1.5		− .41	− .21	− 3.0**
GNP $250–500	.18	.20	.11	1.3				
GNP $500–1,000	.12	.47	.28	3.2**		.31	.18	2.8**
GNP $1,000–2,000	− .10	.27	.12	1.5				
GNP $2,000 +	− .01	.20	.12	1.4				
PQLI residual 1960	− .31	.10	.15	1.9		.10	.14	1.8
GNP growth 1960–80	− .61	− 29.60	− .85	− 10.5***		− 29.55	− .85	− 10.7***

Model	N	r	r^2	adj. r^2	SEE	F
All variables	114	.76	.59	.56	.46	21.6***
Significant variables	114	.76	.58	.56	.46	37.0***

*Significant (p < .05)
**Significant (p < .01)
***Significant (p < .001)

bility that cannot be more fully elaborated in this analysis, namely that the form of GNP growth characteristic of this era in the global political economy has relatively limited impact on basic needs improvements. Moreover, unlike the use of income data among population deciles, the measurement of these variables does not allow any rigorous adjudication of alternative points of view concerning the proportions of growth benefits which flow to various population segments. These data allow us only

Table 3-4. Change in residual PQLI regressed on half-decade growth rates

Variables	Simple r	Two-decade growth			Half-decade growth		
		Beta	St. beta	t	Beta	St. beta	t
GNP $0–250	− .05	− .41	− .21	− 3.0**	− .40	− .21	− 2.9**
GNP $500–1,000	.12	.31	.18	2.8**	.31	.19	2.8**
PQLI residual 1960	− .31	.10	.14	1.8	.09	.13	1.6
GNP growth 1960–80	− .61	− 29.55	− .85	− 10.7***			
GNP growth 1960–65	− .10				− 7.14	− .31	− 4.4***
GNP growth 1965–70	− .29				− 8.14	− .30	− 4.0***
GNP growth 1970–75	− .62				− 8.46	− .41	− 5.8***
GNP growth 1975–80	− .54				− 5.50	− .25	− 3.5***

Model	N	r	r^2	adj. r^2	SEE	F
Two-decade growth	114	.76	.58	.56	.46	37.0***
Half-decade growth	114	.77	.59	.56	.46	21.4***

*Significant (p < .05)
**Significant (p < .01)
***Significant (p < .001)

to observe that basic needs fulfillment improves with economic growth, though not proportionally.

On the reverse question, findings reveal that economic growth was more—not less—rapid among nations with high relative levels of basic needs satisfaction. In a series of analyses, the GNP growth rates over various intervals were regressed on relative basic needs attainment at the earlier point in time and the dummy variables for income level. In all cases, that basic needs performance was a positive predictor of future growth rates, with or without controls reflecting the lower growth rate found among the poorest nations. For the entire two-decade period with the appropriate controls, the t value was 6.8. Thus, nations with initially greater basic needs fulfillment produced more rapid subsequent growth, not the slower growth predicted by orthodox understandings of the sources of basic needs provision. This is especially striking because our previous analyses have already established that relatively high PQLI levels are likely to be retained after economic growth. Thus, it can be said that the future economic performances of nations with higher than average levels of the PQLI are successful not only in relation to the standards of basic needs theorists, but also according to the criteria of more growth-centric analysts. There is nothing in these findings to suggest that growth versus equity trade-off considerations would be an appropriate argument against a basic needs development orientation. Furthermore, in a final analysis, short-term changes in relative PQLI performance were found to be unrelated to subsequent growth rates. For further details of these time-series results, see Moon and Dixon, 1988.

Chapter 4
Economic Systems and Paths of Development

Paths of Development

GNP per capita serves as a proxy for economic development, which is itself an umbrella concept: a continuous, linear *summary* of multiple processes that are *individually* discontinuous, nonlinear, and far from universal (Todaro, 1981; Chenery and Syrquin, 1975; Morris, 1984; Furtado, 1979). But development patterns differ sufficiently across nations that it has become customary to acknowledge the existence of a number of alternative *paths* of development. On some paths, one or another of the "normal" development processes is accelerated or delayed; on others, these processes themselves operate differently or interact with others in unique ways. In particular, basic needs provision is believed to lag GNP growth along several of these development paths.[1]

Rather than try to decompose development and identify the relationship between PQLI and each development component, this empirical analysis tackles the problem of identifying the economic processes most responsible for basic needs provision in two ways. Some theoretically prominent processes (such as industrialization) are especially

---

1. Despite the generally good fit between GNP per capita and PQLI, basic needs provision does not follow as a normal and universal consequence of aggregate national wealth. While increasing wealth is certainly a plausible causal mechanism, so too are changes in labor productivity, technical progress, urbanization, family size, demographics, fertility, industrialization, class formation, savings rates, tax incidences, state strength, cultural norms, and many more dimensions known to be highly correlated with—indeed, to collectively constitute—what we call "development."

well tracked by indicators of particular development dimensions (e.g., the sectoral distribution of the labor force). I replace GNP with such alternative indicators when they are both more closely associated with variation in basic needs provision and more theoretically explicit than GNP. Other processes are more easily represented by aggregating them into broader "modes of production" such as state socialism or subsistence agriculture. For these, I test for differences in the GNP-PQLI relationship across system types.

Economic systems can be distinguished most generally by certain fundamental properties of production processes and their reflection in other structural arrangements of the political economy. These overall system types can be characterized broadly as "modes of production." They are distinguished by the principal productive forces of the economy and by the relations of production through which they are organized (Laclau, 1971; Amin, 1976; Foster-Carter, 1978; Ruccio and Simon, 1988). The type of product produced is a useful proxy for the pattern of inputs to that production. In this chapter, I single out differences between agricultural and industrial systems for an extended discussion, with briefer treatments of some especially significant subtypes: subsistence agriculture and agriculture differentiated by the relative intensity of capital, labor, and land use. Part IV considers the basic needs performance of sectors closely connected to the global system, especially plantation agriculture, mining sectors, and other export enclaves. Though these economic system types differ most obviously in their products, these differences carry implications for the relations of production as well as the superstructure of the political and social systems that result. Apart from the relations of production implicit in product categorization (e.g., the relative autonomy of the landowner/worker in a subsistence system versus the strongly hierarchical class relations and tight labor control in the plantation system), it is also necessary to distinguish capitalist from socialist systems and, among the former, those involved in autonomous versus dependent development.[2]

Mode of production is highly collinear with other variables in the analysis, however. For example, the distinction between agricultural and industrial systems is simultaneously a distinction between relatively poor and relatively rich systems. Socialist political economies are also marked by states with an elite committed to socialist ideology and

2. Because the distinctions are designed to identify differential basic needs performances, they do not necessarily accord with those that might be drawn for other purposes. For example, differences among land tenure systems are treated only superficially whereas export-oriented industrial sectors are distinguished from import-substitution ones.

a political program that follows from it. Thus, on empirical grounds it is difficult to distinguish the effects of state ownership of the means of production—the usual defining characteristic of state socialist systems—from the effects of state policies in health, education, and welfare which are mandated by the view that the state's legitimacy rests on achievement in those areas. Insofar as the latter is universal among contemporary state socialist systems, though the behavior to which it inclines the state need not be confined to these systems, it is difficult to isolate the effect of the relations of production from simple government policy.

Socialism: The Absence of Markets

The previous analysis of the basic needs propensities of capitalist systems highlighted several processes that tend to lower basic needs provision. In order to anticipate systematic differences in the basic needs performance of capitalist and socialist systems, I briefly consider each of these processes as they apply to socialist political economies.

Inequalities resulting from the functional distribution of income and the distribution of the means of production are sharply limited in socialist systems. With a much lower percentage of income deriving from ownership of capital and land, inequality levels are likely to be much lower. Income differences across skill categories of workers remain, but they appear to be lower than their capitalist counterparts (Lane, 1976). Sectoral inequalities are more difficult to assess. Certainly the sectoral composition of socialist and capitalist economies is markedly different (Gregory, 1970). In Eastern Europe, for example, industrialization patterns are independent of the scale and resource considerations that are so significant in the determination of Western European patterns (Gregory, 1970: 127). These patterns also change more rapidly in a command economy with central administration. Although sectoral differences clearly exist in income levels, they are small relative to those in capitalist nations. The rural/agricultural versus urban/industrial cleavage is a constant. Damaging external articulations are infrequent in socialist nations that approximate autarky, but are becoming more common (Bunce, 1983). In sum, available data suggest a general pattern of lower inequality in socialist nations (Echols, 1980; Wiles, 1974).

It is also evident that socialist states possess a much greater command over social resources, with a considerably greater ability to extract, mobilize, and target the surplus on the problems of basic needs. Of course, this ability may not be reflected in enhanced basic needs fulfillment—though it seems likely—both because lagging collective goods are probably not so great a problem in the relatively wealthy nations with state socialist systems and because the *capacity* to target basic needs is different than the actual *propensity* to do so.

Finally, unproductive consumption is different in form in capitalist and socialist societies. Certain elements are common across systems. Spending for the military and internal security forces, for example, is high in both groups of nations, though rather higher in socialist states, in part because of the broader development role typically played by the military (Wolpin, 1981). "Private waste" is surely higher in capitalist nations—advertising, insurance, and so on—whereas "public waste" (corruption, planning inefficiencies, and bureaucratic bloating) is the dominant form in socialist states.

To test the contention that state socialist systems provide higher levels of basic human necessities relative to level of development, a dummy variable for state socialism is initially entered into the previous analyses.[3] If the effect is as expected, however, we should model the superior performance of socialist nations as involving not merely an intercept effect but a slope effect. That is, the difference between the basic needs performance of socialist and capitalist nations should increase with level of development if a higher proportion of the total societal resources is devoted to basic needs provision in one than the other. Thus, in the bottom half of Table 4-1, an interactive formulation is also introduced. This step, however, does not significantly improve the prediction of the simple additive specification.[4]

Because the presentation of results in Table 4-1 establishes a pattern that is duplicated in most succeeding tables, it is worthwhile at this point to take note of its basic structure. Notice that the table reports the results for the model when fully estimated, and, in the last three columns, when it is reestimated with variables removed which do not meet the $|t| > 1$ retention criteria (and have slope estimates smaller than their standard errors). Because all (both) variables are significant in the simple additive case, the two sides of the upper half of the table are identical, but in the multiplicative case reported in the bottom half of the table, the right side illustrates the reduced model estimates without the "state socialism" interaction term found to be insignificant in the full model estimation. This deletion of the insignificant variables is necessary to prevent the inflation of standard errors of estimates

3. Socialist nations are considered to be those governed by a Communist party as of January 1, 1969. The data are from Blondel (1969).

4. This issue should not be forgotten, however. Later in the chapter I introduce a measure of economic development superior to logged GNP, and in its presence the interactive specification is shown to be clearly superior.

Table 4-1. The basic model of wealth and socialist effects (with an additive and interactive specification)

ADDITIVE FORM		All variables			Significant variables		
Variables	Simple r	Beta	St. beta	t	Beta	St. beta	t
Logged GNP/cap	.80	16.49	.77	14.4***	16.49	.77	14.4***
State socialism	.30	17.25	.18	3.3**	17.25	.18	3.3*
Model	N	r	r^2	adj. r^2		SEE	F
All variables	120	.82	.67	.67		16.33	119.8***
Significant variables	120	.82	.67	.67		16.33	119.8***

INTERACTIVE FORM		All variables			Significant variables		
Variables	Simple r	Beta	St. beta	t	Beta	St. beta	t
Logged GNP/cap	.80	16.73	.78	14.4***	16.49	.77	14.4***
State socialism	.30	27.35	.28	2.8*	17.25	.18	3.3*
GNP × socialism	.29	−.01	−.12	−1.2			
Model	N	r	r^2	adj. r^2		SEE	F
All variables	120	.82	.68	.67		16.30	80.7***
Significant variables	120	.82	.67	.67		16.33	119.8***

*Significant (p < .05)
**Significant (p < .01)
***Significant (p < .001)

caused by the specification error implicit in the retention of "irrelevant variables."

From the top half of Table 4-1 we capture most vividly the effect of state socialism, as the parameter estimate indicates that such systems possess a PQLI level more than 17 points higher than would be expected on the basis of GNP alone.[5] Further, the inclusion of the

5. The use of purchasing power estimates of GNP would be preferable, but these are not available for the state socialist nations. Recall, however, that the estimated relationships using the alternative measures do not shift as much at the income levels of the nine Eastern European nations as at lower levels, so there is no reason to suppose that these price distortions are seriously compromising our ability to estimate socialist effects.

Nor need we be concerned with possible errors in translating the NMP figures of the "material product system" into the GNP figures of the "national system of accounts." The translations used here were provided by the USACDA (1980), the source of data for GNP of all nations. The major difference between capitalist and socialist systems persists, however, when nonmonetized measures of development level are used, especially the percent of labor force in agriculture, which is used throughout much of the subsequent analysis. Moreover, the sheer size of the coefficient precludes the effect being an artifact of measurement error. Consider that the actual PQLI figures of seven of the nine Eastern

dummy variable improves the r^2 from .64 to .67 and reduces the standard error from 17.00 to 16.33. The effect is significant at the .001 level.

Nonetheless, there are two problems in confidently crediting state socialist systems with superior performance in the provision of basic needs. First, the sample contains only eleven state socialist nations, most concentrated at relatively high income levels. Thus, it is difficult to tell how universal the effect may be, especially over broader income ranges. Second, the experience of Cuba, whose PQLI of 82 on a per capita income of $465 seems to confirm that socialist effects can be achieved even among the relatively poor, exemplifies the ambiguity of the explanation. It is difficult to isolate the mechanisms that account for this performance as uniquely socialist because of the complex of changes brought about by the Cuban revolution (MacEwan, 1981). On the one hand, major asset redistributions, especially land reform, substantially altered the connection between the functional and the size distribution of income which is characteristic of capitalist political economies (Griffin and James, 1981). Similarly—again uniquely socialist— the state took over many key functions that directly influence distributions of both income and access to key infrastructural services. For example, actions that increased real wages, made pensions more universal, decreased wage gaps horizontally across and vertically within sectors, introduced subsidies for food, and instituted public rather than private provision of medical care all have a decidedly socialist flavor (Seers, 1974).

On the other hand, many of the other measures—though they are empirically associated with socialist governments—are by no means restricted to them. Enhanced emphasis on education, the diversion of public investment and consumption to functions especially benefiting the poor, bias toward rural rather than urban development, and so on are more closely tied to regime goals and ideologies than to the structure of the economy (Streeten, 1981). The two are by no means independent, but they are also not identical. Further, there is an inherent difficulty in distinguishing socialism from capitalism. Though the basic structure of the economy is usually more clear-cut than the state's ideo-

European countries (all save Yugoslavia and Albania) are between 90 and 93. This basic needs performance was achieved on per capita GNPs (as estimated by ACDA) ranging from $1,100 to $3,700, with an average of about $2,400. The best-fitting regression model reported in Table 3-1 (which *includes* the socialist nations) predicts a PQLI of about 80 at the average income level of this group and requires a per capita GNP of over $4,200 to attain a PQLI of 90 and over $5,000 to reach 93. These latter figures are well beyond the conceivable limit of measurement error. Most vividly, West Germany and East Germany have identical PQLI levels (93); even the most casual observer could not fail to recognize that the difference in aggregate national wealth between these two is real, not artifactual.

logical commitment, there are nations, such as Yugoslavia and Tanzania, which have rather unique systems that are difficult to classify as a pure case (Bunce and Hicks, 1987).

Thus, though there is some ambiguity concerning the precise mechanisms responsible and consequent uncertainty as to whether capitalist systems might approximate these results by emulating these governmental policies, there is no doubt about the empirical fact that state socialist systems perform markedly better in the provision of basic needs than do capitalist nations of similar income levels.[6] This finding not only sharpens our prediction of PQLI levels for both socialist and nonsocialist nations (though the impact on the former is of course markedly greater than the latter); it also strengthens our conviction that basic needs performance can be understood better in light of particular principles concerning the allocational and distributional propensities of capitalism than by mere reference to aggregate levels of wealth or income. Thus, we are encouraged to pursue the search for those developmental paths that perform relatively well and relatively badly in the provision of basic needs.

Economic Structure

It is frequently argued, especially among theorists of dependency and dependent development, that structural change in the productive processes of the economy—not GNP growth—is the primary development process relevant to welfare improvements. Although I postpone the detailed examination of the dependency perspective until Chapter 8, I do seek a measure of the structural transition whose relationship with basic needs provision is more reliable. This search is guided by the pattern reminiscent of modernizing Europe: rising incomes associated with the transition from a largely agricultural to a largely industrial economy. In the contemporary Third World, considerable growth in GNP has occurred which has not been based on this transition, with the result that some relatively high-income nations retain quite traditional economic structures. Following dependency understandings, I hypothesize that in such cases basic needs levels will be more surely

---

6. The confidence in the outcome derives not only from the strength of the findings, but also from the support offered by a number of studies whose different approaches converge on the same general point. For example, the income distributions of socialist nations have been shown to be more egalitarian than others (Gurley, 1979; Ahluwalia, 1974; Wilber and Jameson, 1981; Echols, 1980). Wolpin (1981) shows spending priorities and health inputs to be more favorable for socialist systems. Moreover, all these results are theoretically expected.

associated with the economic structure—and the host of political and social attributes which follow from it—than with simple income levels.

The first question is whether economies dominated by the agricultural sector will perform better or worse in the provision of basic needs—relative to income, of course—than largely industrial economies. What is unique about the agricultural sector and how does it systematically differ from the industrial sector?

Most nonindustrial branches of production are marked by low levels of technological development and correspondingly low levels of productivity.[7] This pattern is discernible both between relatively industrialized and relatively nonindustrialized economies and between industrial and agricultural sectors within the same economy. The latter is illustrated by the fact that in the Third World the percentage of the labor force employed in agriculture is typically about twice the percentage of GNP produced by agriculture (Todaro, 1981: 253). This fact reflects much lower levels of capital usage in the agricultural sector, a pattern documented by a survey of eighteen Third World countries in which only about 12 percent of investment during the 1950s and 1960s occurred in the agricultural sector, less than half the percentage of GNP produced by that sector (Szcepanik, 1970).[8] Thus, the distinction

7. Although this low productivity is normally thought to arise from the nature of agricultural production itself, the role of the demand side and the politics of exchange should not be ignored. Because productivity measures ultimately depend on assumptions about final goods prices, the domestic and international politics of price determination—which generally work to lower relative prices of agricultural goods—cannot be divorced from this characterization. These politics may stem from inherently economic processes like differential income elasticities of demand for so-called inferior goods, which agricultural produce tends to approximate. This position formed the heart of the Prebisch critique of comparative advantage as a reliable guide to national interest in Latin American production decisions. It is challenged, however, by Emmanuel (1972), who places the politics of labor-management wage bargaining and the politics of market domination by core states and firms at the forefront of the argument. In most respects, however, the ultimate source of claims on the social surplus (i.e., relative factor and final goods prices) is irrelevant to our concern with the provision of basic needs relative to economic development. That is, so long as the same set of prices constitute the metric for judging productivity in agricultural and industrial sectors, the surplus produced in each—however defined—ought to be capable of supporting proportional levels of basic needs.

8. The poor productivity of agriculture is not universal, however, and cannot be considered inherent. First, the pattern varies across levels of development (Chenery and Syrquin, 1975). Productivity in agriculture relative to the economy as a whole is about 70 percent in the poorest nations and falls to 50 percent in middle-income countries. After that it rises steadily again, as agricultural technology is modernized at a lag after technology enters industry and as surplus agricultural labor is absorbed by the rest of the economy. Second, even this pattern of variance is far from universal; the very low figures

between industrial and agricultural production overlaps several other dimensions used to characterize both whole economies and sectors within them.[9]

Because of low levels of productivity, the economic surplus generated by agricultural processes is smaller than that of more advanced modes of production (Myrdal, 1968). From the standpoint of conventional economic measures, such sectors contribute relatively less to gross product and economies dominated by them manifest low levels of income. On this basis one would also expect low levels of basic needs fulfillment, but it is less clear whether such nations should perform *proportionately* differently from more industrialized ones. To think of this principally as a question about the shape of the curve between national income and basic needs fulfillment, however, would ignore major differences between agricultural and industrial systems. For example, output levels typically fluctuate much more in agriculture than in industry (Brooks and Grilli, 1979). This fluctuation tends to lower the level of welfare expected on the basis of a year-to-year average income. That is, more damage is done in bad years than can be repaired in good years because, for instance, basic health care requires continuous rather than sporadic inputs. Thus, basic needs levels will be lower in systems where income is spread unequally over time. Indeed, the effect of "inequality over time" may be as significant as the inequality among individuals.

Within the agricultural sector, inequality among individuals—the so-called size distribution of income—has both a different basis and a different shape than in industrial systems. Although the size distribution partially reflects the functional or factor distribution of income in both systems, the relevance of the various cleavages between factors differs considerably. Class inequalities in industrial economies relate principally to differential access to capital and are manifested in the relative proportion of final goods costs allocated to wage rates, on the one hand, and profits and interest on the other. By contrast, in agricultural systems land is as scarce as capital but less substitutable, so that class is determined principally by land ownership. What can be said about the relative size of these inequalities?

---

characteristic of poor nations were not present in the early histories of some newly settled areas like New Zealand, Canada, or Argentina (Chenery and Syrquin, 1975: 53).

9. Agricultural production is often characterized as a "peripheral process," especially in contrast to the "core process" of capital-intensive industrial production (Wallerstein, 1979). Dependent development is distinguished by the intensification of capital usage in some sectors without either a spread of that technological and capital growth to other sectors or the increase of the proportion of the labor force employed in the more advanced sectors.

It is extremely difficult to generalize about inequalities in landhold-ings because they vary enormously across nations. In much of Latin America, for example, the stark contrast between latifundio and mini-fundio probably exceeds the inequalities in capital holdings between the rich and the poor of the industrial sector, whereas in most of Africa the relatively egalitarian land distribution would not seem capable of generating the same inequalities as the wealth differentials in other sec-tors. I return to this huge variance in landholding patterns below as a significant element in the differentiation of various agricultural forms, but for now it offers a barrier to any systematic generalization about the inequality propensities of agricultural and industrial systems. Like-wise, it is not obvious whether the systems can be differentiated on the basis of inequalities generated by unemployment and underemploy-ment of resources. Certainly labor is far more frequently underutilized than either capital or land, a tendency that has a major impact on the size distribution of income, but differences among the latter two are not immediately evident.

In one important respect class cleavages differ in industrial and agri-cultural sectors, however. Technological progress in the industrial sec-tor typically leads to the need for highly skilled labor and thus the creation of a structural position between capitalist and unskilled la-borer. Although it is possible that at some stages of development this change introduces another cleavage that can lower relative basic needs fulfillment, it seems likely that more often it will act to stabilize income distribution by preventing a single massive cleavage. It also provides a mechanism for fundamental change in the political economy which may eventually be significant for basic needs. Thus, some class in-equalities may be easier to reduce in the industrial than in the agri-cultural sector because of the market response to the development of human capital. With stratification of the labor market—either through "skilling" of segments of the labor force or the upward pressures on wages owing to labor organization—intermediate categories of workers develop. By contrast, output changes in agriculture are more likely to occur without great infusions of capital, technological innovation, or specialized skills in the labor force, instead responding to very simple mechanization, other inputs like fertilizer or new seeds, or demand changes. Thus, no comparable "middle class" in agriculture is likely to develop; indeed, the continuation of market pressures interacting with initial conditions tends to increase rather than decrease the gap in asset ownership and with it the income differential.

There are also price effects unique to agricultural systems. First, the greater fluctuations characteristic of agricultural prices operate similarly to output fluctuations in lowering welfare levels expected on the basis of a year-to-year average income. Second, the well-known price gap between urban and rural sectors has less clear net implications. Certainly the lower food prices characteristic of rural areas raise basic needs purchasing power above the levels suggested by income. However, the prices of other goods and services especially relevant to basic needs, such as health care and potable water, tend to exhibit the reverse pattern. At the level of whole economies, normalizing income according to a common market basket of consumption (purchasing power parity) can limit the effect of price distortions, but this is only a partial solution since the market basket used is not one relevant to basic needs satisfaction (Kravis et al., 1975). Moreover, there is no similar procedure to adjust for intersectoral price differences within a single economy.

In sum, the cross-cutting arguments do not make a clear case for expecting either industrial or agricultural systems to outperform the other in basic needs provision. Ahluwalia's (1974) collection of data indicates that household income inequality is smaller in rural areas, though that conclusion does not consider the other elements in basic needs determination which seem generally to point in the opposite direction. In particular, "cross-time inequalities" and the logistical problems of providing infrastructure at the lower population densities of rural areas suggest that agricultural sectors may lag. The major differences *among* agricultural systems, however, make it difficult to characterize them as a group.

At least two interrelated dimensions define agricultural systems within which the dynamics that provide basic needs levels vary. The first relates to factor endowments and the mix of inputs in the production function, while the other concerns the use of output.

Different agricultural systems utilize quite variable levels of technology and land.[10] The sub-Saharan African pattern, for example, is based on very low levels of technology but relatively abundant land, whereas the South Asian pattern consists of somewhat greater technological sophistication applied to markedly smaller plots (Bell and Duloy, 1974).[11]

---

10. This difference is especially clear if we compare noncommercial peasant agriculture with North American agribusiness. That the latter's use of technology has more in common with the industrial than the agricultural sectors in most other economies is revealed by huge differences in labor productivity. Todaro (1981: 41) opines that estimates of agricultural labor productivity in North America as much as thirty-five times greater than that in Asia and Africa are overstated but within an order of magnitude. The productivity gap between developed and less developed countries more generally appears to be in the range of ten to fifteen times (Todaro, 1981: 257).

11. The differences in productivity determinants across these two cases may be summarized by noting that the South Asian problem derives from the diminishing marginal

Lenski and Lenski (1974) label the former "horticultural" and the latter "agrarian" societies. Though the two may yield similar levels of income and even similar traditional measures of productivity, they are actually very different systems. The most obvious immediate difference is the much greater population density supported by agrarian systems, whose productivity per unit of land is much greater than in horticultural systems—even though productivity per unit of labor is quite similar. From the standpoint of basic needs, the higher population concentrations and greater urbanization make the logistical problems of providing collective goods like water, sewage, transportation, education, and other infrastructural and utility systems somewhat more tractable in the South Asian pattern.

The more typical Latin American pattern involves both more advanced technology and more abundant land, thus yielding higher productivity. Overall rural production is still well below technical possibilities, however, due to extremely high inequality in landholdings which leads to underutilization of land and various suboptimal mixes of production factors. "Minifundios" are too labor-intensive while "latifundios" undercultivate arable land (Berry and Cline, 1979).

For our purposes, differences in factor mixes are important for two reasons. First, it is evident from the discussion of Bell and Duloy (1974) that these different patterns suggest that different policy initiatives may be neccesary to increase the living standards of the poor. Second, though it is less clear that the political and social dynamics of such systems constitute greater or lesser barriers to basic needs provision, it is apparent that the structural relations among key actors are very different. How these differences are manifested in the political arena is considered in Parts III and IV of the book.

There is another more important difference among agricultural sectors, however. The socioeconomic formation of subsistence agriculture is a special case of an agricultural system marked by both a characteristic location on the dimension of technological sophistication and a unique attribute of nonmonetized output.[12] With the geographical and sectoral spread of global capitalism, of course, there are no longer any

---

productivity of abundant labor on scarce land at low levels of technology, whereas most African economies suffer from the diminishing marginal productivity of abundant (though poor-quality) land at low levels of technology.

12. I avoid the more general distinction between capitalist and precapitalist modes of production, however. It is, of course, notoriously difficult to draw for both theoretical and empirical reasons. Above all, the articulation of quite different modes of production within sectors and within nations is a primary feature of the contemporary global system, which is undeniably dominated by capitalism. Thus, the remaining precapitalist sectors—however defined—are clearly different from the classic picture of largely autonomous modes of production.

exclusively subsistence agricultural economies, and even the purely subsistence sector within most predominantly capitalist economies is small and declining rapidly. Nonetheless, subsistence agriculture remains important in many current systems and the stamp of its historical presence has continuing impact in many more. Clearly, the size of that sector, its connection to more modern sectors, and its relevance to patterns in the contemporary political economy are highly variable across nations. Because the extraction and distribution of the economic surplus in these systems contrast sharply with those of other systems, their variable role across economies may be a significant factor in cross-national differences in basic needs provision.

Truly subsistence agriculture carries resource allocation and mobilization implications not found in even similarly poor agricultural sectors that produce for a market. While agricultural systems in general are marked by lower levels of inequality than industrial systems, and "horticultural" systems—within which subsistence cultivation is most common—tend to even smaller individual differences, subsistence economies are especially egalitarian (Lenski and Lenski, 1974). An important reason is that the nonmonetization of final goods in subsistence economies also leads to nonmonetization of landholdings. With little commercial value, land is not so routinely bought and sold, offered for collateral, or rented; consequently, landholding patterns are much more egalitarian than in commmercial agricultural sectors. Theoretically, rent-wage imbalances are a less significant factor in the size distribution of income. At the practical level, the wealth-concentrating role of the moneylender is much reduced (Todaro, 1981: 263–67).

The common assumption that inequality predicts poorer basic needs performance than would be possible with a more equitable distribution of income and wealth seems to imply that subsistence systems would produce near the maximum levels of welfare possible for a given income level. In fact, there are good reasons to suppose that subsistence systems promote very low levels of welfare and consistently underperform market-based systems of equal income.

First, the *consumption* basket at the individual or small-group level must be nearly identical to the *production* basket because even internal trade levels are low when the output is nonmonetized. This, of course, is the defining characteristic of a subsistence sector.[13] Consequently, not only are the productivity advantages of specialization forgone rela-

---

13. The use of the term "subsistence" in this context is ironic and misleading. It refers not to the outcome of such processes but to their goal. Individual-level sustenance is the maximum that such systems can provide; more often they meet the less exacting standard of reproduction of the economically necessary population, which is compatible with the very high infant mortality rates, very short life expectancies, and very low levels of literacy which are characteristic of these systems.

tive to systems that produce primarily for a market, so too are such "consumption efficiencies" as a more diversified diet. Second, non-monetized production makes the extraction of surplus even more sharply limited than would be the case if products could be easily marketed. Because neither savings rates nor taxation rates can be positive fractions, let alone significantly large, the surplus cannot be as easily mobilized for the purpose of supplying the collective goods that are so essential to the provision of basic needs. Given the greater logistical problem posed by smaller land densities, subsistence economies yield almost no increment of basic needs from collective goods or even personal investment.[14]

Systems with such limited capacity for both generating surplus and monetizing it manifest low levels of investment and thus slow growth. Indeed, the pace of change generated by micro-level processes is likely to be quite slow. It may be equally significant that systems without the capacity to generate collective goods are also incapable of the major changes associated with the larger-scale undertakings of institutions. In the modern world, of course, contact with other societies cannot be prevented, and the weakness of domestic institutions implies a vulnerability to the domination of others. The course taken by such societies in terms of economic development, state formation, institutional growth, policy making, class alliances, and ultimately the welfare of the poor may be as much a product of outside forces as of the internal dynamic, which is too ineffective at reproduction to withstand the external pressures.

In fact, recognition that the provision of basic necessities requires both minimal levels of collective goods and regular, broadly distributed individual expenditures leads me to speculate that at low levels of wealth the principal determinant of basic needs provision will be the former, whereas at higher levels, the latter issue is more central. In both cases, however, the economic processes strongly interact with the political and social ones, as considered both in this discussion and throughout the remainder of the book.

Dualism, Disarticulation, and Uneven Development

The real question of interest, however, concerns not so much the basic needs performance of sectors as that of whole economic systems. The

14. It might be considered that the absence of fluctuating prices in subsistence farming might remove one source of risk which plagues commercial agriculture. That is probably true, but outweighed by the greater risk that output short-falls may drop basic needs provision below the sustenance point in the absence of even the very limited security offered by the possibility of credit.

latter may have as much to do with the interaction of these various sectors within a single economy as the inequality within each sector (Swamy, 1967). In particular, sectoral and geographic unevenness can have serious basic needs implications. When sectors are not articulated in ways that permit growth in one sector to spread to others, it is possible that growth that raises GNP will have no positive impact on basic needs levels; indeed, several mechanisms could cause its impact to be negative.

First, where there are large leakages from the economy, the income multiplier effects may be quite small (Caves and Jones, 1973). When many of the factor inputs come from abroad and much of the output is sold externally, backward and forward linkage effects will be sharply limited. If profits flow overseas or a sizable percentage of the wage bill is concentrated in the hands of a few with tastes for imports, linkages will be restricted. The wealthy in poor, open economies are likely to spend and invest their money abroad, thus limiting growth potential and spread effects.[15]

Second, the development may be predatory on other sectors or regions because the growth node attracts an inflow of capital, skilled labor, and entrepreneurship as well as a disproportionate share of limited funds for infrastructural development. Other sectors are drained of the inputs for development as the best of human and nonhuman resources are attracted by a growth pole that offers greater opportunity. This dynamic is central to capitalist development—indeed, fundamental to the explosive growth potential of capitalism as an economic system—and is manifested in countless ways, well known in a variety of literatures. It forms, for example, the basis of the damaging overmigration from rural to urban areas (Todaro, 1976; Portes and Walton, 1981), the decapitalization of the periphery (Frank, 1966), the sunbelt-snowbelt dynamic in the United States, the international "brain drain" phenomenon, and many other "backwash effects" (Myrdal, 1957).

Third, price effects undermine the living standards of all those who do not benefit directly from the uneven development. As incomes in one sector rise, prices follow. Price rises will generally lag income increases within the growth enclave, but the effect in other areas will be

15. These are the familiar conditions cited by dependencia theorists as the root of the failure of Latin American growth to produce true development. In particular, sectoral and geographical unevenness is encouraged by enclaves resulting from multinational corporation investment, extractive industries with high capital/labor ratios, or limited-input, external demand–oriented enclaves like cash crop sectors. The leakages are greatest in nations with small, ineffectual, and dependent governments, high import propensities, and limited contact between sectors owing to their articulation with external rather than internal markets.

either uncompensated price increases (falling real incomes) or supply shortages. In either case, the fall in basic needs provision in stagnant sectors may equal or exceed the rise in the growth nodes.[16]

Fourth, uneven sectoral development also exacerbates the functional distribution of income because rapidly growing enclaves are ordinarily marked by a higher profit ratio than the sectors from which productive factors are taken. Thus, the share of profits in the national income will rise (Lewis, 1976: 33).

While sectoral and geographic unevenness is a common feature of capitalist economies, the most widely discussed example of it is "dualism," the sharp cleavages found in many Third World nations between rural agricultural and urban industrial sectors, and discussed, in different ways, by nearly all theorists of economic development. An advanced, capital-intensive, modern, urban, industrial sector frequently exists side by side with a backward, labor-intensive, traditional, rural, agricultural sector.

Though difficult to measure, four dimensions of dualism help to explain its highly variable magnitude across nations. First, nations obviously vary in the relative size of these two sectors. The concept is most relevant to basic needs performance in nations at moderate levels of development. Among very poor nations the modern sector is not large enough to generate substantial inequality. At high levels, the reverse is true; the number of the rural poor is too small to greatly affect overall levels of well-being, even if measured by distribution-sensitive indices like the PQLI.

Second, the gap between sectors varies directly with the capital intensity of the advanced sector and inversely with the capital intensity of the agricultural sector. The lower the level of dualism, the lower the inequality associated with this split. In practice this observation implies that relatively labor-intensive industrialization and relatively capital-intensive agriculture would be expected to produce higher levels of PQLI. Both elements of the argument are readily supportable, the first on the basis of fuller employment of labor than is possible otherwise, the latter on the basis of increased productivity where the majority of the poor live. The reverse pattern of factor intensities, which is far more common (especially in highly dependent, export-oriented, MNC-dominated nations), suggests poorer basic needs performance. This underperformance would be exacerbated by the intersectoral flows of urban overmigration, capital drains, and so on.

Third, dualism can be most profound when some sectors are better integrated with external economies than with the remainder of the na-

16. This seems to have been the case in the "Brazilian miracle" (Fishlow, 1973).

tional economy. Thus, though modern trade theory argues that trade will increase the relative return on labor in labor-abundant nations (Caves and Jones, 1973), a large foreign sector may nonetheless lead to underperformance by inducing greater sectoral inequality, especially with an extractive or MNC-financed export enclave with high capital/labor ratios.

At the same time, the articulation of these key sectors to external economies rather than to the internal economy encourages greater inequality in the functional distribution of income as well. Consider that the interests of capitalists in an economy with a small foreign sector are mixed: increases in the wage bill may threaten profits, but when taken collectively they also increase demand (de Janvry and Garramon, 1977; Portes and Walton, 1981). When demand is largely external, however, wage increases are a deadweight loss likely to be resisted through extraeconomic avenues (e.g., government repression) that are less available in systems where demand counterarguments will be raised by other capitalists. Thus, a large foreign sector undermines an important bargaining position for labor and, by compromising the case for diminishing inequality, probably lowers basic needs provision relative to self-contained economies with more mixed incentives. Additional elements related to dependent relations are considered in later chapters.

Fourth, the connections between sectors vary, though there is probably less empirical variance across countries in this regard than there is theoretical variance across theorists. Controversy exists over both the extent of the contact between sectors and the impact of that articulation. Many suggest that the contact is relatively limited but see it as either mostly benign or positively helpful for development. They emphasize that the rural sector exports surplus food to sustain the workers in the industrial sector and to provide foreign exchange revenues for the importation of needed investment goods. At the same time, the agricultural sector also provides a market for industrial goods and a source of labor which can be calibrated to the demand for it. This contact is not only helpful for industrial growth, it also provides an outlet for surplus labor, whose near-zero marginal productivity is a drag on overall rural development (Lewis, 1954; Fei and Ranis, 1961). Thus, this view argues that the agricultural sector sustains the industrial one, yet the former is little affected by the latter and then in a mildly positive way.

By contrast, many see the rural sector as tightly incorporated into the overall economy and sharply conditioned by it. The contact is dominated by backwash effects so that dualism is not merely an indicator of great inequality, it guarantees the continuation and exacerbation of that cleavage. Further, it places an upper limit on feasible growth, the shape of which is also more likely to have a negative than positive impact on the poor. For our purposes, this view implies basic needs levels lagging conventionally defined development indicators. Articulation with precapitalist modes of production which absorb a substantial share of the costs of reproducing the labor force (through the production of cheap food and the maintenance of excess labor supply) is a major theme in most "unequal exchange" arguments, whether framed at the international or intersectoral levels (Portes and Walton, 1981; Emmanuel, 1972; Amin, 1976; Wolpe, 1975).

At the same time, the developmental patterns that arise in dualist economies frequently manifest an "urban bias" that goes beyond the natural dynamics of capitalist markets (Lipton, 1977). For political reasons, planners respond more to the problems of politically powerful and volatile urban dwellers, thus pursuing policies that reinforce the urban-rural imbalance which would be present in any case. Griffin (1981: 5–6) argues, however, that the alleged sectoral bias is actually an accidental manifestation of class bias. Although it appears to produce intersectoral consequences, the cluster of policies at issue—licensing, foreign exchange allocations, credit availability and interest rates, expenditure targeting, etc.—actually produces even greater *intra*sectoral distributional consequences, including the impoverishment of rural workers and the growth of an informal urban sector of dubious benefit to urban workers.[17]

The Structure of Production and Basic Needs

Given these theoretical expectations, we now turn to the first of the empirical analyses linking economic structure with basic needs performance. The working hypothesis is that the distribution of the labor force across the agricultural and industrial sectors is a better predictor of basic needs levels than standard GNP measures.[18]

17. The basic needs implication of the growth of the urban informal sector involves interesting complications discussed in Chapter 5.

18. Though the bulk of this discussion has emphasized the purely economic differences among alternative development paths, subsequent chapters show that alternative modes of production are also important for various other political and social correlates of structural change. For example, GNP growth derived from improved terms of trade, monopoly gains from natural resources, highly sectoralized export promotion, or net factor flows need not be accompanied by such transformations as the growth of the urban working class, middle class, and autonomous national bourgeoisie; the creation of a strong, nationalist state; formation of integrated and autonomous networks in education and communication; and, perhaps most important, the rise of effective political actors, institutions, and policies that represent mass interests. By contrast, GNP growth

Table 4-2. Correlations between development measures and PQLI (broken down by income segments)

Wide income ranges

Variables	All (N = 98)	$90–$300 (N = 28)	$300–$2,300 (N = 48)	$2300+ (N = 21)
GNP/cap	.715	.287	.450	.600
Logged GNP/cap	.861	.324	.488	.610
PPP/cap	.807	.381	.604	.503
Logged PPP/cap	.881	.410	.590	.536
% labor agriculture	−.900	−.544	−.719	−.179

Narrow income ranges

Variables	$90–$2,300 (N = 78)	$90–$150 (N = 15)	$150–$300 (N = 14)	$300–$1,300 (N = 39)	$1,300–$2,300 (N = 9)
GNP/cap	.650	.118	−.389	.428	−.254
Logged GNP/cap	.724	.117	−.357	.428	−.258
PPP/cap	.759	.429	−.092	.545	.396
Logged PPP/cap	.774	.415	−.147	.526	.402
% labor agriculture	−.824	−.574	−.360	−.640	−.800

Though an imperfect indicator, the percentage of the work force employed by agriculture and industry taps this critical developmental dimension.[19] Of course, labor force measures are collinear with aggregate wealth indicators, but it is argued that the relationships of basic needs provision with the former will be stronger than those involving GNP per capita and, indeed, will appear even net of their effects.

Table 4-2 confirms the significance of these developmental processes by showing the correlations between five development indicators and the PQLI. To uncover differences in these relationships across levels of development, the table is broken down by income groups, some of which overlap. It is most striking that the share of labor force in agriculture is more closely related to PQLI than is overall GNP per capita, whether the latter is measured conventionally or by the purchasing power parity reestimates and whether in logged or unlogged form. Moreover, this is true

derived from industrialization is much more likely to involve both the economic transformations identified with classical, autonomous development (technological progress, increasing employment, infrastructural improvement, etc.) and the political processes that affect basic needs. It is thus argued that GNP growth is less important than structural transformations measured by changes in labor force distributions across sectors.

19. The variable for the percentage of the labor force in agriculture is V285 from *World Handbook III* (Taylor and Jodice, 1982).

not only for the sample as a whole, but for six of the seven income ranges separately. The seventh—nations above $2,300—is of marginal importance, however, due to the limited variance in basic needs performance within the group. It is also not surprising that sectoral labor force changes would fail to account for much variance at this level of development, since the transition to a largely industrial economy is essentially complete at this stage. In fact, though of course these indicators are highly collinear, with this segment removed, the gap in explanatory power between the percent in agriculture measure and even the best-fitting of the GNP specifications (the logged version of the purchasing power párity estimate) is substantial.

One other developmental dimension—the importance of subsistence agriculture—is of considerable interest, but data for it are more difficult to come by. Adelman and Morris's (1967) compilation of ordinal rankings for circa 1960 on the percentage of the labor force in subsistence agriculture is the only measure available. Its use is somewhat questionable for several reasons. The time point does not fit the rest of the indicators used in this or most subsequent analyses. The data themselves are of questionable quality. Finally, it lowers the sample to 67 when included in the same analysis as GNP reestimates.[20] Nonetheless, because of this dimension's centrality to the question of the relevance of mode of production for basic needs provision, it is included in a regression of PQLI on the percentage of the labor force in agriculture and logged GNP (corrected for price distortions). That regression is reported in Table 4-3, and though its results cannot be accepted without some caution, they are suggestive indeed. The strong negative coefficient is in line with expectations and indicates that movement away from subsistence agriculture is a significant factor in enhanced basic needs levels. Regardless of overall growth in wealth or income, and even without shifts in overall employment levels in the agricultural sector, subsistence sectors—despite their presumed lower inequality—appear to do very badly in the provision of basic needs. In fact, within some ranges the importance of the subsistence sector appears to be a better predictor of PQLI than the size of the agricultural sector as a whole. When the analysis was rerun for various income segments, the relative importance of the subsistence sector was inversely related to level of development.[21] Furthermore, in no case was

20. Unfortunately, the Adelman and Morris sample contained no state socialist nations, so that dummy variable, proved so helpful a predictor earlier, could not be included in this analysis.

21. It is never an easy decision to use data of questionable quality. In this case, the results of multiple analyses—most not reported in detail here—suggest that the effects reported are not the consequence of measurement error. For one thing, the results are quite

Table 4-3. PQLI regressed on labor force and GNP measures

Variables	Simple r	All variables				Significant variables		
		Beta	St. beta	t		Beta	St. beta	t
Logged PPP/cap	.71	2.43	.08	.7				
% labor agriculture	−.80	−.29	−.27	−2.2*		−.33	−.31	−2.8**
% labor subsistence	−.85	−.49	−.56	−4.8***		−.51	−.59	−5.3***

Model	N	r	r^2	adj. r^2	SEE	F
All variables	67	.86	.75	.74	11.97	62.8***
Significant variables	67	.86	.75	.74	11.92	94.8***

*Significant (p < .05)
**Significant (p < .01)
***Significant (p < .001)

any GNP measure even marginally significant in the presence of the labor force measures.

The very strong performance of the labor force measure suggests that we now attempt to replicate the model of state socialist effects first estimated with a GNP measure in Table 4-1.[22] Not only do we need to reaffirm the state socialist effect when our specification of level of development improves, we also want to reexamine the somewhat surprising finding that state socialist effects can be adequately modeled as shifting the intercept but not altering the slope. A comparison of Table 4-4 with Table 4-1 highlights two significant differences from the earlier analysis.

First, the effects of state socialist systems are shown to be markedly greater with a proper specification. In the additive model, not only does the parameter estimate for the state socialist dummy variable increase in size—from about 17 to nearly 20—but the standard error declines markedly and the overall r^2 changes more significantly. Second, the interactive specification is now shown to be markedly superior— but in precisely the

---

robust across different samples. Further, the behavior of the model across income segments is coherent and perfectly in accord with the reasonable expectation that subsistence sectors would become less and less important as level of development increased. Moreover, these same analyses strengthen our conviction that the size of the agricultural labor force is a significantly better predictor of basic needs than GNP, since no GNP measure appeared as a significant predictor after inclusion of any or both labor force figures in any of the income-segmented analyses. This robust result would be highly unlikely if the difference in explanatory power of the indicators was artifactual.

22. Naturally it would be desirable to include the subsistence measure of Adelman and Morris, but doing so would entail reducing the size of the nation sample more dramatically than is compatible with the general character of the study. In fact, it would reduce the sample by nearly half. Thus, both this analysis and my further work retain the larger sample at the expense of a theoretically promising dimension, but one whose measurement is, in any case, problematic.

Table 4-4. Basic model of labor force structure and socialist effects (with an additive and interactive specification)

ADDITIVE FORM Variables	Simple r	All variables Beta	St. beta	t	Significant variables Beta	St. beta	t
% labor agriculture	− .87	− .87	− .85	− 20.3***	− .87	− .85	− 20.3***
State socialism	.30	19.94	.20	4.9***	19.94	.20	4.9***

Model	N	r	r^2	adj. r^2	SEE	F
All variables	120	.89	.80	.80	12.78	232.5***
Significant variables	120	.89	.80	.80	12.78	232.5***

INTERACTIVE FORM Variables	Simple r	All variables Beta	St. beta	t'	Significant variables Beta	St. beta	t
% labor agriculture	− .87	− .89	− .87	− 21.0***	− .89	− .87	− 21.6***
State socialism	.30	− 3.09	− .03	− .3			
% labor × socialism	.24	.57	.26	2.7	.51	.23	5.7***

Model	N	r	r^2	adj. r^2	SEE	F
All variables	120	.90	.81	.81	12.45	166.0***
Significant variables	120	.90	.81	.81	12.40	250.8***

*Significant (p < .05)
**Significant (p < .01)
***Significant (p < .001)

opposite direction to that postulated. That is, contrary to the original expectation, the gap between the basic needs performance of capitalist and state socialist systems declines—not increases—at higher levels of resources. To see this, observe that the coefficient for the interaction term is + .51; that is, the expected value of PQLI for socialist systems is greater than that of capitalist systems by an increment of .51 times the percentage of the labor force in agriculture. At the sample mean (about half the labor force in agriculture), this translates to a gap of about 25 PQLI points, whereas among the more structurally advanced (i.e., less agricultural) nations, the figure would be considerably smaller. This gap is more in line with the gap actually observed with respect to the Eastern European nations, which was established in note 5 of this chapter to be about 10 to 15 points. At the same time, the expected gap among the poorest nations in the sample would be much larger—as much as 40 points for a nation with 80 percent of its labor force in agriculture—and closer to that observed between Cuba and capitalist nations at similar levels of development.

The explanation for this effect returns us to the curves and scatterplots of Chapter 3. We know that the deviations of actual PQLI from the values expected on the basis of development level alone decline with levels of development. Simply put, allocational mechanisms appear to matter much less in systems whose overall resources are sufficient to sustain basic needs despite distributional inequities or resource inefficiencies. The greatest difference can be made—and apparently is made by socialist political economies—at relatively low levels. Stated differently, the curve of basic needs levels relative to development levels is flatter for socialist political economies than capitalist ones, in large measure because the superior record compiled at lower levels makes further progress more difficult for socialist states. By contrast, the underperformance of capitalist systems allows progress to be more rapid, even though at all income levels the PQLI of capitalist nations remains considerably below that of their socialist counterparts.

The above analyses address the major arguments concerning the basic needs propensities of general modes of production (monetized agriculture, subsistence agriculture, capitalist industrialization, and socialist industrialization). Earlier discussion also identified several more specific features of an economic development path thought likely to carry basic needs consequences. In particular, I considered elements of contact between the foreign sector and the global capitalist system. Even though the incorporation of economies into the global capitalist system has profound implications for the structure of the economy, I postpone a discussion of those linkages to Chapter 8. At that point a more thorough and integrated analysis will enable us to represent more of the dynamics associated with dependent development as a distinctive mode of production. The mechanisms by which those linkages affect basic needs involve effects transmitted through the political system as well as those operating more autonomously in the economic sphere. Thus, it will be advantageous to consider the proximate effects of domestic politics before tracing the dynamic interactions of internal and external factors and their more distal impacts on basic needs provision.

In summary, basic needs performance improves with level of development, but it does not follow that such improvement is necessary, automatic, or universal. The search for an understanding of the mechanisms that generate differential basic needs performance has thus far yielded only preliminary inferences into the most important of the processes of basic needs provision.

It is evident that the logarithmic relationship between GNP and PQLI conceals a more fundamental relationship involving the timing of certain structural processes, especially the shift of the labor force from the agricultural to the industrial sector. Beyond the point marking the essential end of structural transformation in productive processes, basic needs improvement slows dramatically while the variation in national experience correspondingly narrows. This finding does not reveal the responsible mechanisms, however. Though the simple explanation—at higher income levels the trickle-down of aggregate wealth floods the problem—may be correct, it is also well known that structural features of the economy, polity, and society narrow markedly with maturation. In particular, nearly all wealthy societies have evolved either a democratic or a state socialist political system, both of which—as we see below—perform particularly well in the provision of basic needs at all income levels. This issue must be revisited when a more complete model of basic needs determination—including its political components—becomes available. That is the task of the next chapter.

Chapter 5
Social and Political Dimensions of Development

Social and Political Correlates of Development

The previous analysis of economic structures hinted at effects that lie in the social and political realms. In this chapter I consider in greater detail two sets of related processes. First, structural change in the economy substantially alters the behavior of individuals by affecting their opportunities and constraints. The two examples analyzed in this chapter—the migration decisions related to urbanization and the family size decisions related to fertility and the demographic transition—illustrate the significance of the view of economic development as much more than rising aggregate income. The changes in economic structure that accompany GNP growth along some—but not all—development paths carry social and political implications by shaping individual decisions. In turn, these decisions affect basic needs outcomes both directly and indirectly. For example, the life chances of the individual rural-to-urban migrant are thought to improve, yet the aggregation of these decisions brings about the overurbanization widely thought to undermine the welfare capacity of the system as a whole.

The second process by which economic structures affect basic needs fulfillment involves power distributions among political actors. Markets, while allocating goods and services, simultaneously allocate wealth, political power, and leverage on the many processes that govern the distribution of the economic surplus. Thus, as economic development proceeds, structures of political power tend to evolve in patterned ways. In this chapter, I begin the investigation of the dynamic impact of these changes on basic needs levels by considering the relative importance of key economic and political groups. Part III of the book then builds on this analysis by investigating the character of the institutions that govern society.

Urbanization and Rural Migration

Urbanization resulting from large-scale rural migration is an especially interesting process from the perspective of our earlier analysis. First, although increasing urbanization is widely regarded as a natural component of development, it is a dimension that varies quite widely across nations. Thus, it is a visible example that the variance I have previously identified with alternative *economic* development paths has its counterpart in alternative paths of *social* development. Second, urbanization is thought by many development theorists to carry profound implications for both the immediate well-being of citizens and the prospects of a nation for future welfare gains. If so, it should be a partial predictor of PQLI.

Chenery and Syrquin's (1975) analysis identifies most development processes as occurring according to a nonlinear but monotonic function, typically marked by a relatively rapid change followed by a leveling off. Although most processes can be accurately represented by a similar functional form, they nonetheless tend to occur at quite different points in the developmental history. The timing of urbanization is especially illuminating in juxtaposition with indicators of processes whose transition occurs relatively early in the developmental sequence—such as shifts in sectoral production shares (e.g., percent of GDP originating in agriculture)—and those that usually occur relatively late, such as labor force allocations (e.g., percent of labor force in agriculture).

In nations below a GNP per capita of $100,[1] 71 percent of the labor force is in primary sectors, which produce 52 percent of GNP, while 8 percent of the labor force is in industry, which produces 13 percent of output. Above $1,000, the labor force shares and production shares are nearly equal, though this gap—which reflects differences in productivity across sectors—never quite disappears. Productivity in agriculture, for example, averages about 70 percent of the economy-wide figure in the poorest countries, declines to about 50 percent in nations

1. The numbers are from Chenery and Syrquin (1975) and refer to 1964 U.S. dollars at factor cost. The translation to 1970 U.S. dollars at market prices—the metric used in the remainder of the empirical analyses—requires multiplying by a factor of roughly 1.5.

with income per head around $500, and then gradually rises as (1) agricultural technology is modernized at a lag after technology enters industry and (2) surplus agricultural labor is absorbed by the rest of the economy. Relative service sector productivity, by contrast, begins around 150 percent and falls slowly from about $500 until it finally dips below that of industry above $1,500. Relative to both industry and agriculture, capital substitution is limited in the service sector.[2]

Thus, for a long period in the transition, labor is more productive and better compensated in the industrial sector than in the agricultural sector. Of course, natural adjustment processes—such as urban migration—operate to equalize factor returns across sectors. Urbanization, which can be seen in part as the attempt of workers to shift from a less productive sector to a more productive one, is less rapid than productivity gains but much more rapid than employment changes. High levels of urban underemployment are thus a component of the "overurbanization" nearly universal in the Third World. Urbanization begins at about 12 percent of population, reaches 50 percent at around $450, and stabilizes at about 75 percent above $2,000. This timing leads that of labor force shares, which begin at about 8 percent industrial and reach equality between industry and agriculture (at about 30 percent each) when aggregate income reaches about $800.

Thus, urbanization is often represented as a natural consequence of economic development; indeed, in this sample ($N = 95$), the zero-order correlation between logged GNP and urbanization is $+.79$. Still, urbanization is very much more rapid in some nations than in others; after all, more than a third of the variance remains unexplained by level of development. Although space does not allow any extensive discussion of the factors that account for differential urbanization, a search for urbanization correlates among the variables used elsewhere in this study does reveal patterns that may be useful in interpreting later findings. First, not unexpectedly, the share of the labor force in agriculture is more closely tied to urbanization levels ($r = -.83$) than is GNP ($r = +.79$), a reminder that differences between agricultural and industrial development patterns go beyond wealth to encompass a range of social features. Second, alternative economic development paths carry implications for urbanization; for example, even after controlling for labor force shares, urbanization levels are smaller among nations marked by large foreign trade sectors, especially those involving substantial plantation and mining operations. Third, colonial histories appear to be relevant, with former British colonies being markedly less urban than either long-independent nations or former French colo-

2. O'Connor (1973) makes a similar point about lagging productivity in the service sector and especially the public sector in advanced industrial societies.

nies, even after controlling for both economic factors and the modest, but discernible, differences between urbanization in the various regions of the world.

These correlates of urbanization are important to us in part because urbanization may directly affect basic needs levels through either of two cross-cutting mechanisms. On the one hand, overurbanization seems to tax service delivery systems beyond their limits (Todaro, 1976; Abu-Lughod and Hay, 1977). Yet, on the other hand, the known propensity of urban PQLIs to remain substantially above rural ones suggests that other factors are at work (Chenery et al., 1974). Greater land densities in urban areas ease logistical problems and offer economies of scale in the provision of infrastructure. It is also thought that urban problems tend to be afforded priority over rural ones because the concentration of the poor in cities may give them greater political leverage to force government policies to respond to their plight (Lipton, 1977). The urban underemployed may represent the first step in a developing working class whose economic position and political power is actually midway between the rich and the very poor.

It is difficult to net out these effects, especially since urban growth is concentrated in the urban informal sector whose character undermines the easy dualist dichotomy between advanced urban and backward rural sectors (Rao, 1974). The basic needs impact of this type of development is far from clear. The informal sector provides surplus labor that is perpetually underemployed and immediately available to place downward pressure on wage rates in the formal sector. But, because of the sensitivity of the PQLI to the very poorest, and the relative prosperity of the fully employed workers in the urban formal sector, depressing wage levels in the urban formal sector may not degrade the overall PQLI if balanced by the increasing size of sectors that sustain higher basic needs levels. Further, the movement between rural and urban areas—both cyclical population movement and repatriation of wages—may help to balance and stabilize the economies of both areas.

Still, though health and welfare conditions in urban slums and squatter settlements are poor, they are not generally worse than in the rural areas from which the inhabitants have migrated. The easier logistics of service delivery seem to marginally outweigh the negative consequences of crowding. Social indicators seem to indicate that this is true, and the continuation of urban migration leads many to believe that expected utility is evidently greater in the urban slums than in rural areas. If the desperately poor freely choose migration—a point that, of course, remains in dispute—perhaps analysts should take their word that urban life represents a better prospect of fulfillment of basic needs than rural life.

This consideration suggests another benefit of examining urbaniza-

Table 5-1. Two basic economic models, augmented with urbanization

Variables	Simple r	Logged GNP model			Labor force model		
		Beta	St. beta	t	Beta	St. beta	t
% labor agriculture	−.89				−.89	−.89	−19.8***
Socialist × agr.	.14				.58	.16	3.6***
Logged GNP/cap	.81	12.63	.60	6.3***			
Urbanization	.74	.31	.26	2.7**	−.01	−.01	−.1
Model	N	r	r^2	adj. r^2		SEE	F
Logged GNP model	95	.83	.68	.67		15.69	98.2***
Labor force model	95	.90	.81	.81		11.99	200.8***

*Significant ($p < .05$)
**Significant ($p < .01$)
***Significant ($p < .001$)

tion rates. If rapid urban migration results from greater than usual disparities in income potentials across sectors, variance in urbanization rates may coincide with the relatively large gaps in productivity and factor intensity associated with notions of dualism and sector inequality. If so, an urbanization measure becomes an indirect proxy for features of uneven sectoral development not easily captured by cross-national measures but readily visible to participants in the process (i.e., urban migrants).

In order to ascertain the net effects of urbanization, Table 5-1 reports the results when the urbanization measure is added to both the economic control models identified previously. Though the zero-order correlation between PQLI and urbanization (+.74) indicates that urban societies are markedly more effective in the provision of basic needs than predominantly rural ones, it appears that the effect is due almost wholly to factors already represented in the economic model constructed in Chapter 4. The left side of the table indicates that the inclusion of urbanization significantly improves the logged GNP prediction of PQLI ($t = 2.7$), but the insignificant coefficient shown on the right side indicates that the labor force in agriculture measure accounts for the variance in PQLI just as well.

From this evidence I conclude that there is no indication that "premature" urbanization is a net detriment to basic needs provision. That is not to say that urbanization processes are unimportant for basic needs determination. The result may reflect a washing out of the two direct effects that were hypothesized to operate in contrary directions. Moreover, it is possible that some of the superiority of the labor force measure as a basic needs predictor reflects its tapping of the urbanization dimension.

Fertility and the Demographic Transition

A second important social dimension of development concerns the set of decisions surrounding fertility and its role in the demographic transition through which both fertility and mortality rates decline. Like "premature" urbanization, a disequilibrium in the demographic transition can be represented as a timing gap between mortality changes, which occur relatively early in the process, and fertility changes, which occur relatively late. Fertility declines are thought to represent family planning decisions that reflect changing opportunities for female employment, changing financial pressures, changing expectations of the survival rates of children, and changing alternatives to large families for old age security (Kasarda et al., 1986; Bulatao and Lee, 1983). Each of these is presumed to follow from economic development, and consequently fertility declines are assumed to be a natural, automatic consequence of aggregate growth and the associated decline in mortality. Of course, neither cultural adaptation nor adjustments in economic calculus are instantaneous, and the resulting lag between mortality and fertility changes manifests itself in the damaging population growth that is such a significant problem in many Third World countries.[3]

The demographic transition remains a popular characterization of a change often argued to be a more or less universal consequence of economic development, but more recent analyses have argued that fertility reductions are importantly mediated by social and cultural changes more conditioned by developmental *paths* than by aggregate income *levels* (Nolan and White, 1983, 1985; Hout, 1980). The argument hinges on differences in the incentive structures for individual family planning decisions associated with different development paths. In particular, the demographic transition may be delayed or distorted by inequality, which leads to a slower fall in fertility because the poor retain high fertility until *they* rather than the *average* family attain higher incomes (Bell and Duloy, 1974: 119; Kocher, 1973). Further, processes that keep wages near subsistence and maintain an economic role for children will sustain a strong incentive to have children and thus keep fertility "unnaturally" high (Hout, 1980). The precise development paths that retain a large economic role for children are not clear, though the considerations must include not only wage rates but economic structures and cultures, such that rural areas and subsistence sectors are likely to have higher rates of child employment than urban ones of similar level of development.

---

3. Age distributions also have great leverage on raw birthrates, so population growth continues for some time after average fertility levels reach the equilibrium point. This too accounts for much of the built-in lag.

Nolan and White (1985) and Hout (1980) argue that dependency predicts to these conditions, and indeed they find a positive effect of dependency measures (some of which I consider in a later chapter) on
fertility. Moreover, Nolan and White (1985) report that in a panel design, development leads to declining fertility (and economic role
change of women) only in the semiperiphery and not the periphery.

All of this leads me to wonder if the differences in development
paths captured in this book's earlier economic models (and refined in
later chapters) can account for some differences in fertility rates. I
would certainly expect so for two reasons. First, the developmental
dimensions were chosen in part to identify economic structures that
produce inequalities. Second, the intimate causal connections between
fertility and infant mortality (the latter of which is a component of the
PQLI) probably imply similar determinants. Thus, a simple model of
fertility based on the economic dimensions discussed elsewhere was
estimated. The results confirm that fertility declines are sensitive to differences in economic development path as well as level of development. Indeed, all the factors significant in predicting PQLI are also significant in this model. The distribution of labor across sectors is more
important than income level (though that too is highly significant) and
state socialist political economies have markedly lower fertility levels.
Moreover, when the dimensions of external dependence discussed in
later chapters are included, significantly higher fertility levels are found
in nations with a large foreign trade sector and a large mining sector,
especially if penetrated by multinational corporations. The multiple r is
above $+.91$.

This finding is important for an understanding of the mechanisms
through which development paths affect basic needs levels. In fact, the
potential significance of demographic effects as mediating mechanisms
in these kinds of relationships is highlighted by Nolan and White
(1985), who argue that the *primary* effect of dependency on growth may
be on the denominator rather than the numerator of GNP/population
(See also Bollen, 1977, and Chirot and Hall, 1982.)

High fertility levels are frequently regarded as a drag on improving
basic needs attainment for several reasons. Most concretely, they place
great pressure on generally inadequate medical and health systems.
Because basic needs measures are made especially sensitive to the welfare of the very young by the inclusion of an infant mortality component, fertility measures are likely to strongly affect PQLI in a quite direct way. High fertility levels are also thought to exacerbate problems
of inequality which translate into relative underperformance in basic
needs provision. Ahluwalia (1974: 30), for example, offers three possible mechanisms to explain his finding that population growth leads to

Table 5-2. Basic economic model, augmented with birthrate

Variables	Simple r	All variables			Significant variables		
		Beta	St. beta	t	Beta	St. beta	t
% labor agriculture	−.86	−.60	−.59	−6.6***	−.65	−.63	−10.1***
Logged GNP/cap	.82	1.29	.06	.7			
Socialist × agr.	.27	.36	.17	4.0***	.36	.17	4.0***
Birthrate	−.83	−.64	−.28	−4.1***	−.67	−.29	−4.5***

Model	N	r	r²	adj. r²	SEE	F
All variables	113	.91	.84	.83	11.56	138.2***
Significant variables	113	.91	.84	.83	11.53	185.1***

*Significant (p < .05)
**Significant (p < .01)
***Significant (p < .001)

lowered income shares for the poor. First, population growth reproduces the labor surplus, which holds down wages relative to interest rates, rents, and profits. Second, population growth is usually more rapid among the poor, thus diluting limited capital (especially inherited farmland) more rapidly than among the richer and less fertile. Third, growth in lower income groups is more rapid than in upper groups, thereby increasing the number of poor relative to the number of rich.

A series of cursory analyses was conducted in which the fertility measure was added to various other economic determinants of basic needs provision. Because the fullest models contain dimensions of economic development path not elaborated until later chapters, only the simplest of these are presented in tabular form here. Nonetheless, three observations are warranted. First, fertility rates are obviously important even after the effects of the level and path of development are included. Table 5-2 illustrates that birthrate is a better zero-order predictor of the PQLI than logged GNP and nearly as good as the labor force measure. Furthermore, it retains explanatory power and statistical significance even in a model that also includes indicators of development path beyond those included in the Chapter 4 model of economic effects illustrated in Table 5-2 (e.g., trade centrality, multinational corporations, mining sectors, plantations, and so on). Second, including birthrate lowers most of the other coefficients in the various models, suggesting that fertility mediates many of the effects we have observed. Third, it seems likely, however, that the empirical effect of birthrate is rather greater on the indicator—the infant mortality component of the PQLI—than it is on the underlying concept: the physical welfare of the poor.

Thus, it seems prudent to remember the potentially important impact of the fertility rate, but misleading to retain it as a causal factor in future models. At the same time, the use of a cross-sectional design, which is necessary for other reasons, does present a formidable limitation at this juncture. The potential for misinterpretation of the causal direction of the relationship is very high in this case. In fact, the arguments that infant mortality declines are causally and temporally prior to birthrate declines seem as strong as the obverse ones, though multicollinearity and serial correlation starkly limit our capacity to sort out the reciprocal causation.

The Effects of Class Actors and Economic Groups

No discussion of the social and political dimensions of development would be complete without treating the impact of development on the creation of economic actors and on differential growth of political power among competing actors. Markets allocate power as surely as they allocate wealth, and determine welfare nearly as directly as they set prices and volumes. Furthermore, because actors reciprocally shape market structure and context, they are a linchpin in the interactions among development path, growth rates, distributional effects, and basic needs provision. Later chapters describe the role of economic actors in shaping the part played by the state in development processes, and Part III of the book considers in more detail the effects of the political system and the orientation of the state on basic needs outcomes. In particular, I want to recast and reinterpret my earlier discussions of the allocation of the economic surplus and both the functional and size distributions of income.

Thus far the arguments have been couched in a way that suggested that economic principles could largely or even fully explain the outcome patterns. The relative scarcity of labor and capital, for example, was portrayed as the major determinant of wage levels relative to rents or profit. Urban/rural cleavages were presented as a consequence of the dynamism of markets and the uncoordinated accumulation of many micro decisions based on narrow profitability criteria. These explanations are partial, however, and potentially misleading if they are taken to be indicative of general "laws" of development which cannot be violated or altered. Rather, these allocational principles must be seen as only one source of the distributional outcomes, which also have a significant social and political side. Moreover, the principles themselves are highly contingent on a social, political, and institutional context that cannot be neglected if we desire either a full picture of the determinants of basic needs provision or an identification of the changes necessary for societies to rapidly alter PQLI levels.

Economic actors can play a dramatic role in altering distributions of income, opportunity, and life chances through both direct and indirect action. Directly, wage rate determination can be seen as the outcome of relative class power as much as the consequence of labor supply and demand. Where the institutional power of the organized working class is relatively great, the bargaining position of any subunit of it is enhanced. Thus, the greater the strength of organized labor, the more egalitarian the income distribution, and the better the relative provision of basic needs. Naturally, the obverse is also true; the greater the power of a traditional rural elite, the more the functional distribution of income emphasizes returns to land and capital, and the lower the wage levels and other remunerations to labor power.

Indirectly, we must also consider the overall orientation of the state apparatus—which I discuss in detail in Part III—as a major consequence of the orientation and action of political elites. Of course, the legal framework within which bargaining over income occurs, the side on which the coercive forces of the state can be expected to intervene to alter both bargaining processes and outcomes, and the theoretical and normative outlook of powerful actors all profoundly influence outcomes relative to basic needs and other indicators of the distribution of national product and aggregate wealth.

At the same time, of course, many of these structural elements are closely identified with particular development paths. Most of the analyses in this vein are found in Part IV of the book, which focuses on the interaction of global economic structures and elements of the domestic political economy, including class structures and the nature of the competition among classes and economic actors. However, at least one such linkage is implied by the analysis thus far. The social structure of a nation with a largely agricultural economic structure is likely to differ markedly from that of a more industrial nation. Traditional rural elites are likely to be more powerful and more dominant and to have less need of alliance or compromise with other actors. Their dominance/ is likely to be visible in the makeup of the state and its orientation toward distributional questions, including the priority to be attached to basic needs provision.

It would certainly help our understanding of the sources of variation in basic needs provision to enter into the analysis indicators of class strength. Operational problems make this difficult, however, and some related theoretical considerations suggest that its value may be somewhat dubious. Most evidently, the relative strengths of classes are difficult to gauge even in concrete cases and all but impossible to measure with precision cross-nationally. Certainly the *size* of the class is an important factor, but its organization, its access to institutions, and its leadership are at least equally significant. Class consciousness is a notoriously difficult concept to measure or even predict in the short term. Further, much of the power of classes derives from a structural position that interacts strongly, though not necessarily predictably, with the economic structure. Bell (1974), for example, considers the organizational prospects of classes to depend on the existence of competing "primordial attachments" of tribe, region, and ethnicity.

Moreover, many of the most significant class effects involve even less visible phenomena, such as the class alliances that magnify the political power of all alliance members. Urban capitalists and urban workers may either conflict violently or unite in support of lower food prices, for example, depending on conditions and strategies. A peasantry seeking land reform may become a partner to an urban alliance or the greatest source of opposition to it. In some production systems the welfare of the poor can become instrumental for the interests of elites, whereas in others the poor must press politically against elites whose interests lead them to resist strongly. In short, the conditions of class power are far from clear and the means to measure it even indirectly are not present in this study.

Nonetheless, the centrality of class concerns leads me to try at least a first cut before the more elaborate analyses of Parts III and IV. Consequently, I introduce three variables derived from the Adelman and Morris (1967) data on their limited sample of nations. The variables are meant to tap the power and importance of key groups: the middle class, the urban working class, and traditional rural elites. The limitations of the variables are illustrated by the measure of the importance of the middle class, which is predominantly an indicator of (1) the percentage of the population employed in certain "middle class" occupations and (2) the percentage of those positions occupied by indigenous as opposed to expatriate elements. The former taps the *size* of the middle class, whereas most theories emphasize that its central mission in transforming the political system depends more on its *strength* and *orientation*. We would expect size to be largely a function of the economic development pattern; the others are less generalizable. The foreign component, though potentially significant for the orientation and sensitivity of elites to the plight of the poor, surely taps only one limited dimension.

Table 5-3 reports the results of two preliminary analyses, the first using logged GNP and the second using the percentage of the labor force in agriculture as the basic model. From the estimates of the right side of the table, it appears that the importance of the middle class predicts superior basic needs provision whereas labor and traditional elites do not act to alter basic needs levels significantly. We must remember, however, the weaknesses of the data. For example, since the

Table 5-3. Basic economic model, augmented with measures of the strength of class actors

Variables	Simple r	Logged GNP model				Labor force model		
		Beta	St. beta	t	Beta	St. beta	t
% labor agriculture	−.81				−.42	−.40	−4.0***
Logged GNP/cap	.66	5.63	.24	2.9**			
Middle class	.81	.59	.62	7.4***	.45	.48	5.0***
Labor	.49	.14	.17	2.3*	.09	.11	1.5
Traditional elites	−.16	.06	.09	1.3	.04	.06	.9

Model	N	r	r^2	adj. r^2	SEE	F
Logged GNP model	70	.85	.73	.71	12.55	44.0***
Labor force model	70	.87	.76	.74	11.93	50.5***

*Significant (p < .05)
**Significant (p < .01)
***Significant (p < .001)

inclusion of the middle class variable dramatically reduces the impact of multinational corporations, it is likely that a substantial fraction of its predictive power derives from its differentiation of indigenous from expatriate elements rather than the power of the middle class relative to others.

Caution is also warranted because of the context of the analysis and the small sample of nations. For example, the labor force measure of economic structure already implicitly contains nearly three-fourths of the variance in the political power of economic groups. Whether the remaining variance picks up disproportionate class power or merely measurement error is far from clear. It is worth noting, however, that the estimates of the predictive power of class strength are much greater—but the overall fit much reduced—when aggregate wealth replaces economic structure as the control. This fact suggests that these elements of class strength partially explain why the *path* of development is significant for the determination of the PQLI, even after controlling for *level* of development.

Several other key actors are deliberately excluded from the above analysis because they are not so closely identified with particular levels of development. The effects of the military and state personnel, the impact of multinational corporations, and the class dynamics associated with plantation development and reliance on foreign trade are taken up in later chapters.

Politics and the State: Allocations by Governmental Institutions

Chapter 6
Effects of the State and Political System

From Market Processes to Government Policies

We have seen in Part II that markets—if left unbridled—tend to allocate resources in ways that yield suboptimal basic needs fulfillment. Part II emphasized marginal productivity explanations of class and sectoral inequalities, but the same conclusion can be reached from a number of theoretical angles that emphasize other economic formulations.[1]

By contrast, Part III pursues political explanations of basic needs levels which encompass extraeconomic factors. This is not to say that such factors are independent of the processes discussed in the first two parts of the book. To the contrary, some political effects may be seen as the mediating mechanisms between economic and social development, on the one hand, and basic needs provision, on the other. This is so because markets do more than allocate final goods and factor inputs; they also allocate wealth, access to infrastructure and institutions, and political power. And, like income, they allocate these other determinants of life chances—hence life chances themselves—unequally as well. Thus, inequalities are produced not only by a freely functioning market system that allocates short-run income, but also by the longer-

---

1. Certainly, the conclusion that markets yield inequality is more universal than orthodox economic pricing theories of factor inputs (Samuelson, 1967). Friedman (1962), for example, finds income inequalities to result from individual differences in skill endowments; relative tastes for leisure, risk, and nonfinancial rewards; and chance. Davis and Moore (1945) present a functionalist theory that views income inequality as a necessary allocation mechanism to ensure that the most talented occupy the appropriate jobs.

term implications of that allocation process for the wealth and political power distributions that reinforce and intensify inequalities.[2]

In Chapter 5 we briefly considered the political and social factors relating to class and political power, but that discussion and the accompanying empirical analysis inadequately treated the major manifestation of political power—control over the state. Part III approaches the problem from the other end by focusing more explicitly on the effect of the state on basic needs provision. To begin, Chapter 6 investigates the size and strength of the state apparatus and then moves to characterizations of the orientation of its policy program. First, it considers orientations that derive from the pressures embodied in the nature of state-societal relations, especially in the context of a democratic political order. Second, the independent effect of ruling regime ideology on the policy priorities of the state is examined. Chapter 7 then takes up the special role of the military within state-level processes, ranging from the impact of socialization imbued by military service to the spending priorities induced by military participation in policy making.

The Role of the State in Basic Needs Provision

The state is a key institution for basic needs provision for a simple reason. If the natural propensity to inequality is to be minimized, the productive capacities of the economy must be *directed* toward the provision of basic needs. That direction must be accomplished outside a system dominated by the logic of capital accumulation and microeconomic rationality; that is, it must occur in the political realm. As Lindblom (1977: 89) observes,

> For organized social life, people need the help of others. In one set of circumstances, what they need from others they induce by benefits offered. In other circumstances, what they need will not willingly be provided and must be compelled. A market system can operate in the first set of circumstances, but not in the second. Its limitation is conspicuous when compared with an authority system.

2. As will be seen below, this argument does not imply that the state or the political system is epiphenomenal, a mere reflection of economic or even social structure. Such economic reductionism founders on the obvious differences in state size, strength, form, and behavior among nations with relatively similar economic structures. At the same time, empirical patterns in state attributes make it clear that some forms of economic organization *are* quite prone to be associated with distinctive political orders. Furthermore, the causation is reciprocal though probably asymmetric. For the most part, however, this chapter treats the political effects as largely autonomous, though the implicit linkage is frequently very near the surface.

There is no better example of the inability of market systems to provide necessities than the plight of the Third World poor. For those who possess nothing to offer in exchange for the resources that would increase their life chances, only an authority system—the political instrument of the state—offers aid.[3]

The numerous pathways through which the state can influence basic needs levels reflect the complexity of the state as an agent of change and the multifaceted nature of its role within the political economy. In subsequent sections, I trace the major modes of causation which flow through the state and note the major impediments these roles must confront.

We must begin by observing that the modern state is frequently involved in direct economic production and is always an important employer. Thus, contrary to the notion that the state can be seen as "outside" the economic system, it is not only an important influence on the economy, and not only significantly dependent on its outcomes, but is actually a key participant in its operation. Thus, in the next section I consider the state as an economic sector and treat the growth of that sector as a dimension of development. Like the agricultural and industrial sectors, the state sector manifests distinctive allocational propensities as its size varies in predictable ways with level of development (Chenery and Syrquin, 1974). This sector's leverage on distributional outcomes via employment effects requires that we investigate elements of its production function which may affect distributional outcomes (e.g., wage levels, resource efficiency, and capital intensity). Quite apart from the controversial impact of government *policy*, it is not clear whether we should consider the state as an economic sector a positive or negative influence on basic needs.

3. Virtually all analysts have assumed that the state is the only effective means to either overturn market-generated outcomes or to impel the market to generate different outcomes (Cutright, 1967; Ward, 1978; Chenery et al., 1974). With respect to the former, there are other possibilities in societies that maintain alternative and potent nonstate institutions. Of these, organized churches appear the most likely. Consequently, a cursory analysis of the effects of religion and related cultural factors is conducted in Chapter 9. Extended families are another possibility, though they operate on a much smaller scale and it is by no means clear that they always *improve* distribution. Their impact on aiding the reproduction of labor by bridging the urban informal sector and the traditional rural sector is addressed briefly in Part IV.

With respect to influencing market forces—as opposed to post hoc compensating for their effects—the organized power of trade unions is a partial exception to state monopoly. However, their effect is complex in systems in which members of organized labor are located in the upper income deciles and enjoy greater income stability and wealth than the poor. Moreover, it is ordinarily assumed that their power can arise only with the aid of the state and that, outside of the limited impact of wage bargaining, the major expression of such power is through the instrumentality of the state (Martin, 1975). The distinctive role of organized labor in plantation economies is considered in Chapter 9.

The most dramatic basic needs effects, however, are thought to revolve around the special role of state policy, which distinguishes it
from other institutions or sectors. Most obviously, the state may contravene the operation of inequality-producing market mechanisms by
redistributing assets or income. Redistribution may take place through
patterns of taxation and expenditures or even more directly via the
provision of collective goods and infrastructure, which are crucial to
basic needs.

More subtle are the pathways that Skocpol (1985: 21–27) calls
"Tocquevillian." Patterns of state activity "affect political culture, encourage some kinds of group formation and collective political action
(but not others), and make possible the raising of certain political issues (but not others)." Thus, the state may systematically improve the
bargaining position of the poor by imposing an institutional and legal
framework favorable to their interests. In this way, the allocational
mechanisms of the economic and political system are made to function
within a context that alters their propensity to yield suboptimal levels
of basic necessities. Through laws governing labor-management and
landowner-peasant relations, for example, the state may alter significantly the relative power of various groups in ways that have implications for their success in nonstate political interactions such as collective bargaining (Herring, 1983; Evans, 1979). The most dramatic
extremes—on the one hand, minimum wage legislation, and on the
other the prohibition of union organizing—exemplify the leverage of
government action on the operation of market mechanisms.

Next, the strength of the state is treated as an indicator of the institution's *capacity* for such action. Because such distributional outcomes
also require that the state be *disposed* to act in ways conducive to basic
needs fulfillment, the following two sections consider *dispositional* arguments rooted in the *goals* of state action. I then introduce the first empirical analysis, which seeks a general impact of state size on basic
needs, and attempt to disaggregate state effects by program area. I
then consider variations in state disposition which originate in state-
societal relations—specifically the impact of democratic mechanisms. A
consideration of ideological differences in the orientation of ruling regimes is followed by a more elaborate empirical analysis of state effects
on the PQLI. For now, we return to the impact of the state sector.

State Sector Size as a Developmental Dimension

Much like the size of the industrial sector, state sector size is a variable
dimension of development which marks both alternative development

paths and different levels of development. Operationally, state expenditures grow with level of development along a curvilinear path not unlike the monotonic function that describes industry share of GNP, though the overall slope—or the total change over the range—is not quite so great. Below per capita income levels of $100 in the Chenery and Syrquin study, government revenue averages about 12 percent of GNP, rising to an average of 31 percent above $1,000.[4] The size of the state sector is also a more variable property of nations at similar levels of development than other sectoral attributes. About 38 percent of the variance in government revenue as a percentage of GNP can be accounted for by level of development.[5]

This variance makes it important to ask if development patterns marked by a relatively large state sector are more or less productive of basic needs than those with a relatively small state sector. To approach the impact of the state on basic needs from that vantage point, I return to the questions of inequality and inefficiency I have used to compare capitalist with socialist systems and agricultural with industrial sectors.

As before, the inequality considerations concern both intrasectoral and intersectoral inequality. It would appear that income inequality is much lower in the state sector than in either the industrial or agricultural sectors because of the relatively minor role of rents, profits, and interest. Exceptions may occur in cases where illegal income is a significant component of government revenues (e.g., the Somoza family in Nicaragua and Emperor Bokassa of the Central African Empire), but seldom in nations dominated by democratic institutions, which offer legal remedy to corruption, or leftist ideologies, which afford little legitimacy to vast wealth gaps.

The implications of public sector wage levels for intersectoral inequalities are more difficult to gauge. Wage rates in state-owned enterprises in the Third World tend to be higher than in the private sector (Bardhan, 1974). Moreover, throughout the public sector productivity tends to be lower than in private sectors with comparable wage rates. This is true not only in the sense that the same operations tend to be performed more efficiently in the private than in the public sector. Many purely public sector activities—the military, for example—are *inherently* more inefficient both by a production function criterion and in the sense of output rationality when physical well-being is the stand-

---

4. By contrast, the percentage of GNP originating in industry increases from about 12 percent to about 37 percent.

5. This fact makes it slightly less predictable than the industry share or primary product share of GNP (about 48 and 46 percent, respectively) and markedly less predictable than labor share in agriculture (about 55 percent).

ard. Public sector wage rates are thought to be disproportionate to productivity for at least three reasons. First, labor market competition
forces public sector wage rates to keep at least apace of wages in the
most advanced sectors, within which productivity is much greater
(O'Connor, 1973). Second, public sector salaries have been historically
high in much of the Third World dating from the colonial and early
postcolonial period in which salaries were calibrated to metropolitan
living standards (Murray, 1963; Magubane, 1985). Third, the absence of
profit-making imperatives lessens the downward pressure on wages.

Thus, through employment effects the state may tend to increase
sectoral inequality much as an advanced sector does in a dualistic economy, even though the major mechanism does not involve differences
in capital intensity. Further, the propensity of state employment to be
concentrated in urban areas will also tend to exacerbate urban-rural
cleavages, which are associated with relatively low levels of basic needs
provision (Lipton, 1977).

At the same time it is generally acknowledged that levels of inefficiency and waste are larger in the state sector than elsewhere. Most of
the explanations for this tendency are too well known to require elaboration here (Larkey et al., 1984); for our purposes, the importance of
the argument lies in its consequences for basic needs achievement.
Conservatives argue that public sector growth—"'Leviathan' run
amuck" (Colella, 1979: 6)—produces such severe "system overload"
that policies are actually counterproductive for aggregate welfare
(Friedman, 1962; Beer, 1977). Indeed, Anton (1984: 53) observes that
Drucker (1969) "even claimed that government seemed able only to
make war and inflation—and the writer was not totally convinced (of
the former)."

How various state activities affect *private sector* efficiency is more controversial, though there is probably agreement across the ideological
spectrum on the general shape of the curve. Relatively modest government activity to maintain the competitive climate and sustain necessary
institutions and infrastructure surely increases efficiency (Polanyi,
1944; Rueschemeyer and Evans, 1985). A powerful state capable of
maintaining the integrity of a functioning institutional structure and a
workable economic and political system is essential. Without it, the
unrestrained behavior of powerful economic and political actors undermines the efficiency of the system—not to mention the welfare of the
poor—by limiting the economic competition that gives capitalism both
its dynamism and its philosophical justification (Hirschman, 1958;
North, 1979). While static efficiency need not yield long-term growth
prospects, the inability of the state to balance the power of other actors

tends to undermine both (Skocpol, 1979).[6] These arguments are more closely associated with the left, but even conservatives do not dispute that such state actions—if limited—are beneficial.

Nor do most of those on the left deny that at very high levels of government intervention to regulate private sector activity (usually for extraeconomic purposes), the state's efforts probably reduce efficiency (Friedman, 1962). Unfortunately, most contemporary governments are lodged in the middle, which is contested theoretical terrain. Thus, it is not clear how the state sector affects net efficiency, nor whether those efficiency reductions that may occur are balanced by parallel improvements in the provision of basic needs through other mechanisms.

The Capacity of the State for Welfare Enhancement

Despite the importance of the state as an economic sector, most analyses of the role of the state emphasize the consequences of its policy outputs. The remainder of this chapter thus focuses on the distributional effects of state policy rather than the employment effects of the state sector. The state is thought capable of providing basic needs through several sets of actions.

First, it is ordinarily presumed that the state's fiscal policy is redistributive and progressive.[7] The sheer size of government revenues—which range from nearly 20 percent to over 50 percent of GNP—creates the financial potential for the state to serve as the central allocator of society's wealth. Through progressive revenue-raising measures, on the one hand, and need-based welfare expenditures on the other, substantial redistributive effects are certainly *possible*.[8] Indeed, the more optimistic reformers and "grow now, redistribute later" development policy advocates often seem to consider government revenues a society's "discretionary income." Such a view of redistributive *potential*

6. The clearest example is the tendency of monopolies to arise in the absence of state antitrust action. The consequences are negative both for aggregate growth because of efficiency losses and for egalitarian distributions because of skewed incomes from rents. More broadly, the prevalence of extraeconomic bargaining advantages—especially among multinational corporations and large landowners unopposed by the state—are thought to yield similar outcomes.

7. Of course, a large state need not be actively redistributive in order to bring about greater equality. At least some cross-national differences could arise given only the weaker assumption that state expenditures are less skewed than those of the private sector.

8. On the expenditure side, redistribution can take a variety of forms from direct cash payments to subsidies of certain outputs or critical wage goods (especially food).

must be balanced, however, against the recognition that these funds are far from unclaimed; indeed, they are probably the object of greater competition than private consumption funds.

There are especially sharp limits to redistribution in the context of the great inequalities present in most Third World countries. Both income and wealth "become embodied in goods—Mercedes, luxury apartments, college educations—which cannot be redistributed. There is no way to turn a Mercedes into bicycles or a luxury apartment into public housing. Thus, incomes become a stock which cannot be redistributed" (Wilber and Jameson, 1979: 14). As considered in greater detail below, however, the chief barriers to redistribution are not financial or logistical, but deeply political, involving a central feature of all societies—the political power and resistance to change among those whose current comfort produces profound and activist conservatism.

As a consequence, the extent of these effects is highly variable crossnationally. Indeed, Hewitt (1977) has roughly estimated their redistributive impact among a group of advanced industrial societies. More elaborate investigations to identify the groups that gain and those that lose from government programs also have been conducted for individual nations (especially the United States), but the analysis is far too complex and the quality of available data on both the budgets and the macroeconomic processes of most nations far too limited to extend the analysis cross-nationally.

The state can also make a great impact on basic needs via the less politically charged path of investing in collective goods that "transcend . . . the financial and mental horizons of capitalists" (Baran, 1957). Indeed, many of the inputs that yield the greatest return in basic needs terms are the infrastructural and collective goods, which are seldom provided from private funds. The bulk of educational needs, transportation and communication systems, and fresh water and waste disposal services are always either provided directly or heavily subsidized by the state (for example, through teacher training or school construction). At high income levels where inefficiencies are more easily absorbed, a trade-off between public and private provision of infrastructural needs can occur, but among the poor there is no feasible alternative to state provision of these collective goods (and services) that weigh so heavily in basic needs provision.

Rather than "correcting" the misallocations of the market system after the fact (e.g., by providing income supplements to the unemployed) or "competing" with the market (by providing infrastructural goods and services, for example), state action may instead intervene directly in the process to steer market outcomes. Through economic incentives and restrictions, investment may be channeled to those purposes with the greatest leverage on the physical well-being of the poorest groups.[9]

This enumeration of the pathways through which the state can influence basic needs levels is helpful in framing an empirical analysis. It points, however, to a fundamental difficulty in resolving the question of whether the growth of the state is more likely to enhance or limit the provision of basic needs. The operationalization of any concept involving the state must confront its multidimensional character, yet most cross-national studies of macroeconomic growth or inequality have used two theoretical labels almost interchangeably—state size and state strength. Measures of the former are relatively unproblematic and tap reasonably well dimensions of state activities which influence basic needs through more or less direct economic pathways. This study follows the precedent of many recent studies that operationalize state size as the expenditures of the central government as a percentage of GNP (Rubinson, 1976, 1977; Weede, 1980, 1983; Weede and Tiefenbach, 1981a; Hewitt, 1977; Jackman, 1975; Bornschier et al., 1978; Chase-Dunn, 1975; Evans and Timberlake, 1980; Meyer and Hannan, 1979).[10]

9. Redirecting investment involves both direct government expenditures and inducements to alter the investment patterns of the private sector. Among the former are infrastructural investments that act directly on basic needs, such as health and educational expenditures. The latter include incentives to alter credit policies and to redirect investment in sectoral and geographical terms (Tullis, 1983; Chenery et al., 1974; Streeten, 1981; Griffin and James, 1981).

10. The specific data are from the U.S. Arms Control and Disarmament Agency (1980). To avoid possible yearly fluctuations, the study employs the constant dollar ratio averaged for three consecutive years (1969–71, or, in a few cases, the closest available years). Even this relatively routine measure presents two potential problems. First, the use of central government expenditures rather than total government expenditures risks biasing results by drawing an improper distinction between relatively centralized and relatively decentralized states. Nonetheless, there is theoretical reason to prefer emphasizing the central government since most of the arguments concern the state as a unitary actor. Moreover, there are technical and empirical reasons as well. Data are both more available and more comparable for central government expenditures; coverage of local government accounts is far from thorough in most of the Third World and highly variable across states. To confirm the superiority of the central government measure, the initial analyses were tried using both approaches. Probably for a combination of these two reasons, all the empirical results tend to be a little stronger using the central government measure, though the difference is not large. Moreover, an inspection of results for individual countries known to occupy the extreme ends of the government centralization scale does not reveal any likely distortion resulting from this choice.

Second, in a continuing effort to maintain the general character of the analysis, estimates of state size for state socialist nations are also included. Though net material product and gross national product are not identical measures of national output, and despite difficulties in directly comparing state budgets, ACDA does estimate this state size measure for centrally planned economies. Furthermore, in an earlier analysis (Moon and Dixon, 1985), centrally planned economies were excluded from the parameter estimation with no significant effect.

A budgetary measure of state size captures quite well the likely impact of the state along several of the sets of causal avenues described
above. The measure parallels that used to indicate the relative size of
other economic sectors. The fiscal redistributive potential of progressive taxation and transfer programs will show up in such a size measure. So, too, will the purchase of collective goods and infrastructural
investment.

Measures of state strength—which must capture more elusive state
effects—are far more difficult to construct, however. In terms of erect-
ing and maintaining an institutional structure capable of restraining the
power of other actors or steering outcomes through agenda setting and
other "Tocquevillian" mechanisms, a state may be *strong* without being
large.[11] Its strength may derive from exceptional organizational ability,
widespread popular acceptance of its role, or an ability to mobilize—if
necessary—resources not directly within its budgetary control. Because
the provision of basic needs frequently involves competition for resources among economic groups, a key issue in state strength involves
its alliances with some powerful actors and its autonomy from others.

Moreover, an effective state must be not only powerful, but competent. Skocpol (1985: 16) considers the stability of administrative control
as well as loyal and skilled officials to be critical to overall policy competence. Max Weber emphasizes that officials must be housed within
"an extensive, internally coherent bureaucratic machinery" (Rueschemeyer and Evans, 1985: 50). State effectiveness will also vary with the
"policy instruments" at the disposal of the state (Skocpol, 1985: 18);
large variations in these instruments are themselves a consequence of
institutional dynamics in individual national histories (Stepan, 1978;
Katzenstein, 1978; Fainstein and Fainstein, 1978). In part for this reason, Krasner (1978: 58) introduces the further complication that policy
competence may vary greatly across policy areas.

Unfortunately, there are no good cross-national indicators of these
dimensions of state strength. Those so far proposed are contaminated
with diverse conceptual elements that would only confound the analysis. Two examples will suffice to illustrate the problem. It is often
argued that centralization of power through a single-party system increases the power of the state by eliminating political rivals who would
otherwise constrain state behavior (Meyer and Hannan, 1979). While
that is no doubt true, gauging state strength in this way confuses it

---

11. Indeed, Stepan (1985) makes the point that economic size may actually weaken the
state by politicizing economic issues, creating opposition to the state, and thus lowering
its capacity to enforce its decisions.

with ideological disposition and structural arrangements. Totalitarian regimes are strong but far from autonomous from sources of support like the military; moreover, such regimes have ideological orientations, program priorities, and spending patterns that are likely to have at least as great an effect on basic needs performance as does state strength.[12]

One might also try the absolute fiscal size of the state as a proxy for state strength vis-à-vis foreign actors. Since fiscal size is strongly related to the overall size of the economy, however, the measure contains unwanted variance involving the many correlates of economic size.[13] For all these reasons, the current analysis incorporates only the fiscal size measure, though many of the other considerations can be reintroduced in later analyses that include these other dimensions.

Sources of State Disposition toward Basic Needs

Moreover, though the size or strength of the state is an important element in the determination of basic needs levels, most of its importance derives from the leverage it affords the political and economic program of the state. Of course, the effect of that program on the welfare of the poor may be highly variable across nations; certainly, characterizations of it vary dramatically across theorists. Sometimes the welfare of the poor is seen as a relatively high priority, while in other nations or for other theorists state action appears indifferent to basic needs performance. In short, state strength tells us relatively little about the uses to which state power will be put. Thus, even though a strong and competent state is usually seen as a *necessary* condition for needs satisfaction, we must seek a theoretical defense of the proposition that states actually *will* act in the way they are *capable* of acting.

There are three plausible sources for the *disposition* of the state to pursue basic needs provision as a relatively high priority. The first,

12. Indeed, some superficially plausible indicators of the ability to enforce state decisions—size of internal security forces, for example—fail in a more dramatic way. Democratic states are strong in the sense that their legitimacy—and the voluntary compliance that flows from it—are sufficiently great that force is seldom used, while states that lack legitimacy maintain trappings of power which may actually signify its absence.

13. Chenery and Syrquin (1975) establish that the development patterns of large versus small countries are very different. They find, for example, that large nations—especially at middle income levels—are marked by (1) much higher savings rates, (2) lower levels of capital inflows, (3) considerably higher investment rates, (4) slightly more rapid growth from 1950 to 1970, (5) lower levels of government revenue, (6) a larger industrial labor force, (7) somewhat greater urbanization, and (8) marginally higher levels of education. Most of these obviously have nothing to do with state strength.

variations of which I take up in the next two sections, rests on certain inherent dynamics of state formation and universal propensities among state personnel. According to these formulations, state strength is more than a *partial* explanation of international differences in the provision of basic needs; one variant also considers a strong state to be a *sufficient* condition for relatively favorable treatment of the poor because large states are more *disposed* toward as well as more *capable* of basic needs enhancement. While that is by no means axiomatic, several plausible arguments assert that state capacity *does* tell us something about the disposition of the state.

Related ideas suggest that in all nations the state bureaucracy's personnel—a class in itself by some formulations—have a characteristic outlook. Theorists disagree sharply, however, about its policy consequences. The next section considers arguments that the state is a natural ally of the poor and that nations with a relatively large and powerful state are thus likely to provide basic needs in greater measure than others. The following section discusses the reverse arguments—that the state is a natural opponent of the poor and, consequently, that nations marked by large states will tend to underperform in the provision of basic needs.

The other two theories of the source of basic needs commitment view the state as neither universally supportive of nor universally antagonistic toward the welfare of the poor. Instead, they suggest that the impact of strength or size of the state on the provision of basic needs should be modeled as an interaction with the disposition of the state to pursue such goals. One suggests that the basic needs disposition is provided by democratic institutions, which permit mass political pressure to push state policy in directions that account for basic needs provision. The other emphasizes the ideological commitments of state personnel, which are rooted partially in economic structure and historical precedents and thus differ systematically and widely across nations.

The State as Promoter of the Welfare of the Poor

Any argument that the state is disposed to contravene the allocational processes of the economy—especially in opposition to the rich and in support of the poor—would need to confront two interrelated questions. First, how can the state remain isolated from the competing claims on the social surplus which swirl all around it? More specifically, if the state is a product of the very same unbalanced social forces that prevent optimal needs levels, how does it then resist expressing the class bias of the forces that gave birth and provide sustenance to it?

Second, given that the state can somehow effect such an insulation, why would its policy priorities tend to favor the poor and, more broadly, basic needs?

The tension between the view of the state as, on the one hand, insulated from social forces and supportive of basic needs and, on the other, a product of its social environment, is exemplified by the positions of Weber and his critics. In his work on the behavior of bureaucracies (Gerth and Mills, 1946), Weber advances a managerial conception of the state. As an institution standing outside the economic process of capital accumulation and the political process of class competition, the state is said to seek the common interest through the rational logic of the technician. Most important, the state is not class-biased and not especially sensitive to political pressures emanating from outside the state. Such a perspective thus places great emphasis on the character of the elites who constitute the state bureaucracy since their freedom of action is assumed to be relatively great. Consequently, by assuming that "elites of various organizations cooperate in supporting the overall development of societal resources," such managerial theories become vulnerable to several objections (Alford, 1975: 149). The most damaging of these rest on the doubt that there is, in fact, a unique and socially optimal resource development and distribution program. If there are several competing programs that vary in their implications for existing social or economic groups, there are still further doubts that state bureaucracies, composed as they are of elite representatives of certain of those groups, will choose among them in an unbiased manner. Alford, in fact, goes so far as to label the Weberian view "utopian."[14]

Yet the assumption persists that the state is capable of actions that are class-blind or even vigorously supportive of the poorest and weakest segments of society. This assumption is justified only if state structures can be severed from the conflict among social groups. Several views suggest that the sheer size of the state apparatus engenders internal dynamics strong enough to largely shield state policy from the more distant social forces, which can only weakly constrain it.

These dynamics center around the socialization processes of bureaucratic organizations. Best developed in the literature on bureaucratic politics in foreign policy decision making, this position emphasizes the tendency of individual bureaucracies to adopt characteristic perspectives on the proper mission of the organization (e.g., Halperin, 1974).

---

14. Such arguments probably take on even greater force in Third World nations where the personnel occupying the state bureacracy are even less likely to be socioeconomically representative than they typically are in advanced industrial democracies.

This internally defined ethic both constrains the behavior of individuals—thus preventing them from acting in accord with any externally derived identification—and shapes, over time, the values and priorities they hold individually. Career interests and psychic pressures interact to produce an organization committed both individually and collectively to a mission relatively independent of pressures from outside the bureaucracy. Further, such effects occur universally whenever a bureaucracy achieves sufficient size and should thus be a generalized phenomenon of any strong state.

Indeed, the realist tradition in international relations frequently explains the universal pursuit of the "national interest" in similar terms. The powerful dynamics generated by individual agencies also occur at the level of the state itself. Krasner (1978: 10), for example, argues forcefully that bureaucrats are relatively homogeneous and commonly committed to a single set of "ambitious ideological goals related to beliefs about how societies should be ordered." These arguments suggest that a unique state perspective may well arise, even though they cannot dismiss the penetration of state processes by more general social forces.

Still, in the formulation of that perspective, state bureaucrats must shift their loyalties either to the state bureaucracy itself or to the nation as a whole, and in neither case is it obvious that basic needs levels would necessarily benefit. In the latter case, it is not implausible that the provision of basic human needs would form one component of a policy imperative, especially since the "national interest" concept Krasner has in mind is similar to Pareto's idea of the "utility of the community." Nevertheless, there is nothing certain about the place of basic needs in such a hierarchy of national goals.

The former possibility is exemplified by what Caporaso (1982: 105) characterizes as the "state-for-itself" conception, which identifies the state as "neither an impartial arbiter of group claims nor as a vehicle of the ruling class, but rather a combination of individual careers and organizational interests that are primarily self-serving." If by "self-serving" we understand that state policies work in the interest of state bureaucrats, then we need one more assumption about the linkage between mass welfare and bureaucratic interests to justify the expectation that such a state would provide basic needs in larger measure than the freely functioning economy without state intervention.

One possible linkage is the argument that the interests of state bureaucrats are dependent on the perceived legitimacy of the state and that legitimacy, in turn, is dependent on at least a minimal provision of welfare needs. Such an argument is to be found in its structural form in the neo-Marxist position of O'Connor (1973), though it is also supported in a more indirect way by eclectic theories of domestic conflict and revolution (e.g., Gurr, 1970; Hibbs, 1973). Justifications for this idea based on pluralistic mechanisms in the context of democratic systems are discussed later in this chapter.

In sum, then, a number of views identify the size and strength of the state as a plausible predictor of relative performance in the provision of basic human needs. The large state, in these views, has both a greater *capacity* to engage in welfare-enhancing programs and policies, and also, through the internal dynamics of the state itself, a greater likelihood of holding the *disposition* to make such efforts.

The State as Opponent of the Poor

Other perspectives on the state question the necessary relationship between state strength and the disposition to seek outcomes favorable to the poor. It is argued that freedom from external pressures is at least as likely to produce a parasitic or predatory state as one committed to social welfare (Reuschemeyer and Evans, 1985). Especially in less developed nations, state personnel are likely to form a homogeneous technocratic elite with cohesive bonds that encourage "corporate" behavior (Benjamin and Duvall, 1985). Thus, the state is not an impartial arbiter in competition over the surplus, but rather a self-interested player whose power is likely to achieve gains at the expense of others—and probably to the detriment of overall basic needs levels (Duvall and Freeman, 1983).

Even if certain role influences do incline state bureaucracies toward basic needs provision, the commitment required to undertake actions that directly confront the interests of powerful, entrenched, and strongly motivated social groups may well be considerably greater than that engendered by such role effects. To rely on the good will of civic-minded state bureaucrats to ensure relatively egalitarian division of the social surplus ignores the strong resistance that distributive policies generate (Tullis, 1983).[15] Moreover, redistributive policies most often must fight not only political forces, but the propensity of the market as well (Rueschemeyer and Evans, 1985).

This is not to say that the state will never contribute to the provision of basic needs, only that such action should not be expected without some more compelling source of such a disposition. Later sections con-

15. This is the chief criticism leveled against "grow now, redistribute later" development strategies. Unless the growth process redistributes political power, there is no pressure for the later redistribution of economic gain and, in fact, considerable pressure against it (Weaver and Jameson, 1981).

sider as potential sources the effect of popular pressures via democratic procedures and/or ideological orientations that motivate and constrain state behavior. In the absence of these or comparable forces, the balance of theoretical arguments seems to imply that the state will actually divert the social surplus away from basic needs provision.

Admittedly, it is most usual in the West to view the state as a natural ally of the poor, since the growth of the state in European and European-derivative polities of the twentieth century has come largely under the auspices of electorally successful parties of the (social democratic) left and has taken the form of the contemporary welfare state (Hicks and Swank, 1984; Cameron, 1978; Alt and Chrystal, 1983).[16] This view, however, confuses one historical datum with theoretical necessity.[17] In fact, many functions of the capitalist state may be quite antithetical to the welfare interests of the poor. None other than Adam Smith pointed out long ago that a prime function of the state is "to protect the rich against the poor, to protect those who have property against those who have none at all" (Smith, 1976: 715). Many modern analysts who concur with Smith's candid observation (e.g., O'Connor, 1973) would go even further, claiming that the eventual purpose of most state action is to benefit the rich by strengthening the process of capital accumulation and ensuring reproduction of the system.[18]

Milliband's (1969) instrumentalist theory of the state is even less ambiguous in its implications for the welfare of the poor. He contends that the state—far from insulated from broader social forces—is deeply embedded in the structure of the political economy and thus never far from its capitalistic origins. In particular, his argument rests on the strand of Marxist thought which identifies the capitalist state as an instrument with which one class maintains dominance over another.[19]

---

16. Various empirical analyses have confirmed that state growth is most rapid among those advanced industrial societies with a history of governance by parties of the left. Even among those that identify other sources of state growth and minimize the effect of social democratic government, the ideological dimension remains. In particular, the right is sometimes held to be a greater constraint on state growth than the left is a spur to it (Hicks and Swank, 1984). But the assumption that state growth is directed toward the benefit of the poorer rather than the richer strata is much less frequently challenged, either in theoretical circles or in popular political debate.

17. State growth in other parts of the globe is not so closely identified with either a particular ideology or a functional distribution of income.

18. Of course, ultimate purposes and more immediate consequences need not coincide. O'Connor, most obviously, would readily admit that many state actions designed to perform a legitimation function (e.g., welfare) bring about improved prospects for the poor—at least in the short term—even though they are motivated by a desire to maintain a system sharply antagonistic to their longer-term interests.

19. Engels (1969: 258), for example, contends that "the state is nothing but a machine for the oppression of one class by another." The Communist Manifesto (Marx and Engels,

Though many state theorists from various ideological currents disagree with Milliband's position, the crux of the debate recently has been the degree to which the state can be made "relatively autonomous" from its source of social support (Gold et al., 1975; Block, 1977; McGowan and Walker, 1981). Although most theorists assume that intervention on behalf of redistributive goals requires considerable state autonomy, it has also been suggested that such intervention itself increases the tendency of elites to reassert state control and thus reduces state autonomy (Habermas, 1975).

Interestingly, the identity of the state's supporting class has been at issue much less frequently. In fact, the expectation that the state will operate in ways that do not foster the welfare of the poor seems quite widespread across the ideological spectrum (Lindblom, 1977). It is central to structural neo-Marxism, implicit in most formulations of corporatism since the poor are not represented, and not strongly contested even by most pluralistic formulations. The most colorful expression of the notion that the class makeup of the state bureacracy dictates its likely policy consequences, however, remains that offered by Bardhan (1974): "More often than not the local administrative machinery is manned by people belonging to the families of the rural oligarchy and the urban elite. . . . To quote a Bengali rural proverb, 'if there are ghosts inside your mustard seeds, how would you use the seeds to exorcise the ghosts?'"

Budgetary Measures and Program Enumeration

As a first-cut test of the effect of state strength on basic needs, the budgetary indicator of state size is added to the regression model estimated in previous chapters. The analysis is conducted not only over the entire sample but also among nations below the $2,300 per capita income level, which earlier analyses showed to represent somewhat of a break point in basic needs provision. This division also corresponds roughly to a distinction some theorists have drawn in the operation of the state in different social contexts. Most directly, Benjamin and Duvall (1985) argue that property rights are held paramount in less advanced nations, whereas the state supervises their infringement by "quality of life" rights in advanced industrial societies. The results are

---

1969: 37) is also quite explicit on this point: "The bourgeoisie has at last . . . conquered for itself, in the modern representative state, exclusive political sway. The executive of the modern state is but a committee for managing the common affairs of the whole bourgeoisie."

Table 6-1. Adding state size to basic economic model

Variables	All nations				Nations < $2,300 GNP/cap			
	r	Beta	St. beta	t	r	Beta	St. beta	t
% labor agriculture	−.87	−.91	−.89	−22.0***	−.80	−.89	−.80	−14.1***
Socialist × agr.	.24	.59	.26	6.3***	.34	.60	.33	5.4***
Govt. expenditures	.18	−.34	−.11	−2.5*	.18	−.36	−.12	−1.9

Model	N	r	r²	adj. r²	SEE	F
All nations	120	.91	.82	.82	12.14	176.5***
Nations < $2,300	92	.85	.73	.72	13.20	79.4***

*Significant (p < .05)
**Significant (p < .01)
***Significant (p < .001)

illustrated in Table 6-1. It appears that the net effect of state size may be mildly negative, with the parameter estimate meeting the .05 standard of statistical significance among all nations and just missing it for the sample with the relatively developed countries excluded. There is no evidence, however, for a fundamentally different process at work in the two samples. Quite obviously, this variable warrants continuing attention in subsequent analyses.

While the fiscal size notion may roughly capture our concerns with the size of the state sector as a developmental dimension and its "employment" effects, most of the theoretical interest in the state hinges on treating the state as an instrument for the furtherance of particular goals or strategies. Specifically, I suggested earlier that the effect of the state may involve an interaction between state capacity and state disposition. By measuring state size I have treated the former but have captured the latter only by rough inference.

Before proceeding to theoretical treatments of the sources of state disposition, however, I want to consider a more direct approach to the measurement of variance in the state's efforts to supply basic needs. If the effects of different government programs on basic needs levels differ, the most obvious approach to the effect of the state is to enumerate the programs thought to have the greatest leverage, obtain measures of their scope in each nation, and test individually their presumably differing impacts. This approach conforms most closely to that of policy analysts discussed in the introductory chapter, though consequently it is somewhat at odds with the political economy emphasis of the rest of this study. In empirical terms, the success of this approach hinges on several considerations. First, one must be able to enumerate the programs that have the greatest leverage on basic needs levels. Second, data on these programs must be available and comparable for a large number of cases. Third, the effect of these programs on basic needs levels must be straightforward and additive. Fourth, the individual impact of each program—represented by the parameter estimate—must be sizable enough to overcome the noise of measurement error and cross-national variation, represented by the standard error. There appear to be problems with each of these assumptions.

The first step is to enumerate the programs most likely to carry implications for the welfare of the poor. On the revenue side, the progressivity of taxation is widely regarded as a key determinant of the redistributive character of state fiscal policy. Unfortunately, comparable data on tax incidences by income or wealth group are available only among the relatively few nations whose tax structure is similar. Statutory tax rates are more widely available, but the inference of actual tax burden is highly speculative in the face of huge cross-national differences in rules for income exclusion. Even in the United States, whose tax code is surely the most studied in the world, there is little agreement on the actual progressivity of income taxes—let alone the entire system of taxation by local, state, and federal governments and taxes on income, wealth, consumption, and production.

Unwilling to allow such a significant feature of state policy to remain unanalyzed, cross-national researchers have sought a proxy for progressivity. Several studies have employed available data on the proportion of tax revenues derived from direct taxes, which are normally progressive, and from indirect taxes, which are usually more regressive (Hewitt, 1977). This measure is quite crude, however, because the variance in actual progressivity of income taxes and in the regressivity of indirect taxes is probably greater than the variance in the proportion of revenues derived from each. Indirect taxes, in particular, encompass a range of different revenue sources with enormously different progressivities: luxury import taxes, excise taxes, food taxes, property taxes, and so on. Even this crude breakdown is available for a smaller sample of nations than one would prefer. Still, in the absence of other options, this variable is included in the analysis below.[20]

On the expenditure side, the comprehensive enumeration of programs is even more difficult. Certainly government spending on health and education is an obvious candidate for consideration. By any definition of basic needs, one would expect the welfare of the poor to be strongly affected by health and education expenditures; such measures as infant mortality and literacy would seem to be especially responsive.

20. The data source is *World Bank* (1980d) and is an average for several years around 1970.

Unfortunately, the level of specificity of available data is inadequate to produce the kind of policy analysis desirable from the perspective of development administrators. The most interesting questions from this angle concern the relative efficiency of differently conceived programs in these areas. On the medical side, for example, this comparison requires data on the distribution of medical spending across such categories as preventative versus curative services, high-technology versus "barefoot doctor" investments, and centralized versus decentralized treatment centers. On the education side, the relevant issues concern the emphasis afforded elementary education, higher education, vocational training, life skills, and reading and other subjects. As much to illustrate the problem as to contribute to the analysis, data from the same ACDA publication that produced the state size data are included in the model estimation below.[21]

A statutory rather than a budgetary measurement approach would consider the existence of programs providing social insurance rather than the amount of money spent on them. This approach, which has been used by others (Jackman, 1975), is facilitated by the data presented by Bornschier and Heintz (1979) on the number of social insurance programs in effect for each nation in each year. These have been aggregated so that each nation is characterized by the number of "program-years" of experience it accrued between 1934 and 1967. It should be noted that this measure contains a time element, which differentiates it from the other measures, which use a "snapshot" approach; indeed, if continuity of effort or long causal lags are significant components of basic needs provision, this aspect of the measure may be more central than its nonbudgetary quality.

The effects of the enumerated programs are tested by adding the indicators for each to the regression equation of Table 6-1. The results when all are entered together are given in Table 6-2; they appear to indicate a substantial positive impact for social insurance program experience (SIPE) but virtually no effect for health or education expenditures nor for the progressivity of taxation.[22] In fact, the parameter estimate—though not nearly significant—is actually of opposite sign from expectations for both health expenditures and taxation.

---

21. The data are for education and health spending as a percentage of total central government spending, averaged over the years 1969, 1970, and 1971.

22. When the analysis is restricted to nations below $2,300 GNP per capita, the social insurance variable is no longer significant ($t = 1.3$). One suspects that this fact implies that social insurance programs are far more effective in the developed countries, which can afford to fully fund them, even though their impact appears to remain positive—if small—even in the Third World. However, the decline in significance may be simply attributable to the reduction in variance of the independent variable within this sample.

Table 6-2. Adding enumerated programs to state expenditure model

Variables	Simple r	All variables				Significant variables		
		Beta	St. beta	t		Beta	St. beta	t
% labor agriculture	− .89	− .82	− .82	− 11.7***		− .78	− .77	− 12.6***
Socialist × agr.	.10	.41	.08	1.6		.50	.24	5.5***
Govt. expenditures	.03	− .39	− .12	− 2.1*		− .28	− .09	− 2.1*
Direct taxation	.49	− .15	− .10	− 1.8				
Health spending	.22	− 1.69	− .06	− 1.1				
Education spending	.33	1.82	.10	1.6				
Social insurance	.73	.10	.17	2.4*		.09	.15	2.5*

Model	N	r	r^2	adj. r^2	SEE	F
All variables	95	.91	.83	.81	11.92	58.8***
Significant variables	109	.92	.84	.83	11.36	135.2***

*Significant (p < .05)
**Significant (p < .01)
***Significant (p < .001)

Several limitations constrain our interpretation of Table 6-2, though much can be learned from it. First, all of these indicators have missing data, and simultaneous inclusion lowers the size of the sample from 120 to 95. To partially alleviate the problem, each of the four measures was tested separately, permitting a sample of between 105 and 119, but the results confirm that only social insurance program experience is significant. Second, the reduced nation sample is far from a random subset of the larger one. The obvious difference is the exclusion of most of the socialist nations, the most dramatic impact of which is the now insignificant coefficient for socialist effects.[23]

A third constraining factor concerns the relationships among the independent variables, especially those involving development measures such as agricultural labor force. The apparent decline of explanatory power for the labor force measure as one moves from Table 6-1 to Table 6-2 (the t declines from − 22.0 to − 12.6) helps to clarify one of the "political" mechanisms whereby development leads to improved basic needs provision. That is, SIPE may be thought of as an intervening

23. This insignificance is *not* due to collinearity between social insurance program experience and socialism, which would allow us to interpret SIPE as a mediating mechanism for the socialist effect. Over this sample, socialism has a much reduced zero-order correlation and only a marginally significant parameter estimate in the presence of the labor force measure alone. Thus, this reduced effect is almost entirely a consequence of the relatively few socialist nations remaining in the sample and hence the small leverage these few data points have on the overall equation.

mechanism for bringing the fruits of economic growth to the poor. The specification of Table 6-2 suggests that developmental paths that feature structural change in the economy—but without corresponding institutional changes in the state's role in guaranteeing the spread of developmental benefits—engender living standards for the poor which fall below expectations based on development of the economy alone. This point is key to an understanding of the central thesis laid out in Part I: economic development is an umbrella concept that hides beneath it a range of collinear but variable processes. To represent development as monolithic limits our ability to understand the shape of the curve representing basic needs improvement relative to GNP growth even while it allows us considerable statistical power to predict it. As a corollary, deviance from the curve cannot be understood—nor government policies advocated to encourage positive deviations—until the components of development are separated.

A related point concerns the role of education spending, which is portrayed in Table 6-2 as an insignificant influence on basic needs provision (including literacy). Such a counterintuitive outcome must be seen in the context of the overall analysis: the bivariate correlation between education expenditures and the PQLI is a highly significant $+.32$. However, education spending contributes an insignificant increment to the explained variance of the previous model precisely because much of the variance in education expenditures is already contained in the model. Education expenditures are correlated with each of the other independent variables: government expenditures (.54), state socialism (.32), and the labor force measure $(-.27)$.

Apart from the enumerated programs, there are others—some of which entail large fiscal consequences and some of which do not—which may well affect basic needs levels (e.g., population control, family planning programs, food subsidies). They are not included here for several reasons. The effects of most of these are quite indeterminant because of lack of specificity in budgetary categories, and measurement is nearly impossible because of variance across nations in the emphasis of programs with similar names. More important, the effects of any one of these programs are likely to be small enough to make detection difficult if not impossible. This does not mean, of course, that such programs do not work; it means only that their marginal effects on the overall life expectancy of the population are quite small. The implication, from the standpoint of detecting empirical consequences, is that strategies to detect the impact of government policies should attempt some form of aggregation.

Moreover, from both the explanatory and prescriptive standpoints, including individual programs as autonomous elements of a political economy explanation misleadingly treats the components of state policy as exogenous factors when they are more appropriately considered intervening mechanisms. Simply put, this approach begs the most interesting question and one that runs parallel to that of the entire study: why do some nations give higher priority to the satisfaction of basic human needs than others? Of course, at the same time, the evidence that state-sponsored social insurance raises the level of basic needs provision does provide an important clue concerning where to look for the ultimate sources of internation gaps in welfare performance.

Political Democracy and Basic Needs

This section considers that political democracy may be a source for the disposition of the state to adopt a certain pattern of policy choice. This pattern, however, is defined not by its specific program composition but rather by the social groups that would be expected to benefit from it and therefore press for its adoption. In fact, the presence of this pattern of policy choice is treated as an unmeasured causal variable. It is represented indirectly by indicators tapping conditions that predict both the political power of these social groups to translate policy preferences into state action and an institutional context favorable to the exercise of that power.

In particular, representational perspectives on the state recognize that the marked differences in content of government policy across states reflect as much a disposition to undertake certain policies as a fiscal capacity to do so. Further, representational perspectives view this disposition as the product of direct pressures from social groups and individuals on the state itself, mostly in the form of demands on the social surplus. Unlike managerial and bureaucratic conceptions of the state, which highlight internally generated cues for action, this perspective emphasizes the existence of mechanisms that allow such demands to be effectively pressed from outside the bureaucracy (Lenski, 1966). MacPherson (1973: 188), for example, attributes to state personnel a role much different from that seen by the Weberian theorists discussed above. He considers state personnel to be "mainly inert recipients of pressures from interest groups. When the output of laws and orders is treated as the result of the input of pressures, it matters little what persons are in office as the government. The government, as the mechanism through which decisions are made, becomes in effect as impersonal and anonymous as the market in the economic model."

This perspective thus reintroduces the importance of the connection between the state and the political economy within which it resides. Attention to such a connection is not, of course, unique to pluralistic conceptions; it is also central to the above-cited positions of Lindblom, Milliband, and O'Connor. The position advanced by pluralists contains, however, a characterization of state-societal relations which is markedly different from—though not completely incompatible with—that of the latter two neo-Marxists. O'Connor, for example, postulates a universal need for the capitalist state to affirm its own authority—through either the use of force or the maintenance of legitimacy—while also sustaining the conditions required for capital accumulation. Even so, he recognizes that the state faces strategic and tactical options in bringing about these outcomes which range from repression to welfare policies and that different states adopt quite different policy mixes. That variance is accounted for by the different structural relationships between the state and society found in various nations. The pluralist perspective identifies the existence of democratic institutions as a key aspect of that structural relationship and the central variable that determines the state's position on this and many other policy trade-offs.

In fact, in what Hewitt (1977) concisely labels "the simple democratic hypothesis," pluralist perspectives imply that the existence of democratic institutions—especially the enfranchisement of all citizens—virtually guarantees relatively egalitarian policies. Since the provision of basic needs will surely rank high on the political agenda of the poor, their ballot box power should be translated into state policies that enhance the PQLI.

This optimistic assessment of the ability of representational processes to guarantee agreeable policy outputs rests on two additional premises which may not hold. First, democratic theory assumes the existence of a quite pluralistic society such that persistent cleavages (especially class-based ones) across issues do not develop. Second, either the political institutions or the political culture must mandate the maximum protection of minority rights consistent with majority rule. Either or both premises are necessary to guarantee that a persistent minimum winning coalition does not develop which can invalidate the ballot box power of the weakest strata as thoroughly as formal disenfranchisement. Many theorists, including those discussed above and some others considered below, have questioned the universality of these assumptions across all the nations that are ostensibly democratic. Moreover, state action can be welfare-degrading precisely because of its responsiveness to multiple interest groups if they succeed in supplying benefits for themselves while shifting the costs to the collectivity (Elkin, 1985; Aranson and Ordeshook, 1985; Olson, 1982).

Still, the expectation that democratic systems will outperform nondemocratic ones in the provision of basic needs is not without a response. Since democracies, especially in the Third World, exhibit very short life spans when these premises are not at least partially met, another argument linking democratic forms to welfare performance is exposed. The presence of functioning democratic institutions probably entails not only the existence of certain procedural mechanisms but also, by implication, a social and political milieu favorable to their functioning as expected by the simple democratic hypothesis. As noted earlier, domestic conflict and political instability result when legitimacy cannot be maintained. Although a state that is not responsive to its populace may survive, it cannot survive as a *democratic* state (Wilkinson, 1977). The procedures of democratic institutions are simply too frail to withstand the stress resulting from a political system that is not pluralistic. Thus, the mere persistence of democratic institutions implies that they have been at least somewhat successful, whether because of the approximate accuracy of the above assumptions or through some other mechanism.

Indeed, this argument reminds us that direct ballot box power is not the only link between democratic systems and basic needs performance. In systems with long histories of democratic *forms*, even periodic departure of the system from actual democratic *behavior* need not eliminate the upward pressure on basic needs levels. In Latin America, for example, the legitimacy of the state has come to be seen as at least as dependent on policy impacts associated with fairness or egalitarianism as it is on the form of political interaction between state and society. That is, where democratic forms generate democratic rhetoric, the state is capable of deflecting public dissatisfaction with procedural attributes of a regime by citing its welfare performance. Of course, all regimes have similar options, but the point is that even badly flawed democratic systems tend to generate an ideology that is more egalitarian and more welfare-oriented in its performance standard than systems not constrained by even insincere public expression of democratic values and ideals. Thus, even without fully functioning democratic institutions, at least the extremes of behavior associated with Bokassa or Duvalier are much less likely in partially democratic nations. Moreover, democratic institutions usually provide a substantial level of popular legitimacy even when they are relatively ineffective in translating popular preferences into state policy. Such legitimacy is far preferable to the inefficient expenditure of public resources to purchase compliance through clientelism or repression. For this reason alone, democratic systems should outperform others in basic needs provision.

The structuralist theory of the state articulated by Poulantzas (1973) further deemphasizes the causal role of functioning democratic institutions. He too is dubious about the conception of the state as standing apart from the political economy; in his view the character of the state provides insight into the nature of the political economy from which it springs. In fact, he identifies the state as the representation of the balance of class forces in society, a balance that in capitalist societies always favors the dominant class but is still highly variable across time and nations. Thus, the state cannot be expected to be a major instrument for redistribution against the will of dominant economic interests, but neither will it perform on behalf of dominant classes without constraint, as in Milliband's more instrumentalist formulation. Instead, the effect of the state can be expected to vary, though it will surely go no further than the level of reformism necessary to reproduce the system.

What this means concretely will vary from system to system, of course, but the presence or absence of democratic institutions will not much affect it. This is not because democracy does not work, but rather because democratic forms do not arise except in those circumstances where the balance of class forces brings it about. Thus, according to this view, democracy is simply the expression of class forces, never the negation of them. Democracy, then, does not stand as an *exception* to the relationship between the balance of class forces and state policy, but rather as an *example* of the class struggle at a particular historical conjunction. Although state policy may be the instrument by which the poor are made better off, democratic processes are not the source of this improvement but a manifestation of a class power that lies elsewhere. None of this is to say that ballot box power is unimportant, of course, only that some theoretical perspectives consider the empirical relationship between democracy and the provision of basic needs—though surely not spurious—to be less theoretically central than is implied by representational perspectives. Consequently, as we see below, the stronger—and more meaningful—correlation is argued to be between welfare outcomes and commitment to a socialist policy program.

Even from perspectives closer to mainstream pluralism, doubts about the effectiveness of electoral control remain. As Hewitt (1977: 451) puts it, "Political democracy is not a sufficient condition for the achievement of a more equal society. The crucial matter is what the mass electorate *does* with the franchise." By implication, democratic processes do not always bring about an orientation favorable to the interests of the poor.

The electorate may fail to steer state policy in a direction beneficial to the poor either because the electoral mechanism does not work as hypothesized in the ideal democratic model, or because the policy instruments are poorly chosen. The former possibility returns us to the premises of democratic theory. Ballot box power may be insufficient if the position of elite theorists such as Mills (1956) is correct, namely that the political resources of groups vary so dramatically that even "one man, one vote" procedures fail to equalize them. Certainly such a danger is feared by liberal reformers who advocate restrictions on campaign financing and the like. More dramatically, Schumpeter (1954: 263) notes that small groups may be able to "fashion and, within very wide limits, even to create the will of the people." And, at a minimum, Lindblom (1977) asserts the existence of the "privileged role of business" as a universal characteristic of advanced capitalist polyarchies. Such "corrections" to democratic theory are probably even more essential in the much less pluralistic societies of the Third World.

Further, the increasingly administrative character of modern government shifts much important decision making into agencies less bound by citizen preferences and thus—by some accounts—more open to bureaucratic discretion. For many theorists, however, that "discretion" implies a greater orientation toward preserving a property-based market system than improving the living standards of the poor (Elkin, 1985). Thus, even social welfare programs are more likely designed to pacify the poor than to improve their access to basic needs (Piven and Cloward, 1971, 1977).

Even if democratic processes were to allow the poor to *dictate* policy, it cannot be guaranteed that policy would necessarily serve to provide basic human needs. Alternative strategies for bringing about such effects exist, and the choices among them are by no means clear. Voting studies from a variety of nations have observed that the relation between class-related demographic variables and policy preferences is not so strong as some representational approaches might suppose, suggesting that differences in ends-means judgments are probably a necessary supplement to class interests in the understanding of mass policy preferences. Of course, it has long been known that electoral behavior is relatively badly predicted by apparent economic interests and perceptions, even though more recent research has increasingly sharpened the formulation of this linkage with respect to the criteria used by voters. It remains that the polling place is the scene of some of the most irrational, nonrational, and indeterminantly rational political behavior known to social scientists. To expect electoral choices to engender the economic interest maximization of voters requires a number of dubious assumptions about the priorities of voters. Further, the political and economic sophistication of the electorate—not notably great in most poor countries but significantly variable cross-nationally—is no doubt a factor of some importance. Moreover, policies often carry long-term implications that are strikingly different in direction from their politically relevant short-term effects.[24] For all of these reasons, then,

---

24. A "pro-labor" policy that permits unions to bargain themselves into capital flight and unemployment is but one, albeit highly controversial, example.

democratic processes alone may not provide for the welfare needs of individuals.

More generally, if we rely on the presence of democracy as the predictor of a state's disposition for basic needs provision, we cannot say much about the enormously diverse policy orientations that exist among nondemocratic nations. This is a crucial omission because there are theoretical reasons to expect the emergence of need-based programs even in the absence of electoral forces that press for them.

Ideological Orientation and Basic Needs

With respect to more or less democratic nations, we return to Hewitt's observation that "the crucial matter is what the mass electorate *does* with the franchise." Unlike the empirically rare case of direct democracy, in representational democracies what the electorate does is select not individual policies, but rather *leadership* that is identified with certain goals and priorities as well as broad theories about how such goals can be achieved. In short, they select an ideological orientation that they expect will be manifested in countless policy actions concerning issues hopelessly beyond their expertise, including most of the highly technical issues that can influence the provision of basic needs.[25] The implication is that the electoral approach may work only where a tradition of class struggle and organization provides workers a common set of purposes and a political organization that advocates them (Petras, 1978: 72).

Together with the weakness of democratic linkages, this limitation of the electoral approach suggests that the poorest elements of society may be better protected by an ideological orientation that assigns relatively high priority to the protection of their interests—roughly, the ideology of the left—than by the electoral power of democratic processes. If so, the varying performance of states in providing for basic human needs is better explained by the ideology of the state than by the processes that bring it about. In this connection, it is important to note not only that democratic processes do not always bring about an orientation favorable to the interests of the poor, but also that such orientations do not arise exclusively in·democratic systems.

---

25. Some of the most obvious of these issues and their effects are discussed in the previous section, but many more entail implications for resource distribution or efficiency though they are not primarily seen as redistributive in nature. The latter include, for example, exchange rate policy, commercial policy, investment controls, and banking regulations. The range of policies with potential implications is far too broad to enumerate, let alone measure and test.

Indeed, most neo-Marxists would argue that they are *less* likely to occur in capitalist systems—whether democratic or not—and that the major difference in policy orientation, especially on issues of class interest, is to be found between capitalist states, on the one hand, and authentically socialist states, on the other. Differences within the two groups will be dwarfed by differences between them. Still, differences that do exist within the capitalist group must be explained by the interests of the dominant classes and not by the strength of electoral challenges to them. Although the degree to which the interests of the dominant class require equality would seem to vary considerably across nations, it is not obvious how that factor can be captured. In particular, the complex relationship between food prices and rural incomes, on the one hand, and the reproductive costs of labor, on the other, would seem to preclude any simple characterization of the structures most likely to produce equitable outcomes. There have been plausible suggestions that equality is greater in relatively closed economic systems in which the income of the poor is seen by capitalists to represent both a wage bill (which is to be minimized) and aggregate demand (which is to be maximized) (de Janvry, 1981). This suggestion is taken up in Chapter 8.

The precise ideological dimension expected to distinguish systems is only slightly more clear. There is little doubt that the common right-left dimension is thought by most to be of dominant importance. Certainly many theorists have contended that a political economy organized according to socialist principles will be more egalitarian, and, indeed, our previous empirical work verifies that such systems do provide a larger measure of basic needs than comparable capitalist systems. It is not clear, however, whether that effect derives principally from the organization of the political economy (which lacks a significant functional distribution of income and other attributes of capitalist economies) or from the ideological makeup of the ruling regime, which is doctrinaire Marxist.

More broadly, then, the standing of democratic socialism or welfare state socialism is in dispute. Indeed, the theoretical and empirical arguments on both sides are exceptionally clear and, in isolation, compelling. The resolution of their varying weights seems to hinge, then, on empirical test. On the one hand, it is evident from both the policy program and the rhetoric of the socialist parties of Western Europe that their commitment to the welfare of the working class and the poor is more unequivocal than that of either their own nation's parties of the center and right or the comparable party of the left in, for example, North America (Brooks, 1983; Hicks and Swank, 1984). The class makeup of their constituencies confirms that such a judgment is widely shared, and it would thus not be unreasonable to anticipate that the effect of the state in nations dominated by such parties would be similarly distinctive.

On the other hand, it is argued that the socialism of Western Europe is dramatically different from that of Eastern Europe. Obviously the theoretical tenets of the respective socialisms differ, but even if they did not, the constraints imposed by both the domestic and international capitalist system are substantial enough to deflect policy a considerable distance from party philosophy (e.g., Mitterrand's France and Nyerere's Tanzania). The positions of populist left regimes in the Third World are more difficult still to characterize. With a number of alternative conceptualizations of the relevant dimension and relatively little theoretical guidance, empirical analysis must begin the task of sorting the consequences of ideological orientation.

Empirical Findings on the State and Basic Needs

We now turn to the measurement of the key dispositional variables. Previous cross-national studies have represented somewhat different conceptions of political democracy with a variety of measures that vary in sophistication and theoretical breadth. The best of these is Bollen's composite index, whose six component indicators encompass the range of theoretical dimensions of democracy as it is understood in the West: (1) press freedom, (2) freedom of group opposition, (3) absence of government sanctions, (4) fairness of elections, (5) executive selection, and (6) legislative selection. (For sources and other details, including results of a confirmatory factor analysis, see Bollen, 1980.) This measure has received sufficient use in other studies to be widely recognized and accepted (Bollen, 1983; Bollen and Grandjean, 1981; Bollen and Jackman, 1985a; Weede, 1982; Moon and Dixon, 1985; Dixon and Moon, 1986; Moon, 1987). In order to minimize the effect of sudden changes or unusual observations, the measure employed here is an average of Bollen's index for 1960 and 1965.[26]

26. Given the recent decolonization of many nations in the sample and the relatively rapid pace of political change in its wake, either observation individually (especially that for 1960) may give a false picture of the actual political system that existed by the early 1970s. The mean of the two figures should reduce the danger dramatically, but to further mute potential fluctuations and to capture changes occurring after 1965, it is desirable to include at least a third data point for the early 1970s. Unfortunately, data sources for two of the six constituent elements (numbers 1 and 4 above) have not been updated. Nevertheless, an experimental measure was constructed for 1973 (the last available year in the remaining data sources) as true to the original as available data permitted. Four of the

The measurement of the ideological orientation of the ruling regime presents a similar variety of available measures but a much greater problem in choosing among them. Ideology is a notoriously difficult concept to capture empirically and all estimates of it are necessarily flawed. From a theoretical standpoint, the essential requirement is a scheme to distinguish regimes holding a roughly leftist orientation from those of a more conservative bent, but even this very rough categorization may be difficult to apply in some cases (Hewitt, 1977). The current study adopts the codings of Blondel (1969), who classified the ideological norms of over 130 ruling regimes as of January 1969. Blondel's characterization of regimes bears more upon the broad norms of the political system as a whole and the expectations of its major participants than upon the particular views, preferences, or even policies of the current government, though the latter is clearly relevant to the former and persistent long-term differences between the two are assumed to be minimal.[27] Blondel's schema of seven broad categories

---

six updated components are identical to those used by Bollen, and the remaining two are conceptually similar, though definitely not identical. In an earlier study, the 1973 measure was averaged with that of the other two data points and the result was used to replicate a regression model whose political components were similar to that considered here. With but one exception, there was virtually no change in the resulting parameter estimates; the lone exception was a strengthening of the democracy effect substantial enough to increase the overall fit of the model. Specifically, the estimated impact of democracy increased by nearly a third while its standard error remained unchanged.

Despite these agreeable findings, I hesitated to incorporate the updated measure into the main analysis due to concern for comparability of measurement. That same concern prompts the use of only the two-point average in this study. We know that the two substituted components are not as highly correlated with the remaining ones as in Bollen's original. We also know that the correlation of the 1973 measure with those for 1960 and 1965 is relatively modest (.69 and .78 respectively) compared with the correlation between Bollen's measures (.91). More important is what we do not know: Bollen's confirmatory factor analysis established the error structure of his 1960 and 1965 measures, but we have no reason to suppose that the 1973 measure is similarly well behaved. Thus, the Bollen average is used in the main study, though the findings using the update suggest that the democracy effects are unlikely to be inflated—indeed, they are probably slightly deflated —by the "snapshot" character of the democracy measure.

27. Once again, concern about the validity of this measure prompted an investigation of alternatives and their effects on the overall results. In the process of the earlier study, a pilot analysis was conducted with a smaller sample of nations. Use of several other published measures—which were highly correlated with both one another and the Blondel measures—produced quite similar results to those used in the main study (Moon and Dixon, 1985). This outcome should not be too surprising since Janda's (1980) detailed analysis of about ninety political parties has shown that subjective ideology ratings can discriminate in a fairly reliable fashion among party political programs. Indeed, even Western estimates—by both government officials and academic analysts—coincide quite closely with those of official Soviet publications. Thus, although more specific program analysis or concern with specific questions of ideology is problematic cross-nationally, rough right-left scales are apparently not especially controversial, and on the basis of our

of norms was collapsed for this study into a three-way classification of leftist, rightist, and centrist regimes.[28]

A model to test these claims was created by adding to the specification of Table 6-2 the continuous measure of political democracy and the pair of ideological orientation dummy variables. In recognition of the theoretical arguments suggesting an interaction between *capacity* and *disposition*, however, an interaction term for each with state size is also included.

It was immediately apparent that the inclusion of democracy and ideological orientation as predictor variables reduces the independent explanatory power of social insurance program experience below the level of statistical significance. This finding suggests that social insurance program experience should be considered a mediating mechanism through which state disposition affects basic needs accomplishment. Insofar as the existence of social insurance programs is collinear with other aspects of state policy, the apparent direct effect of SIPE—barely reaching the threshold of statistical significance in any case—is probably inflated by the omission of relevant variables. Further, although social insurance programs almost certainly improve basic needs levels (though the magnitude of their independent impact is in doubt), there remains the theoretical question of whether these programs ought to be represented as autonomous and exogenous or simply reflective of state disposition.

In part, of course, this is a matter of theoretical taste. Empirically, however, SIPE is decidedly not theoretically autonomous or empirically exogenous. In fact, over two-thirds of the variance in social insurance program experience can be accounted for by aspects of the political economy, principally levels of development, ideological norms, and the presence of democracy.[29] Together with the marginally significant increment to explained variance provided by SIPE, this finding sug-

---

earlier survey it appears that Blondel's measure is the best available for the purposes of this study. It is available in a large sample for the correct time point, the measures have face validity, and they have the advantage of having been used by others (Delacroix and Ragin, 1978).

28. Blondel's (1969: 533) original classification of regimes employed the following seven types of norms: (1) authoritarian conservative, (2) traditional conservative, (3) liberal democratic, (4) populist right, (5) populist center (and unclassified), (6) populist left, and (7) radical authoritarian. Categories 1, 2, and 4 are treated as rightist regimes; categories 3 and 5 are centrist; and categories 6 and 7 are coded as leftist. Unlike in the earlier study (Moon and Dixon, 1985), the variables are not effect-coded; instead, they are coded more simply and conventionally as dummy variables, though as explained in the original that coding will not affect the significance of the results.

29. The statistical analysis is presented in Chapter 10, which sorts the channels through which the structure of the political economy affects state orientation, state policy, and, eventually, basic needs levels.

gests that social insurance can be treated as an intervening mechanism without major cost. As a practical matter, the loss of eleven cases to missing data on social insurance does not seem justified, and future specifications consequently omit this variable.

Table 6-3 thus reports the results of the model when estimated with SIPE omitted. This analysis demonstrates that political democracy is a significant predictor of enhanced basic needs provision, a result that accords with previous studies using a different economic control model (Moon and Dixon, 1985; Dixon and Moon, 1986; Moon, 1987). It is also compatible with a range of studies which have shown that democracy diminishes income inequality, though there is some dispute about the technical merits of the empirical work (Bollen and Jackman, 1985a; Hewitt, 1977; Stack, 1978; Jackman, 1974, 1975; Rubinson and Quinlan, 1977; Bollen and Grandjean, 1981; Weede, 1982; Cutright, 1967). The interaction term is completely insignificant, however, in the presence of the dummy variable, clarifying that the positive impact of democracy is not contingent on the fiscal size of the state. This outcome may imply that the effects of democracy are not carried principally by programs with clear expenditure implications, but rather by the other actions undertaken by governments with distributional and allocational consequences. Indeed, our earlier discussion of the effect of democratic expectations on the structuring of political behavior was reminiscent of the "Tocquevillian" dimension of state influence not captured by budgetary measures.

By contrast, however, including an interaction term of state size with the dummy variables representing right and left norms offers a different picture than a simple additive specification, which, in an analysis not shown, suggested the absence of significant ideological effects. Most interestingly, these results offer an important amendment to our earlier interpretation of state size as a negative predictor of basic needs levels. Though the results of Table 6-1 might have implied that a larger state carried negative implications for basic needs attainment through features common to all state sectors (e.g., efficiency, inequality, waste), this analysis emphasizes that such effects are not universal. Instead, these effects vary with the ideology of the ruling regime, strongly suggesting that the principal effects of the state lie in the policy realm rather than in characteristic features of the "production function" in the state sector. In particular, increasing state size is associated with a higher PQLI among states with leftist norms but a lower PQLI among those of the right. Among centrist states, no pattern emerges.

These effects are seen most clearly in the coefficients displayed on the right side of Table 6-3 for the additive and interactive terms involving rightist norms and state size. Technically, both the additive and the interactive terms are needed for a proper estimate of the main

Table 6-3. Effects of democracy and ideology (with interactive specification)

Variables	Simple r	All variables			Significant variables		
		Beta	St. beta	t	Beta	St. beta	t
% labor agriculture	− .87	− .81	− .79	− 16.8***	− .80	− .78	− 17.7**
Socialist × agr.	.24	.64	.29	5.3***	.60	.27	6.2**
Govt. expenditures	.18	− .27	− .08	− .5			
Democracy	.47	.10	.11	.8	.15	.15	3.1**
Rightist norms	− .38	2.71	.05	.3	8.26	.14	1.8
Leftist norms	.11	− 10.94	− .14	− .9			
Right × govt. expend.	− .38	− .37	− .14	.9	− .60	− .23	− 2.9**
Left × govt. expend.	.16	.32	.12	.7			
Democracy × govt. expend.	.45	.00	.03	.2			

Model	N	r	r^2	adj. r^2	SEE	F
All variables	120	.92	.85	.84	11.46	68.2*
Significant variables	120	.92	.85	.84	11.34	125.2*

*Significant (p < .05)
**Significant (p < .01)
***Significant (p < .001)

(universal) effects and the interaction (conditional) effects of ideological
norms and state size. In practice, this specification allows us to distinguish between the strikingly different effects of increased state size
within each of the three ideological categories of regime orientation.[30]
We observe a striking difference in sign between the main effect ($t =$
1.8) and the interactive effect ($t = -2.9$) of rightist regimes, which
implies that large states with right-wing ideologies perform quite badly
whereas small states with similar ideologies are capable of basic needs
performance better than would be otherwise predicted.[31]

30. A proper understanding of the propensities of left, right, and center governments
requires the simultaneous examination of the parameter estimates and mean values of all
the independent variables in the sample. The additive effects of the norm variables must
be treated as adjustments to the intercept while the interactive effects are represented as
different slopes between PQLI and state size for each of the three groups of nations. A
graph could render two-dimensionally the relationship between state size and PQLI. At
high levels of state expenditures, the left achieves the best results and the right the
worst; at very low levels, the reverse is true. Near the mean of state size (21 percent of
GNP), the expected PQLI is very similar. This analysis, however, assumes that all else is
equal. The mean size of the state also differs systematically between groups and the
mean level of democracy similarly varies, as do all the other variables in the equation.
Elaborations of the net impact of these countervailing factors become quickly intractable
at this level of complexity. For a detailed examination of these effects based on a much
simpler model, see Moon and Dixon (1985).

31. As we shall see in further analyses, the specification of rightist effects consisting of
a positive main effect and a negative interactive one nearly always appears, but it is not

The hypothesis linking leftist norms to superior performance in the provision of basic needs is not supported by the analysis, however.[32] But before such a conclusion is accepted, several counterarguments must be considered which contend that the rightist effects are muted by the composition of the control model. Further, it can be argued that the results do not deny the effects of leftist ideology at all, but rather clarify them and stipulate more clearly where they occur.

First, it must be remembered that at least three forms of leftist norms may be distinguished—roughly, state socialist, social democratic, and populist left—and not all need have similar implications for basic needs levels. Of these, the strongest expected ideological effects—those of state socialism—are already contained in the economic control model in the form of the interaction term involving the dummy variable for state socialist political economies. Further, the Blondel scheme codes the social democratic states of Western Europe as liberal democratic regimes on the basis of their participatory norms. Consequently, the initial analysis included them as centrist rather than as leftist regimes, though their position on a right-left dimension is certainly ambiguous.[33] Thus, in the above model estimation, the leftist norm variable represents only the effect of populist left regimes of the Third World. A reanalysis distinguishing the three leftist orientations was undertaken, using Blondel's measure of the strength of the social democratic party among liberal democratic regimes. The results are quite clear: state socialist nations are superior providers of basic needs, but leftist ideology that falls short of commitment to wholesale alteration of

---

very robust. Often, the main effect falls below not only the level of statistical significance but the level at which it is retained in the final step equation. Nonetheless, the interactive effect is *always* the stronger and the interpretation that the negative impact of rightist regimes increases with state size remains intact. Although the inclusion or exclusion of the interactive effect alters little the conclusion that rightist regimes underperform their leftist and centrist counterparts, the interactive effect is retained because it clarifies that the apparent negative effect of state size is largely a phenomenon associated with rightist regimes rather than being a more universal effect that might be interpreted as a sectoral consequence.

32. Though the theoretical discussion emphasized the effect of the left, the finding that the most striking distinction is between the right and the nonright is not especially surprising. After all, it is consistent with the findings of others who have approached the question in terms of welfare effort rather than welfare outcome. For example, Hicks and Swank (1984) have shown that rightist party participation in Western democratic governments has systematically slowed the growth of certain types of welfare payments while centrist and leftist parties are not significantly different from one another (Castles, 1982).

33. This ambiguous position may help explain the lack of a significant difference between the propensities of leftist and centrist governments in the above model estimates. With state socialist nations omitted from the former category and many of the governments having attributes of both centrist and leftist norms, no sharp distinction is possible between the left and the center.`

the political economy has no such effect. Neither in its social democratic nor populist form does leftist ideology produce levels of basic needs significantly different from centrist regimes (the omitted category in the dummy analysis).[34]

A second caveat warns that the economic control model is also known to predict to the ideology of the ruling regime; thus, its inclusion will tend to lower the estimate of ideological effects through multicollinearity.[35] The most obvious of these, of course, is the known relationship between level of development and various elements of the political system, including both the presence of democratic forms and the ideology of the ruling regime. Indeed, it has long been argued that these political attributes represent the mechanisms that lie between economic development and outcomes such as diminishing income inequality.[36]

In the following chapter, I continue the process of specifying with more clarity the operation of the state and its ideological makeup. For now, the estimates of Table 6-3 are adopted as the working model of basic needs provision with complete confidence that even the marginally significant variables represent factors whose causal impact is probably somewhat understated.[37]

34. This null result is extremely robust. Whether the specification is additive or interactive, whether the control model uses labor force measures, Kravis or conventional GNP estimates, whether estimated over all countries or only the nonrich, neither the democratic nor the populist left has an impact on basic needs levels different from that of the centrist group, net of other factors.

35. This factor becomes even more central in later chapters, which improve upon the economic control model by incorporating elements of dependent development and the characteristic structures and international exchanges associated with it.

36. Indeed, the labor force measure is a better correlate of PQLI than GNP in part because it better predicts political outcomes. As a result, the apparent independent effect of the political variables declines as the economic control model improves. As a first cut at an analysis that is pursued in greater detail in later chapters, a reanalysis was undertaken which replaced the economic control model with simple logged GNP, thus replicating the specification used in most previous analyses (Moon and Dixon, 1985; Grosse and Perry, 1983; Drewnowski and Scott, 1966). The results of this analysis give much greater weight to both democratic and ideological effects, with the t value of democracy increasing from 3.1 to 3.7 and the interactive and additive form of the rightist norm effect increasing to -4.6 and 3.3 from -2.9 and 1.8, respectively.

37. Reestimating the relationships after eliminating that range of cases where the economic control model is already a very accurate predictor (i.e., nations above GNP per capita of $2,300) yields results insignificantly different from those reported above.

Chapter 7
Effects of the Military

The Role of the Military in Basic Needs Provision

The variables examined in Chapter 6—state strength, democratic institutions, and regime ideology—by no means exhaust the political determinants of basic human needs. The role of the military has also occupied a central position in most analyses of the political dimension of economic development. Wolpin (1981: 4) is most clear in placing the military center stage in developmental dynamics: "The struggle for socio-economic development *presumes* success in constraining domestic militaristic tendencies" (emphasis added). Few challenge the importance of the military in shaping social outcomes, but the assessment of the net effect of the military is controversial indeed. The strident rhetoric of political actors is mirrored in the research literature on the connection between the military and development. Both political actors and researchers concede the significance of the question "Does the military aid or hinder development?" but no one has fully answered it.

Various theoretical and empirical treatments have reached strikingly different conclusions. Some argue that the military stunts the growth of the economy while others contend that the military efficiently mobilizes the resources necessary for long-term growth. More broadly, critics charge that the military tends to arrest the development of the political system, to distort the allocation of resources toward nonproductive functions, and to turn the organs of government against the citizens it is designed to serve. A more sanguine view holds that the military is a progressive force, not only in establishing stability but also in achieving effective policy implementation by exercising control over actors who would thwart social change.

Empirical literatures have developed concerning several plausible causal linkages, including the differential performance of military and civilian regimes, the economic impact of military spending, and the developmental role of the military as an institution. For two reasons, however, these empirical studies have failed to resolve the theoretical dispute. First, they have not recognized major differences between these various military effects nor carefully specified the interactions among them. If—as I suspect—these causal effects are cross-cutting, this is a serious omission since measurement approaches that merge them or research designs that treat them in isolation will tend to obscure, distort, or minimize their impacts.

Second, the simple distinction between military and civilian regimes has been exaggerated while the social and political context of military effects has been neglected. If the investigation is framed within a more comprehensive study of the political economy of basic needs provision, the effect of the military on resource allocation can be more sharply focused and the state role in shaping welfare outcomes can also be more fully specified.

Even a cursory literature survey demonstrates that ascertaining military effects on development requires that alternative characterizations of the role of the military be distinguished. Some of the apparent contradictions result simply from imprecision and ambiguity in causal claims. For example, one must distinguish the direct policy-making role of the military within military regimes from the more indirect policy influence wielded via the constraints that a powerful military may exercise on civilian regimes. Further, even without policy influence, the military remains a significant institution in the social and cultural life of a nation and a potentially powerful force in shaping developmental outcomes.

The military must also be recognized as a major economic sector. Indeed, it has particular significance because its size and pattern of resource allocation vary so much across nations. Moreover, because military spending so strongly affects the overall pattern of state expenditures, its leverage on resources targeted to basic needs may be especially great. Finally, apart from the military as an agent of developmental outcomes, the presence of military regimes or a large military establishment can be considered an indicator of other social, economic, and political conditions. All of these matters are discussed in detail later in this chapter.

In sum, a disaggregated look at military effects within a controlled model will allow us to reconcile many of the contradictory claims and to interpret more accurately the controversial role of the military in social development. To begin, I introduce the literature on the role of military regimes, within which is found most of the major strands of causality considered in the broader literature of military effects on development. Indeed, there is implicit in this literature a causal model of military effects which serves a valuable heuristic role, though empirical analysis demonstrates that certain of its linkages and mediating mechanisms are dubious.

Military Regimes and Basic Needs: Mediating Mechanisms

Although many argue that military regimes are detrimental to the interests of the mass citizenry (Vagts, 1959; Milliband, 1969), others contend that the military is often not only a positive force in national development but even a natural ally of the poor (Levy, 1966; Halpern, 1963). Most arguments center on one of four mediating mechanisms, each sketched here but more fully discussed below.

First, it is said that when military personnel occupy civilian roles the hierarchical organization of the military introduces discipline and efficiency in place of waste and corruption. The result is superior state performance, which I speculate may extend to enhanced basic needs provision.

A second mechanism involves the characteristic political outlook, value priorities, and ideological dispositions of military officers. Some accounts suggest that the officer corps acquires through socialization a greater commitment to the "national interest." Others stress, however, that military regimes represent the ascendancy of norms that are flagrantly antiparticipatory and frequently tied to interests that are distinctly antagonistic to the type of social change which could improve basic needs levels. Thus, theorists disagree on whether military regimes possess a distinctive state disposition to undertake welfare-oriented packages of redistributive programs, collective goods provision, and initiatives for economic and social structural changes.

A third impact of military regimes concerns the strengthening of the military as an institution and the broadening of its role as a modernizing force in social development. As the size of the military increases under the nurturing of military regimes, its capacity to penetrate the social order and to transform it through the socialization implicit in military training similarly increases, perhaps with benefits for the poor.

Finally, the growth of the military has budgetary consequences said to shift the allocation of societal resources. The positive modernizing

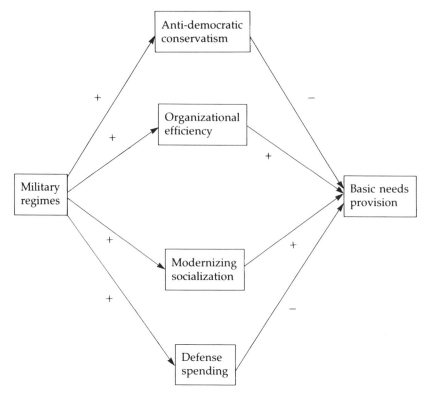

Figure 7-1. Military regimes and developmental mechanisms

consequences of the military's expansion are usually balanced against the growth and distributional consequences of military spending. Most often—though by no means universally—the economic effects of the military sector are seen as negative for basic needs levels.

The general structure of the argument is summarized in Figure 7-1. Three potential flaws in "reduced form" models of the effect of military regimes on developmental outcomes are immediately evident. First, contrary to the assumptions, military regimes may not consistently lead to these four mediating mechanisms. Indeed, the empirical literature introduces some doubt concerning the consequences of military regimes for each of them. Second, the right-side predictions are themselves contested, as exemplified by both the lively literature that disputes the growth consequences of military spending and the controversies concerning ideological effects aired in Chapter 6. Third, the causal impacts of these four mechanisms may net to zero while retaining significant but cross-cutting individual explanatory power. That idea is certainly plausible since the dominant theoretical claims concerning ideology and spending suggest negative effects whereas the most-cited contentions concerning organizational efficiency and modernizing socialization imply the reverse. In order to clarify and test these theoretical linkages, the remainder of the chapter is devoted to fleshing out these mechanisms and the major connections among them.

The Orientation and Organization of Military Regimes

Supporters of military regimes frequently base their case on the central role played by nationalism and patriotism in motivating the coups that bring the military to power. It is argued that the professionalism of the officer corps is sustained by a socialization that develops "a sense of public service and national guardianship" (Janowitz, 1964). As a result, military governments come to power committed to a reversal of the problems associated with civilian leadership. The diagnosis offered by Park Chung Hee of the reasons for the 1961 coup in South Korea is typical:

> "I want to emphasize and re-emphasize, that the key factor . . . was to effect an industrial revolution in Korea. . . . Prices continued to rise. Currency expansion was posing a serious threat to the Korean economy. . . . The national economy was dragged in the mire. But the previous regime remained insensitive and slept on . . . the morality of the Korean people was completely gone; intrigues, slander, and libel were rampant. Adversely affected by such social traits [the] nation's youthful people sought only their own fortunes, tried to lead an indolent life, drifted themselves into hedonism." (Lovell, 1970: 170–72)

Typical too is Park's representation of the contribution of the subsequent military government: "The army represents discipline, dedication to duty, patriotism, and the subordination of individual self-seeking to the public necessities. . . . Western democratic institutions . . . have caused deleterious effects. . . . Therefore, we have to establish a new system, whatever the form it may take" (Lovell, 1970: 172–73).

The case for the superior performance of the resulting military governments relies heavily, of course, on a comparison with a previous regime notable for corruption, inefficiency, and instability. Although this characterization of previous civilian governments is frequently self-serving and value-biased, it does need to be taken seriously. Simply put, military governments do tend to arise in circumstances where civilian governments have failed.[1] This fact complicates our evaluation of

---

1. Of course, in many circumstances the instability induced by the politically active military is a major reason for the failure.

military regimes in that any regime arising in such circumstances is likely to confront problems that constrain success in basic needs performance.

In such circumstances, basic needs levels could benefit from a military intervention that would curb corruption and check the drift toward chaos and stagnation. If the professionalism of the military is real and its devotion to the national interest sincere, the structure of military command might yield a closer approximation to Weber's ideal of bureaucratic organization than can be found in the civilian sector, at least in the most backward countries. More effective policy making and more efficient implementation may result from the reduced corruption and better organization found in a hierarchical state that relies on the rationalism and modernism that are developed through the military's commitment to discipline. Whether the same approach that makes the trains run on time can improve basic needs provision is an open question. Finally, it can be argued that military regimes are better able to defend the state than their civilian counterparts and are consequently able to maintain a level of stability and order which will allow state strength to yield developmental dividends.

From both the standpoint of the motives of military coup-makers and the actual record of military regimes, however, each of these arguments must confront rejoinders. Most basically, although coups do occur most often in failing political systems, it is not evident that they are usually motivated by a commitment to the military's role of national guardianship in the face of a state in need of reform. Thompson's (1973: 44–45) authoritative study of 229 coups between 1946 and 1970, for example, found that only nineteen could be "judged to be 'strikingly' reformist in nature" and notes that "one is forced to conclude that the desire for societal reform remains fairly atypical of contemporary military coups." Indeed, grievances of a "professional" character "are often used to mask more materialistic personal or corporate motives." Consequently, military coups should not be expected to frequently rescue the system from corruption, instability, or ineffectiveness. In fact, on each of these counts, military regimes are themselves highly suspect.

That corruption may persist in military regimes is suggested by the rather large role that the "corporate" interests of the military appear to play in precipitating coups. Thompson (1973: 12–13) extracts from a large literature seven dimensions of these corporate interests—autonomy, hierarchy, monopoly, cohesion, honor, political position, and resources—several of which have implications for the personnel and budgetary resources directed toward the military establishment (Finer, 1975; Needler, 1963; Luckham, 1971; Lee, 1969; Bebler, 1972). Indeed, the linkage between military regimes and the military budget is the most frequently cited explanation for flagging socioeconomic performance by military regimes. The discussion below treats the effects of military spending independently, however, and the empirical analysis to follow questions the necessary relationship between regime composition and budgetary priorities. Moreover, it cannot be assumed that increasing military allocations are corrupt nor that military spending contributes less to development than alternative expenditures.

Nonetheless, it seems likely that where corporate interests motivate seizure of power the programmatic as well as budgetary priorities of the resulting regime will emphasize values and interests more central to the military than to the poor. Of course, case studies have had no difficulty in chronicling flagrant corruption in individual military regimes (Lang, 1972; Crouch, 1978; Maynard, 1978; Stepan, 1971; North, 1979; Martin, 1966; Nkrumah, 1969). Indeed, Kennedy (1974: 58) portrays corruption as absolutely inevitable:

> The army which intervenes with relatively clean hands may campaign against corruption, a few offenders may be jailed, and some may even be shot, but the command of resources in "soft" states soon leads inexorably to a diversion of resources. In an atmosphere where status and prestige are bound up with power and wealth, the scarcity of income among the pious is in conflict with the aspirations of the ambitious; either they succumb to the opportunities or they slide down the social scale.

Such corruption may be muted or channeled in less costly directions by the professional socialization of the military culture, but whether the net effect of corruption makes military regimes, on average, less obstructive of basic needs achievement than civilian regimes remains an empirical question. It is important to recall, however, that favored treatment of the military can occur without military seizure of power; indeed, it frequently occurs in an attempt to forestall it.

Neither is it evident that military regimes introduce greater stability into political and economic life. In the first place, military regimes themselves are frequently very short-lived. Welch's (1978: 147) observation is most telling on this point: "Close to two-thirds of governments that assumed power by means of coup d'état are themselves ousted by the same means; only one in twenty post-coup governments gives way to a civilian government." This is, in part, the consequence of the motives that generate both the original and subsequent coups. Thompson's (1973) study not only identifies "subcorporate" interests—especially intramilitary and factional grievances—as the most frequent motivation for coups; he also recognizes that they are "probably most responsible for the 'musical chairs' quality of coup chains and cycles."

Because leaving civilian office and/or the military inevitably involves a substantial loss in power, prestige, and wealth (Lang, 1972; Chorley, 1943), praetorians seldom return to the barracks or retire to private life willingly. The consequent battle for ascendancy among factions must surely occupy a high enough priority to detract from the effort of the state to further basic needs. Thus, instability is as likely to result from a military coup as to be diminished by it. As Abrahamsson (1972: 144) puts it, "The result of a coup d'état is often not primarily more order, but simply a different ruling clique."

Finally, even while in office, military regimes may not be any more competent or efficient than the civilian ones they replace. Though the discipline of military organizations may exceed that of most civilian governments, it is not clear that the management skills are easily transferable (Janowitz, 1964; Vagts, 1959; Feld, 1971). Some contend that the organizational abilities of the military are taxed to the limit in maintaining social order and controlling competing factions, leaving little opportunity for the promotion of developmental policies (McAlister, 1966). Moreover, the characteristic approach of military regimes to gaining compliance—exercising coercion rather than achieving legitimate authority—undermines, more than enhances, the state strength necessary to achieve communitarian goals like basic needs (Wolpin, 1981: 25; Huntington, 1968). Thus, the efficacy of military governments in achieving goals may be obscured by the negative impact of their choice of development goals or by side effects of their implementation style.

The sum of these arguments is difficult to compute, but it should be noted that in many areas the dispute is between those who believe that military regimes are superior to civilian ones and those who believe them to be no better. In the case of two mechanisms, however, there is a strong suggestion that military regimes are systematically worse than their civilian counterparts. The first of these—the level of military spending—is considered later in this chapter, but at the moment we turn to the second: the characteristic ideology of military regimes.

The Ideology and Outlook of Military Regimes

To anticipate the pattern of behavior of any state—and its consequences for social outcomes—we need an understanding of the dominant ideology and outlook of its leadership. The previous chapter emphasized that the state cannot be in any sense autonomous unless state personnel shift identification from their social position to either the state itself or the nation as a whole. With respect to military regimes, there is little agreement on how far that process typically progresses. Adekson (1978: 32) lays out the parameters of the debate: "The military qua military is a special class-in-itself, not in the orthodox Marxist sense, but in the sense in which a bureaucracy is, and therefore has its interests and motivations often independent of (though they may also coincide with) those of any one of the conventional classes in society."

Two lines of argument depart from this point. One emphasizes the autonomy of the military regime resulting from the combination of military socialization—the "military mind" or "military culture"—and the unique structural location of the military. As a "class," the military depends not on ownership or control over the means of production, but rather on a monopoly of the instruments of violence and access to the allocative instrumentality of the state apparatus. In this sense, the military is independent of society and the military regime autonomous enough to allow it to pursue social goals such as basic needs which may challenge the interests of dominant classes.

Whether or not the regime will exercise that autonomy in the interest of the poor, of course, is another matter—and there is reason to doubt it. For several reasons, officers tend to shift their allegiance to the military institution itself rather than to any welfare-based conception of the state. This allegiance is partly a matter of self-selecting a compatible ideological environment; several empirical analyses confirm that professional military men tend to value orientations that are elitist, politically conservative, and authoritarian (Vagts, 1959; Abrahamsson, 1972; Lang, 1972). They also tend to be hostile to egalitarianism (Levy, 1971; Bienen, 1971; Van Gils, 1971; Nun, 1969). This self-selection operates together with military socialization to generate greater conservatism than exists in the public at large as well as unusual commitment to the military as an institution. In poor countries, that institutional loyalty is also tied to material circumstances. For many, the military represents a unique path to social mobility (Kling, 1956; Needler, 1966). Moreover, once a military career is under way, officers find little prospect of shifting to the civilian sector without a major loss of income or, especially, status, or both (Chorley, 1943; Lang, 1972). Indeed, military rank also represents an avenue to power and wealth that can support a patron-client relationship (Bebler, 1972; Kennedy, 1974). Thus, while the military regime may be autonomous, it is more likely to pursue its own corporate interests or its ideological identification, neither of which is likely to afford high priority to basic needs.

A second perspective sees the behavior of the military as flowing from the original class background of its officer corps. Although military recruitment patterns do vary from country to country, the officer corps always underrepresents the poorest strata of society (Chorley,

1943; Abrahamsson, 1972; Otley, 1978; Dye, 1976; Stepan, 1971; Horowitz, 1969). It has been suggested that the military is less socially conservative in ex-colonial societies where the traditional upper class was discredited or nonexistent, but recruitment is very seldom concentrated below the lower middle class level and is frequently well above it (Wolpin, 1981; Janowitz, 1964; Huntington, 1968; Levy, 1971). Moreover, alliances are invariably formed with actors less ambiguously committed to the status quo—either big business (Etchison, 1975; Porch, 1977), traditional agrarian elites (Wolpin, 1981), or foreign powers (Woddis, 1977). Thus, it is no mere coincidence that the interests and motivations of the military "coincide with those of conventional classes." The alliances typically formed between the military and other classes suggest an orientation more receptive to the interests of the wealthy than those of the poor. The resulting conception of the national interest is not likely to favor the provision of basic human needs.

In sum, from a variety of vantage points, we should expect military regimes to be conservative and antiegalitarian in economic priorities, authoritarian in participatory norms, and protective of corporate interests. Of course, there remain controversies about the impact of the political views of the military on welfare outcomes. On the one hand, the antidemocratic character of most military governments and the conservative economic policies usually associated with them have led some to believe that they possess a capacity to mobilize resources in a way superior to that of civilian regimes (Welch, 1970). They may be capable of generating more rapid economic growth through increased efficiency, enforced savings and restricted consumption, suppression of industrial disputes, work rate increases, and the transfer of agrarian surpluses to industry (Benoit, 1973; Kennedy, 1974; Deger and Smith, 1983).

From the perspective of this analysis, however, most of these effects seem to imply attainment of growth rates at the expense of the urban working classes and, especially, the rural poor among whom the attainment of basic needs typically lags; thus I would expect basic needs provision *relative to GNP* to fall. Many theorists agree, as reflected especially in the literature on bureaucratic authoritarianism in Latin America. There the recent ascendancy of the military is identified as an indicator of regime domination by a coalition of elites whose political program affords very weak priority to the interests of the rural poor, though it may emphasize aggregate growth (O'Donnell, 1973; Most, 1980). Schmitter's (1971) finding that military rule is associated with more inequitable tax structures together with higher rates of growth is also supportive of the expectation that military regimes will underperform

Table 7-1. Effect of military regimes (both with and without other state effects)

Variables	Simple r	Reduced model			Extended model		
		Beta	St. beta	t	Beta	St. beta	t
% labor agriculture	− .87	− .89	− .87	− 20.8***	− .80	− .78	− 17.7***
Socialist × agr.	.24	.51	.23	5.7***	.61	.28	6.2***
Democracy	.47				.15	.16	3.1**
Rightist norms	− .38				7.63	.13	1.6
Right × govt. expend.	− .38				− .57	− .22	− 2.7**
Military regime (months)	.09	.01	.01	.3	.03	.03	.8
Model	N	r	r^2	adj. r^2	SEE		F
Reduced model	120	.90	.81	⁄ .81	12.45		165.9***
Extended model	120	.92	.85	.84	11.36		104.1***

*Significant (p < .05)
**Significant (p < .01)
***Significant (p < .001)

in the provision of basic needs relative to aggregate measures of national income or wealth.

The Empirical Record of Military Regimes

To begin the evaluation of military regime performance, I add an indicator of military regime presence to the model constructed in Chapter 6. For this purpose, Jackman's (1976) data on months of military rule during the 1970s were augmented by data from Blondel (1969) and Banks (1971).[2] The results are shown in Table 7-1. On the right side, the control model is that of Table 6-3 which includes the political effects of democracy, state size, and regime orientation. Of course, since military regimes have been associated with characteristic locations on each of these dimensions, it may also be useful to identify the "reduced form" impact of military regimes. That impact includes the "indirect effects" brought about by the military character of the regime but mediated by these other factors. Naturally, the omission of these factors

2. Alternative characterizations of regimes as military or nonmilitary are surprisingly divergent. However, experimentation with alternative data sources yielded no significant differences in the results. The reader is directed to Jackman (1976: 1090–91) for a fuller description of the criteria used in his coding. In addition to his sample of 77 countries, this analysis includes 43 other nations. However, on the basis of the data of Blondel (1969) and Banks (1971), all but one of these 43—Greece—were reported to have had no military regimes during the decade (Dixon and Moon, 1986).

may also represent a misspecification, so the right-side formulation is certainly the preferred one. Nonetheless, the left side of Table 7-1 is useful in illustrating the effect of military regimes on the basis of the control model of Table 4-4, which does not contain the political factors. In neither case is there any evidence of a unique effect of military regimes, whether the antidemocratic and rightist character of most military regimes is controlled or not.[3]

These results can be set within the context of several quantitative analyses that have also investigated the link between military regimes and various aspects of the pace and distribution of development. Those findings, too, have been mostly inconclusive. Some support the view that military regimes generate more rapid economic growth, usually at the expense of the poorer elements of society. Berg-Schlosser's (1984) analysis of a sample of African nations revealed that military regimes produced the highest growth rate in GNP per capita and the smallest progress in the PQLI of any of the four government types he considered. Tannahill (1976) finds that among ten Latin American countries military governments are associated with higher growth rates but lower social welfare spending and more regressive taxation than their civilian counterparts. By contrast, Weaver (1973), Schmitter (1971), and McKinlay and Cohen (1976) all report no significant differences on several measures of regime performance in a larger sample of Third World nations.[4]

These equivocal conclusions may reflect the cross-cutting arguments found in the previous sections, a possibility I consider in a multistep empirical analysis below. One theorist, however, more boldly synthesizes the arguments concerning the orientation of the military in the following well-known passage:

> As society changes, so does the role of the military. In the world of oligarchy, the soldier is a radical; in the middle-class world he is a participant and arbiter; as the mass society looms on the horizon he becomes the conservative guardian of the existing order. Thus, paradoxically but understandably, the more backward a society is, the more progressive the role of its military; the more advanced a society becomes, the more conservative and reactionary becomes the role of its military. (Huntington, 1968: 221)

3. Alternative measures based on different conceptual and theoretical formulations include the characterization of Blondel (1969) concerning the presence of military support as the technique by which a regime retains power; he also considers the length of military rule. Neither shows a significant effect.

4. Wolpin (1981) provides a more comprehensive summary and critique of this literature, together with a reanalysis. None of the studies utilizes the PQLI nor positions the question of military regimes in the context of an overall model of political and economic influences on development outcomes, however.

The inconsistent empirical findings cited above have prompted tests of Huntington's more complex "interactive" thesis by both Nordlinger (1970) and Jackman (1976). Both reasoned that if Huntington were correct, the presence of military regimes would predict positively to development in "backward" nations and negatively in more advanced ones. Although Nordlinger's analysis shows limited support for the intuitively appealing Huntington thesis, Jackman's replication and reanalysis identifies technical problems that invalidate those conclusions. Further, Jackman's more elaborate analysis uncovers no intervening effect by level of development, size of the middle class, nor region.

Nonetheless, the intriguing suggestion of differential effects for military regimes at different levels of development warrants a test using basic needs as the outcome dimension. The argument seems plausible because key determinants of military orientation may well exhibit systematic variance by level of development: the class character of recruitment patterns, the presence of alternative sources of social mobility, the identity of potential alliance groups, relations with external actors, and the status of the civilian political system in which the military intervenes.

To test for these effects, dummy variables were created representing various income levels; each was multiplied by the military regime variable. Both the individual dummies and the interaction terms were entered into the regression equation simultaneously. In the absence of theoretical guidance as to the specific points of inflection at which the role of the military is to change, several alternative cut-off points were tried provisionally and the corresponding interactive specifications were estimated. The results were not at all robust. In fact, two initial analyses using arbitrary but plausible cut-offs produced precisely opposite conclusions, one suggesting that military regimes were positive at low levels of development but negative at higher levels, while the other showed the reverse pattern. More elaborate analyses using finer income divisions were undertaken in order to search for the points of inflection where the slope of the interactive term changed. Statistically significant interactive effects can be created in this way, but they are theoretically uninterpretable. For example, military regimes appear to have strong positive effects between income levels of $300 and $500 per year, but marginally significant negative effects both immediately above and immediately below that range and insignificantly positive effects at the very lowest income levels and above $1,100.[5] Nor did a regional breakdown produce evidence that military regimes perform

5. Both Table 7-1 and several subsequent analyses were also replicated with nations above $2,300 GNP excluded. The results were not significantly different.

differently in different geographical areas. All in all, though marginally significant parameter estimates do occasionally appear, the results are so inconsistent and unpatterned that I reluctantly conclude that Huntington's intriguing thesis fares no better in this analysis than in Jackman's. Indeed, there is strong pressure to concur with Jackman's final assessment:

> We can conclude that blanket statements portraying military governments in the Third World as either progressive or reactionary are without empirical foundation. This implies that many observers may have been mistaken in attributing unique political skills to the military, whether directed toward progressive or conservative ends. We can also conclude that military regimes do not assume different mantles as countries of the Third World become wealthier. In short, the simple civilian-military government distinction appears to be of little use in the explanation of social change. (Jackman, 1976: 1097)

Nonetheless, the underlying reasoning of Huntington remains of interest. If the performance of military regimes is thought to vary—with their ideological disposition or their propensity to divert social resources to the corporate interests of the military establishment—we can test for these effects *directly* rather than *indirectly* through the postulated but apparently false relationship between these propensities and level of development.

Moreover, despite the finality of Jackman's conclusion concerning military regimes, we must continue to regard the status of military effects on development as an open question. This is so for two reasons, illustrated by Figure 7-1. First, the mechanisms by which military regimes affect development—ideological orientation, organizational efficiency, defense spending, and modernizing socialization—may net to zero while retaining significant but cross-cutting individual explanatory power. Second, the last two mediating mechanisms may operate quite independently of any effect of military regimes.

The Military as a Modernizing Institution

Though the view is by no means unchallenged, both theoretical and empirical studies have identified the scope of military participation in society and the strength of military institutions as a spur to economic development. The military *as an institution* has been regarded as a positive force in promoting economic growth and, somewhat less clearly, the equality associated with the provision of basic needs. The core of this expectation lies with the "modernizing" impact of the military.

These modernization arguments have two distinct components. Some theorists emphasize the impact of military leadership on the priority assigned economic growth by state policy and, thus, on the pace and style of development which follow. Naturally, this variant has much in common with the above discussion of military regime effects, though obviously the military need not assume power directly in order to influence state policy. An alternative approach emphasizes the process of "nation-building" which results from the individual-level acculturation provided by military service. This view has more in common with theories of human capital investment and mass socialization.

The positive contribution of the military to national development is a persistent theme in the literature of the 1950s and 1960s (Jackman, 1976). Lovell's (1970: 10–11) overview of case work from five disparate nations summarizes the conclusion of the literature: "Professional training of the military in every case has inculcated a sense of dedication to the nation's advancement and welfare, a commitment to modernization, to technological progress and efficient organization of the economy that sets the military apart from most other groups within the society." Pye (1962) attributes this attitude in part to the comparative perspective of the military in seeing the backwardness of the traditional society against the backdrop of the increasing sophistication in military technology available elsewhere. Gutteridge (1970) notes that service abroad is especially influential in this respect. Von der Mehden (1970: 220) similarly observes that "military life leads to a closer attachment to the material values of Western mechanical civilization, efficiency with regard to administration, national survival and unity, and authority." Thus Levy (1966: 603) concludes that the military is uniquely efficient at "combining maximum rates of modernization with maximum levels of stability and control." In sum, there is widespread agreement that the military is especially effective at promoting the modern attitudes that the "modernization theory" of economic development has long regarded as a key element in the transition from traditional to modern political economies (Weaver and Jameson, 1981; Portes, 1976; Valenzuela and Valenzuela, 1978).[6] Of course, these arguments are also related to the contentions about the efficiency and discipline of military regimes discussed above.

Modernization effects may be more strongly associated with mass socialization through military service, however, than with the influence of military organizations in national decision-making circles. For the

6. The literature in a similar vein is extensive; the most prominent works are by Welch (1970), Johnson (1962), Halpern (1963), McAlister (1966), Bienen (1971), Needler (1966), Pye (1959), Lieuwen (1960), Janowitz (1964), and Finer (1962).

individual, military training is "the vehicle for upward mobility and provides the opportunity for teaching people the relationship between effort and reward" (Kaldor, 1978: 59). And Benoit (1973) has observed that soldiers usually must learn such valuable Western skills as "following and transmitting precise instructions; living and working by the clock; noticing and reading signs; spending and saving money. . . . The shaking-up experience involved in transforming tradition-bound peoples into modern urban types is unpleasant and difficult and usually resisted. Military discipline provides a mechanism for speeding up the process." From this perspective, then, the military provides a kind of vocational training which amounts to a considerable investment in human capital—indeed, one that is expected to yield dividends in the fuller and more efficient employment of resources (Weede, 1983). Lovell (1970: 12) goes further yet when he declares: "Military establishments have become vast educational institutions in developing nations, exposing thousands to new skills, modern equipment, improved managerial techniques, and effecting a transformation of attitudes that reaches the draftee and the village reservist, but is found most profoundly among the regular officer elite."

At a broader level, the military represents a means of promoting mobility and breaking down regional, ethnic, or religious divisions, a process that fosters nation building. For example, Duncan (1978) has gone so far as to attribute to the Cuban military the primary role in forging a new "modal personality and common national identity" with developmental consequences directly relevant to both growth and distributional issues.[7] Several of these processes carry implications for inequality and for service delivery to the poorest elements of society. The military is frequently responsible for the construction of public works and infrastructure, for example (Pye, 1962; Duncan, 1978). The repatriation of military pay to rural villages is also thought to be a significant form of interregion transfer in many poor countries. It is likely to be of particular significance when access to currency is otherwise limited, for example, in largely subsistence areas. In fact, if military recruitment shifts excess labor out of rural areas and transfers a share of military pay in the opposite direction, a considerable redistributive effect with basic needs implications could accrue from both halves of the transaction.

A rather different approach has yielded a similar empirical expecta-

7. Oddly, Wolpin (1981), whose Marxist analysis stands in stark contrast to the conservatism of most proponents of this view, is perhaps the most optimistic of the theorists about the *potential* of the military for such contributions. However, he expects such an outcome only via the "communist military subordination model" likely to arise from the experience of social revolution led by a radical guerrilla military organization.

tion concerning the size of the military establishment. Weede and Tiefenbach (1981a) identify military participation as a factor in reduced levels of income inequality. Following the initial suggestions of Andreski (1954) and Lenski (1966), and partially replicating the empirical analysis of Garnier and Hazelrigg (1977), they find that military manpower as a percentage of the population—the military participation ratio—is inversely related to various measures of inequality. Their reasoning proceeds from identification of the military participation ratio as a rough indicator of a nation's security threat which in turn imparts some military value to the mass population and, still more speculatively, encourages the wealthy to share income. Titmuss (1958: 86) puts it most simply: "The aims and content of social policy, both in peace and war, are thus determined . . . by how far the cooperation of the masses is essential to the successful prosecution of war. If this cooperation is thought to be essential, then inequalities must be reduced and the pyramid of social stratification must be flattened." Thus, in this formulation it is not military participation *itself* which produces social benefits, but rather the policy imperatives that flow from the condition of threat *implied* by the presence of a large citizen army.

The Effects of Military Spending

Despite the modernization perspective, research on the connection between the military and development has been concentrated on the special impact of military spending. It should be immediately clear, however, that the issues of military personnel and military spending are anything but independent of one another. I return to the interrelationship between these two elements below, but for the moment treat the arguments that bear directly on the impact of military spending on economic growth and basic needs, exclusive of the modernizing effects of military training.

Several analysts have detected positive cross-sectional correlations between military expenditures and growth rates, which they have attributed to a combination of resource mobilization and demand inducement effects (Benoit, 1973, 1978; Whynes, 1979; Kennedy, 1974). Benoit argues that among less developed countries, capacity utilization is often quite low and military spending can be expected to move the economy closer to full employment of resources. The argument is essentially Keynesian and does not rely on any special growth-inducing propensity of military over civilian spending. Rather, it is argued that the demand for military spending may make growth-inducing expansionary monetary and fiscal policies more palatable and also lead to tax increases, which shift resources away from consumption (especially luxury import consumption) and toward greater domestic investment.

On the other hand, a range of theorists question the results of these studies and offer a strong theoretical counterpoint to the resource mobilization arguments.[8] In the first place, reluctance to engage in deficit spending is hardly a common affliction of contemporary governments, and it is far from evident that military spending would be the most beneficial form it could take. Second, even proponents argue that the largest contribution comes from the diversion of revenues raised through progressive and defense-justified tax increases into expenditures with more direct welfare implications (i.e., nondefense) (Faini et al., 1984). On the first point, evidence for the progressivity of tax structures is slim. On the second, global trends suggest that the growth of military spending is more likely to come at the expense of civilian spending than the reverse (Duchin, 1982). Even if true, the argument appears to beat itself: the positive developmental consequences come from the subsequent shift away from military spending, not from the initial military spending itself.[9] Also, the inflationary effects may offset or even dominate the aggregate demand effects; as with all Keynesian policies, there are at least as many value trade-offs and welfare shifts— especially across time and class—as absolute welfare gains.

More important for our purposes, most of these analysts also imply that whatever economic growth may occur through military spending is paid for by increased inequality and reduction in the provision of basic needs for the poor. They decry the "defense burden" as a massive shift of resources from a productive welfare-enhancing function to one whose benefits are at best dubious and at worst absolutely negative. The clearest mechanisms are lower investment levels due to depressed savings if tax rates increase, or inflation resulting from underfinanced expansion of government spending if they do not (Deger and Smith, 1983; Deger and Sen, 1983). The latter in particular can be

8. Since these studies deal with aggregate growth, the details of their empirical methodology and findings are not directly relevant to our concern with the provision of basic needs. Thus, they are not rehearsed here. Many contend, however, that several serious technical flaws account for the misleading results. For a general critique, especially of the widely assailed but very influential analysis of Benoit (1973), see Ball (1982), Terhal (1981), Lim (1983), Faini et al. (1984), Smith and Smith (1979), Deger and Smith (1983), and Deger and Sen (1983).

9. Several works also note that inclusion of foreign resource inflows eliminates most or all of the significance attached to military expenditures as a spur to growth. Interestingly, Benoit deliberately includes as part of the effect of military spending the increased foreign aid that often flows to regimes with large defense expenditures. Such reasoning may well mistake the causal mechanism responsible for the aid–military expenditure correlation and thus misrepresent the indirect effects of military spending. For the source of external support of military regimes, see Wolpin, 1981: 27–42.

expected to have extremely harsh consequences for the poor (Terhal, 1981).

The distributional consequences of the type of macroeconomic growth induced by military spending also appear undesirable. It is often pointed out, for example, that it is the poorest elements of society that have the least to gain from any benefits of military expenditure (such as higher rates of economic growth) as well as being most likely to feel its negative consequences (such as higher rates of inflation). The same might be said of the effects of foreign exchange shortages, which frequently result from the large import component of defense spending for weaponry. If military expenditures are financed by debt, the consequences are only delayed. If they are financed instead by cutbacks in the development budget, it is even more clear that the defense burden is greater on basic needs than on aggregate growth.[10] Further, such effects may become self-reinforcing if reductions in social programs generate protests that in turn reap repression (Luckham, 1978).

Recalling the rural nature of the most serious basic needs deprivation, Kaldor's (1978: 71) simple summary of the distributional patterns is telling: "Military expenditure is paid for largely out of surplus product generated in the countryside . . . but it is spent in the metropolis and in the towns."

A Theoretical and Empirical Summary

To begin the empirical analysis, a simple measure of the size of the defense budget—military spending as a percentage of GNP—is added to the model of political and economic effects first estimated in Table

---

10. There is a similar question of even greater breadth, which unfortunately cannot be treated in the depth that it deserves in the context of this analysis. What is the source of the money spent on the military? Much of the emotionally charged debate on military spending turns on this very issue. Consider two extreme answers, for example. Should military spending come at the expense of spending on health care and education, there is very little doubt that the net impact on the provision of basic needs would be highly negative. Should military spending be financed by a confiscatory tax on luxury imports, one imagines the result could be strongly positive. Against what standard, then, is military spending to be evaluated? Duchin's (1982) interesting analysis suggests very different growth trajectories under different assumptions about the purposes to which money freed by disarmament would be put. The only correct answer to the question "What is the impact of military spending on the provision of basic needs?" is the rejoinder "Compared to what?" The pragmatic answer of this analysis is empirically derived; the comparison is implicitly with the profile of uses to which the money is put by the nations in the sample. The point is more than a curiosity; it suggests that no general answer to the question is possible. Benoit (1973) ducked the problem in another way, by making an arbitrary assumption about the investment-consumption mix that would have resulted from forgone military spending.

Table 7-2. Effects of military expenditures (without other military effects)

Variables	Simple r	All variables				Significant variables		
		Beta	St. beta	t		Beta	St. beta	t
% labor agriculture	−.87	−.81	−.79	−17.3***		−.80	−.78	−17.7***
Socialist × agr.	.24	.62	.28	6.3***		.60	.27	6.2***
Democracy	.47	.13	.13	2.5*		.15	.15	3.1**
Rightist norms	−.38	6.52	.11	1.3		8.26	.14	1.8
Right × govt. expend.	−.38	−.53	−.20	−2.5*		−.60	−.23	−2.9**
Military spending	.09	−.37	−.05	−1.1				

Model	N	r	r^2	adj. r^2	SEE	F
All variables	120	.92	.85	.84	11.33	104.7***
Significant variables	120	.92	.85	.84	11.34	125.2***

*Significant (p < .05)
**Significant (p < .01)
***Significant (p < .001)

6-3.[11] The results are displayed in Table 7-2. The obvious finding is a null one: the parameter estimate for military expenditures is negative, but it is neither large nor statistically significant. From this initial analysis, it appears that military spending does not have the anticipated negative impact on distributional welfare.

Even though the parameter estimate is not significant, however, it is of the expected sign. Moreover, the presence of military spending in the regression equation does produce changes worthy of our attention in the other parameter estimates. Specifically, the reduced estimates of democracy and ideology suggest military spending as a mediating mechanism for their effects. A comparison is facilitated by the juxtaposition of the left side of Table 7-2, whose model contains the military expenditure variable, and the right side, which is estimated without it (thus repeating Table 6-3). First, the t value of the democracy variable declines from 3.1 to 2.5 in the presence of the military expenditure variable. Though still statistically significant, that diminished direct effect hints that democracy may improve basic needs in part by holding military spending below the level expected in nondemocratic nations. Second, both the main and interactive effects of rightist norms exhibit a similar decline, the former from a marginally significant t value of 1.8 to an insignificant one of 1.3, and the latter from −2.9 to −2.5. This finding suggests a relationship between ideological norms and military

11. The measure of military expenditures is directly comparable to the measure of overall state size used in the previous chapter. It is total military expenditures as a percentage of GNP, averaged for the period 1969 to 1971. The data source is USACDA (1980).

spending priorities which warrants further attention. Consequently, I return to that theme below on the basis of more direct evidence for the role of political factors in shaping military budgets and a better specification of the overall effect of military factors on basic needs.

It is obvious, however, that this specification may be flawed by the omission of at least one relevant variable, namely the military manpower measure, which serves as a proxy for the modernization effect achieved through military training. The estimation error is both potentially very large and of predictable direction in a situation such as this. First, the manpower size and the budgetary size of the military establishment are obviously related at both the conceptual and the empirical levels. The statistical colinearity between the two ($r = .76$) is sufficient to strongly affect parameter estimates, though not nearly large enough to pose serious problems for the differentiation of causal influences.[12] Second, the expected effects of the two independent variables are in opposite directions: military spending is expected to impede basic needs provision while military training is expected to enhance it. Causal structures of this sort characteristically yield artificially deflated parameter estimates unless the relevant variables are included together in the regression equation. The cross-cutting effects "wash out" one another in analyses involving only one of the two variables.

To check for this effect, a measure of manpower size is added to the model to complement the military spending variable.[13] The resulting model estimates displayed in Table 7-3 are dramatically supportive of the above lines of argument concerning the differential effect of military spending. A number of interesting features of this model serve as the basis for further analysis.

As hypothesized, the larger the share of manpower devoted to military service, the more satisfactory is the basic needs level. This effect is statistically significant even when it is estimated in an equation that does not contain military spending ($t = 2.4$ in an analysis not shown), but it is dramatically enhanced by the inclusion of military spending (t

12. For a more complete discussion of the diagnostics on this question, see an earlier paper (Dixon and Moon, 1986). It examines not only the r^2 values of each independent variable regressed on all the others but also the eigenstructure of the regressor matrix (Belsley, Kuh, and Welsch, 1980). There is no evidence of any degradation of estimates due to extreme collinearities.

13. The measure is number of active duty military personnel per 1,000 population, derived from USACDA, 1980. Once again, the variable is an average of 1969, 1970, and 1971 data. Similar measures that use military personnel as a percentage of the work force or male work force are correlated extremely highly over the more limited samples for which they are available. When the analyses of this chapter are replicated over such samples, the results are virtually identical. The choice among alternative indicators is thus not consequential.

Table 7-3. Effects of military expenditures and manpower

Variables	Simple r	All variables				Significant variables		
		Beta	St. beta	t		Beta	St. beta	t
% labor agriculture	−.87	−.74	−.72	−15.8***		−.74	−.72	−15.8***
Socialist × agr.	.24	.61	.27	6.7***		.60	.27	6.6***
Democracy	.47	.14	.14	2.9**		.13	.13	2.8**
Rightist norms	−.38	4.92	.09	1.1				
Right × govt. expend.	−.38	−.48	−.19	−2.4*		−.30	−.12	−3.1**
Military spending	.09	−1.56	−.21	−3.8***		−1.69	−.22	−4.3***
Military manpower	.38	.92	.23	4.4***		.94	.24	4.5***

Model	N	r	r^2	adj. r^2	SEE	F
All variables	120	.93	.87	.86	10.52	106.8***
Significant variables	120	.93	.87	.86	10.53	124.3***

*Significant (p < .05)
**Significant (p < .01)
***Significant (p < .001)

= 4.5 on the right side of Table 7-3). Of course, it can be argued that the latter estimate overstates the positive developmental impact of military manpower size because it represents its partial effect while holding constant military spending. Given the definitional linkage between military manpower and the military budget, however, the statistical control cannot be duplicated in the real world since it is hardly possible to substantially increase the size of the military while holding constant its budget. In this sense, the "total" effect of military manpower (t = 2.4) is a more realistic appraisal of the sum of military manpower's two contrary effects, a positive impact of military training and a negative drag effect of paying for it.

By the same token, the negative estimate of military spending is similarly inflated. Though its magnitude is striking (a t value of −4.3), military spending appears significant only in the presence of the military manpower variable. In fact, the latter introduces what might be termed an "elaboration effect," which transforms the meaning of the military budget variable. A statistical control for the manpower size of the military establishment enables us to crudely decompose the budget and focus on the central attributes of the priorities revealed by it. Simply put, it is now evident that the effect of military spending—like that of government spending more generally—depends critically on what the expenditures are used to purchase and at what price. Further, both the theoretical discussion above and that of the literature more broadly imply exactly the result represented in Table 7-3: military spending is harmful when devoted to overly generous pay levels to military personnel and to the purchase of relatively capital-intensive weaponry and equipment. Let us review the lines of argument concerning these differential effects of military spending.

Many of the objections to military spending apply with much-diminished force to labor-intensive expenditures at salaries comparable to those of civilian sectors. Under these conditions, incomes earned out of the military budget will tend to be less skewed than spending that contains a larger component of profits or rents. A low ratio of budget to manpower suggests that foreign weapons purchases are limited, thus reducing the diversion of scarce foreign exchange which so often cripples development plans that require importation of technology for industrialization. Similarly, if domestic weapons manufactures are relatively modest, there is little distortion of industry toward production functions at variance with factor endowments, an economic feature that frequently undermines balanced and egalitarian growth by idling labor resources. The familiar argument that capital-intensive, high-wage industry decreases employment and increases inequality can certainly be extended beyond the private sector to the military (Ball, 1982; Weaver and Jameson, 1981; Wolpin, 1981).

Also, labor-intensive expenditures are excepted from many of the doubts concerning the resource mobilization effects of military spending. The key issue is whether previously "idle capacity" is being mobilized—in which case the effects are almost surely positive—or whether the resources are merely being diverted from one function to another. If the latter, the consequences are surely negative for basic needs, both because the competition for resources will yield inflation and relative factor price changes that will harm the poorest most and because the military sector is less likely to produce goods that meet basic needs. But the existence of large labor surpluses, common in Third World countries, implies that manpower spending—especially at relatively low wages—is more likely to meet the test than spending on capital-intensive equipment (Whynes, 1979). Even Benoit (1973) acknowledges that investment-depressing (and therefore growth-depressing) effects occur when military expenditures are capital-intensive. Indeed, this study's earlier discussion of modernization effects fits neatly with this strand of argument; together they suggest a strong case for expectation of a differential impact of military spending according to the composition of the budget.

Of course, labor-intensive military spending does forgo some of the very advantages said to characterize such programs. Kennedy (1974), for example, argues that the initial stages of industrialization are eased by specialization in weapons and other military hardware because the markets are more stable and better protected than in branches of indus-

trial production in which competition from the better-established industries of other nations would have to be faced immediately. Further,
much of the modernization effect is thought to revolve around the role
of military technology in both stimulating the drive for growth among
military leaders and providing the training to military conscripts which
spurs growth upon release. It appears, however, that the bulk of the
modernizing impact of the military is not a consequence of technology-
related factors, but rather is more directly related to individual-level
factors and mass effects.

Finally, another approach to understanding the effect of the composition of the military budget considers that the ratio of military expenditures to military manpower may be thought of as a reasonable proxy
for several significant distinctions between types of armies recognized
in the literature. Kaldor (1978), in particular, distinguishes between the
preindustrial and the industrial army. Examples of the former are mass
armies based on the infantry or cavalry such as the retinue armies of
precolonial Africa or the nineteenth-century militias of Latin America.
They are notable for their reliance on the soldier and not the weapon,
but the organizational and orientational consequences go far beyond
the economic characteristic of being labor-intensive.

Most important, these armies—pro-development and contributory to
basic needs provision in our formulation—are built on conscripts. At
once conscription implies a process more likely to sample proportionally from various classes and thus to avoid the upper-class bias of
more elite and more "professional" armies. Second, it also results in a
more widespread distribution of the effects of military training, because with the greater turnover rate a higher proportion of the population would have received military exposure than might be expected on
the basis of the current size of the military. Third, the army is less
likely to acquire the kind of professionalism which yields corporate interests sought through higher budgets, more advanced equipment,
higher pay rates, and greater political influence. It is not hard to see
why the impact on development of these two different types of armies
may differ markedly.

This line of reasoning might seem to suggest a return to Huntington's thesis that the character of the military changes with the social
structure of the system that gives rise to it. Although this idea is partly
true, it does not imply the interactive thesis that Jackman suggests as
an operationalization of it. In the first place, the Bedouin levies of the
Middle East or the caudillos of Latin America are rooted in a social
structure badly mirrored in indicators of "level of development" (Kaldor, 1978). Second, the real roots of many contemporary military organizations lie not in the domestic setting, but abroad. Many authors

refer to the powerful impact that external political socialization has had, particularly in the case of American influence in Latin America (Wolpin, 1981; Price, 1971; Needler, 1966; Grand Pre, 1970; Hobsbawm, 1973; Horowitz, 1967). The effect of colonial heritage is also felt in the character of the military establishment that evolves subsequent to independence (Gutteridge, 1970; Bebler, 1972). Finally, the orientation of the military results from factors unique to the case, especially the historical circumstances surrounding militarized independence or revolutionary movements, witness the special stamp placed on the military by Fidel Castro or Pol Pot. Thus, the proportion of expenditures to manpower must be seen as an indicator of an important attribute of the military organization, but one that is autonomous from—or, at any rate, certainly not reducible to—any single attribute of the corresponding society.

The Military Budget as a Mediating Mechanism

It does appear, however, that these attributes of the military budget may be mediating mechanisms that transmit some developmental effects of other features of the political system. Thus, to shed some light on the sources as well as the consequences of these budgetary priorities, an analysis was conducted in which military spending, military manpower levels, and the spending/manpower ratio were used as dependent variables.[14] The results have interesting implications for our conclusions concerning the effects of democracy, ideological norms, and military regimes.

Although it is evident from the results of Table 7-4 that neither the size nor the composition of the military budget is especially well predicted by economic and political attributes, there are interpretable results. First, by both measures richer nations devote a higher percentage of their resources to the military than poorer nations. Second, democratic nations expend substantially less than nondemocratic ones, a

14. In effect, this ratio combines the other two measures in such a way that it will have a value of 1 if the military is as large in manpower terms (troops as a percentage of total population) as in budgetary terms (expenditures as a percentage of GNP). Similar measures when applied to civilian sectors—as they were implicitly in Chapter 4—are thought to capture the capital intensity or relative wage rates of a given sector. In this case, the calibration is somewhat different in the two measures—military spending does not accrue only to men under arms but to all employees of firms that provide goods or services to the military. In part for this reason, the mean of the sample on this variable (about .78) does not give us a comparable measure, but nonetheless, the ratio is a reasonable proxy for the general notion of military spending that is either capital-intensive or flows to higher military salaries.

Table 7-4. Determinants of military expenditures and manpower

Variables	Simple r	Military expenditures			Military manpower		
		Beta	St. beta	t	Beta	St. beta	t
% labor agriculture	−.15/−.37	−.04	−.31	−3.1**	−.13	−.50	−5.0***
Socialist	.37/ .32	2.24	.17	1.6	3.01	.12	1.1
Democracy	−.29/−.12	−.05	−.38	−3.1**	−.08	−.33	−2.7**
Rightist norms	−.12/−.10	−1.04	−.14	−1.4	−.44	−.03	−.3
Military regime	.11/−.09	.02	.16	1.8	−.00	−.01	−.1

Model	N	r	r²	adj. r²	SEE	F
Military expenditures	118	.51	.26	.22	3.30	7.7***
Military manpower	118	.52	.27	.23	6.29	8.2***

*Significant (p < .05)
**Significant (p < .01)
***Significant (p < .001)

contrast especially vivid with state socialist systems. Indeed, this linkage is strong enough to account for a portion of democracy's positive effect on basic needs levels, though it tells us nothing about the source of state socialist systems' success in welfare provision. Third, marginally significant estimates hint that right-wing regimes may spend a little less than otherwise expected and military regimes slightly more, but neither has any impact on the manpower size of the military. Fourth, these differences suggest—and a regression analysis using the spending/manpower ratio as the dependent variable (not shown) confirms—that military regimes favor a military establishment with a higher ratio of expenditures to manpower than other regimes, even those with rightist norms. This outcome is explicable as a consequence of the corporatist interests of the military in both higher pay and more elaborate equipment but not higher troop levels, because larger mass armies do as much to threaten the position of military leaders as to enhance it.

These relatively weak findings are in line with the mixed evidence reported in Zuk and Thompson's (1982) survey of thirteen empirical studies. Five studies indicate that military governments spend more on defense than civilian governments while one says they spend less. Five others produce null or ambiguous results, and two suggest a curvilinear relationship. Some of that ambiguity may be attributable to the tendency noted above for both rightist and military regimes to have smaller overall budgets than nonmilitary and leftist regimes. Thus, their *slightly* higher military spending as a percentage of GDP constitutes a *significantly* higher percentage of the state budget devoted to the military. A regression analysis (not shown) with the latter as the dependent variable confirms the higher priority afforded military spending by military regimes ($t = 2.8$).

These results also may suggest a mechanism to account for the interactive effect between rightist ideology and the state size measure documented in the previous chapter. It is certainly plausible that the poor basic needs performance of large right-wing governments is as much a consequence of the size or composition of the military budget as any more general policy orientation. In order to test this possibility, the analysis of the previous chapter is repeated with state expenditures broken into their civilian and military components.

First, the additive analysis reported in Chapter 6 was altered by replacing the one state size measure with two variables reflecting the civilian and military budgets as a percentage of GDP. The original raw parameter estimate for state size was $-.31$, but the reanalysis seems to indicate that military expenditures are more harmful than civilian ones; the betas are $-.58$ and $-.25$ respectively when the budget is split apart. The former, however, is estimated with considerably more error than the latter—perhaps because the labor intensity of the military is uncontrolled in this analysis—with the result that the t values are virtually identical.

Second, a partial replication was undertaken of the interactive analysis that revealed that greater state size was detrimental to basic needs only in the presence of right-wing governments (Table 6-3). Just as the state size measure was replaced by separate variables for civilian and military spending, the interaction term between state size and rightist norms was replaced by separate interaction terms for the two budget categories. The results presented in Table 7-5 are clear. The interaction between *civilian* expenditures and rightist norms is strong, whereas there is no significant differential effect of *military* expenditures. Thus, the source of the poor basic needs performance of right-wing regimes apparently lies less in the military than in the civilian sphere. Indeed, replacing the interaction term of state spending with one involving only civilian expenditures improves the overall fit of the model and increases the significance of the various parameter estimates; the t value of military spending increases from -1.1 to -1.6; the additive effect of right regimes moves from $t = 1.3$ to $t = 1.5$ and the interaction term from -2.5 to -2.8. Thus, the specification of Table 7-5 is adopted as the working model for subsequent analyses.

Military Participation in Politics

Having completed our analysis of the three measurable mechanisms said to mediate the relationship between military regimes and develop-

Table 7-5. Distinguishing the effects of civilian and military expenditures

Variables	Simple r	All variables				Significant variables		
		Beta	St. beta	t		Beta	St. beta	t
% labor agriculture	−.87	−.81	−.79	−16.8***		−.81	−.79	−17.4***
Socialist × agr.	.24	.65	.29	6.4***		.64	.29	6.6***
Democracy	.47	.13	.13	2.5*		.13	.13	2.5*
Rightist norms	−.38	6.54	.11	1.1		7.06	.12	1.5
Civilian spending	.17	.02	.01	.1				
Military spending	.09	−.64	−.09	−1.7		−.52	−.07	−1.6
Right × civilian	−.39	−.70	−.23	−2.3*		−.67	−.22	−2.8**
Right × military	−.23	.35	.03	.6				

Model	N	r	r²	adj. r²	SEE	F
All variables	120	.92	.85	.84	11.32	78.9***
Significant variables	120	.92	.85	.84	11.24	106.7***

*Significant (p < .05)
**Significant (p < .01)
***Significant (p < .001)

mental outcomes, we can now return to the discussion of the cross-cutting effects suggested by both the literature and the current empirical analysis. Specifically, we are now in a position to evaluate the adequacy of the "causal model" sketched in Figure 7-1. Recall that a null effect of military regimes on basic needs performance—such as that suggested by Table 7-1—could occur for three distinct reasons. First, military regimes may not produce the four hypothesized intermediate consequences: organizational efficiency, conservative ideology, enlarged social role for military service, and increased military spending. We now know that military regimes are associated with conservatism and rather higher military spending, though they are not associated with greater manpower levels.[15] Second, the mediating mechanisms themselves may not function as predicted. To the contrary, we know that military spending and rightist norms do lower basic needs attainment while military manpower increases it. Finally, the cross-cutting mechanisms may wash out one another, thus inviting a misleading null inference.

It appears that the final explanation is the correct one. To complete the analysis, the military regime variable is reintroduced into the model of Table 7-5. In the presence of measures of three of the proposed

15. The absence of a suitable measure of organizational efficiency prevents a clear evaluation of this alleged property of military regimes. As is argued below, however, it is not implausible that the variable for the existence of military regimes is a proxy for this effect when the other three mechanisms are controlled.

Table 7-6. Military effects on basic human needs

Variables	Simple r	All variables			Significant variables		
		Beta	St. beta	t	Beta	St. beta	t
% labor agriculture	−.87	−.75	−.73	−16.2***	−.75	−.73	−16.3***
Socialist × agr.	.24	.67	.30	7.3***	.67	.30	7.3***
Democracy	.47	.15	.16	3.2**	.15	.15	3.2**
Rightist norms	−.38	1.77	.03	.4			
Right × civilian	−.39	−.41	−.14	−1.8	−.34	−.11	−3.0**
Military spending	.09	−1.92	−.26	−4.6***	−1.97	−.26	−4.9***
Military manpower	.38	.97	.25	4.5***	.99	.25	4.7***
Military regime (months)	−.25	.07	.08	2.2*	.07	.09	2.3*

Model	N	r	r^2	adj. r^2	SEE	F
All variables	120	.94	.87	.87	10.36	96.9***
Significant variables	120	.94	.87	.87	10.32	111.5***

*Significant (p < .05)
**Significant (p < .01)
***Significant (p < .001)

causal mechanisms—ideology, military spending, and military manpower—it is plausible that this variable is now tapping the uniquely
military character of the ruling regime, the hypothesized superior organizational efficiency of military over civilian leadership. The results
of Table 7-6 seem to confirm this outcome. Indeed, the inclusion of this
variable not only improves the overall fit of the model, it also boosts
the size and significance of the parameter estimates for the related factors. The effect of military regimes is seen to be small—at the mean
value of months of military rule (19), the expected PQLI is only about
1.5 above the level expected of a nation without any experience with a
military regime. It is, however, statistically significant (the t value of
2.3 is significant at the .02 level), and it rounds out our understanding
of other military and political effects.

Even so, we have not quite exhausted the factors we must consider.
Military participation in policy making is not limited to the presence of
military regimes. Indeed, it can be argued that the distinction between
civilian and military regimes is in many circumstances an artificial one.
Ronfeldt (1974: 110–11) represents a common position among Latin
American scholars: "Neither of the two ideal polar-types—purely military or civilian rule—is or has been particularly common in Latin
America. The empirically common fact is rule by civil-military coalitions, regardless of who formally occupies the chief executive offices."

It is certainly true that civilians play a large role in military regimes,
and that the military represents a significant force in formally civilian-

led regimes as well (Sarkesian, 1978; Zolberg, 1969). This blurring of categories is no doubt a factor in the failure of many statistical studies—including my initial effort—to find significant performance differences between civilian and military regimes (Tannahill, 1976; Schmitter, 1973; Thompson, 1975; McKinlay and Cohen, 1976; Jackman, 1976). Simply put, the attributes thought to cause the underperformance of "military regimes" are also frequently present in civilian-military "coalitions" usually coded as "civilian regimes."

Though the military receives a higher percentage of state-controlled resources in military regimes, the contrast is no more dramatic than the military/civilian distinction itself. The influence of the military on budgetary allocations is powerful wherever the military maintains a strong political presence. This influence may be somewhat higher when the military role is prominent enough for a civilian-military coalition to be coded as a "military regime," but it is far from absent in other cases. The corporate interests of the military are protected by civilian leaders who recognize the reality: "A regime can survive for a time when the civilian bureaucracy opposes it. But no regime can survive if the military does not at least acquiesce in its rule" (Wriggins, 1969: 65). Thus, in a system with a politically active military and, consequently, an ever-present threat of a coup, the spending priorities may not be radically altered by its actual occurrence. There is evidence, for example, that government resources are frequently diverted to the military in order to forestall a coup; indeed, for this reason, military spending is about as likely to increase before a coup as after it (Zuk and Thompson, 1982). This pattern implies that the most meaningful distinction may lie between systems with an intervention-prone military and those without one (Wolpin, 1981). Of course, this chapter aims to remove the confounding influence of military spending and military regimes by measuring the resource consumption of the military and including it as a separate variable.

Even this approach has its limitations, however. Weaver (1973: 64–65) observes that "military budgets and the overall costs of maintaining a military establishment are extremely difficult to measure since without exception Latin American governments hide military appropriations in several budget categories." It seems plausible that deliberate underestimation of the military burden would be largest in countries where the military had the greatest influence.

A second consideration also suggests that the appropriate distinction implied by the theoretical arguments is that between systems marked by a politically active military and those in which the military is subordinated and nonthreatening to civilian leaders. J. J. Johnson (1964: 143–44) has observed, for example, that "without the military, every government in the Latin American orbit would be farther to the left than it is now." Once again, the inclusion of the ideological measure helps in sorting out the role of this mechanism said to mediate the relationship between military regimes and basic needs performance.

These arguments remind us, however, that the presence of a politically active and intervention-prone military may dramatically transform the operation of a domestic political system. Regimes faced with imminent replacement surely must adopt a more limited time horizon in gauging alternative policies, for example. This result can hardly be beneficial for the relatively long-term commitment to investment in human capital and infrastructure required for basic needs gains. Moreover, the rapid regime changes associated with an active military also disrupt the normal economic processes that affect both the growth and distributional aspects of basic needs provision, especially if accompanied by broader-scale instability or political conflict.

Thus, the interpretation of the military regime variable as a proxy for the unique style of state management associated with military regimes is not fully justified. Naturally, the general approach of trying to isolate one characteristic of military regimes by successively removing other characteristics is never completely satisfactory. The difficulty is that military regimes are sufficiently multifaceted that the list of enumerated features can never be exhaustive, with the result that the main effects always remain something of an amalgam of the nonenumerated attributes. In this case, the operation of a military regime remains confounded with the presence of a politically active military.

One approach—itself flawed but potentially instructive—is to examine the functional form of the relationship between military regimes and basic needs performance. In particular, we can distinguish between systems in which military regimes have been dominant for a long period of time and those in which the military has been in power more briefly. Effects found in the latter may be interpretable as a consequence of a politically active and intervention-prone military whereas those in the former more truly reflect the actual impact of military governance.

An empirical analysis does produce a pattern compatible with this interpretation, though the results are not strong enough to yield great confidence in a distinct causal model of the dynamics. For example, it is clear from a number of analyses (not shown) that the positive parameter estimate for military regimes is principally a consequence of the higher PQLI to be found in nations with a lengthy period of military rule. That is, the poorest basic needs performance is to be found in nations that have experienced some, but not extensive, military rule. Both nations that have *never* experienced a military regime and those that have been *predominantly* ruled by the military outperform the middle category. The exact source of this pattern is not clear. Indeed, the relative weakness of the effect together with the technical problem of skewness which dogs the attempt to identify this sort of functional form makes it difficult to be sure that it is not a statistical artifact. Nonetheless, we suspect that military rule may have a positive impact on basic needs when it is sustained long enough to dominate the negative effect of an active military.

It must be remembered, however, that the positive impact of military regimes is small, far from robust, and at most an extremely "partial" effect. That is, military regimes may be progressive for basic needs levels only when we control for the greater military spending, the more conservative ideological orientation, the lower levels of democracy and, it appears, the greater political activism of the military which military regimes imply. The "reduced form" result—the effect of military regimes without those controls—remains almost exactly zero. Military regimes are successful only in relation to *comparable* civilian regimes—rightist, nondemocratic, and wasteful in the use of military resources. Furthermore, at least two alternative paths of political development are unequivocally superior: state socialism and political democracy.

PART IV

Distal Influences
on State, Society,
Economy, and
Basic Needs

Chapter 8
Dependency Elements of Economic Structure

Distal Effects

As we have seen in Parts II and III, predominantly "domestic" theories of basic human needs provision are capable of accounting for a large percentage of the cross-national variance in PQLI. Both liberal and Marxist theorists argue, however, that national development processes cannot be fully understood without reference to their global context. External factors are neither marginal in importance nor exogenous in origin. Indeed, the internal/external distinction is inherently artificial and can be drawn sensibly only for a given time slice; today's internal development feature reflects yesterday's external relations, for example. Beyond a recognition of the importance of the external environment, of course, schools of thought do not agree on the identification or evaluation of external effects (Valenzuela and Valenzuela, 1978; Portes, 1976; Rostow, 1960; Inkeles and Smith, 1974; Chilcote and Johnson, 1983; Warren, 1980; Bauer, 1972; Johnson, 1967). The analysis of Part IV focuses on the theoretical family comprised of the world system perspective (Wallerstein, 1974a; Chirot, 1977; Chase-Dunn, 1981), the "dependencia" tradition (Cardoso and Faletto, 1979; Frank, 1966; Evans, 1979), and related eclectic theories that emphasize external determinants of development (Bornschier, 1981; Galtung, 1971).

As we shall see, the variety of interpretations within this single "school" of thought share the conviction that internal theories are severely limited by their focus on "proximate" effects. Thus, Part IV considers a number of the more "distal" effects required for a comprehensive explanation. Chapter 8 examines the *geographically* distal influences of the global economic system, including the effects of international economic transactions. Some of these simply refine the previous model by explaining additional variance, but others dissolve the boundary between internal and external altogether. In the process, they shift our attention to internal developmental features that are induced by those transactions and help us to understand how alternative developmental trajectories have arisen. Examining these linkages then deepens the previous explanations by setting them within an overall causal structure that permits the stipulation of mediating mechanisms. Chapter 9 then deals similarly with *temporally* distal influences, especially the impact of colonialism. The analysis traces the continuing effect of past events and conditions through contemporary features that represent historical residue from the past.

Structural Location and Modes of Production

Both world systems and dependency theory argue that the global economic system has evolved a single division of labor and a corresponding social and economic structure within which each nation is embedded (Chase-Dunn, 1981; Wallerstein, 1974c; Frank, 1966). The developmental impact of the global system on the political economy of contemporary nations is profound, but it varies according to the location of the individual nation within the hierarchical structure. Most commonly it is argued that core nations benefit, at the expense of nations more peripheral to the system, in terms of both higher growth and greater social harmony born of greater equality. Neither could be achieved without the surplus transfer provided by a continuous flow of economic transactions with poor and dependent nations (Baran and Sweezey, 1966).

Through multiple and complex mechanisms the political and economic systems of poor countries have been penetrated by external actors, incorporated into the world system, and in the process fundamentally transformed. Their developmental paths are altered so profoundly that the resulting systems no longer function according to the same social principles, obey the same economic laws, or yield the same developmental consequences as nations that have developed more autonomously. They are incapable of self-reproduction (dos Santos, 1970), and their growth is not only slow (Baran, 1957) but fitful (Amin, 1976: 259), sectorally narrow, and uneven (Amin, 1977: 352). Rather than being reinvested in future growth, their surpluses are plundered (Jalee, 1968), repatriated through super-profits (Frank, 1969;

Hymer, 1972), lost in terms of trade deterioration (Prebisch, 1959), and extracted through unequal exchange (Emmanuel, 1972). Their state institutions are weakened (Delacroix and Ragin, 1981; Rubinson, 1977), their class structures are distorted (Petras, 1978), even their demographic transition (Nolan and White, 1985) and their urbanization patterns (Portes and Walton, 1981; Timberlake, 1985) are disrupted. In short, the "laws of motion" of core-periphery relations are said to yield growth processes and developmental outcomes that are unique to the periphery. For our purposes, the significance of these contentions lies in the suggestion that the basic needs performance of the periphery will lag that of the core.

This litany of differences has led some to argue that the forms of economic organization found in different structural positions—even though all are ostensibly capitalist—actually constitute distinct modes of production (Magubane, 1985; Chilcote and Johnson, 1983). Even where Third World industrialization has occurred, the resulting political economy is said to be but a pale reflection of core capitalism. Its mode of production has instead been characterized as "peripheral capitalist" (Amin, 1976) and its change process as "associated-dependent development" (Cardoso and Faletto, 1979). This conception has two implications for the route by which our analysis seeks to identify the effect of structural position on basic needs provision.

First, these theorists usually contend that the differences between nations occupying each structural position are not of degree, but of kind. One can divide nations into the dominant and the dependent (dos Santos, 1970), or distinguish the structural position of core from periphery, but finer gradations are inappropriate. Indeed, even the creation of an intermediate third category (e.g., "semiperiphery") is theoretically problematic and empirically challenging (Wallerstein, 1974c; Kentor, 1985; Moon, 1987a). Dependency theorists have been especially vociferous in denouncing measurement approaches that conceive "dependency" as a continuous variable that can be used to characterize the degree to which a nation is dependent (Valenzuela and Valenzuela, 1978; Duvall, 1978; Cardoso, 1977). At best, several discrete "situations of dependency" can be delineated (Cardoso and Faletto, 1979). Empirical researchers in the world systems tradition have struggled to define the membership of the three structural locations (categories) in discrete terms, even when their devices have involved continuous variables (Timberlake and Lundy, 1985; Snyder and Kick, 1979; Gidengil, 1978).

The second implication of this conception is that these structural locations obviously are not unidimensional phenomena, but rather "syndromes" of multiple, related features (Mahler, 1980; Chase-Dunn, 1983). Moreover, no single dimension of dependency is an adequate proxy because the control mechanisms by which dominant-dependent relations are maintained change much more rapidly than the structure itself (Magdoff, 1969; Frank, 1969; Valenzuela and Valenzuela, 1978). The move away from primary product production, for example, need not involve a change in structural location (de Janvry, 1981; Emmanuel, 1972). These variations complicate precise measurement schemes and encourage broader-scale and more abstract treatments that emphasize the relatively stable, but unfortunately less visible, *structures* of dominance rather than the more accessible—but potentially misleading—*patterns* through which they are manifested.

Despite obvious theoretical and empirical difficulties, this "core-periphery" imagery of structural position continues to dominate recent writing on the external component of national development. For the purposes of this analysis as well this broad conception is a handy device for organizing disparate causal mechanisms.

The "Core-Periphery" Imagery of Structural Position

Core-periphery imagery is now commonplace, yet its meaning is seldom stated with the precision required for quantitative analysis. One source of definitional looseness is the persistence of two related—but not identical—themes concerning the essence of structural position. First, world systems formulations invariably emphasize the economic structure known as the international division of labor (Caporaso, 1987). Its critical elements concern the nature of the goods being produced by each nation and the productive processes they employ. Wallerstein expresses this understanding of structural position: "The core-periphery distinction . . . differentiates those zones in which are concentrated high-profit, high-technology, high-wage diversified production (the core countries) from those in which are concentrated low-profit, low-technology, low-wage, less diversified production (the peripheral countries)" (1979: 96–97).

Though the most easily measured proxy for this conception is the relative level of processing found in the export and import baskets (Galtung, 1971), the core-periphery distinction is also intended to connote disparities in capital/labor ratios, factor productivity, and means of labor control, as well as such related differences as product differentiation, price and income elasticities of demand, opportunities for oligopolistic or monopolistic marketing actions, dynamic forward and backward linkages, and a host of other factors that make the production of certain types of goods preferable to others.

The second basic theme of this tradition has to do with power. While accepting division-of-labor distinctions as absolutely critical—indeed, most identify dependency theory's birth with Prebisch's (1959) analysis of the liabilities inherent in primary product export reliance—dependency theory formulations more often emphasize the political and social structure of dominance-dependence (power) relations. Thus, particular actors (e.g., multinational corporations, hegemonic states, or international economic institutions) and particular transactions and interactions (e.g., military intervention, compliant policy actions, or decapitalizing monetary flows) embody the dominance of the core. Galtung's (1971) identification of "feudal patterns of interaction" also parallels this stress on actors and power.

Although there is no overt inconsistency in these two formulations, their juxtaposition does reveal both the multidimensionality of core-periphery concepts and the degree to which they are embedded in a particular theory of international political economy. The coherence of these positions is maintained by the theory that dominance in political relations yields the capacity to structure production and exchange relations in ways that both favor the interests of the dominant actors and reproduce their power relations. Reflexively, these economic relations strongly condition political relations among classes and nations. Even though such recursive causal relationships no doubt exist, they surely yield patterns far from the statistically perfect ones implied by the definitional concepts of core and periphery. Moreover, quite different formulations of these causal dynamics are to be found even within broadly similar theoretical works (Chilcote and Johnson, 1983; Caporaso, 1987).

This multidimensionality becomes even more striking when we leave the conceptual realm of division of labor or dominance-dependence relations to enter the empirical task of measurement. Here we encounter two visible dimensions of structural position, each of which also offers both an economic and a social-political face.

On the one hand, the structural position of a nation within the global division of labor is given by the attributes of its internal economic processes. Typically, theorists identify as both the consequence and the indicator of peripheral capitalism the classical components of the mode of production—for example, capital/labor ratios, form of labor control, patterns in factor markets—and secondary effects such as unequal sectoral growth, the absence of sectoral linkages, class inequality, growth of the tertiary, and stagnation. The case for peripheral capitalism as a distinctive mode of production rests even more on the social and political face of this developmental pattern (Veltmeyer, 1983; Johnson, 1983). Class formation and the nature of class cleavages are both the expression of these economic attributes and a key causal factor in their creation and reproduction. The penetrated and internationalized bourgeoisie, the fractionated working class, and the small middle class are distinctive features of the social structure of the periphery, which in turn yields a political system absent a strong, nationalist state and void of effective political actors, institutions, and policies that represent mass interests (Petras, 1978).

On the other hand, structural position must also be understood in *relational* terms. Peripheral nations are not just poor; their characteristic structure is neither a primeval state nor merely a reflection of poverty, but a consequence of international exchange relations, which have both an economic and a political face. On the economic side are the familiar arguments concerning primary product specialization and the unequal exchange to which it gives rise, reliance on foreign capital and the resultant adverse flows, and the general impact of market control on surplus extraction. Core-periphery political relations are marked by constrained choice, policy domination, and the co-optation of peripheral elites. Of course, the attribute and the relational elements cannot be easily distinguished, in part because many of the external flows are strongly related to internal attributes of the economy. For example, primary goods exports are an exchange reflection of primary goods production.

Before proceeding to the measurement issues that this multidimensionality implies, however, we must probe the theoretical arguments that support our guiding proposition: the international division of labor and dominance-dependence relations benefit core nations while they undermine the provision of basic needs in the periphery (and have mixed effects on the semiperiphery).

Structural Location and Basic Needs Provision

The contention that peripheral capitalism must be regarded as a distinctive mode of production with unique laws of motion and inferior welfare performance rests in part on the different historical origins of core and peripheral capitalism. In early Europe, capitalism developed largely autonomously through interactions among indigenous economic, political, social, and cultural forces. External contacts were relatively limited, and both the economy and the polity were considerably more closed to foreign influences than the modern periphery. Moreover, the contacts that did occur were with systems of lesser power; consequently, the transactions could be fashioned into positive spurs to growth and change (Wallerstein, 1974a). In contrast to the experience of early Europe, today's periphery faced a vastly different external environment and one that played a far more active role in structuring its political economy. Moreover, in the case of contemporary dependent development, the articulation to systems of greater economic and political power is said to have had a distorting effect of greater magnitude and "opposite sign." Brett (1973: 284) puts the distinction simply: "Capitalism had evolved organically in the areas of origin, but it was injected into the colonial world from outside and, where necessary, imposed upon unwilling populations there at the point of a gun."

The restructuring of the economies of colonized areas to serve the interests of foreign actors required that traditional societies—many of which originally possessed the capacity for autonomous development—be balkanized and peripheralized, as in most of Africa (Amin, 1972), if not destroyed outright as in most of the Caribbean (Mintz, 1985). The extraction of surplus required not only the establishment of an export sector, but also the alteration of the social and economic structure of the whole society to facilitate its reproduction and growth. In the absence of labor surpluses, for example, labor was diverted to export sectors either by direct coercion or through irresistible incentives (e.g., taxation payable in currency available only through cash crop production). The resulting "colonial capitalist mode of production (CCMP)" (Magubane, 1985: 199)—and the contemporary peripheral structure which is its historical residue—have a number of features distinct from both the formal models of orthodox economic theory and the historical experience of Europe. To be sure, there were important differences among nations in early colonial processes (Amin, 1972)—indeed, these are addressed in Chapter 9—but there are also striking parallels.

Because of an unusually large foreign sector composed of primary product exports, the periphery is vulnerable to a range of exchange mechanisms that lower both the long-term growth prospects and the immediate welfare fruits of any given level of production. The mechanisms of surplus extraction range from Emmanuel's (1972) "unequal exchange" and Prebisch's (1959) declining terms of trade to Kay's (1975) "monopoly pricing." At the same time, inequality levels within these sectors are typically very large, with wage rates lagging productivity, profit rates swollen by rents, and massive concentrations of ownership of land and capital.

An even more distinctive aspect of economic structure in the periphery is the extreme dualism commonly found between a very labor-intensive traditional sector and a capital-intensive modern sector that produces consumption goods for export or luxuries for local elites. Through several mechanisms, the articulation of these sectors is not only a primary source of the reproduction of peripheral capitalism, but also a major cause of lagging basic needs provision.

First, the resulting intersectoral wage inequality yields lower basic needs fulfillment than development paths with more labor-intensive industrialization or capital-intensive agriculture, either of which would tend to equalize the capital/labor ratio—thus, wages—across sectors. Second, the surplus extracted from the agricultural sector in the form of monopoly rents by landowners enters the investment stream that fuels growth in the modern sector. But the resulting backwash effects include low investment and slow technical change in agricultural sectors, which constrain basic needs improvements in rural areas. Third, the reproduction of labor for the modern sector is subsidized by cheap wage goods resulting from low wages in the traditional sector and by cyclical urban-rural migration, which absorbs some of the burden of maintaining the unemployed. Thus, intersectoral inequality will be exacerbated because wage levels are kept low not only by limiting the real consumption of wage earners but also by lowering the price-denominated costs of those wage goods that are consumed. The latter, in turn, means exploiting even further the rural areas, especially through lower food prices (Portes, 1985; de Janvry, 1981: 77–78).

Intersectoral inequality is more prominent in peripheral capitalism than where capitalist development is more autonomous because the connection between capital accumulation and aggregate demand—which was so key to the early development of today's core economies—is largely absent in the contemporary periphery. In relatively closed economies, such as those of modernizing Europe, autocentric development must rely on growth in internal demand formed by some combination of higher income concentrations of the very wealthy, higher wages paid to workers, and a larger pool of consumers (i.e., a proletarianization of the work force). At low levels of technology, the former is limited by the capacity of industry to produce luxury goods; thus, the future of European development was correctly diagnosed to lie in increasing incomes among the masses through the latter two routes. Although the competitive interests of individual capitalists in holding down wages remained, their common interests in market widening and market deepening represented a cross-cutting influence that weakened their resistance to upward pressures on wages in the wage good sectors of both industry and agriculture. Moreover, these upward pressures were fostered by structural and institutional forces that evolved organically out of preexisting mechanisms and ideologies for the maintenance of system legitimacy. This type of political economy is said to be "socially articulated" in the sense that (1) the contextually determined interests of powerful actors are compatible with welfare-enhancing development (capital accumulation ultimately requires quite widespread development and limited class and sectoral inequalities) and (2) real social forces arise which strongly propel development in that direction (powerful trade union movements, state institutions legitimated by process and performance, and welfare- and participation-oriented public ideologies) (de Janvry, 1981).

By contrast, contemporary peripheral nations manifest a vastly different economic pattern, which is both cause and consequence of significant differences in social cleavages and political structures. A massively larger export sector, less muted income inequality, and a foreign market consisting principally of societies at higher levels of development combine to allow exogenously determined foreign incomes to replace domestic wage levels as the determinant of demand; thus, the upward pressure on wage rates disappears. Moreover, the availability of both foreign and domestically produced luxury goods increases the spending capacity of elites and thus the incentives for greater inequality. As a consequence, capital accumulation can continue—indeed, it can accelerate—even while development remains exceptionally uneven and the welfare of the masses stagnates or even retrogresses. Additional mechanisms that cause basic needs levels to lag include higher expenditures for repression to sustain the unfavorable labor conditions, and the expression of these social structures in political arrangements, dominant ideologies, and public programs for infrastructure and welfare.

The logic of these processes also helps explain the necessity of treating peripheral status as a highly aggregate phenomenon very badly approximated by any single dimension measure. De Janvry (1981) emphasizes, for example, that social disarticulation comes in at least two very different-looking forms. Economies dominated by either export enclaves or import-substitution industrialization exhibit social disarticulation with similar consequences, even while such key elements as the level of processing and the size of the foreign sector may be very different. At the same time, the role played by the rural subsistence sector in reproducing the reserve army of labor, which lowers wage levels, while subsidizing those same low wages through episodic employment can also be approximated by the growth of an urban informal sector in other economies (Portes, 1985: 55–56). Thus, even labor force measures would draw a false distinction between two alternative forms of peripheral capitalism. As de Janvry (1981: 40–41) puts it,

> It would clearly be useless to attempt a global schematization of the process through which disarticulation develops, since this process obviously assumes specific forms in different countries and time periods. . . . The emergence of a structural pattern of disarticulated accumulation in a peripheral country is the outcome of a complex and unstable social process. The key dimensions that condition this process are the class structure in

the particular peripheral country and the subjective contradictions that characterize it, the type and acuteness of the prevailing objective contradictions, and the pattern of insertion in the international division of labor and the external possibilities that it offers at a particular historical moment.

Furthermore, the strategic choices made in the process of class struggle, accommodation, and alliance formation are not predictable. Even were this not so, the measurement of class-based social forces presents virtually insurmountable barriers in a study of this type. Though economic structures surely predict roughly to the state of class formation and conflict, and surely these class forces are partially reflected in political system and institutional arrangements, little of this process can be measured directly. Thus, I examine more aggregate notions of structural location before pursuing in greater detail the effects of more variable aspects of peripheral capitalism. It remains an empirical question whether alternative structural arrangements of peripheral capitalism yield differential basic needs attainment. That is, the fundamental importance of the structural position conception versus the characterization of individual causal mechanisms is yet to be determined.

Approaches to Measuring Structural Position

The multidimensional character of structural position lends itself to several measurement approaches. Thus, one could equate the periphery with nations suffering from "social disarticulation" or define the category in terms of level of processing, or openness, or dominance-dependence relations, or class relations, all of which are sensible approaches and accord with frequently cited theoretical viewpoints. Though these approaches blend theoretically because the various elements are thought to be causally intertwined, operationally we are faced with alternative definitions of widely varying measurement tractability. Although these elements are surely correlated, we do not know how highly correlated they are, nor which of the elements are of primary significance for the provision of basic human needs. We must choose between (1) a synthesis involving some method of aggregation and weighting of various factors and (2) an analytic separation of the various components.

Theoretically, the case has been made above for the use of a composite measure, which synthesizes various elements. In essence, reliance on a single indicator is held to be dangerous because each reflects only a single form of dependence or a particular variant of peripheral capitalism. At the practical level, a composite measurement approach is also warranted by the assumption that the elements are highly collinear and difficult to measure individually. Thus, I attempt to capture structural position as a set of discrete categories, then return to examining individual dimensions below.

Composite Measures of Structural Position

To date, the most ambitious effort to create a composite measure of structural position is Snyder and Kick's (1979) use of a block modeling technique. By virtue of similarity among exchange matrices in each of four transaction networks—trade, military interventions, diplomatic representation, and treaties—nations were grouped into ten blocks. These blocks were then collapsed into three groupings that corresponded to a priori notions of the makeup of the core, periphery, and semiperiphery. It is evident, however, that the four transaction networks represent a rather narrow range of structural position components; in particular, they are weighted toward the dominance-dependence face of the concept and quite far removed from its economic division-of-labor roots. The focus on transaction matrices to the exclusion of attribute similarity matrices is also theoretically rather arbitrary. Finally, although trade involves the very processes that constitute and maintain structural relations, the behaviors underlying the other networks are usually portrayed as consequence rather than cause in world systems analysis. Of course, since similar critiques could be launched against any finite sample of dimensions from a multidimensional concept, it seems prudent to examine alternative categorization schemes rather than to rely on any one incomplete measure.

Previous attempts to identify national clusters have pursued several approaches. The most elementary of these have reduced structural position to a simple trichotomy of level of development using production figures such as GNP (Timberlake and Lundy, 1985; Firebaugh, 1985). This approach is atheoretical—or at least theoretically narrow—but it does lend itself to rigorous measurement, albeit on a single dimension.

Alternatively, the measurement approach of Chase-Dunn (1983) is less rigorous in its use of quantitative data but compensates with a sharper focus on the economy's productive structure. While acknowledging the multidimensionality of structural position and the desirability of employing quantitative data, he generates a rough categorization based on a comparative history of countries in the world economy. After setting forth a composite summary of the relevant theoretical dimensions, he notes (p. 77): "Although I combine the dimensions of political-military power and economic competitive advantage . . . , my understanding of what it takes to win in the world economy causes me to weight economic development more than military power in a combined measure of overall position." The resulting emphasis on production techniques closely parallels the economic attribute face of structural position sketched above. Chase-Dunn is forced to concede, however, that "this attempt reveals a number of unresolved conceptual problems" (p. 78). Neither are these problems attacked in any systematic way. Still, the fidelity of the schema to an important dimension of structural position relatively resistant to quantitative assessment warrants its inclusion in this analysis as a complement to Snyder and Kick's measures.

Gidengil's (1978) approach uses a type of cluster analysis on dimensions including level of development, degree of processing in imports and exports, and export partner and commodity concentrations. Her analysis, however, produces five clusters, only two of which have the hypothesized pattern of attributes: one is an ideal type of a "core," the other a "periphery." The remaining three clusters manifest a mixture of attributes which may suggest a semiperiphery, but she does not use the term. Her categorization is discussed below, though her restricted sample of nations and the rather poor theoretical and empirical fit between the "semiperiphery" and her intermediate clusters precludes its use in the formal analysis.

Nemeth and Smith (1985) also employ a block modeling technique on trade matrices. Through a factor analysis, they reduce fifty-five two-digit SITC codes to five clusters of commodities believed to share similar properties concerning degree of processing. Trade levels between nations in each of these commodity categories are then used to construct similarity matrices. The results of their analysis include a somewhat smaller core grouping than most other studies and a markedly larger semiperiphery, split into a "first" and a "weak" or "second" semiperiphery.

Finally, in a reanalysis of the Snyder and Kick data, Bollen (1983) amends their classificatory schema without challenging its basic validity. His approach exemplifies the difficulty in measuring concepts so deeply embedded in theory. Operating from the premise that peripheral status slows economic and political development, he concludes that the political and economic performance of nations can be used to correct mistakes in classification. He identifies six "misclassified" nations, which are outliers in a regression analysis involving development, democracy, and Snyder and Kick's structural position measures. Ignoring the original basis of classification, his schema then assigns to these six the structural position of the grouping of nations to which their level of democracy most closely conforms.[1]

In most theoretical arenas—where the validity of the research design and the adequacy of the measures are more certain than the accuracy of the theoretical claim—such an approach would be unacceptable. With respect to structural position, however, the very outcomes cast as "dependent variables" are internal to the definition of the "independent variables." After all, in many world systems and dependency formulations, these performance attributes are as closely linked definitionally to structural position as are the exchange transactions considered by Snyder and Kick. Thus, while the Bollen procedure leaves one uneasy, the literature's conceptual ambiguity juxtaposed with its theoretical clarity suggests that his revised schema be considered as a complement to Snyder and Kick's original. Still, Bollen's (1983: 477) remarks are clearly justified: "This measurement error makes obvious the need for further attempts to classify countries into the world system positions. Ideally alternative classification schemes would be available so that the analyses reported could be rerun with a new measure to see if the results replicate."

One of the purposes of this chapter is to begin exactly this process of thinking more clearly about the meaning of structural position language, identifying more carefully the appropriate measurement techniques, and assessing more precisely the accuracy of empirical claims. Ideally, of course, empirical analysis would play little direct role in adjudicating alternative measurement techniques, since one cannot know whether through such procedures inaccurate measures are being corrected by valid theory or, alternatively, a faulty theory is being saved by ad hoc amendments to a valid measurement schema.

The first step in probing the utility of the core-periphery imagery requires a comparison of the available measures. That analysis confirms the multidimensionality of the concept, the difficulty in measuring it, and the importance of greater attention to this issue in conceptual, theoretical, and methodological analyses. Simply put, the alternative schemata produce very different groupings of nations with some dramatic disagreements. As Kentor (1985: 36) indicates, the core is quite easy to identify, but the periphery is rather less so, and the semiperiphery is extremely difficult to distinguish from the first two. The schema of Gidengil agrees with that of Snyder and Kick, for example, at rates of

1. Bollen (1983) downgraded Spain, Portugal, and South Africa to the semiperiphery and Taiwan, Iraq, and Saudi Arabia to the periphery. This improved the fit of his model of development, democracy, and structural position, but as we see below, it harmed the overall fit of the model described here, and the changes were not retained in subsequent analyses.

89, 75, and 38 percent of cases, respectively (Kentor, 1985). More detailed comparisons of Snyder and Kick with Bollen, 1983; Nemeth and
Smith, 1985; Chase-Dunn, 1983; and Timberlake and Lundy, 1985, confirm the difficulty of reliably measuring the structural position concepts.

In general, the schemata that share a conceptual foundation produce
relatively similar results.[2] For example, Bollen and Snyder/Kick disagree on only 6 nations, while Chase-Dunn and Timberlake/Lundy diverge on 10 nations. Where the approaches differ, however, there is
remarkably little agreement in the results. Snyder/Kick disagree with
Timberlake/Lundy on 29 nations and with Chase-Dunn on 28; the comparable figures for Bollen are 23 and 24. The Nemeth/Smith codings
resemble neither group very closely, diverging most often from Tim-
berlake/Lundy (35) and least often from Snyder/Kick (28). Even this last
figure is extremely high considering that the joint sample consisted of
only 86 nations. A major factor is the very much larger semiperiphery
of the Nemeth/Smith schema—44 nations—compared with the others
which range from 27 to 30. For that reason, the Nemeth/Smith codings
are excluded from the analyses below which seek to identify groupings
of nations which can sustain a consensus among the alternative schemata.

Convergence is achieved on quite a small percentage of nations.
There are, of course, few problems in distinguishing core from periphery nations, but the semiperiphery category illustrates the extreme difficulty of reliable measurement. Even discounting Gidengil and Nem-
eth/Smith, 46 nations were included on at least one of the four lists of
semiperiphery countries but only 11 of these—less than 25 percent—
were found on all four lists. (In fact, Gidengil agrees on only 2 of these
11 while disagreeing on 2 others and omitting the remainder because
data were unavailable. Nemeth and Smith agree on 6, disagree on 1,
and omit 5.) In even a two-way comparison, only 14 of 43 nations considered by either Snyder/Kick or Timberlake/Lundy could be agreed
upon by both. Furthermore, as we see below, this kernel of 11 nations
contains 4 state socialist nations of Eastern Europe which are theo-

2. The sample of countries coded by each researcher differed markedly, but all contained fewer than the 120 nations used throughout this analysis. To employ each schema
while maintaining comparability between the analyses, I began with the Snyder and Kick
codes, which are the best known and are available for the largest sample. They were
augmented by placing several uncoded poor African and Asian countries in the periphery. The only controversial case was Kuwait, classified as periphery on the basis of its
primary product orientation. Treating it as semiperiphery (or even core), as suggested by
its GNP, does not improve the fit. For the other schemata, missing data points were
replaced with the Snyder and Kick codings. The result is mild inflation of the incidence
of agreement among them.

retically dubious, and even the remaining 7 contain some arguable calls—Ireland and India, for example—as well as a striking heterogeneity. In sum, this comparison is not encouraging for the prospects of a composite measure with test-retest reliability. The sharp disagreement over the semiperiphery should make us especially reticent to accept conclusions about this highly amorphous grouping.

Indeed, there is good reason to wonder whether this simple trichotomy of core, periphery, and semiperiphery—however measured—should be understood as a theoretical concept explicit enough to support quantitative empirical analysis. The alternative approach is to consider "structural position" merely a metatheoretical label, much as Duvall (1978) treats the related term "dependency"—useful as a metaphor but not to be mistaken for the multiple causal mechanisms that cluster around it. The implication is that we must decompose and elaborate the metaphor by examining the impact on basic needs outcomes of the various forms of dependency and features of peripheral status.

Such an approach seems to be more in line with the emphasis of dependency and world systems theorizing on concrete, contextually explicit, and historically and geographically specific mechanisms. Moreover, it would be critical if the various forms of dependency and structural position are less collinear than is sometimes assumed, if their individual impacts on basic needs differ, or if their impacts are best represented by a continuous variable rather than as a step-level function. Granting the latter requires that we regard dos Santos's (1972) much-quoted distinction between "economies that are capable of self-sustaining growth and those which can do so only as a reflection of [others]" as a rhetorical flourish—a metaphor—rather than as a model specification.

Beneath the metaphor are possibilities considered in more detail in the following sections, including a more direct examination of the impact of trade. Before embarking on this more elaborate and complex strategy, however, I test the adequacy of the more general synthetic conception of structural position through the use of composite measures of core and periphery status.

Results from the Analysis of Structural Position

We begin by adding world system position as operationalized by Snyder and Kick (1979) to the current model, as estimated in Table 7-6. The results imply that structural location has an effect of only marginal significance, but the partially anomalous pattern of coefficients invites a more careful look. Specifically, after the effects of the current model are controlled, semiperiphery nations perform better than the sample mean, periphery nations worse, and the core nations about the same (though somewhat closer to the latter than the former). Only the contrast between the semiperiphery and the periphery is significant, however, and when the semiperiphery dummy variable is included by itself, the explanatory power of the model is only a marginally significant improvement over the original.

Still, the positive coefficient for semiperiphery is anomalous, since it was expected that both semiperiphery and periphery nations would underperform relative to expectations based on wealth. The finding thus invites a probe of potential explanations, centering on weaknesses in the measurement approach used to isolate the problematic semiperiphery category and ambiguities in the conceptual basis of the core-periphery imagery itself.[3]

One explanation focuses on the heterogeneity of the semiperiphery group which we have found reflected in the disagreements between alternative codings.[4] In particular, despite the contrary insistence of Wallerstein, the presence of three quite different types of nations in this group suggests that the semiperiphery may be nothing more than a residual category. If so, the basic needs performance ascribed to this group of nations may actually reflect attributes of one or more subgroups which are not a consequence of structural position.

Six of the semiperiphery nations in this sample are state socialist systems whose international interaction patterns separate them into an identifiable Eastern Bloc. Although their level of development situates them midway between core and periphery, they do not share the other characteristics typically attributed to the semiperiphery. Most pointedly, their internal political economy is not capitalist, though their external interactions may conform to Wallerstein's understanding of capitalism as "production for a market." Moreover, the regional autarky of COMECON prior to the 1970s so limited their interactions with the global capitalist system that this contact was probably insufficient to structure their internal political economies in ways relevant to basic needs (Bunce, 1985). To equate their largely *external* status with the

---

3. In an analysis not shown, the plausible explanation that the effect of noncore status is already "contained in" the measures of domestic politics is not supported by the pattern of correlation among the independent variables. With the effect of logged GNP removed, the relationship between structural position and domestic political variables is not strong enough to account for the observed relationships with PQLI. Further, attempts to clarify the causal structure through alternative designs were not successful. Significant interaction effects do not exist between structural position and either GNP or levels of democracy. Nor does the full model perform differently when estimated separately for each category of nation.

4. The other codes are introduced below as a comparison.

dynamic linkages of the highly penetrated semiperiphery is at least dubious.

Unfortunately, the appropriate criteria for distinguishing the world system from its "external areas" have never been completely clear. Wallerstein (1985) emphasizes the existence of a single division of labor in which the constituent areas are connected by trade in "necessities" while external areas engage in only "luxury" trade. Unfortunately, that distinction also is not only empirically problematic, but conceptually ambiguous (Amin, 1974b; Sraffa, 1972: 6–7). Moreover, both Sokolovsky (1985) and Chase-Dunn (1980, 1983) contend that there are multiple means of incorporation and many problem cases. In defending the inclusion of Eastern Europe, for example, Chase-Dunn (1983: 79) notes that "commercial exchange is by no means the only relationship that integrates areas into the world system. Culture and, more importantly, politics and engagement in the interstate system are also fundamental."

Maybe so, but if the incorporation is not via economic transactions, and does not result in a capitalist class structure—let alone a *peripheral* capitalist class structure—what can we expect concerning consequences that are argued to flow from these mechanisms? In short, Eastern European nations have internal attributes sufficiently at variance with the usual notions of capitalism and connections with the global capitalist system sufficiently sparse that they could be alternatively characterized as external to the economic system, even if integral to the geopolitical system. There is certainly no obvious reason that we should ascribe their distinctive basic needs performance to an ambiguous location in the global capitalist system when the alternative interpretation—that their state socialist political economy is the key causal factor—is both more compelling theoretically and conceptually clearer. It is similarly difficult to identify attributes that are common to this cluster and the other two groups that make up Snyder and Kick's semiperiphery.

The second problematic group assigned to the semiperiphery contains the diverse nations of Europe's physical perimeter. The common members of what might be called this "semicore" are Ireland and Turkey, while Snyder/Kick add Finland and Timberlake/Lundy include Austria, Luxembourg, and Iceland as well as the southern tier of Greece, Yugoslavia, Spain, Portugal, and Malta. Some of this group have had a substantial colonial experience of subordination (e.g., Ireland), others have been importantly external to the system (e.g., Turkey), while for others economic stagnation has opened a gap with formerly comparable nations. It is not immediately obvious that these nations have more in common with their new "peers" than with their old ones. Nor is it apparent that the global system has had a similar conditioning effect on the political economies of these diverse nations.

The third component of the semiperiphery contains nations usually identified with the Third World and more difficult to distinguish from the periphery than from the core. Some of these (e.g., Argentina) have also suffered status decline, while most are going the other way. These include the newly industrializing countries (NICs) whose social structures also lag behind their newfound prosperity. If it is these structures that determine basic needs provision—or the rapid change in them which is characteristic of NICs—the effect of current semiperipheral status may well be spurious. Also included are simply middle-income countries, ranging from the larger nations of Latin America to the more prosperous nations of the Middle East. Idiosyncratic cases (Israel, South Africa, New Zealand) may also be included here.

Although it is beyond the scope of this chapter to trace further this fundamental ambiguity in the concept of the semiperiphery, a cursory analysis demonstrated that the basic needs provision of these three subgroups is very different. First, the performance of the "semicore" nations is nearly identical to that of the core. Second, among the Eastern European nations (for which the semiperiphery characterization is most dubious) the beta is almost $+9$, while it is less than $+5$ for the "rising periphery," which is more often associated with the semiperiphery concept. Third, none of these effects approached statistical significance when estimated individually.

Of course, the variation in performance among these subgroups must undermine our faith in the ability of simple core-periphery imagery to adequately represent the diversity found within any of the three structural positions. Operationally, since the semiperiphery is both conceived and enumerated somewhat differently by the various schemata, these subgroups are not equally represented by them. As a result, it seems quite likely that the apparent basic needs effect of structural position will be highly contingent on the particular measurement schema adopted. At a minimum, this contingency suggests that we must compare findings that rest on alternative, yet plausible, categorizations. When the analysis was repeated using each of the categorizations discussed above in place of the Snyder/Kick codes, small differences were observed which bracket the initial findings, but do not diverge significantly from them. For example, while the t values for the semiperiphery ranged from 1.0 to 1.6 and for the periphery from $-.8$ to -1.4, none met even the .10 criterion of statistical significance.

Still, it is reasonable to suppose that all these results may be weakened—perhaps even distorted—by the presence of nations that are plausibly coded into more than one category. After all, nations with

Table 8-1. Effects of structural position on basic human needs ("consensus" structural position codes)

Variables	Simple r	All variables				Significant variables		
		Beta	St. beta	t		Beta	St. beta	t
% labor agriculture	−.87	−.70	−.68	−13.1***		−.68	−.67	−13.4***
Socialist × agr.	.24	.61	.28	6.7***		.62	.28	6.8***
Democracy	.47	.14	.14	3.0**		.13	.13	2.9**
Right × civilian	−.39	−.36	−.12	−3.2**		−.34	−.11	−3.1**
Military spending	.09	−2.00	−.27	−5.0***		−2.04	−.27	−5.2***
Military manpower	.38	.89	.23	4.3***		.91	.23	4.4***
Military regime	−.25	.07	.08	2.2*		.07	.08	2.3*
Core	.45	−3.77	−.04	−1.0				
Semiperiphery	.20	−.77	−.01	−.2				
Periphery	−.69	−7.31	−.13	−2.7		−6.98	−.12	−2.7**

Model	N	r	r^2	adj. r^2	SEE	F
All variables	120	.94	.88	.87	10.09	82.5***
Significant variables	120	.94	.88	.87	10.05	103.9***

*Significant (p < .05)
**Significant (p < .01)
***Significant (p < .001)

attributes lying between the ideal types would be less likely to manifest the basic needs performances associated with those types. Thus, before we discard core-periphery influences, it is appropriate to examine the results when only unequivocal representatives of each category were coded. Thus, a "consensus" classificatory schema was created in which nations were coded as occupying a structural position only if four schemata (excepting Nemeth/Smith) concurred in their respective evaluations. This approach recognizes 14 core nations, 11 semiperiphery countries, and 59 periphery nations, with 36 nations (30 percent of the sample) considered "anomalous" and thus unclassified.[5]

Table 8-1 presents the findings of this analysis, with the full model in the left columns and the results when "insignificant" variables are removed in the right columns. Though still not unequivocal, these coefficients are more in line with expectations. In particular, pure periphery nations do yield lower basic needs levels than would be otherwise expected; in fact, their average PQLI is nearly seven points lower than that of the unclassified group. The contrast is not so dramatic with the

5. If we were to exclude those nations with differing codings in the Nemeth and Smith analysis, the consensus cases would reduce to only 9 core, 10 semiperiphery, and 50 periphery nations, leaving 49 nations (43 percent of the sample) "anomalous" and thus unclassified. For this reason, I ignored the Nemeth and Smith codes in identifying consensus cases.

classified members of the core and semiperiphery, though it is still significant and in the predicted direction. The relative performance of the semiperiphery remains slightly better than that of the core, but the estimate contains far too much error for this result to be considered even marginally significant.

Moreover, these divergent results may warn of difficulties more fundamental than simple measurement error. In fact, the extreme heterogeneity of the semiperiphery and the ambiguity inherent in alternative measurement approaches returns us to a question considered earlier. What is meant by the terms "periphery" and "semiperiphery"? The measurement difficulties that erode the robustness of our findings may be a reflection of a central conceptual ambiguity—indeed, a conceptual mistake! We must ask how coherent and accurate are the lists of attributes said to characterize nations in each structural position. Operationally, we must know if these attributes covary in a systematic way that can be captured by a trichotomy. If not, the most basic justification disappears for regarding structural position as a categorical and comprehensive summary of significant attributes of the political economy.

Table 8-2. Analysis of variance and covariance: Structural position and selected world system variables (Snyder and Kick structural position codes)

	Unadjusted group means			Deviations of group means (controlling for logged GNP/cap)		
Variables	Core (N = 21)	Semi-periphery (N = 30)	Periphery (N = 69)	Core	Semi-periphery	Periphery
PQLI	91	72	45	4.6	8.3	−5.0
Labor in agriculture	16	40	63	−4.5	−5.8	3.9
Democracy	86	58	51	16.8	−2.0	−4.2
Rightist norms	.24	.37	.47	−.01	−.03	.02
Govt. expenditure/GNP	21	26	20	−6.7	3.3	.6
Military expenditure/GNP	3.3	6.1	3.0	−.6	2.2	−.8
Troops per capita	9.4	11.7	4.1	.9	4.6	−2.2
Military rule	2	19	24	−.3	2.4	−.9
Trade/GNP	38	46	47	−27.4	−.5	8.6
Partner concentration	12	16	27	−9.0	−5.0	5.0
Commodity concentration	11	31	36	−19.0	1.0	6.0
Raw material exports	41	67	84			
Mineral exports	18	26	25	−16.1	.4	5.5
Export fluctuations	6.0	8.7	10.1	−2.0	−.2	.8
Multinational corporations	59	42	95	−82	−43	48
Never a colony	.90	.37	.12	.40	.04	−.15
Independent in 1945	1.00	.72	.40	.07	.08	−.06
GNP/cap	4,829	1,423	711			

The coherence of the core-periphery schema can be gauged by its discriminating power with respect to attributes theoretically associated with nations in each structural position. Thus, an analysis of variance and covariance was performed to determine if nations in each of the three positions have distinctive values on the variables commonly associated with them. From the group means presented in the first three columns of Table 8-2 it is apparent that nations occupying each structural position (using the Snyder/Kick codes) do tend to exhibit the pattern of attributes ascribed to them. Economically, periphery nations are poor, agricultural, penetrated by multinational corporations, and have external relations marked by a large foreign sector, high reliance on raw material exports, and high partner and commodity concentrations. Politically, they are nondemocratic and rightist with a tendency to military government and a colonial past. With few exceptions, core nations exhibit the opposite characteristics. Semiperiphery nations are frequently lodged between the two extremes. There are certainly significant deviations from simple linearity, however. With respect to state strength and the military, for example, the semiperiphery is distinctive. Further, the semiperiphery more closely approximates the periphery in some respects (e.g., trade reliance, commodity concentration, mineral exports) and the core in others (e.g., partner concentration).

Moreover, there is reason to question whether the general pattern is sufficiently strong to warrant considering these categories theoretically meaningful. Much of the similarity within categories is surely explicable alternatively as a pattern resulting from similar level of development. Dependency and world systems analysts argue that the effects of structural position go beyond the expectations based on GNP per capita, such as those documented by Chenery and Syrquin (1975). To test this claim, an analysis of covariance was performed in which the linear effect of logged GNP per capita is removed from the various dependent variables before the discriminating power of the dummy variables is assessed. With that effect removed, the adjusted mean deviations presented in the last three columns of Table 8-2 represent the mean difference between the nations of each category and the sample as a whole.

These results suggest a less unified theoretical concept. There are few significant political differences between the periphery and semiperiphery beyond those expected on the basis of income. With respect to levels of democracy, frequency of rightist governments, and colonial past, for example, the differences are barely distinguishable. On the economic side, the results include some countertheoretical patterns. For example, the labor of semiperiphery nations is relatively less concentrated in agriculture than in the core when corrected for income level, and the size of the state and the strength of the military are greatest in the semiperiphery.

The most direct test of the discriminating power of the schema is a discriminant function analysis in which the variables often said to characterize structural position are used to "predict" the category into which the nation should be placed. When the consensus coding scheme is used to create inductive profiles of each of three categories, about 90 percent of these 84 nations are found to lie closer to the profile expected of their structural position than to either of the other two. However, among the 36 nations for which no consensus exists, only about a third are correctly placed by this "prediction." The lesson is clear: for about three-fourths of the nations of the system, structural location is a fairly good summary of a range of political and economic attributes. The remaining quarter, however, signify that the structure of the international system is not so rigid as is often supposed. More specifically, the semiperiphery takes on the flavor of a residual category whose membership is not nearly so readily definable as the core and the periphery. Even the latter two ideal categories provide roughly accurate descriptions of less than two-thirds of the nations in the sample, and there remain exceptions even within these groups. Thus, our interpretations of the effects of structural position must be made with caution and with awareness of the need for greater attention to the mechanisms responsible for any of the statistical patterns.

Of course, the difficulty of constructing a more encompassing roster of each structural position or a more accurate ideal type for each in terms of economic and political attributes is due not to coding flaws, but rather to the simple fact that the attributes themselves are not especially collinear, as demonstrated by a zero-order correlation matrix of variables selected from Table 8-2. In Table 8-3, the coefficients above the diagonal are the zero-order Pearson r's. Though a number of these are significant, none are above the level of .50 which marks 25 percent of explained variance.

By the same argument as that advanced above, however, the generally sizable correlations may be explained in large proportion by the more general correlate of level of development. To eliminate this factor, the partial correlation coefficients—with the effect of logged GNP removed—are reported below the diagonal in Table 8-3. The correlations do not appear to meet the usual standards for combining items into an index. Indeed, a principal components analysis reveals that only 25 percent of the variance in the matrix containing all of the variables in Table 8-2 can be accounted for by the first extracted factor. That is, a concept of structural position does not very adequately summarize the features usually associated with this imagery.

If elements commonly associated with umbrella concepts are not highly correlated, then we must question the empirical and logical co-

 8-3. Zero-order and partial correlations: Selected structural position and world system variables

	(1)	(2)	(3)	(4)	(5)	(6)	(7)	(8)
griculture		−.20	.39**	.35**	−.02	−.06	−.50**	−.87**
rade/GNP	.09		−.01	.28*	.44**	.34**	.13	.22*
artner concentration	.16	.09		.24*	.25*	−.03	−.13	−.36**
ommodity concentration	.31**	.41**	.13		.35**	.50**	−.28*	−.31**
lultinational corporations	.20	.45**	.38**	.47**		.43**	.17	.14
line exports	.19	.41**	.03	.63**	.47**		−.06	.13
emocracy	−.29*	−.03	.03	−.30*	−.00	−.22		.44**
ogged GNP/cap								

 E: Zero-order correlations appear above the diagonal, first-order partial correlations below the diagonal (controlling for
 d GNP/cap).
 ignificant (p < .01)
 gnificant (p < .001)

herence of the concepts. Indeed, the analysis presented here suggests that these concepts are more a heuristic device than a category for causal analysis. Far from suggesting that the world systems/dependency family is incapable of offering insight or explanatory power, however, this study suggests that key social outcomes such as the provision of basic human needs can be understood fully only through a consideration of the issues raised by this rich body of theory. Unfortunately, simplistic core-periphery concepts, which are a highly visible component of world systems theory, appear to be of little value for scientific purposes.

If this is so, our probing of external effects may more appropriately focus on particular features of peripheral capitalism or dimensions of dependency—including those illustrated in the last two tables—rather than using composite measures to treat peripheral capitalism as a distinctive mode of production with its own basic needs tendencies. One of the most important features of peripheral capitalism is the pattern of trade associated with it.

Trade and Basic Needs

From nearly all theoretical perspectives trade is seen as an essential element of national development which exerts great leverage on the welfare of individuals. In the context of this study, a measure of trade reliance or openness is especially useful as an alternative approach to capturing one key distinctive aspect of peripheral capitalism: the unusually large size of the foreign sector.[6] The use of this continuous measure in place of the discrete categories employed above permits finer gradations of the extent to which the processes hypothesized as central to associated-dependent development are at work. This method is appropriate if the theoretical contention that dependent capitalism yields poorer basic needs performance is accurate, while the methodological principle that dependence is a discrete variable is not.[7]

Trade may affect the basic needs performance of nations through a variety of mechanisms, some of which are quite direct whereas others are less proximate. For example, the availability of trade opportunities is central to the calculus of economic elites which is said to sustain social disarticulation. Though cleavages exist in all nations between sectors that rely on domestic demand and those that do not, the relative power of each varies cross-nationally. Since the size of the foreign sector captures, albeit roughly, the proportion of economic actors who are free of the cross-pressure of wage levels as determinants of relevant demand, a measure of trade share is a reasonable proxy for this operationally elusive concept. More broadly, trade reliance is a rough indicator of the tendency of dominant classes to look outward for political resources, socioeconomic orientation, and consumption goods, all to the detriment of the development of a political and social milieu likely to afford basic needs a high priority. Previous studies have cited these linkages in posing trade reliance as a predictor of inequality.[8]

But trade must be conceived of as more than a control mechanism for maintaining the core's subordination of the periphery or the dominant classes' position within the domestic social structure. It is also a flow of economic resources which permits the national consumption basket to differ from the national production frontier. All theorists recognize that the product composition of these two baskets will vary enormously— and proportionally with the relative size of the foreign sector. There is less agreement concerning the use value differences between the consumption and production baskets and the relative capacity of the two to provide for basic human needs.

On the one hand, the well-known liberal view, dating from the classical gains from trade arguments of Smith and Ricardo, is that trade

6. Foreign sector size is operationalized by total trade as a percentage of GNP. Similar measures have been used in many studies of inequality and growth. For surveys of the voluminous empirical literature, see Mahler, 1980; McGowan and Smith, 1978; Dixon, 1983; and Weede and Tiefenbach, 1981b. The data for 1965 are taken from Taylor and Jodice, 1982.

7. See McGowan and Smith, 1978, for a discussion of the relative merits of considering dependency a discrete category or a continuous variable.

8. See Mahler, 1980; McGowan and Smith, 1978; Dixon, 1983; and Weede and Tiefenbach, 1981.

permits efficiencies of scale and optimal allocations of resources which yield a consumption basket containing greater use values than the production basket. The implication is that large trade shares should be associated with higher welfare levels (though the latter need not include basic needs improvement).

The contrary expectation follows from the recognition that economies structured to exploit comparative advantage also risk the constraining effect of fluctuations in export earnings and import capacity which result from rapid changes in international prices and currency values (MacBean, 1966). Since basic needs levels are as sensitive to over-time fluctuations in resource inputs as cross-individual inequality, this may be an important consideration in limiting the basic needs impact of higher growth, even if such growth does occur. Neoclassical theory also observes that imports constitute a leakage that weakens multiplier effects on growth and spread effects on intersectoral integration (Singer, 1950; Myrdal, 1968).

Further, a variety of radical economic arguments associated with dependency and world systems theory single out mechanisms involving surplus extraction and transfers, which occur both internationally (from South to North) and within societies (from poor to rich). Both tend to lower basic needs fulfillment.

Most of these arguments center on the determination of relative prices of imports and exports. This "terms of trade" argument was set forth most powerfully by Prebisch (1959, 1962), who contended that the long-term trend of prices for primary products relative to manufactured goods was downward. Since the comparative advantage of poor nations lies nearly universally in the former, welfare growth could be expected to lag in the periphery. There is no shortage of mechanisms available to explain this tendency. Within neoclassical theory, the most frequently cited factors include the income elasticity of demand for primary products. An extension of Engels's law—the percentage of income devoted to food purchases declines with income level—suggests that demand for primary products will grow less rapidly than total demand, thus constraining price movements. Lack of product differentiation or quality improvements, price ceilings imposed by substitution, and simple excess capacity have also been cited as factors. Evidence on global trade percentages suggests that consumption of primary products has declined relative to total consumption, though the evidence that terms of trade changes have been so uniform is much less clear. Beyond specialization in primary products, the product cycle and related theories of trade determination suggest that the periphery will always be relegated to trade specialization in less profitable branches of production (Vernon, 1979; Emmanuel, 1972).

For our purposes, however, arguments concerning systematic variation in the welfare contributions of similarly priced import and export
baskets are more directly relevant. If relative price levels systematically
favor developed nations, the trade of the periphery could constitute a
negative flow of resources which would lower welfare levels relative to
more closed economies and, especially, relative to those that *gain* from
these perverse price arrangements. Consequently, we could expect that
the PQLI of periphery nations would vary inversely with their level of
trade, whereas the reverse would be true among core nations.

Three mechanisms of surplus extraction and transfer are discussed in
the literature. The first, termed "unequal rewards," concerns the lower
wage rates that prevail in the periphery as a consequence of both excess labor supply and the lower labor productivity associated principally with low levels of technology and capital/labor ratios. Because of
this known wage gap, the exchange value of goods produced by any
given quantity of labor will be higher in the core than in the periphery.
Since welfare effects—including basic needs levels—follow, one would
expect them to be proportional to the difference in wage rates and the
productivity gaps they reflect.

A second source of value transfer is Emmanuel's (1972) "unequal exchange." Emmanuel contends that core-periphery trade constitutes a
transfer of value in that the exports of the periphery contain more embodied labor than imports of the same monetary value. Once again,
wage rates are seen to differ, but this time not primarily as a consequence of productivity differences. Indeed, Emmanuel is not directly
comparing wage rates within the same sector at all since his theory
applies to trade involving two commodities, each of which is produced
in only one of the two trading nations. Wage rates do not track productivity gains in peripheral nations due to labor market conditions, which
themselves reflect a host of social and political forces as a complement
to economic factors. Where labor is in a disadvantageous bargaining
position—excess labor supplies, absence of trade unions, and other
factors associated with the social and political face of peripheral location and dependency—wage rates will lag. As a result, final goods
prices in sectors located primarily in such geographical areas will lag
those that are concentrated in the core. Not only does this gap reduce
growth prospects in the periphery, it also suggests that trade will increase welfare in the core but lower it in the periphery.

Finally, a third argument locates the surplus transfer in "unequal
trade." Unlike the above theoretical treatments, this idea questions the
presumption that trade is free and that prices are set by competitive
markets. Due to the natural advantage of core countries in dominating
marketing arrangements, exerting monopoly power, and controlling

capital, currency, and finance markets, trade involves a welfare loss to the periphery beyond the consequences of free markets postulated above. That is, the relevant mechanisms involve not so much production prices as distortions in market prices—including those resulting from trade barriers erected by government policy.

For all these reasons, we expect trade to have implications for basic needs levels. To test this expectation, a measure of trade reliance is added to the current model. The results show a small negative effect, significant only at the .10 level ($t = -1.3$ when the periphery dummy is included in the model, $t = -1.9$ when it is omitted). In one sense, of course, these results should not be a surprise since the theoretical arguments suggest causal factors that may cross-cut in their effects and consequently wash out in a statistical analysis. I consider several elaborations of this basic additive model in turn.

First, the arguments concerning the welfare implications of trade are almost always cast in a conditional form that emphasizes differential outcomes depending on structural location. The negative effect of trade for the periphery is said to be balanced by its positive effect for the core. We can capture this formulation with an interactive specification involving structural position dummies and trade volumes.

The analysis suggests that trade may affect basic needs differently across nations, but the suggestive results are too weak to be considered conclusive. Specifically, trade seems to have a significant negative effect on basic needs levels in the periphery, just as most of the theoretical threads imply. Contrary to expectations, however, a similar effect—though much smaller and statistically insignificant—appears among core nations. Finally, the effect of trade levels on PQLI in the semiperiphery varies with the coding schema—mildly positive with the Snyder/Kick codes and mildly negative with the "consensus" codes—though the size of the coefficient fails the test of statistical significance in all cases.

The difficulty of interpreting complex interaction analyses together with the dubious conceptual status of the structural position dummies combine to mandate caution about conclusions based on relatively weak findings. Table 8-4 illustrates the problem. Conventional tests for the significance of interaction terms evaluate the marginal variance explained by the addition of multiplicative terms to an equation already including the dummy variables representing the main effects. With the three dummy variables, the main effect of trade, and the three multiplicative terms included, none of the seven estimated coefficients even approaches statistical significance. Nor did the addition of the three interaction terms yield a significant increment of r^2. Yet, the final step of a backward regression reveals a quite sizable and statistically signifi-

Table 8-4. Effects of structural position on basic human needs (interactions of trade with "consensus" structural position)

Variables	Simple r	All variables			Significant variables		
		Beta	St. beta	t	Beta	St. beta	t
% labor agriculture	− .87	− .73	− .71	− 12.8***	− .73	− .71	− 16.0***
Socialist × agr.	.24	.63	.28	6.6***	.65	.29	7.4***
Democracy	.47	.15	.16	3.2**	.15	.15	3.3**
Right × civilian	− .39	− .32	− .10	− 2.6**	− .28	− .09	− 2.5*
Military spending	.09	− 2.02	− .27	− 4.9***	− 2.06	− .27	− 5.3***
Military manpower	.38	.87	.22	4.1***	.92	.23	4.5***
Military regime	− .25	.06	.08	2.0*	.06	.08	2.2*
Core	.45	− 1.41	− .02	− .2			
Semiperiphery	.20	.73	.01	.1			
Periphery	− .69	− 2.59	− .05	− .5			
Trade/GNP	.00	.00	.00	.1			
Core × trade	.39	− .09	− .04	− .6			
Semiperiphery × trade	.16	− .03	− .03	− .3			
Periphery × trade	− .43	− .08	− .09	− .9	− .10	− .11	− 3.0**

Model	N	r	r^2	adj. r^2	SEE		F
All variables	120	.94	.89	.87	10.12		58.8***
Significant variables	120	.94	.88	.88	9.98		105.6***

*Significant (p < .05)
**Significant (p < .01)
***Significant (p < .001)

cant coefficient for the interaction of trade and the periphery. The most obvious interpretation involves three observations. First, the initial parameter estimate suggests that trade does exert a downward effect on basic needs provision. Second, however, the relatively large standard error of that initial estimate implies that the effect of trade varies too greatly across cases to yield a powerful and consistent universal estimate. Third, some of this variance in trade effect seems to be associated with gross characterizations of structural position, though the findings are too weak to be accepted without further probing.

A second elaboration takes account of the concession by many dependency analysts that trade may carry two sets of cross-cutting welfare implications. Trade that enhances GNP growth may carry welfare effects, though these gains remain less significant for the poor than GNP originating in wholly domestic enterprises. If this description is accurate, it would be necessary to reinstate a logged GNP measure, which has fallen out of our analysis since it was displaced by the labor force measure as an indicator of economic structure in Chapter 4. When logged GNP is added to any of the models of this chapter to reflect the impact of trade on production-based and price-metric levels of development, the positive contribution of the GNP measure is statistically significant and the negative effect of trade is enhanced. It appears that trade's mildly positive effect on growth is insufficient to overcome its dampening effect on relative basic needs provision, though the model fit improves if both factors are taken into account.[9]

The third elaboration involves a return to the postulated syndrome of effects surrounding the pattern of trade relations said to be common among periphery nations, especially high partner and commodity trade concentrations and distinctive commodity specializations. It may be these patterns that explain the propensity of trade to depress basic needs levels in the periphery, but not elsewhere.

Dimensions of Trade Relations

Some of these arguments can be tested directly. It is said, for example, that longitudinal fluctuations in export earnings are harmful to welfare in general and basic needs in particular. The reasons are too obvious to require detailed treatment. Briefly, such fluctuations complicate planning at every level from the individual family to the national government, particularly when trade is the dominant source of scarce foreign exchange and, ultimately, a significant share of the income of the poor. Moreover, fluctuating revenues are liable to bonanza concentration in a few hands, in part because they are resistant to institutionalized distribution (through wage labor bargaining, for example). To test this thesis, a measure of export revenue fluctuation and an interaction term with the size of the export sector were added to the current model.[10]

The results, though far from conclusive, seem to confirm the emerging picture. When added to the basic model by itself, the measure of export fluctuation was negatively associated with PQLI, though the parameter estimate was not nearly statistically significant ($t = -.9$). The interactive form, which takes account of the greater importance of the fluctuation in nations with a large foreign sector, offered a superior fit ($t = -1.4$), though the parameter estimate remained too small to be considered statistically significant. Finally, in the presence of these measures, the differential effect of trade in the periphery was reduced. The conclusion: the greater export fluctuations characteristic of the pe-

9. Obviously, the positive effects of trade on growth—which clearly exist—are not necessarily net effects. Indeed, there is good reason to suppose that the causal mechanisms surrounding trade of various forms, in various circumstances yield a variety of cross-cutting effects. Sorting them out is well beyond the bounds of this study.

10. Unfortunately, data availability decreased the sample size to 105 nations under this specification.

riphery—a propensity documented in Table 8-2—probably help explain the contrast between the welfare-dampening effect of trade in the periphery and the more neutral or even positive impact elsewhere. It must be emphasized, however, that although the results are consistent with this interpretation, their weakness permits no more than the claim of a plausible working hypothesis.

A second refinement of the trade arguments suggests that the concentration of trade with a single developed nation partner accentuates the various problems discussed above. The penetration of class processes by socialization from abroad and the reliance on exchanges dominated by powerful actors who can manipulate them to their advantage are more severe when trade is partner-concentrated. Exchange rate policy and commercial policy decisions may be pushed away from welfare optimal choices by the influence of both foreign and domestic foreign-penetrated actors, for example (Moon, 1982). Partner concentration measures similar to the one used here have been employed by other studies of growth and inequality (Mahler, 1980; Dixon, 1983; McGowan and Smith, 1978; Tyler and Wogart, 1973).[11] Results of this test are discussed below.

A third refinement considers the commodity concentration of exports, a feature of the trade of periphery nations more often singled out than any other in both theoretical and empirical analyses (Mahler, 1980; Dixon, 1983; Kaufman et al., 1975; Dolan and Tomlin, 1980; Ragin and Delacroix, 1979; Walleri, 1978; Galtung, 1971; McGowan and Smith, 1978; Weede and Tiefenbach, 1981b).[12] The arguments are many and multidimensional. Export fluctuations in both price and volume are more severe when the commodity basket is narrow (Michaely, 1967; Massell, 1964). The export elite is even more single-minded and less likely to suffer cross-pressures of multiple interest. The export enclave is also less likely to be integrated into the remainder of the economy if concentrated on a single export, thus increasing sectoral inequality. A commodity concentration measure is thus included in the analysis.

The results of both concentration measures follow the pattern of export fluctuation. The estimated effects are negative, insignificant, and stronger in the interactive than in the additive form. They also reduce the differential effect of trade. Although the direction of these effects is correct, they are too small to produce any confidence that a major causal mechanism is at work. Viewed in the context of our broader

11. The measure is an average of 1965, 1970, and 1975, as reported in Taylor and Jodice (1982).

12. The measure is an average of 1965, 1970, and 1975, as reported in Taylor and Jodice (1982).

knowledge, both theoretical and empirical, however, these results support the judgment that the welfare-dampening effect of trade is indeed mostly a consequence of the particular type of trade in which periphery nations are most often engaged.

The findings of this section are individually contestable but take on greater plausibility when seen together. Moreover, while the periphery is not a category of analysis in which we have a great deal of confidence, it does appear to serve us reasonably well as a general summary for a series of attributes that are neither strongly related to one another nor powerfully associated with basic needs levels. In fact, the findings tend to support the notion that structural position is a kind of syndrome of weakly related elements, each of which exerts an individual effect on basic needs too small to be reliably estimated, but which collectively must be recognized as causally consequential. Conceptually, this result is not far from the justification used in support of composite measures of structural position. Operationally, it is the basis for utilizing the final estimates of Table 8-4 as the working model for further analysis, retaining the periphery trade variable as a marker representing a syndrome of trade effects that are numerous but individually too small to be estimated reliably.

There is one remaining element of trade patterns, however, whose empirical impact is individually visible and whose theoretical import is fundamental. A host of theories suggest that the key to the maximization of trade benefits and the minimization of trade costs lies in the appropriate choice of export product specialization (Lenin, 1965; Baran, 1957; Magdoff, 1969; Galtung, 1971). Contrary to the assumptions of most orthodox trade theory from Smith and Ricardo to Heckscher-Ohlin, the welfare implications of the choice of export branch have been viewed as monumental by more radical theorists. Some of the reasons for this have already been discussed, beginning with Prebisch's (1962) influential treatise on the limitations of development centered on primary product exports. Indeed, Emmanuel's (1972) "unequal exchange" thesis is an elaboration of one piece of the argument. Furthermore, many of the elements described above—export fluctuations, commodity concentrations, sectoral imbalances—are components of the more general proposition that welfare levels are not as great in societies specializing in certain types of primary products as in those with export advantages in manufactured products.

The case has been stated with respect to two specializations in particular. For well-known reasons, agricultural products tend to embody a variety of export characteristics undesirable for long-term growth and disastrous for equality and basic needs provision: unstable prices, unstable production, stagnant technical change, lagging relative demand,

)

intensive reliance on heavily concentrated land resources, the absence of forward and backward linkages, large leakages from the domestic economy, and so on (Delacroix, 1977; Ragin and Delacroix, 1979; Delacroix and Ragin, 1981; Rubinson and Holtzman, 1981). Sharing most of those drawbacks, specialization in mining products introduces additional problems, especially a capital intensity and a penetration by multinational corporations which are thought to foster intersectoral inequality and encourage resource loss through a variety of reverse capital flows (Chase-Dunn, 1975; Bunker, 1985; Ragin and Bradshaw, 1985). Mining sectors are also usually separated from the remainder of the economy in an "export enclave" whose lack of integration substantially reduces spread effects and overall societal welfare benefits.

To test for these effects, a rough measure of export composition is required. World Bank data permit the identification of exports representing four broad sectors: food, other agricultural products, mineral products, and industrialized goods. The former three are combined as a measure of primary product specialization while the mineral category is treated individually as well. The results from the analysis of raw materials exports follow the pattern seen above with other characterizations of export attributes: the effect on basic needs fulfillment is negative, stronger in interaction with foreign sector size, but below the level of statistical significance. It also reduces the periphery interaction with trade. Of course, the absence of a strong effect is certainly not surprising since the model already contains collinear predictors, especially a measure of the labor force in agriculture.

The sectoral range of primary products is also large enough to contain several cross-cutting effects. When the mineral export variable replaces the raw material measure, it is evident that economies reliant on mineral production are marked by basic needs levels significantly below those of otherwise similar nations. As with the trade effects discussed above, however, there is evidence for a dual effect, namely that mining processes—probably because of their capital intensity—produce higher increments of GNP per unit of labor than other sectors but lower relative basic needs payoffs. Thus, to fully capture these crosscutting effects it is necessary to reinstate the logged GNP measure. When both GNP and the mining variable are included in the analysis, it becomes clear that mineral exports raise GNP with a consequent enhancement of basic needs—but one that is more than offset by the declining propensity of those resources to be targeted on basic needs. Thus, the mineral export sector again illustrates the principle that different forms of economic organization and patterns of production yield vastly different relationships between aggregate economic growth and broadly distributed mass welfare improvements. In short, while GNP matters, how that GNP is created matters more.

Export Enclaves and Foreign Capital

Of course, the mineral export sector is far from the only example of the "export enclave" syndrome so frequently cited as a source of serious distortion by dependency theorists and a variety of social scientists (Chase-Dunn, 1975; Sylvan et al., 1979). Indeed, the character of the dependency situation is said to have changed greatly during the last quarter century, paralleling the shift of the foreign sector out of traditional extractive industries toward a greater variety of enterprises whose defining characteristic is foreign ownership and/or control. Such control can be exercised through a variety of mechanisms including manipulation of high debt burdens and access to foreign exchange, capital, technology, and even foreign markets; but the most visible contemporary manifestation remains the penetration of Third World economies by multinational corporations (MNCs). The effects of MNCs have been treated theoretically in great detail elsewhere (Hymer, 1972; Biersteker, 1978) and their empirical effects on growth and inequality documented by several persistent researchers (Bornschier and Chase-Dunn, 1985).

For our purposes, these arguments suggest that MNCs should lower basic needs levels by introducing class, sectoral, and regional inequalities; by yielding a greater return to owners of capital than to sellers of labor power; by fostering negative capital flows and leakages through mechanisms including transfer pricing and rents on technology and sundry services (entrepreneurship, management, marketing); and by entering into alliances with local capital and the state which discourage progressive social and political movements. More broadly, MNCs represent another avenue through which social disarticulation can be created and sustained.

When a variable representing MNC penetration is entered into the analysis at this stage, however, there is no robust effect.[13] Not only are the parameter estimates well below the level of statistical significance, there were no consistent effects that could be interpreted as elements

13. The measure is taken from Bornschier and Heintz, 1979. It has been used in a variety of studies of growth and inequality, most notably in the aforementioned analyses of Bornschier. There is no indication that the reduced sample ($N = 110$) for which the variable is available had any influence on the results. The potentially differential effect of MNCs on nations in different structural positions likewise had no effect on basic needs.

of peripheral status as in the case of commodity concentration, partner concentration, export fluctuation, and raw material specialization discussed above.

Before we dismiss the effects of MNCs, however, it is important to observe that significantly negative effects *were* observed in earlier analyses that omitted some of the variables now found in this analysis. First, significant negative effects appear in the absence of the mining variable, which is, not surprisingly, quite collinear with the MNC measure. Comparison of analyses with both measures individually as well as together seems to indicate that mineral exports have a larger effect than MNC ownership in that sector; still the collinearity of both the measure and the phenomenon it represents must be kept in mind. From a practical standpoint, large-scale mineral exporting sectors usually imply the presence of MNCs. This fact may help explain why other studies have found negative effects of MNCs on inequality; most of those analyses have not included a measure for mining.[14] Second, an additional increment of MNC effect on basic needs is removed with the inclusion of the state socialist dummy, implying, perhaps, that one of the mechanisms through which state socialism protects basic needs is the exclusion of multinational corporations.

One final example of an export enclave completes the analysis of this chapter and points the way toward the analysis of Chapter 9. Plantations have been a major feature of a number of peripheral political economies for more than a century. They seem to possess many of the characteristics associated with various forms of dualism: sectoral and social disarticulation, regressive domestic elites, foreign ownership and resultant resource leakages, and specialization in primary products subject to commodity concentration, partner concentration, and export fluctuations. Thus, a dummy variable representing the presence of a dominant plantation sector is included in the analysis.[15]

The results presented in Table 8-5 are counterintuitive. The effect of plantation status on basic needs levels is positive and, simply put, huge. The parameter estimate—nearly fourteen PQLI points—is comparable in magnitude to the measure of democracy or the state socialism dummy; the *t* value of 5.2 is more significant than any variable in

14. It may also be that the results reflect the differences in the dependent variables. Many of the mechanisms said to carry the effects of MNCs involve income inequalities relevant to the industrial working class, and most analyses show that the strongest effects of MNCs are on the income shares of the middle and upper—not the lower—quintiles. By contrast, basic needs—and the PQLI—are more substantially weighted toward the poorer strata and the rural sectors less directly affected by MNCs.

15. The measure comes from Beckford's (1972: 14–15) landmark study. The nations he considers "plantation economies" are coded 1 while "plantation sub-economies" are coded .5.

Table 8-5. Final model of contemporary determinants of basic human needs

Variables	Simple r	Model of Chapter 7				Final contemporary model		
		Beta	St. beta	t		Beta	St. beta	t
% labor agriculture	−.87	−.75	−.73	−16.3***		−.51	−.50	−7.4***
Socialist × agr.	.24	.67	.30	7.3***		.58	.26	7.2***
Democracy	.47	.15	.15	3.2**		.13	.14	3.4***
Right × civilian	−.39	−.34	−.11	−3.0**		−.29	−.09	−2.9**
Military spending	.09	−1.97	−.26	−4.9***		−1.66	−.22	−4.7***
Military manpower	.38	.99	.25	4.7***		.87	.22	4.8***
Military regime	−.25	.07	.09	2.3*		.08	.10	3.1**
Periphery × trade	−.43					−.12	−.13	−3.8***
Mineral exports	−.12					−.07	−.07	−2.1*
Logged GNP/cap	.80					5.28	.25	3.8***
Plantations	.06					13.69	.16	5.2***

Model	N	r	r^2	adj. r^2	SEE	F
Chapter 7 model	120	.94	.87	.87	10.32	111.5***
Final contemporary model	120	.96	.91	.90	8.79	102.1***

*Significant (p < .05)
**Significant (p < .01)
***Significant (p < .001)

the equation save the labor force and state socialism interaction. From the standpoint of theorizing about contemporaneous economic effects, this positive estimate is an anomaly. An explanation centered on more temporally distal effects is presented in Chapter 9. It probes in much greater detail the profound implications of the presence of plantation economies in the colonial past for the type of political economy likely to arise in the contemporary period.

These findings complete the analysis of the contemporary political economy, while simultaneously demanding a far greater elaboration of the historical dimension of contemporary economic structure. The current model is a powerful and robust predictor of basic needs levels: the adjusted r^2 reaches .903 and the standard error falls to 8.79. It is also— with a single major exception—theoretically compelling. We now turn to the analysis of this and other examples of historically distal effects on mass citizen welfare.

Chapter 9
Colonialism and Other Historical Influences

Current Structures and Historical Processes

Despite the predictive success of this model of basic needs performance, current social conditions cannot be fully understood without an
examination of the histories that produced them. Temporally distal influences must be examined for two reasons. First, some processes relevant to basic needs are long-term in nature and stable over time. Moreover, the institutional residues of past structure and process often
remain more visible than the influence they continue to exert on the
process and performance of contemporary systems. This visibility is at
once a blessing and a curse. For predictive purposes, such contemporary manifestations can serve as a proxy for these long-acting—but relatively transparent—social forces. For explanatory purposes, however,
the evidence encourages confusion concerning whether the chief causal
mechanism is a contemporary feature (such as a large plantation sector)
or a historical dynamic (such as the long-term sociopolitical consequences of plantation colonialism).

Second, satisfying explanations require that certain basic needs predictors themselves be treated as the outcomes of understandable historical processes. Unfortunately, individual national histories exhibit
greater variation than implied by ahistorical approaches that assume a
single, universal, linear development path and thereby lose both the
complexity of the individual case and the sense of process.

Despite the significance of historical influences, broad-scale cross-national research is inherently limited in the degree to which individual

histories can be investigated. As in our more detailed treatment of development path rather than simple development level, however, this study attempts to recapture at least some of the individual historical variation that is necessarily lost by the general cross-national approach. The method exploits the proclivity of the historical processes that influence current system performance to also leave behind a discernible record. In particular, because system structures remain intact over considerable periods, reasonable inferences of the structural past may be made on the basis of current system attributes. In a study such as this, of course, the richness of individual national histories must be forgone, but the relatively common experiences of clusters of nations can be captured by identifying especially revealing contemporary structures and known historical influences.

In particular, most nations in our sample were exposed to colonialism recently enough that unmistakable evidence remains in the form of economic structures, political institutions, and social and cultural features ranging from language to ethnic makeup. Nearly 50 percent of the 120 nations emerged from their colonial period in the last half-century, and many of these only a decade or so before the measurement period for most of the variables in this analysis. The terms of that colonial incorporation remain stamped on the fundamental features of the contemporary political economy of these nations, though no doubt to a degree that varies with the length, intensity, and recency of that colonial penetration. Later sections sketch arguments focusing on the type of colonial development characteristic of the empires of the leading colonial powers within various regions.

By all accounts, the colonial experience of plantation colonies was especially intense, with profound and fundamental consequences for the future political economy. Thus, this chapter's probe of historically distal influences on basic needs begins with the last finding of Chapter 8. The explanation for the basic needs success of plantation economies is sought in the historical processes that brought them about.

The Economic Effects of Plantations

The presence of a major plantation sector within the political economy of a contemporary nation may affect basic needs directly while it also reflects the outcome of a dynamic historical process originating in a colonial plantation economy. Consequently, any performance characteristic of such a nation—such as a distinctive propensity to provide a relatively high level of basic needs—may result from unseen past processes for which the currently visible historical residue may serve as a proxy. Thus, we must augment our inquiry into the basic needs implications of current plantation sectors with an investigation of the basic needs impact of other social forces produced by that same colonial past.

Moreover, the historical view should help us place current effects within the proper context. In particular, the basic needs propensities of plantation economies must be seen against an appropriate baseline. One baseline, the political economy existing prior to the introduction of plantations through colonial processes, presents the obstacle of documenting an historical counterfactual. We cannot specify the course of autonomous future development which would have occurred in the absence of colonial intervention. However, the immediate impact of early plantation development in steering the economy away from a predominantly subsistence orientation is more or less clear, and the comparison with the basic needs performance of subsistence systems gives us one handle on the distinctiveness of the plantation.

A second approach is to consider the alternative means of exploitation found in other colonial areas and the patterns of colonial development which stemmed from them. The most obvious comparisons include the hacienda system found throughout Latin America, incorporation into the global trading system via mineral exploitation, and imperialism centered on trading networks which left the production process organized predominantly through peasant agricultural systems largely intact. The latter is probably the best contemporary approximation to the historical counterfactual of autonomous development.

Of course, the history of many plantation economies literally began with the colonial experience. None of the aboriginal culture, society, or economy of the Caribbean, for example—indeed, none of the native population—survived the initial colonizing contact. Even where the break with the precolonial past was less complete and occurred more recently, the institution of the plantation was a remarkably dominant historical event. In most instances, it became the core economic activity almost immediately and quickly transformed the majority of the remaining economic sectors, while subordinating and peripheralizing them (Beckford, 1972). In this sense, the presence of a major plantation sector signals to contemporary analysts that the preincorporation history is likely to be less important than in cases where more superficial penetration allowed greater continuity in indigenous development processes. It also suggests a simpler development dynamic than that which resulted from colonial experiences that grafted one system onto another and yielded unique hybrids of indigenous and alien political and moral economies. Because of this wholistic transformation, we are better able to identify a central plantation archetype than we are to find the common core in the more variegated experience of colonies of settlement or trading outposts.

There can be no question that the early impact of the plantation was as a modernizing institution. That is not to say that the immediate effects were in any way benign—let alone beneficial to basic human needs—especially since the institution of slavery, which was itself ultimately lethal as well as destructive of mass welfare, was imposed in many places because of a labor shortage resulting from outright genocide. Nonetheless, it is a fact that large-scale infrastructural development—especially communication and transportation systems but also water supplies and health facilities—arose earlier in plantation areas than in colonies whose exploitation required less intensive transformation of the political economy. The beneficiaries, of course, were often generations separated from the victims whose labor "purchased" the infrastructure at exorbitant human cost.

Furthermore, the mechanisms carrying these developmental effects have been diverse. The rapid introduction of Western economic forms to largely undeveloped political economies had fundamental consequences for social, cultural, and political forms as well. We begin by considering the plantation narrowly as a form of economic organization by examining its direct impact on production.

In relation to previous agrarian production modes in colonized areas, plantations were extremely efficient economic operations. Indeed, they remain so today, a fact that no doubt explains at least part of the capacity of plantation economies to support relatively higher levels of basic needs than economies similar in the proportion of the population found in the agricultural sector. In cost-of-production terms, this efficiency dates from the period in which slavery was the dominant form of labor control. Given the ease with which new labor could be imported, even the requirement of reproducing the labor supply did not require that labor costs reach the level of individual subsistence. Still, the efficiency was not entirely the product of production costs lower than would be possible if the legal rights and economic options of free laborers had forced wages to meet or exceed the level of true labor reproduction.[1]

Relative to the form of agricultural production found elsewhere, this efficiency is also discernible in labor productivity as well as productivity defined in terms of other factor inputs. Yields per acre were

1. Interestingly, the dehumanizing, frequently lethal conditions under which slaves worked on plantations probably contributed to the benefits plantations today convey on prevailing wage rates. Resistance to employment on plantations dating to this period forces wage rates to be relatively higher on plantations than elsewhere (Beckford, 1972: 19).

much greater than in other sectors, for example. Some of this productivity again is due to more intensive exploitation of the individual
worker, but it also results from major differences between the production functions of plantation agriculture versus subsistence sectors or
haciendas. First, the introduction of plantations usually involved a
quite dramatic influx of "capital," defined both conventionally and
more broadly to include various nonlabor and nonland factors of production. Narrowly, agriculture became more mechanized with a markedly increased capital intensity due primarily to investment from
abroad. Improvement in the land itself occurred initially through irriga-
tion and draining operations and later through the introduction of
chemical fertilizers.

The higher level of capital inputs and greater technological sophistication were both augmented and made possible by the enhanced
economies of scale associated with cropping specializations found in
neither subsistence nor hacienda agriculture. In relation to the former,
of course, both the factor intensity and the sheer size of cultivated plots
increased dramatically, so that improved mobilization and concentration of productive resources added to the gains associated with the
inflow of resources.

Greatly enhanced output was as much a consequence of the more
rationalized production process adopted by plantation enterprises.
Plantations represented a markedly more advanced managerial organization than alternative colonial forms. In terms of production techniques, plantations used strict supervision and a hierarchical labor
structure reminiscent of industrial production. More important, investment and marketing decisions reflected management expertise, freedom from constraints, and leverage on markets and other actors not
found elsewhere.

For example, the cropping choices of plantations are optimal for
maximizing factor returns because they reflect comparative advantages
that lie in both demand factors and production functions. In the Caribbean, for example, sugarcane is the most efficient converter of solar
energy, yielding larger quantities of usable organic matter per land unit
than any other crop (Calvin, 1974). Furthermore, the pattern of international demand for cash crops means that they are almost always more
remunerative than subsistence crops. In the Caribbean, there is no
question that raising sugarcane is far and away the most productive
use of land, even when international prices fall to a century-low level
(Hagelberg, 1985). Like other plantation crops (such as tea in Ceylon),
sugar production was introduced into the area in which it is now concentrated from outside. In that sense, sugar production in any form
owes its origin to the plantation enterprises. Of course, even after its

introduction peasant producers are constrained from adopting this same specialization by risk factors as well as competitive disadvantages in marketing and production. Thus, in relation to the classical comparative advantage argument, plantations were the instrument through which the gains from trade were initially introduced and they remain maximizers of output per unit of factor input. Aggregate welfare, including basic needs, can be expected to follow, though obviously the relationship is far from perfectly proportional.

Central to many of the differences between plantation production and subsistence or hacienda agriculture is the unadulterated incentive to maximize productivity in the former. Stemming from the profit motive that dominated the calculus of foreign owners of plantations, this incentive was given greater urgency by the harsh verdict of price-sensitive international markets in judging operational success. By contrast, the hacienda, which dominated the agricultural sectors of most of Latin America, was typically headed by an owner in residence whose mixed motives included the maximization of other social goals (Wolf and Mintz, 1957). The underutilization of land and underemployment of labor still characteristic of the latifundio-minifundio pattern of Latin American development had its roots in the land concentration of the colonial period. These more subsistence-oriented production systems also lacked the plantation's comparative advantage gains from trade and single-product economies of scale.

Moreover, the bottom-line orientation of plantation owners has sustained a continuing drive for productivity gains not found in alternative forms with a less powerful push for profit. For example, "capital" contributions have gone beyond incremental improvements in tools and equipment to include more productive and disease-resistant seed varieties and a range of superior farming practices. Indeed, agricultural research to improve output—funded by plantations or plantation-dominated governments—has been a major factor in plantation production gains relative to those of other crops and other production patterns (Edwards, 1961). By contrast, techniques of subsistence farming on small plots by family labor have changed very little over the centuries.

Many of these efficiency advantages remain today. Plantation productivity continues to be higher than peasant production within the same sectors, partly because of economies of scale and partly because of better factor inputs, especially superior land and better access to capital and technology. The upward pressure this productivity exerts on wage rates more generally could help plantation economies avoid some of the "unequal exchange" Emmanuel associates with the agricultural sector in most poor economies. Certainly if any increment of increased productivity is reflected in worker wages, the basic needs

performance of plantation economies ought to exceed that of less productive systems with a similar percentage of the work force in agriculture. Indeed, as we see below, there are good reasons for anticipating
that a substantial fraction of productivity gains will be reflected in the
welfare of plantation workers.

Balanced against the seeming greater efficiency of plantations, however, are the social costs associated with them. Beckford (1972: 154–82)
argues that the profit calculus of plantation owners—especially when
they are vertically integrated multinational corporations—yields resource allocations that are grossly suboptimal with respect to such social values as aggregate economic growth and sectoral equality. The
private rate of return for plantation owners—which reflects microeconomic efficiency—is said to greatly exceed the social rate of return,
which involves broader issues. Within the plantation sector itself, this
gap seems no worse than in other methods of incorporation. For example, there is no indication that the underutilization of land in plantation
economies is any more pronounced than in the typical agrarian patterns of Latin America, almost all of which feature equally huge inequalities in landholdings. In contrast to the more typical Asian pattern, the use intensities of all factors except labor are sufficiently
greater that higher productivity compensates for the somewhat higher
percentage of undercultivated land.

Beckford is even more concerned, however, about the aggregate
macroeconomic outcome of the articulation of the plantation sector
with other sectors. In particular, it is possible that plantation sectors
manifest higher levels of basic needs fulfillment, even while their impact on the remainder of the economy may mute or even reverse that
effect from the standpoint of the system as a whole. His arguments
about competition between plantations and peasant producers echo
concerns about backwash effects found elsewhere in the literature on
both dependent development in general and multinational corporations in particular. For example, sharp dualism produces sectoral inequalities and exacerbates class inequalities, which are especially pronounced in the advanced sector due to high rents and concentrated
scarce factors of production (especially land, but also capital). Continuing foreign ownership may also divert much of the productivity gain
into leakages from the domestic economy.

In comparison with the highly integrated and sectorally balanced
economies of the industrialized countries, as Beckford is surely correct
in saying, plantations yield vast disparities of income, wealth, and life
chances. Neither is there a question that the growth dynamic of the
plantation is, by the same standard, less autonomous and more constrained by various forms of resource leakage and the absence of self-

sustaining domestic linkages. For our purposes, however, the relevant question is whether the dualism of plantation economies is more or less damaging to basic needs than the dualism characteristic of all dependent economies. Are plantation economies more capable of basic needs fulfillment than economies with a similar percentage of the work force employed in agriculture, for example? In particular, how is the basic needs capacity of the system affected by the introduction of a plantation sector to a political economy largely subsistence in orientation?

Narrowly, of course, the plantation sector has a basic needs propensity much superior to that of the subsistence sector. The latter's poor productivity not only yields relatively low output, it also lacks the capacity to monetize and mobilize even the small surplus it may be capable of producing. Thus, surplus cannot be concentrated and invested in either future development or socially necessary infrastructure, which would provide basic needs both directly and indirectly. In this sense, the plantation is both more dynamic and more immediately beneficial to welfare. Indeed, we know from previous analyses that the subsistence sector yields a much lower level of basic needs than any other agricultural form. The statistical results of Chapter 4 indicated that for the seventy-two nations in the Adelman and Morris sample an ordinal measure of the size of the subsistence sector was an even better predictor of basic needs levels than the agricultural labor force generally. To test for the robustness of this finding with a superior control model encompassing known political effects, the analysis was rerun. Indeed, even when added to the predictively powerful current model, the size of the subsistence sector remains a very highly significant drag on basic needs provision ($t = -3.9$).

Thus, the plantation could improve basic needs provision simply by diverting some labor from a backward to a more productive sector. But the plantation does more than augment an indigenous economy; instead, it replaces it. A combination of the economic advantages of the plantation and the political power of their owners rapidly drove out alternative economic forms in most of the colonies in which plantation enterprises were introduced.[2] The statistical analysis of the Adelman and Morris sample of nations cannot confirm this linkage as one of the pathways between a plantation past and a basic needs present, but

2. Of course, there are cases (e.g., much of Central America) in which the plantation economy is not coextensive with the nation as a whole. That is, the plantation dominates the lowlands area, which is only a subeconomy within the broader national economy. Still, this situation is relatively rare, being found only in those countries with dramatically different geographical regions that mandate different cropping patterns as well as forms of agricultural organization.

plantation economies are marked by an unusually small subsistence sector compared to nations with otherwise similar economic attributes ($t = -1.7$).

At the same time, this suggests that plantations do not usually possess either of the two attributes associated with the classical pattern of an export enclave. First, unlike most advanced industrial sectors, most plantations dominate their respective economies in the sheer size and scope of their operations, as shown in the statistics produced by an International Labour Organization survey of thirteen plantation economies in the mid-1960s. In five of these countries, more than half the cultivated land was devoted to plantations and in four others the percentage exceeded 25 percent. The plantation share of exports was above 60 percent for all the nations except India and Peru, neither of which is coded as a plantation economy in this study. Labor force statistics are available for only a handful of countries, among which plantations employed more than half the agricultural labor force in several (ILO, 1966).

Second, plantations are usually much more highly integrated into the surrounding economy than the export enclaves formed by mineral operations or even industrial export platforms.[3] Indeed, they are usually better integrated than the rural and urban or the agricultural and industrial sectors of most nations. The linkages are not only those familiar as backwash effects (e.g., investment concentrations and worker migrations), but also some that constitute spread effects. Part-time employment on plantations is common among peasants, for example. Prevailing plantation wage rates thus dominate local labor markets, usually pushing wages upward. Moreover, payment of monetized wages diverts production away from subsistence cultivation, encourages consumption patterns that influence attitudes, and introduces mobility opportunities and social differentiation. In all of these attributes, the plantation has more in common with industry than with traditional agriculture. Further, the capital intensity and wage rates of the plantation sector are usually intermediate between those of an advanced industrial sector and a traditional agricultural one, a position that should help reduce the inequality implicit in sharp dualism. Many nonplantation producers also cultivate the plantation crop, so that they benefit

---

3. Beckford (1972: 15–16) cites Liberia, Kenya, Rhodesia, and South Africa as exceptions. The latter three are marked by far greater settlement migrations than are common among plantation colonies. Indeed, alternative modes of exploitation—both minerals and large settler farms and ranches—better characterize both the colonial period and the subsequent development of these political economies. Liberia, of course, is even more idiosyncratic in its pattern of migration.

from marketing and processing arrangements as well as relevant technical information.

The Sociopolitical Effects of Plantations

The contribution of the plantation is broader and more profound, however, than this narrow economic analysis suggests. Now, as then, the plantation is far more than an economic sector; the plantation destroys not only the subsistence economy, but also the social, political, and cultural order that rests upon it. Most obviously, its economic dominance is both cause and consequence of the political dominance of plantation owners. From the earliest days, the plantation colony constituted a total social mobilization geared to increasing productivity. The role of the colonial administration was assumed by dominant planter interests after independence, but the singular devotion to this end was largely unchanged. The immediate goals of maintaining a favorable labor surplus and a pliant work force motivated a wide range of adaptive behavior and had far-reaching future implications. The result was a harnessing of social, political, and cultural forces which prevented the divergence of resources to cross-cutting goals. Even the creole languages of the Caribbean reinforce cultural patterns associated with the plantation (Alleyne, 1985). At the same time, they represent a break with previous cultural traditions and one of the means by which older social structures are fractured and disabled.

The implications of this sweeping structural change for system performance are seen similarly by a range of theoretical orientations. Marxist perspectives identify the changes as necessary to eliminate growth-restricting political structures and to free the forces of production for an ultimately progressive if temporarily painful transition to a newer, more efficient form. Writing on India, Marx (1943: 67) recognized British capital's "dual mission: one destructive, the other regenerating—the annihilation of the old Asiatic society, and the laying of the material foundations of Western society in Asia." Modernization theorists recognize the transition to more Western attitudes and perspectives as a necessary complement to both economic growth and political development (Myrdal, 1968). At the level of the individual, the requirement of creating "modern man" is perhaps put best by Nehru (1961: 46): "You can't get hold of a modern tool and have an ancient mind. It won't work." Finally, the same conclusion comes from Olson's (1982) view of steadily ossifying political structures that impede system performance until cyclical forces eliminate existing associations, alliances, and rent-protecting groups. Periodic destruction is necessary to clear away the residue of no longer relevant adaptations to no longer current circumstances. In short, primordial loyalties seen as retrogressive to plantation development are displaced far more totally by the new order than is common on colonial development paths that retained a role for indigenous elites and left intact economic, social, and political structures.

Not all of the impacts of the plantation were deliberate creations of plantation interests, however. The wholesale transformation of the political economy set in motion dynamics to which no social system is immune. While the plantation's dominance of the macroeconomy continues to the present day, the social, political, and cultural life of these nations has adapted to the social institution of the plantation in a way that distinguishes them not only from other societies but from their own early form as well.

From the beginning, the plantation was a "total institution," containing a rigidly hierarchical social order that defined the relationships between individuals and the terms on which groups could form (Goffman, 1961; R. Smith, 1967; Best, 1968; Thompson, 1957).[4] In fact, the slave trade associated with the plantation colonies of the Caribbean meant that even the ethnic makeup of the population was a consequence of this total institution. The resultant distinctive ethnic mix of the Caribbean is responsible for the cultural developments of these societies as well as the political and economic features with which this study is most concerned (Mintz and Price, 1985).

But the slave trade, together with the form of labor control it implied, laid the seeds for stark social cleavages in which race and class mutually reinforced a social consciousness whose parallel with the Marxist view of the social effects of industrialization is striking. The plantations—which brought together large numbers of exploited, abused, and socially alienated workers—were the sweatshops of the Third World. In the early period, the combination of horrible conditions and the close physical proximity of sizable concentrations of the like-minded produced frequent slave revolts. Even after the abolition of slavery, the organization of production featured unskilled labor heavily supervised by authoritarian management of different color as well as class. Planta-

---

4. Coexisting with these rigid caste lines, reinforcing race and class considerations and the deep cleavages of interest and ideology which follow from them, is a kind of paternalism which emerges from the melding of the economic function of the plantation with the reality that the plantation was also a fully self-contained social and cultural order as well. Still, this process did not go so far as in the hacienda of Latin America nor in the more organic peasant-landowner relationship characteristic of Asia. Paternalism has ebbed with the decline of the planter class and its replacement with absentee landlords or multinational corporations.

tions thus became breeding grounds not only for discontent and for resistance, but, in later periods, for the structures through which individual protests were replaced by more organized demands for welfare gains. In particular, an organized trade union movement occurred in plantation economies far earlier in the developmental sequence than was common elsewhere in the Third World.

The ultimate positive consequences for basic needs levels arise through a unique set of intermediate mechanisms. With the abolition of slavery, the imposition of free wage labor within the economic parameters of a plantation economy yielded a singular pattern of social cleavage. The growth of working class consciousness parallels the similar development common to an industrialization path, though it occurs at a markedly lower level of aggregate output and social wealth. However, largely for that reason, it is not accompanied by an economic differentiation that permits the rise of a middle class to arbitrate class struggle. Neither, however, do rigid and polar class alignments produce the social dynamic of violence and repression characteristic of other massively unequal agricultural societies. Paige's (1975) analysis of the unique combination of upper class and lower class options sheds light on the plantation economy's special potential for implicit class compromise. The favorable basic needs outcome is particularly interesting because it arises out of a pattern of political institutions much different from that found elsewhere.

Several factors converge to focus the discontent of plantation workers on the precise terms of the capital-labor bargain, namely the wage rate and working conditions. In such a pervasive social institution, workers do not find themselves torn by alternative explanations of their plight or drawn to competing avenues of redress. Peasants in other systems cope with multiple evils and multiple agents of each: credit markets, land concentrations, rents, crop prices, middlemen, state officials, global markets, shopkeepers, and so on. Plantation workers are paid a money wage by plantation owners who embody all these roles: they control the markets and the state; they even provide company stores. In short, the plantation is wholly responsible for the workers' level of welfare—and the workers know it. There are no feasible alternatives to plantation work in the form of other means of livelihood. There are no feasible alternatives to plantation protest in the form of other social institutions (e.g., a responsive, autonomous state). Indeed, there are few targets of radical political action, since land reform is hardly an issue where control of the land would be so ineffectual for improving welfare. The advantages of plantation owners stem from total domination of markets and institutions, not from land ownership. In fact, in the era when multinational corporation ownership is far more prevalent than an indigenous planter class, the bulk of the profits are to be found in the domain of trade—shipping, insurance, marketing, brokerage, etc.—and not in the domain of production (de Silva, 1982).

Furthermore, physical proximity and the relative absence of competition and social cleavages among proletarianized workers make organizing comparatively easy. By contrast, peasants whose incomes derive more directly from land are more physically isolated, more differentiated among themselves in wealth and income, and less united in identifying the central source of their problems and solutions. As a consequence, the power of worker organizations in plantation economies is relatively great and it is directed rather simply at wage levels.

At the same time, many of these same attributes make it easy for plantation owners to acquiesce to worker organization and the higher wage demands that result. These may be considered a small price to pay for the continuance of a disciplined, efficient, and responsible work force. Moreover, with ample profits derived from other sources and the wage bill being a smaller percentage of total production costs, plantation owners are less hostile to labor movements than hacienda owners, whose economic inefficiency and source of income make them more vulnerable to class-based movements. Moreover, in these circumstances, lower class action is also likely to be directed against land ownership and to assume a more radical character. With both upper and lower class incomes rooted in land ownership, the zero-sum situation fosters political conflict often leading to violence.

Thus, class conflict in the plantation economy is relatively easily channeled toward wage and working condition bargaining. The impact on basic needs is evident. The plantation, due to its efficiency and productivity, extracts a greater surplus than other agricultural forms. Furthermore, that surplus is allocated via a system rather more favorable to the interests of workers than is typical in other agricultural development paths. Moreover, destructive conflict is minimized.

The uniqueness of this result must be seen not only in the contrast with alternative agricultural paths, but also in relation to the route of industrialization with which it shares some key attributes. Principal among these is that labor unions flourish. In industrial societies, however, the impact of labor unions on worker welfare is felt along at least three causal avenues, of which only wage bargaining is found among plantation political economies. Labor unions in industrial nations typically serve as a foundation for political parties that seek to alter the balance of class power or, at a minimum, the nature of the institutional setting within which the conflict is resolved. Socialist parties stress the adoption of leftist principles in a wide variety of state policies while more moderate parties press strongly for democratic institutions within which the parties can function as lobbyists for the interests of the working classes they represent. As our earlier analysis makes clear, both paths—democracy and socialism—are associated with higher levels of basic needs provision than in other political systems, but neither is created by the forms of labor union activity found in plantation economies.

In plantation economies, class-based political activity such as that initiated by unions achieves some measure of success in wage bargaining, but it is much less influential in shaping the nature of political institutions than in industrial nations.[5] The result is an historical process that has left two important and visible current structural legacies. First, an organized trade union movement occurred far earlier in the developmental sequence than was common elsewhere in the Third World. Indeed, the rural and agricultural origins of these unions are unique.

Second, however, the limited aspirations of the union movement prevented the occurrence of either of two frequent political correlates, one believed to be favorable for basic needs, the other detrimental. In industrializing nations, reformist political parties centered around unions often arise to represent working class interests. These parties, however, typically form within a democratic dynamic that features both facilitative political institutions and a ready source of political allies. In particular, organizations to protect working class interests usually develop only after a substantial middle class has formed and successfully pressed for democratic institutions, especially representation through electoral processes. Seeking an ally in the working class, the middle class encourages the expansion of democracy, especially the extension of the franchise, which in turn fosters a political and legal framework favorable to working class organization. Real economic gains for the lower classes thus arise via both direct union activities and the political parties that are associated with them. Plantation economies, however, lack the substantial economic differentiation necessary for the occupational basis of a middle class to develop. Thus, lower class interests are being represented politically at a time when the middle class has yet to coalesce. As a result the political framework within which labor parties can arise is not present.

The detrimental correlate of class-based political activity is the resultant political conflict. Lower class mobilization certainly can occur out-

5. This suggests that the unions' basic needs impact will be much reduced, a fact reflected in my analyses. It must be recalled that the superior performance of the plantation economy—though real enough—is relative to expectations based on economic structure. Plantation economies are still poor, agricultural, trade-dependent, peripheral nations; their PQLI scores do not approximate those of industrial nations.

side democratic settings. Indeed, that is the general pattern in the agricultural political economies of the contemporary Third World. When mobilization does occur, however, it is ordinarily associated with radical political activity and responsive state repression. The spiral of political violence and retrogression in political development undermines basic needs as well as aggregate citizen welfare more broadly (Dixon and Moon, 1989). However, because of the absence of a radical orientation in the working class movement, the plantation economy does not share this pattern either. In fact, the legacy of the plantation economy is a state absent serious political challenge. The state thus remains relatively small and passive, neither forced rightward in political posture nor motivated to assemble a repressive force in the form of large military establishments. Still, this passivity occurs in a context that is anything but promising for the rise of democracy. There is no middle class to press for democracy, there is no egalitarian tradition to rally democratic ideology, and there is a vast imbalance of class forces if expressed in the traditional political arena. Indeed, the unlikelihood of democracy accounts for some of the channeling of discontent into the relatively narrow area of wage bargaining and protest over working conditions.

The outcome is thus an arrangement that yields enhanced basic needs, without any of the immediate instruments our previous analysis identifies.[6] Industrialization is not required, democracy is not required, committed socialist parties are not required. Nonstate actors produced by a unique form of economic and social development can lead to basic needs fulfillment by a rather different path. As a consequence, the most intense grievances can be deflected without violence, but these are quite narrowly focused on economic matters, leaving the structures of dominance largely intact.

What evidence can we find for this interpretation? First, the strength of organized labor is substantially greater than one would expect from economic structure. The presence of early labor unions in various plantation economies is documented by Paige (1975: 49–50). Moreover, in

6. The future implications of the cross-cutting attributes of plantation political economies are difficult to net out. The political and social side of the plantation political economy contains these important sources of dynamic evolution. By contrast, the economy itself is, at this stage of its development, quite stagnant. Initially, of course, plantations mobilized underutilized factors of production—including land, labor, and capital—and concentrated them in sectors of comparative advantage on international markets. Moreover, access to international markets for the factor inputs themselves also expanded the production frontier. Considerations of static comparative advantage have long since been displaced, however, by concerns over the economic dynamism implicit in these commodity specializations. The result seems to be the picture we have uncovered: relatively slow economic growth, but on a path that provides rather higher basic needs levels than alternatives that yield higher growth rates but proportionally poorer basic needs performance.

the sample of nations with adequate data (N = 71), plantations are associated with a far more significant role for organized labor than would be expected on the basis of sectoral labor force shares (t = 2.9).[7] Beyond a doubt, unions arise "out of sequence" relative to the more usual pattern in which unions arise only after a significant share of the labor force has shifted to the industrial sector.

By the same token, however, the usual political manifestations of union strength do not appear. Union organization ordinarily leads to the foundation of a left-leaning working class party and a strengthening of a corresponding right-leaning party, for example. In our sample, the strength of union movements is a very strong predictor of class-based and ideological party systems (t = 4.2). Yet, the party system is no more class-rooted nor ideological in the plantation system than in other political economies at comparable levels of economic development (t = .8).[8]

Indeed, the plantation has no visible impact on most of the political mechanisms identified in previous chapters. In particular, plantations are not associated with greater social insurance program experience (t = −.2), greater levels of contemporary social insurance programs (t = −1.6), higher levels of democracy (t = .7), or lower levels of rightist (t = .1) or leftist (t = −.5) governments. Given the usual impact of labor strength on these same intermediate variables, the absence of such linkages for plantation economies suggests that a quite different form of political economy has evolved.[9] In particular, it ap-

---

7. The variable is the strength of the organized labor movement, an ordinal measure described by Adelman and Morris (1973: 52–54). The original prediction equation contains all the relevant indicators of national economic structure and international structural position used in previous analyses in addition to the plantation dummy. The reported t value is that obtained when the plantation variable is added to the final model, which excludes, in stepwise fashion, the independent variables whose parameter estimates do not meet the .10 standard of significance. The only other predictor in the final model was labor force structure (t = −4.5); the overall adjusted r^2 was .30. These exclusions do not appreciably affect the size of the plantation parameter, whose t value in the original equation was 2.7.

8. The variable is an ordinal representation of the basis of the party system, where the highest scores are assigned nations in which parties are class-based and arrayed along a left-right ideological continuum. The coding is described in Adelman and Morris (1973: 50–52). The procedures for model specification and parameter estimation are as reported in note 7.

9. Labor strength is especially associated with higher levels of democracy (t = 5.2) and a longer history of more elaborate social insurance programs (t = 2.3). Neither is a characteristic of plantation economies; indeed, plantations are actually significantly less likely to have social insurance programs in place around 1970 (t = −2.3). There is also a weak tendency for labor union strength to be found in nations without rightist (t = −1.3) or leftist (−1.6) regimes. Again, plantations seem to have little impact.

pears that working class organization in the private sector has not yielded any substantial impact on state policy. Thus, its basic needs impact must be found largely outside the realm of state action.

Because of the very fact that working class interests have yielded neither radical action nor political parties that support a far-reaching political program, upper class reaction to working class strength has also been far more muted than might be anticipated. In particular, since control of the state has not been a focus of class conflict, the state has not become an active agent in repressing progressive forces; thus military establishments have remained small.[10]

The importance of these effects on basic needs varies. The analysis of the smaller sample ($N = 71$) leaves little doubt that some of the plantation effect is a product of the two-step path involving the subsistence sector: plantations reduce the subsistence sector, which in turn significantly slows basic needs attainment. The impacts of some of the political effects are well documented in previous chapters, but they are also already contained in the current model even without the plantation dummy. Other impacts are more problematic. It is clear that the plantation has encouraged the growth of labor unions, a plausible linkage to improved basic needs performance. The evidence is far from persuasive that the presence of unions can account for the performance of plantation economies, however, because net of other effects, unions do not themselves predict to a significantly higher PQLI ($t = .5$).

Of course, this lack of effect may result from the ambiguity noted previously in organized labor's class position when viewed in the cross-national aggregate. In some cases—the plantation seems to be a particularly prominent instance—organized labor would raise the prevailing wage rate at the expense of capital's share of the surplus, benefiting the poor in a way reflected in enhanced PQLI. Where organized labor represents workers within the advanced sector of a dualistic economy, however, the effect on PQLI may actually be negative if wage demands are met by further transfer of the surplus from the rural sector to the advanced urban sector. The peculiar origin of the plantation economy's labor movement together with the far less segmented labor markets means that organized labor's wage bargaining is much more likely to have positive basic needs consequences in plantation

10. The plantation dummy predicts less frequent military government ($t = -.8$), lower levels of military manpower ($t = -2.4$) and military spending ($t = -1.9$), and lower spending per soldier ($t = -1.7$). Of course, not all of these are statistically significant and most are associated more generally with high levels of unionization. Even with the unionization measure included, however, the sign of the plantation parameter remained negative in the case of the three latter variables ($t = .2$ for months of military government).

political economies than elsewhere. Moreover, given the crudeness of the various measures and the size of the sample, the insignificance of the parameter estimate is hardly conclusive, though it does call into question the importance of this pathway from plantations to basic needs performance.

Colonial Forms and Subsequent Patterns of Development

The discussion of the plantation economy illustrates that historical factors have weighed heavily in generating contemporary levels of basic needs. Clearly, it is important to consider the colonial roots of contemporary structural forms. Plantation development was, of course, a vastly more transforming process than the less intensive colonial experience centered around alternative means of extracting and transferring wealth. For that reason—and because plantations are so distinctive—I give much less attention to most other forms of colonial contact. One dramatic contrast, however, offers an interesting and revealing parallel with contemporary system structure, namely the differential effect of mining on the one hand and large-scale agriculture on the other.

Colonialism centered on the transfer of wealth through the expropriation of precious metals occurred in the early colonial period of parts of both South America and central and southern Africa. This pattern produced the same drain of resources and a similar destruction of indigenous structures, but without enhancing economic productivity or implanting the seeds of dynamism—however incomplete and dependent—which are found in plantation economies. Mineral exploitation required only a minimal transfer of population and resources, principally in the form of a military presence and a supportive administrative organization. Thus, the mining sector remained relatively small and was little integrated with the remainder of the economy. Beyond elementary transportation, no infrastructural development occurred. Although mining yielded enormous wealth, the leakage was nearly complete. The establishment of a colonial state with a mission singularly defined in terms of external interests produced social and political effects that were entirely destructive. The continuance of poor basic needs performance from these systems—documented in both individual nation studies (Peemans, 1975; Katzenellenbogen, 1975; de Silva, 1982; Szentes, 1985) and my earlier statistical analysis with contemporary mining shares of exports—is hardly surprising.

Other forms of colonial development have been identified, though relative to plantation development their lack of distinctiveness, the absence of clear theoretical arguments, and inadequate data do not enable us to make any definitive judgments concerning their impact on subsequent basic needs. Nonetheless, a brief reference to them helps to emphasize the routes by which early development can influence contemporary performance.

With respect to Africa, Amin (1972) has identified three broad economic development patterns. The first, the "Africa of the colonial trade economy," is empirically associated with traditional West Africa. In this style of development the colonial presence is minimal though its implications are quite broad. The administration of these colonies emphasized the creation of trade without requiring the direct supervision of production, which was left to dependent elites. The progressive developmental impact of this form of surplus extraction was even smaller than that of mineral operations since it involved no capital or technology transfers, no dramatic increase in productivity, nor any political development of note. It did, however, require the fracturing of preexisting economic, political, and social patterns in order to produce a labor supply and a dependent, submissive social system.

The second African macroregion, the "Africa of the concession-owning companies," consisted of the traditional Congo River basin. Development in this region was left to private investors with little structuring by colonial authorities. Its pattern includes both plantation and mining development—although the distinction between them has been shown to be extremely significant for future basic needs levels. Finally, Amin places most of eastern and southern Africa in the category of "the Africa of the labour-reserves." Theoretically the defining characteristic involves colonial policies that rapidly create an indigenous proletariat for employment in mines and in settler agriculture. Despite a similarity in the way traditional societies were destroyed, from the standpoint of subsequent political development, a distinction must be maintained between a dynamic sustained by foreign investment in mineral exploitation and one based on agriculture centered on immigrant settler groups.

To be sure, both development styles required the disruption of indigenous societies and the fracturing of economic as well as political relationships. In particular, people had to be freed from rural cultivation and made available for migration to employment centers of external investment. In neither case were indigenous peoples treated well individually, nor were their existing economic dynamics left to develop autonomously. Colonies of settlement, however, can be expected to evolve in very different ways from colonies of exploitation because of the distinctive direction provided by settler groups in establishing a social and political order.

The massive migration from the home country characteristic of "farm colonies" not only implies a different form of economic organization; migrating groups also "carried with them patterns of social organization and definite ideas about the kind of society they wished to create" (Beckford, 1972: 35). Keller (1931) suggests that the resultant colony is likely to be more self-sufficient in economic structure and more like the mother country in population and political institutions. At least in comparison to colonies of exploitation, this resemblance may imply greater popular participation and a larger commitment to equality, particularly since the administration of the settler colony was more likely to be guided by a set of political ideals and interests which treated seriously the future course of development in the colony. Unlike in other forms of colonial development, there existed some concern with the nature of the political system and more broadly with the good of the colony itself. Of course, the perceptions of colonial interest were those of European immigrants, but at least the orientation was something other than a singular devotion to the interests of the metropole. There is a further complication, however. Settlers seek to recreate a political system that resembles—in some ways at least—that of the home country (de Silva, 1982); but because the settlers originated in a wide variety of political systems, it may not be possible to identify a distinctive effect of settler agriculture.

Moreover, although differences across metropoles account for some of the variety in subsequent state forms, as much has to do with unique hybrids. These range from the style of South African development, which sharply distinguishes—after more than two centuries— between natives and immigrants, to that of Latin America. The latter is strongly influenced by immigration (though its scale and scope are highly variant across nations) together with the creation of a large— but, again, variable—mixed-race segment of the population. The range of outcomes is represented by the mostly native hybrid of most of Central America to the mostly European makeup of Argentina and Uruguay. Naturally, political arrangements have adapted to these racial patterns; by and large, pressure for popular participation has been most widespread in those countries not marked by sharp racial divisions.

In any case, it is evident that plantation economies were more thoroughly transformed than colonies marked by different economic forms. Today they stand as a more distinguishable archetype—similar to one another and different from other forms of colonial development—than the complex and variegated hybrids produced by the intersection of various forms of colonial surplus extraction and various metropole origins layered on top of various preincorporation political and moral economies. I return to these complications below, with regard to differences in basic needs propensities of various global regions, but for the moment I consider more tractable questions involving the length and intensity of the colonial experience.

In particular, the above discussion suggests attention to the basic needs impact of a colonial state in which metropole interests guide policy. By contrast, an independent state may be expected to be more oriented toward basic needs achievement for its own citizens. If this view is accurate, an empirical analysis ought to show that basic needs performance in nations with a more recent colonial history lags that of nations gaining independence earlier. Further, the different political forms taken by colonialism associated with the various powers, suggests particular attention to the distinctive legacy of British and French colonialism. Thus, I also examine the empirical evidence for these differential effects before returning to the more complex lines of causation and the necessarily more speculative treatments of basic needs impacts associated with combinations of economic, social, and political aspects of colonial development.

Colonialism and Postcolonial Development

Despite major differences in the economic, social, and political experiences of nations under colonialism, certain common elements suggest that basic needs levels will tend to lag in areas affected by intensive, long-lasting, and relatively recent colonial experiences. I consider two of these elements, one essentially economic and one predominantly political, though they are themselves interrelated. First, the economies are oriented toward what Magubane (1985: 199) calls the "colonial capitalist mode of production (CCMP)," a unique form of "capitalism under the special conditions of colonialism." Second, the political systems are designed to maximize the goals of the metropole, often to the express disadvantage of the colony itself, but always with at least relative indifference to colonial interests. Central to both the above factors are elements of class formation. At the core of the colonial capitalist mode of production and its unique social structure is the overpowering external influence in both creating and sustaining its principal components. As Brett (1973: 284) puts it:

> Capitalism had evolved organically in the areas of origin, but it was injected into the colonial world from outside and, where necessary, imposed upon unwilling populations there at the point of a gun. The process of organic evolution, for example in Britain, produced an indigenous capitalist class which was securely rooted in the social structure and cul-

ture and which, whatever its limits, had necessarily to rely upon internal sources of support to legitimate and defend its claims to social predominance. The dominance of this class in European society was subjected to intense opposition both from the old feudal order and from the emergent working class, but its claims to represent at least one significant tendency within the national culture could never be entirely rejected. But external dominance in the Third World meant that the commanding heights of the new economy and administration were occupied by expatriate groups from the beginning; expatriate groups, moreover, with access to resources derived from their metropolitan base which were far in excess of anything which indigenous groups could hope to acquire in the short run. The crucial question for the long-term development of the society as a whole therefore relates to the effect of their dominance upon the emergence of indigenous social formations which might be capable of replacing them and establishing an autonomous base for the exercise of political and economic power.

What are the implications of the external origins and external support of this expatriate dominant group for basic needs provision? Its development choices will no doubt be as different from those of an indigenous elite as their interests, values, and perspectives. Most obviously, it will be predisposed to outward-looking development strategies, which, if unconstrained by countervailing state policy, encourage greater leakages and higher inequality. The allocation of the surplus both through private investment decisions and state policy will reflect less interest in the future of the domestic political economy than would occur with a more indigenous economic and political elite.

Even after independence, the inheritors of this structural position, whether native elites, descendants of colonists, or some combination, will tend to share this orientation. Moreover, because the power of such classes lies in access to the foreign sector, autonomous and internally coherent development of the domestic economy threatens their interests. Thus, their preferences are for development patterns that emphasize external articulation and accentuate domestic sectoral and geographical disarticulation, conditions that generate inequality and limit dynamism.

The dominant groups are likely to be much different in political outlook as well, sharing less with the mass culture because of "diffusion of the colonizer's cultural tradition" (Magubane, 1985: 199), especially where the elite is actually foreign (so that racism can play a role) rather than merely foreign-supported. In either case, there is little reason to expect state policy to favor the interests of the indigenous poor over those of the powerful and wealthy elites—internal and external, indigenous and expatriate—who dominate the state. At independence, the state will feel few pressures to improve basic needs levels. "In politics,

there were no durable political institutions, no democratic cultural traditions, no widely diffused social ideals, and no full sense of national
identity" (Magubane, 1985: 216). In fact, the state is likely to be corrupt
by virtue of the learned behavior of colonial oppression and the absence of domestic political challenge to the power of those who dominate it.

Indeed, postcolonial elites are likely to be far more dominant than in
a system in which they evolved organically, in part because they face
much weaker competing elites. Of course, the relatively low level of
development and the unfavorable path of development already imply a
small middle class and a weak national bourgeoisie. The monopoly access to the most fundamental resources (external transactions) afforded
by the colonial and postcolonial state implies even greater concentration of political power and more exclusive political dominance. For example, Anastasio Somoza becomes the largest landowner, the largest
coffee merchant, and the unchallenged head of state as a result of
Nicaragua's colonial experience (Paige, 1985).[11]

The expected result is that colonies—and to a somewhat lesser extent, recently independent former colonies—will manifest poorer basic
needs provision than more organically created and evolved systems.
Some of the implied differences, of course, are already captured in the
model. Political factors are represented via the level of democracy and
ideological orientation, while in the economic realm the effects of various trade attributes and the role of multinational corporations have
been isolated in previous analyses.

Nonetheless, the range of colonial effects is sufficiently great that
their distal influences on basic needs are likely to be detected even after
the passage of time has eroded some of their more visible components.
For example, the functional role of the colonial state and its legacies of
personnel, structure, and programmatic makeup must surely affect the
socialization processes discussed in Chapter 6 which dispose the state
to emphasize some goals over others. In particular, the relatively low
priority assigned basic needs by most colonial states is likely to carry
over into the postcolonial state more profoundly than can be captured
by a simple right-left ideological characterization. In addition, even after independence the state sector is likely to be a major source of inequality due to inflated salary levels as well as a source of waste
through corruption and inefficiency. It is also likely to divert resources
to repression and other means of legitimation because of the absence of

11. This example emphasizes the variety of colonial experiences and the difficulty of
generalizing about them. Nicaragua is a case in which economic interests and economic
roots of domination are less important than control of the state's military apparatus, from
the points of view of both internal and external actors.

fundamental legitimacy provided by institutions, political culture, or popular acceptance of welfare performance.

Neither is the full economic legacy of the colonial period adequately captured by our contemporary economic model. The demonstration effect on an externally conditioned elite, for example, yields a greater demand for and acceptance of inequality (Kentor, 1985: 32). Its consequences are undeniable but difficult to measure directly: larger leakages associated with conspicuous consumption of luxury items, greater distortions through foreign schooling, and so on. Moreover, class relations retain the stamp of early colonial development, as in much of central and southern Africa where the use of migrant labor depressed wages and constrained trade-union organization, class consciousness, and skill development in colonies with a need for labor in mines and cash cropping (Magubane, 1985: 211–13).

All of this evidence suggests that the colonial experience lowers the basic needs propensity of a given political economy. Though it seems likely that such effects are related to the length and intensity of the colonial penetration, theoretical and empirical complexities complicate attempts to measure these elements. In particular, gauging the intensity of colonialism requires a better specification than we can produce of the precise dimensions that influence basic needs. Similarly, identifying the length of the colonial experience requires, for example, a resolution of the controversial role of the slave trade in shaping development in West Africa. Was it so profound as to itself constitute colonialism or too marginal in importance to be considered anything other than a trade relationship? At the same time, the character of the colonial period has varied enormously from nation to nation. In sum, a cross-national study of this type is constrained in its ability to capture many colonial effects.

Still, I believe that the effects of colonialism have been deleterious for basic needs levels and that these influences contain considerable inertia, which weakens slowly over time. At least one measurable consequence should result: nations with a more recent colonial experience should manifest a lower PQLI than would be expected on the basis of other attributes and a lower level of basic needs fulfillment than nations whose postcolonial history has been long enough to erode some of these effects.

To test this proposition, we require a metric that captures the declining effect of colonialism over time. Unfortunately, since nearly all nations have experienced some form of colonialism at one time or another, we have available two flawed measurement approaches. First, we could code the length of time of formal independence. This requires, however, a problematic choice of transformation metric. It is

doubtful that the relationship is linear, and any beginning point for
Great Britain or China, for example, would be rather arbitrary. Neither
is it clear what shape this declining influence curve should take. Without theoretical guidance, an empirically derived curve risks false inference because date of independence is so highly collinear with other
items discussed below, most obviously geographic region and the identity of the metropole.

A second approach is to simply select a time point and create a set of
dummy variables reflecting each nation's status at that moment. This
option removes the need for some difficult choices, though, of course,
it introduces another. Which snapshot is the appropriate one? Although the choice cannot be rigorously defended, this analysis selects
the end of World War II as the relevant time frame. This choice causes
about 60 percent of the sample to be considered "independent"; the
remainder achieved independence less than a quarter century before
basic needs levels are measured. This period represents roughly one
political generation.[12]

The results shown in Table 9-1 confirm expectations. Net of the factors contained in the final contemporary political economy model of
Chapter 8, nations that were still colonies at the end of World War II
have a PQLI nearly five points lower than those independent in 1945.
Not unexpectedly, the crudeness of both the measure and the specification cause the parameter to be estimated with considerable error,
however. Thus, while statistically significant, the addition of this factor
improves the overall fit of the model only marginally.

Obviously, this specification is flawed by a failure to distinguish various types of colonial experience. With respect to the huge variation in
economic structure, I have earlier expressed doubt about our ability to
make sense of the great complexity of colonial development paths and
to adequately measure their multidimensionality. It is beyond the capacity of a cross-national study of this type to distinguish, for example,
between the land tenure systems that resulted from various colonial
development strategies. There is one element of colonial administration, however, which seems both theoretically important and tractable
from the standpoint of measurement and specification: we can capture
the distinctive approach to colonialism taken by the major colonial
powers. In particular, the British administrative style contrasts quite
sharply with the colonial patterns of the French, the Dutch, and the
Portuguese.

---

12. It is not known with precision how sensitive the results are to this choice, but a
cursory analysis suggests that the direction of the relationship is extremely robust and
the approximate strength is acceptably invariant with choice of time frame.

Table 9-1. Effects of postwar political independence

Variables	Simple r	Final contemporary model			Current model		
		Beta	St. beta	t	Beta	St. beta	t
% labor agriculture	−.87	−.51	−.50	−7.4***	−.50	−.49	−7.4***
Socialist × agr.	.24	.58	.26	7.2***	.55	.25	6.9***
Democracy	.47	.13	.14	3.2**	.15	.16	3.8***
Right × civilian	−.39	−.29	−.09	−2.9**	−.29	−.09	−2.9**
Military spending	.09	−1.66	−.22	−4.7***	−1.53	−.20	−4.3***
Military manpower	.38	.87	.22	4.8***	.85	.22	4.7***
Military regime	−.25	.08	.10	3.1**	.07	.09	2.8**
Periphery × trade	−.43	−.12	−.13	−3.8***	−.09	−.10	−2.7**
Mineral exports	−.12	−.07	−.07	−2.1*	−.07	−.07	−2.1*
Logged GNP/cap	.80	5.28	.25	3.8***	4.51	.21	3.2**
Plantations	.06	13.69	.16	5.2***	13.32	.16	5.2***
Independence	.60				4.74	.08	2.1*

Model	N	r	r^2	adj. r^2	SEE	F
Final contemporary model	120	.96	.91	.90	8.79	102.1***
Current model	120	.96	.92	.91	8.66	96.9***

*Significant (p < .05)
**Significant (p < .01)
***Significant (p < .001)

Elements of Colonial Administration

There are a number of causal pathways through which the identity of the colonial metrople may be expected to influence subsequent basic needs performance. Several of these involve the varying roles that settlers and other expatriates were to play in colonial development and the relationship those roles implied between the metropole and the indigenous population. Of course, in many colonies, expatriate groups were small and their functions were limited to administration and supervision of production. In fact, settlement was a major goal in relatively few areas, the most prominent cases being French migration to the Maghreb and British settlement of southern Africa and parts of East Africa. Still, in many other areas nonindigenous groups, though small, were the key to development planning, and their influence on political development, though not as profound as in the colonies of settlement, was nevertheless important.

There are discernible national differences in the orientation of nonindigenous groups. The British pattern is especially distinctive in the extent to which settlers and expatriates sought to carve out a political and social entity more or less autonomous from the home country. Of course the greatest expression of this pattern is to be found in the older colonies of North America, Australia, and New Zealand, but it is present in most of the British overseas possessions. By contrast, the French and Portuguese residents of their respective empires sought to faithfully recreate the home country in colonial enclaves. Moreover, it was expected that the civilization of the metropole could be slowly extended beyond the bastions of these expatriate communities, eventually so as to encompass the entire colonial empire. In the short term, the result was that the native population played little immediate role in the actual development of the colonies. Duffy (1970: 178) remarks baldly that "Africans in the Portuguese possessions were regarded mostly as an administrative problem."

By the late colonial period this difference in attitudes toward native populations was reflected in the mission perceived as implicit in the trusteeship role. In the British case, the fundamental relationship between the home country and the colony was one of paternalism between distinctive entities. The pronouncement of the British Cabinet in 1923 is indicative of official policy: "Primarily, Kenya is an African territory, and . . . the interests of the African natives must be paramount, and that . . . if, and when, those interests and the interests of the immigrant races should conflict, the former should prevail" (Baeta, 1970: 436). In this sense, the British role was one of protecting and guiding indigenous development. Although actual policy did not always faithfully adhere to declaratory criteria, these values were an obvious influence, in part due to the significant political weight of the missionary presence in supporting them (Oliver, 1967).

The French, by contrast, sought direct absorption of the colony into the French nation, through the policy of "assimilation" (Crowder, 1964; Morgenthau, 1964). Indeed, though the British unabashedly had their empire, the French insisted on describing their possessions and protectorates as "Overseas France" (Deschamps, 1970). A similar attitude is found in the colonies of other powers. For example, Baeta observes (1970: 433) that the Portuguese territories "have always been officially claimed as part and parcel of the metropolitan area situated overseas." Indeed, the idealism inherent in bringing Christianity and civilization to backward peoples was an important element of national pride. Duffy (1962) notes that "the Portuguese ideal has been that carefully controlled education will in time create an African populace that speaks only Portuguese, embraces Catholicism, and is as intensely Portuguese nationalist as citizens of the metropole." In reality, however, in the case of the French, Portuguese, and Belgians, Africans were held to be subjects of the metropole (Deschamps, 1970; Duffy, 1970; Anstey, 1970).

The difference between an assimilationist and a protectorate orientation also had its counterpart in the manner of governance. The British style of indirect rule allocated a greater role for native populations and encouraged the growth of local institutions. Local elites were active in a muted form of self-governance from the beginning of the colonial era (Kilson, 1970). Much of the local administration was placed in the hands of traditional chiefs, and over time the new educated elite gradually assumed a greater role (Post, 1970).

At the same time, Africans had greater rights to partake of political activities under the British than the French, whereas under the Portuguese and the Belgians, there was virtually no freedom at all in this respect (Anstey, 1970). For example, the legislative councils of British West Africa had appointed African members as early as the nineteenth century (1861 in the Gold Coast) (Young, 1970: 488). Indeed, a proto-democratic form existed within many British colonies. For example, a franchise—albeit a very limited one—was granted in the 1920s for election to these same legislative councils (Kilson, 1970). Though far from autonomous, indigenous elites thus retained enough authority and local institutions introduced enough political development to ease somewhat the burden of creating a polity from scratch at the moment of full independence from British rule.

Elsewhere, the "direct rule" style most often associated with the French was more common. The French certainly employed a much larger number of their own nationals in junior administrative posts than the British (Young, 1970: 494). Like the British, however, they were required to use native chiefs for much local administration. Still, even in this matter there are administrative differences; under the British the chiefs retained much of their traditional role, whereas the French turned them into the lowest level of colonial bureaucrat (Hargreaves, 1969). Nonetheless, the direct rule style actually reached its most extreme form in the case of the Portuguese, whose administrative personnel were much more numerous than those of the French (Crowder, 1970). The central Belgian administrative staff was also virtually entirely European, though in local matters the Belgians more nearly approached the British indirect rule style than any other colonial power.

The other colonial powers also offered less in the way of local institutions than the British. In some French colonies, Africans were appointed to the Chamber of Deputies and the Consultative Council in Paris, while French Equatorial Africa was ruled in a far more authoritarian fashion (Delavignette, 1970). After World War II, all French colonies had elected assemblies, though they grew from being consultative to deliberative to legislative rather slowly, as Paris remained the center of colonial administration. The Belgians and Portuguese did not permit native representation at any level.

Both the administrative structure and the attitudes toward assimilation no doubt had a profound impact on the course of future democratic development, especially in the immediate postcolonial period. Simply put, the former British colonies were far better prepared for independence than the others. A principal factor is the great difference in assumptions about the anticipated length of colonial rule. For the British, eventual independence had long been not only the expected outcome of its protectorate role, but the desired and planned-for future. The transition was eased by a formula dating from the Durham Report of 1839, the British North American Act of 1867, and the Statute of Westminster in 1931. By the time of postwar African decolonization, Britain had the precedents of North America, Australia, and Ceylon to point the way, and the structure of the British Commonwealth to assuage the sting of lost prestige.

By contrast, as late as 1960—when a good number of former British colonies were already independent or well on their way to becoming so—the official Portuguese policy remained that of indefinite colonialism: "We are in Africa and it is our duty to stay there, for ourselves, for the West to which we belong, for the peoples which have been entrusted to us and which have mingled with us in the same moral unity" (Fernandes, 1960: 262). The French position was similar though less rigid—with the notable exception of Algeria, whose independence was resisted with sufficient tenacity to threaten the very fabric of French democracy. The Brazzaville resolution of 1944 is instructive of the link between assimilationist aims and the absence of planning for the rigors of postcolonial independence: "The aims of the civilizing labours of France in the colonies exclude all possibilities of development outside the French imperial system; the eventual formation, even in the distant future of self-government in the colonies, must be excluded" (Young, 1970: 452).

Thus, it is no accident that the postcolonial era in French and, especially, Portuguese territories began later and was accompanied by greater violence than in former British areas. Indeed, while the British acknowledged the likelihood of eventual Indian independence as early as 1917—more than thirty years before the eventual fact—the first promise of independence for the Belgian Congo preceded final fulfillment by less than eighteen months. Thus, the approach of the French, Portuguese, and Belgians had an impact on subsequent basic needs performance through at least two pathways related to the decolonization process itself. First, without acknowledgment of a looming post-colonial future, there could be little planning for it. The results are seen in domestic political institutions that two decades after independence remain weak or nonexistent.

Second, the decolonization process itself left a legacy of militarism and violence. Though most dramatic in the far-reaching consequences of the triumph of nationalist forces in French Indochina, the leadership of the military forces involved in the independence struggle was everywhere influential in postcolonial states. This influence merely accentuated the pattern in which the role of the military even prior to decolonization was far greater in the French than the British territories. Certainly in absolute terms, French colonial armies were markedly larger (Gutteridge, 1970). Moreover, in French colonies, the military often provided the framework for civil administration and services. Most often the result has been detrimental to basic needs performance through mechanisms considered in earlier chapters. By contrast, the former British colonies more often inherited a tradition of civil government and democratic principles as well as an educated class of state personnel minimally capable of assuming command of at least partially formed political institutions.

Though data are inadequate to test the presumption, it seems likely that the basic needs gap extends quite far back in colonial history. The difference between an assimilationist approach and an attempt to foster more autonomous development also had implications for the type of native education that would take place. French "educational policy aimed at making it possible for those Africans who fulfilled the necessary requirements (i.e., by attaining certain levels of acculturation and affluence) to become full citizens of France" (Baeta, 1970: 432). By contrast, the British sought "to provide the African with better equipment for dealing with his own environment and to prepare him for the changes to which this environment will increasingly be subject" (Hailey, 1941: 72–73). The emphasis on cultural assimilation under the French shaped the character of the educational experience and prepared students for a much smaller range of careers. It is also evident that education was far more broadly available under British than French colonialism. For one thing, missionaries played a vital role in basic education, and missionaries were far more prevalent in British than in French colonies (Crowder, 1968; Kilson, 1970). Indeed, in the early part of the twentieth century, 90 percent of the primary education of British African colonies was in mission hands (Groves, 1969).

Missonaries were important in another sense as well. They were effective advocates of native interests in areas such as fiscal impositions and labor questions. In fact, "in British possessions, the clergymen's role as a watchdog often became institutionalized through formal representation on the legislative council" (Groves, 1969: 477). Enhanced basic human needs were often the direct object of such action and surely the result. More directly, missions were also a center for medical care, rudimentary medical training, and even training involving agricultural development (Yudelman, 1975). In the French colonies, early medical care was more often provided through the military (Lasker, 1977).

Through these various pathways, the distinctive national styles of colonialism can be assumed to have affected subsequent economic and political development in ways that have consequences for the provision of basic human needs. The bulk of the arguments seem to suggest that the British approach would yield a postcolonial political atmosphere more conducive to the spread of citizen welfare. In particular, more developed political institutions, a stronger tradition of welfare concern, and a more capable set of political elites form the hypothesized British legacy.

To test this contention, all nations still under colonial administration at the end of World War II were placed into one of three categories represented by dummy variables: British colonies, French colonies, and a miscellaneous category of Portuguese, Belgian, and Dutch. These dummy variables were then added to the model reported in Table 9-1. The results are unmistakable. The average PQLI of former British colonies exceeds that of other recent colonies by nearly seven points. At the same time, though, their PQLI net of other factors remains significantly below that of nations independent at the same time period. In fact, distinguishing the British colonies improves the overall fit of the model significantly, in part by reducing the error with which the parameter for independence is estimated. The new parameter for the long-independent nations—roughly 8.3—is much more significant than the estimate reported in Table 9-1.[13] Although the precise source of the superior basic needs performance of former British colonies cannot be established by a study of this kind, the mechanisms identified in the earlier discussion represent promising avenues for more detailed examination.

13. The reader is cautioned, however, that this does not signify an effect of greater magnitude, since the constant term also changes with this specification. The comparison group is no longer all colonies, but only the non-British colonies; thus, Table 9-2 tells us that independent nations, while enjoying a PQLI 8.3 points above non-British colonies, are only about 1.5 points above British colonies. By contrast, the parameter estimate of 4.7 reported in Table 9-1 represents the gap between independent nations and the remainder of the sample without disaggregating it.

Table 9-2. Effects of postwar colonial status

Variables	Simple r	Final contemporary model			Current model		
		Beta	St. beta	t	Beta	St. beta	t
% labor agriculture	−.87	−.51	−.50	−7.4***	−.48	−.47	−7.2***
Socialist × agr.	.24	.58	.26	7.2***	.54	.24	7.0***
Democracy	.47	.13	.14	3.2**	.13	.14	3.4***
Right × civilian	−.39	−.29	−.09	−2.9**	−.26	−.08	−2.6**
Military spending	.09	−1.66	−.22	−4.7***	−1.58	−.21	−4.6***
Military manpower	.38	.87	.22	4.8***	.85	.22	4.9***
Military regime	−.25	.08	.10	3.1**	.07	.08	2.6*
Periphery × trade	−.43	−.12	−.13	−3.8***	−.08	−.09	−2.5*
Mineral exports	−.12	−.07	−.07	−2.1*	−.08	−.08	−2.5*
Logged GNP/cap	.80	5.28	.25	3.8***	4.88	.23	3.5***
Plantations	.06	13.69	.16	5.2***	12.43	.15	4.9***
Independence	.60				8.34	.15	3.3**
British colony	−.13				6.86	.10	2.7**

Model	N	r	r^2	adj. r^2	SEE	F
Final contemporary model	120	.96	.91	.90	8.79	102.1***
Current model	120	.96	.92	.91	8.41	95.4***

*Significant (p < .05)
**Significant (p < .01)
***Significant (p < .001)

The robust and powerful model presented in Table 9-2 thus becomes the preferred representation of the cross-national determinants of basic human needs. The multiple r of nearly .96 and the standard error of 8.4 are striking testimony to the capacity of this political economy model to account for levels of basic human needs across a wide range of highly disparate cases marked by imperfect data and individual factors that defy generalization. Moreover, the model is theoretically compelling, with all factors related to basic needs by highly plausible theoretical mechanisms. If not a complete answer to the question with which we began—"what accounts for the disparity in basic needs attainment among the nations of the world?"—the arguments summarized in statistical form represent a promising theoretical and empirical framework within which further analysis can proceed.

Interpreting Regional Effects on Basic Needs

Before leaving the empirical investigation, however, we must consider one additional factor. For reasons not yet clear, nations in some parts of the globe are systematic overachievers while others lag behind even those expectations derived from the predictively powerful model in Table 9-2. Because the identification of the mechanisms responsible for this geographical pattern is highly speculative, it may be regarded at the moment as more a descriptive than an explanatory generalization. For that reason I introduce geographical patterns as the last element in this analysis of basic needs determinants and the first element in subsequent probes. In this case the empirical finding with which we would like to deal is indisputable, while the causal mechanisms responsible are diverse and, at our present state of knowledge, rather speculative. Thus I introduce a finding and follow it with several plausible theoretical explanations. This section, then, defines the next major step necessary for a comprehensive understanding of cross-national variance in basic needs levels.

The regional pattern itself is quite evident. Most strikingly, after controlling for the effects previously examined, the nations of Africa manifest much lower levels of basic needs provision than would be otherwise expected. Similarly, the nations of the Middle East underperform, though not so severely. Asian countries, by contrast, are markedly more successful than any other area, though Latin America also exhibits a certain degree of overperformance. The nations of Europe are insignificantly different from predictions and thus represent something of a baseline for our analysis.

Not all the contrasts are statistically significant, and there are several alternative combinations that accurately represent the main elements of the pattern. The most instructive fit—represented by the left side of Table 9-3—emphasizes the underperformance of Africa and the Middle East. That table shows that, on average, African nations have a PQLI about seventeen points below similar nations of Asia and Latin America, while the gap for Middle East countries is a little under eleven points. By contrast, the differences among the omitted categories—Europe, Asia, and Latin America—are not statistically significant.

The right columns of Table 9-3 illustrate the parameters of the final model when estimated after stepwise removal of variables no longer significant. There are two of these, neither of great theoretical importance. The first is the length of military government, a variable whose parameter estimate has never been large and whose theoretical justification has always been a bit elusive. The inclusion of the region dummies induces only a small parameter change, but one sufficient to drop the t value just below the .05 level of statistical significance.

The second variable removed is the interaction term between trade and periphery status. The reader will recall from Chapter 8 that this term represents the negative additive effect of both periphery status and trade, in addition to the negative interaction effect by which trade is more harmful in the periphery than elsewhere. It is thus not hard to

Table 9-3. Adding regional effects to historical model

Variables	Simple r	All variables			Significant variables		
		Beta	St. beta	t	Beta	St. beta	t
% labor agriculture	− .87	− .35	− .34	− 5.6***	− .35	−.34	− 5.6***
Socialist × agr.	.24	.41	.18	5.6***	.38	.17	5.4***
Democracy	.47	.10	.11	3.0**	.10	.10	2.9**
Right × civilian	− .39	− .22	− .07	− 2.6*	− .22	− .07	− 2.6*
Military spending	.09	− 1.03	− .14	− 3.2**	− .86	− .11	− 2.8**
Military manpower	.38	.60	.15	3.8***	.56	.14	3.6***
Military regime	− .25	.03	.03	1.2			
Periphery × trade	− .43	− .04	− .05	− 1.6			
Mineral exports	− .12	− .09	− .09	− 3.1**	− .10	− .10	− 3.6***
Logged GNP/cap	.80	5.91	.28	4.8***	5.52	.26	4.6***
Plantations	.06	7.68	.09	3.3**	6.37	.08	2.9**
Independence	.60	3.70	.06	1.6	4.89	.09	2.1*
British colony	− .13	5.89	.08	2.7**	6.32	.09	2.9**
Africa	− .73	− 15.82	− .25	− 5.9***	− 17.46	− .27	− 6.8***
Middle East	− .16	− 9.99	− .12	− 3.7***	− 10.65	− .13	− 4.0***

Model	N	r	r^2	adj. r^2	SEE	F
All variables	120	.97	.94	.93	7.29	112.3***
Significant variables	120	.97	.94	.93	7.35	127.5***

*Significant (p < .05)
**Significant (p < .01)
***Significant (p < .001)

see why the inclusion of an African dummy variable would lower the variable's apparent predictive value. Because the roster of periphery countries with open economies is so heavily African, multicollinearity between the two terms reduces the statistical significance of both. From the standpoint of compelling theory I would prefer to retain a role for the periphery category rather than the more theoretically ambiguous region dummy, but from the standpoint of a prediction equation, the latter is more effective.

As a prediction equation, the model specification of Table 9-3 is impressive indeed. However, its predictive power—a multiple r of .97, an adjusted r^2 of .94, and a standard error of only 7.34—is no longer matched by a compelling theoretical explanation. I consider, in turn, three plausible mechanisms that could be responsible for these regional patterns and thus could permit us to think of this model as fully explanatory—if still somewhat speculative—rather than merely descriptive. The first two of these explanations are broadly economic in nature, while the third is more directly cultural.

First, the difference may result from variance in the organization of rural production and distributions of asset holding which are known to follow regional patterns. Several dimensions of this issue have been touched on in various parts of the previous discussion. The economies of Africa have retained a markedly larger subsistence sector than is found elsewhere. Even after consideration of the collinear effect of labor force shares and GNP figures, this factor alone is known to account for considerable variance.

Moreover, even in the cash crop sector, the production function of Africa is unique. Most obviously, the capital/labor ratio is extremely low throughout Africa and, especially in relation to Asia, the labor/land ratio is also exceptionally low. The systematic effect of these factors on welfare provision is well beyond the bounds of this study, though the economic effects of asset concentrations and factor intensities on rural poverty have been examined elsewhere (Lipton, 1977; Griffin, 1981). One frequently cited pattern—the greater efficiency and equality of small landholding production—offers one insight into the superior performance of most Asian nations. Furthermore, the social and political consequences of alternative agrarian structures have been much discussed (Moore, 1966; de Janvry, 1981; Paige, 1975, 1985; de Silva, 1982; Magubane, 1985; Ake, 1981). Speculatively, the hacienda culture spawned by the latifundio system of Latin America, for example, provides a means of redistribution which is rooted in neither the market nor state-level politics, thus overcoming more negative basic needs propensities of such highly unequal systems via another path.

A second possibility has been offered by proponents of ecological-evolutionary theory (Lenski, 1966; Lenski and Lenski, 1974; Nolan, 1983; Nolan and White, 1985). This view emphasizes the long-term impact of technoeconomic development, especially the level that had been reached by nations by the time of incorporation into the global division of labor. It is claimed that the disruptive impact of this penetration is mediated by the preexisting institutional and resource base of the penetrated political economy. In particular, so-called horticultural systems would be wholly unable to resist or deflect the intrusion of the world system and the resulting distortion of fundamental social patterns involving fertility and mortality. By contrast, "agrarian" societies—more "preadapted" to basic change—are better able to cope, suffer fewer vital traumas, and respond more vigorously to changing circumstances. Thus, for example, mortality and fertility respond more quickly to subsequent development, so that the demographic transition—which is known to lag GNP change and to assume a dangerous disequilibrium in dependent countries (Hout, 1980)—is less dramatically affected.

Nolan and White (1985) demonstrate that such a pattern—whose implications for basic needs levels are obvious—does appear to exist.

From the point of view of this analysis, the interesting feature of this research concerns the operationalization of the independent variable. The list of 31 vulnerable "horticultural" societies, which suffer greatest disruption of vital rates, is entirely African, while the list of 45 more resistant "agrarian" societies contains 21 Latin American nations, 18 Asian nations, and only 6 among those coded Middle Eastern in our sample. In essence, then, the Nolan and White research represents an approximate replication of the findings of Table 9-3, though without the elaborate controls and with a different conceptualization of the major variables: African nations lag Asian and Latin American nations in performance measures relevant to basic needs. Their theoretical explanation—preexisting technoeconomic development—may be the correct interpretation of this regional pattern. Unfortunately, no adequate data exist which would enable us to more directly and accurately test these competing contentions. In addition to the collinearity necessarily involved in regional patterns, these claims involve sufficient temporal distance and ambiguity in mechanism to make definitive judgments impossible.

A third interpretation—involving culture and religion—is more speculative yet, though crude data exist which offer a very preliminary indication that the speculation may contain a kernel of truth. Cultural and religious factors are known to follow an approximate regional pattern. In particular, Latin America is predominantly Christian and the Middle East largely Islamic. Africa (south of the equator) and Asia are less simply characterized, but they are obviously distinctive both from one another and the previous areas. Since these religious boundaries conform roughly to broad-gauge cultural traditions, a preliminary analysis seems justified.

Though obviously very crude, at least three plausible linkages suggest themselves. First, Islamic culture maintains an extraordinarily rigid division in the treatment of the sexes, which may impede basic needs fulfillment. The constraining effects of this cultural influence may be both direct and indirect. Any inequality—whether class, sectoral, geographic, or sexual—will lower basic needs relative to a society in which resources and therefore life chances are more evenly distributed. Moreover, given the importance of women in all development processes—especially their particular centrality to problems of infant mortality, health care, and nutrition—discrimination in the treatment of women can be expected to have major consequences for basic needs.

Second, the impact of Iberian Catholic culture in Latin America has been associated with two sets of values which may affect basic needs. Dealy (1977) insists that the bundle of norms represented by the conception of the "public man" profoundly influences networks of extended kinship and patron-client relations by imbuing social relationships with a normative and an aesthetic dimension. The net result seems to be an encouragement of a nonmarket, nonstate form for the provision of collective goods and limited, small-scale distribution functions. A more direct religious impact is the linkage recognized by Hout (1980) between fertility patterns and cultural norms associated with Catholic doctrine. The net impact is hard to assess, but a spur to relative basic needs performance is a plausible, if speculative, consequence.

A third religious/cultural connection involves the role of Buddhism in many Asian countries. It is not entirely clear what basic needs linkage may be at work here, though the Buddhist reverence for literacy and education may be the principal factor. In this case especially, the major source of the speculation lies in the empirical rather than the theoretical realm. Though Buddhism is dominant in relatively few nations, the particular nations involved have such a distinctive basic needs record that a causal connection has to be entertained. On the basis of the model of Table 9-3, for example, the nation with the largest positive deviation from expected PQLI level is Thailand. A second Buddhist society, Sri Lanka, is perhaps the best-known example of a society whose basic needs performance exceeds expectations based on GNP (Morris, 1979; Streeten, 1981), and its PQLI exhibits the fourth greatest positive deviation. In the same vein, the two largest negative deviations are Pakistan and Afghanistan, both Islamic countries.

In order to test the religious interpretation of regional patterns, dummy variables were created for the major religious groupings. The original coding is that of Blondel (1969), who identifies nine Buddhist countries and twenty-nine Islamic nations; the former are all Asian, and the latter are centered in the Middle East grouping but also contain nations coded as African and Asian. Although the codings are far from free of controversy, they appear adequate for a first-cut analysis such as this one. Only these two religious variables are at all helpful for predicting basic needs levels, so the analysis presented in Table 9-4 omits the others. It is immediately apparent that these religious groupings are remarkably accurate predictors of relative basic needs levels. In fact, controlling for other factors, Buddhist nations average over thirteen PQLI points above nations in the omitted categories and Islamic nations more than four points below them. The direct comparison between the "regional" model depicted on the left side of Table 9-4 (which duplicates the left side of Table 9-3) and the "religious" model presented on the right side demonstrates that the latter is nearly as predictively powerful as the former.

There are other criteria to be considered, of course. Neither model

Table 9-4. Comparing regional and religious additions to historical model

Variables	Simple r	Regional model			Religious model		
		Beta	St. beta	t	Beta	St. beta	t
% labor agriculture	−.87	−.35	−.34	−5.6***	−.45	−.44	−7.7***
Socialist × agr.	.24	.41	.18	5.6***	.47	.21	6.7***
Democracy	.47	.10	.11	3.0**	.09	.10	2.6**
Right × civilian	−.39	−.22	−.07	−2.6*	−.30	−.10	−3.5*
Military spending	.09	−1.03	−.14	−3.2**	−1.47	−.19	−4.7***
Military manpower	.38	.60	.15	3.8***	.69	.18	4.4***
Military regime	−.25	.03	.03	1.2	.04	.05	1.7
Periphery × trade	−.43	−.04	−.05	−1.6	−.08	−.09	−2.8**
Mineral exports	−.12	−.09	−.09	−3.1**	−.07	−.06	−2.2*
Logged GNP/cap	.80	5.91	.28	4.8***	5.96	.28	4.7***
Plantations	.06	7.68	.09	3.3**	11.74	.14	5.3***
Independence	.60	3.70	.06	1.6	8.03	.14	3.5***
British colony	−.13	5.89	.08	2.7**	6.96	.10	3.1**
Africa	−.73	−15.82	−.25	−5.9***			
Middle East	−.16	−9.99	−.12	−3.7***			
Buddhism	.07				13.41	.13	4.5***
Islam	−.42				−4.08	−.06	−2.1*

Model	N	r	r^2	adj. r^2	SEE	F
Regional model	120	.97	.94	.93	7.29	112.3***
Religious model	120	.97	.94	.93	7.42	108.2***

*Significant (p < .05)
**Significant (p < .01)
***Significant (p < .001)

meets the standard of theoretical clarity represented by the model of Table 9-2, for example. The relationships involving region and religion may be causal, but given the rather weak specificity of our theoretical contentions it seems best to treat these as merely preliminary and suggestive findings. Even so, there are grounds on which to choose between these two models. The religious dummies are somewhat more satisfying theoretically in that they reference a rather more concrete causal mechanism. Moreover, a comparison of the coefficients reveals that the religious dummies are considerably less disruptive of the earlier model estimates than are the regional dummies. The reason is simply that region is more highly correlated with many of the other independent variables, though seldom are those relationships properly causal ones. Generally speaking, single-dimensional predictor variables are preferable to multidimensional ones, which complicate our theoretical formulation by offering multiple interpretations.

Indeed, that very preference motivated the addition of the religious element, principally as an attempt to clarify the source of the geographical patterns observed earlier. The major task is to determine if the religious variables supersede the regional ones; therefore both religious and geographical dummies are entered into the same equation in order to assess the independent contribution of each. Our capabilities, however, are much reduced by collinearities among the predictor variables. The difficulty is twofold. First, assessment of the relative predictive power of collinear variables is constrained by the instability of the coefficients. The partitioning of variance explained is highly dependent on the relatively few cases that exhibit distinctive values on the collinear variables. In its pure form, this classic estimation problem does not arise here because the collinearity is statistically relatively modest. A related problem does occur, however. As we see below, the risks of spurious correlation rise with the homogeneity of these critical groups with respect to unmeasured but potentially relevant other variables. With this limitation in mind, there is evidence that some—but not all— of the region effects can be interpreted as cultural and religious in nature.

On the one hand, the sharply negative African effect remains, despite the collinearity produced by the presence of nine nations coded as both African and Islamic. This collinearity does not greatly diminish the predictive power of either factor; instead, they seem to operate additively and independently. Indeed, one result is that this analysis succeeds in accurately accounting for the horrible basic needs performance of the nations of the Sahel, which appear to suffer the ill effects of both their African and Islamic identities (in addition to their other economic and political attributes, few of which are conducive to basic needs provision). The impact of the Sahel nations on this analysis illustrates the above problem of interpretation, however. It may well be that factors specific to the Sahel produce the poor basic needs performance that has such great leverage on the choice between alternative interpretations of regional effects.

Similar technical problems erode our confidence in the conclusions concerning the other regional dummies, but it does appear that the cultural groupings have reduced or eliminated their effects. In the case of the Middle East, the average PQLI remains somewhat below expectations, but the gap is no longer statistically significant ($t = -1.0$). The case of Asia is even more striking; it appears that the fine basic needs performance ascribed to Asian countries in general is actually found in only the nine countries coded as Buddhist. The five Islamic countries of Asia actually perform slightly worse than comparable countries of the Middle East, though the difference is not significant. The remaining three—India, Nepal, and the Philippines—are also below average.

Given the technical problems noted above and the ambiguity in cod-

Table 9-5. Final prediction model

Variables	Simple r	All variables			Significant variables		
		Beta	St. beta	t	Beta	St. beta	t
% labor agriculture	−.87	−.36	−.35	−6.5***	−.36	−.35	−6.5***
Socialist × agr.	.24	.42	.19	6.7***	.41	.19	6.8***
Democracy	.47	.09	.09	2.8**	.09	.09	2.8**
Right × civilian	−.39	−.28	−.09	−3.6***	−.28	−.09	−3.6***
Military spending	.09	−1.26	−.17	−4.4***	−1.22	−.16	−4.4***
Military manpower	.38	.53	.14	3.7***	.51	.13	3.7***
Military regime	−.25	.01	.01	.6			
Periphery × trade	−.43	−.06	−.07	−2.4*	−.06	−.07	−2.4**
Mineral exports	−.12	−.08	−.07	−2.8**	−.08	−.07	−2.8*
Logged GNP/cap	.80	5.94	.28	5.3***	5.84	.27	5.3***
Plantations	.06	8.47	.10	4.0***	8.30	.10	4.0***
Independence	.60	3.48	.06	1.5	3.58	.06	1.6
British colony	−.13	5.38	.08	2.6**	5.47	.08	2.7**
Buddhism	.07	9.42	.09	3.4**	9.65	.09	3.5***
Islam	−.42	−6.88	−.10	−3.7***	−6.92	−.11	−3.8***
Africa	−.73	−12.36	−.19	−5.1***	−12.68	−.20	−5.4

Model	N	r	r^2	adj. r^2	SEE	F
All variables	120	.98	.95	.94	6.67	127.3***
Significant variables	120	.98	.95	.94	6.64	136.7***

*Significant (p < .05)
**Significant (p < .01)
***Significant (p < .001)

ing some of these countries, it is not clear how much more we know than before about the source of these geographical patterns.[14] Indeed, without a better specification of causal mechanisms, it is possible we have just replaced a geographical mystery with a religious mystery, both of which are theoretically spurious. Still, this is a start from which other researchers may build, whether the tentative conclusions found here are sustained or not. In any case, the addition of these variables has had two impacts. First, it has improved the prediction equation, shown in the final model of Table 9-5, which we can use to assess data problems or other irregularities. Second, because the additions have had so few implications for the previous model estimates, it has secured our confidence in the validity, robustness, and theoretical value of the model presented in Table 9-2.

14. These regional boundaries reflect many other patterns. For example, they also delineate food zones, which may affect basic health via nutrition (McHale and McHale, 1978: 66–75).

Conclusion: Political Economy and Basic Needs

Principles

The statistical model presented in Chapter 9 is a robust and powerful predictor of cross-national variation in basic human needs attainment. Moreover, the model is theoretically compelling in that all of the factors are related to basic needs by highly plausible theoretical mechanisms. Thus, although significant questions remain, we can be confident that the model presented in Table 9-2 is more than a prediction equation: it provides a theoretically informed, rigorously tested, and empirically reliable understanding of the complex determination of basic needs levels.

The building of the model also has focused our attention on aspects of development best seen from the bottom up. To capture these insights I return to the theoretical premises concerning the dynamics of basic needs provision and economic development with which the study began. With the basic model complete, we are now able to revisit these theoretical premises and the methodological assumptions to which they gave rise. Reassessing our starting point can also shed light on aspects of developmental processes that go beyond basic needs issues. Two principles central to the previous analysis are each discussed in more detail in subsequent sections.

First, economic development is neither a single, universal, unidimensional process nor an idiosyncratic experience unique to each nation. Instead we must conceive of several different development paths, each characterized by somewhat different social and political profiles—

a dimension that growth-centric analyses tend to overlook in their focus on GNP.

Second, the role of the state in shaping distributional outcomes is important, but the state cannot be considered separate from the political economy from which it arises. State policy seldom has either the leverage or the autonomy to fully negate the dynamics of the economy and, even when it does, its motivation to affect processes such as basic needs must be provided by concrete forces. Narrowly defined policy analysis misses the critical phenomena, which lie in the realm of political economy.

Both of these themes must also be seen in the context of the unavoidable tension between the conception of political economy dynamics informing the study and the organization of this volume. In order to allow a focused theoretical exposition and a tractable empirical analysis, I have considered—in turn and largely in isolation—four sets of determinants of basic needs levels: economic structure (in Chapters 3 and 4), state-level political processes (in Chapters 5, 6, and 7), external ties (Chapter 8), and colonial histories (Chapter 9). Yet, as noted briefly at several junctures, these four blocks of forces are hardly independent of one another. In this chapter, we must complete our picture of development dynamics by more directly acknowledging the causal connections among these blocks and by focusing the empirical analysis in greater detail on the linkages between them.

Development Path and Basic Needs Performance

Despite the predictable curvilinear relationship between the PQLI and GNP chronicled in Chapter 3, we cannot be satisfied with the representation of development as a single universal process. Economic development is an umbrella concept and GNP a rough guide to only one dimension of it—growth in price-denominated output. Indeed, though GNP represents a dimension that is primary from the standpoint of some theoretical interests, my focus gives emphasis to those dimensions most central to the processes that shape social and political change, distributive patterns, and, through them, basic needs levels. Thus, when restricted to a unidimensional representation the analysis has used a measure of sectoral labor force structure in place of GNP.

The use of *any single* metric, however, to represent multiple dimensions of development overly simplifies the process and obscures variations in national experiences. Consequently, I have sought patterns in these variations in the form of alternative *paths* of development, partly distinguished from one another by reference to forces discussed in the

later chapters. In particular, theories of dependency and radical political economy identify differential development paths rooted in origins
going back to the dominant economic structure and political arrangements of an earlier age. Among economic forms, we can distinguish
development centered around the plantation, the factory, the mine,
and the farm. Implicit are differences in the centrality of trade and
characteristics of its product and partner composition. Also significant
are the political forms associated with alternative colonial histories.

These paths, shaped by historical and/or external forces, are marked
in part by the characteristic profiles of social and political forces associated with them. The discussion of Chapter 9 concerning the social and
political dynamics set in motion by early reliance on the plantation as
an economic form illustrates the extent to which alternative development paths affect basic needs levels via social and political mechanisms, some of which are represented by the other variables in the
model. Although we cannot go into such detail with each of the alternative paths, several observations illustrate the approach further research must take to clarify the dynamics that underlie basic needs provision.

That is, we are now in a position to note not only that basic needs
achievement is more rapid and regular along certain paths than others,
but to begin to untangle the social and political mechanisms partly responsible. In the process, I consider the structural roots of the other
social and political factors we now know to be potent predictors of
basic needs levels. While basic needs performance must be seen to depend on government policy choices and other autonomous social, political, or cultural factors, we must now attempt to assess how autonomous these effects may be. The chapter organization of this volume
may have created visions of independent economic, political, external,
and colonial determinants of basic needs, like the rays split apart by a
prism; but we must now attempt to reassemble a coherent picture of
the general causal structure.

The overwhelming importance of the *structure* of the economy—not
merely its level of output—can be illustrated in several ways. Even
without an elaboration of structural forms, the sectoral distribution of
the labor force is a more prominent landmark in the development land-
scape composed for our welfare-centric eye than is aggregate output.
We have known since Chapter 4 that the sectoral labor shift is a more
powerful predictor of PQLI than growth in GNP per capita; income
growth without structural change does not much improve basic needs
levels. We are now in a position to see some of the explanation for that:
income growth without structural change also does not trigger the political processes known to affect basic needs levels. Labor force share is

a superior predictor of each of the political variables contained in the final model: levels of democracy, the large rightist state, military spending, and troop levels. Further, it also better predicts virtually all of the other social and political determinants discussed in Chapters 5 through 7 but not included in the final model because of sample size limitations or relatively weak predictive power: the strength of the labor movement, the ideological basis of the party system, the political importance of the middle class and traditional elites, urban growth, size of the subsistence sector, and fertility rates.

From the standpoint of understanding the development process, however, the most obvious statistical observation—that sectoral labor force shares are a more reliable predictor of social and political outcomes than GNP—is not the most important. By examining the relationship among these variables when the effect of logged GNP is controlled, we can identify aspects of the social and political profile associated with nations possessing different economic structures. We are especially interested in the retention of a larger share of the labor force in agriculture than would be expected on the basis of monetized aggregate output—a pattern that can arise along a variety of development paths. If industrial production is more capital-intensive and less labor-intensive than is common, the productivity of the industrial sector will drive aggregate national product to a higher level than labor force shares would predict. Such a pattern is thought to be common in the most dualistic economies: those with a technologically advanced, export-oriented enclave. Dualism also can arise when an unusually unproductive agricultural sector—such as one that retains a high subsistence component—leaves a higher population in the agricultural sector than one would expect at any given GNP level.

However it occurs, GNP growth without sectoral labor force shifts has consequences that are interesting indeed. After controlling for logged GNP per capita, large labor force shares in agriculture are associated with massively lower levels of basic needs attainment ($r =$ $-.59$). Some of the mechanisms responsible are similarly clear since such a pattern is associated with a lower incidence of democracy ($-.26$), a weaker labor movement ($-.37$), less class-differentiated party structure ($-.34$), less social insurance program experience ($-.27$), a weaker middle class ($-.60$), and a higher fertility rate ($+.37$).[1] More-

1. All of the reported coefficients are significant at the .005 level, most at the .001 level. Other effects having somewhat weaker impacts include lower levels of urbanization ($-.40$), lower levels of military spending ($-.13$), and a larger state sector ($+.26$). A path analysis depicting these intermediate effects would be desirable, but unhappily the high incidence of missing data on several of them would make it potentially misleading. The

over, elaborations of economic structure which take account of the historical and external dimensions also contribute to our understanding of the incidences of these intermediate social and political mechanisms. As my previous analyses have suggested, development centered around the plantation and the factory produces relatively more effective basic needs provision than development centered around the mine and subsistence agriculture.

Earlier, the prominence of the subsistence sector was observed to predict relatively low basic needs attainment: its impact on PQLI is strongly negative even after controlling for logged GNP ($-.69$) or labor force structure ($-.45$). Some of the explanation can be seen in the distinctive social and political profile of nations with such an economic feature. Even controlling for labor force in agriculture, both the labor movement ($-.28$) and the middle class ($-.39$) are weaker in such systems, and both democracy ($-.22$) and a developed party structure ($-.27$) are less frequent.[2]

Nations specializing in mineral exports are also dramatic underachievers relative to expectations based on either the sectoral labor force ($-.35$) or GNP per capita ($-.38$). In part this failure appears to result from quite distinctive state sector effects: mineral exporters are marked by a considerably larger state ($+.29$), yet less social insurance program experience ($-.21$). Perhaps most telling, the partial correlation between mineral exports and the interaction between state size and rightist norms is $+.36$.

Clearly, mineral exporting is an especially damaging type of peripheral trade, but we can now partially interpret the finding that development relying on other forms of periphery trade is also harmful to basic needs provision. Even after controlling for labor force share, various components of the peripheral pattern are related to known predictors of basic needs levels. The interaction between peripheral status and trade level (as a percentage of GNP), for example, predicts to a significantly larger state ($+.15$) yet a dramatically lower incidence of social insurance program experience ($-.47$); the partial correlation with the large rightist state is a telling $+.22$. Commodity concentration leads to significantly lower levels of democracy ($-.13$) and greatly exacerbates the tendency of trade to increase state size ($+.30$) yet decrease social insurance programs ($-.37$). Like trade more generally, commodity

---

coefficients were calculated for quite different subsamples with N sizes ranging from 120 to 69. Path analysis coefficients would need to be computed over only those cases without missing data on any of the variables—a sample of fewer than 40.

2. Military governments are also less frequent ($-.30$), but military spending tends to be somewhat more capital-intensive though not significantly greater in size.

concentration is also associated with a higher incidence of military governments ($+.25$) and increased likelihood of the capital-intensive pattern of military expenditures ($+.12$) that has been seen to lower basic needs levels. Finally, when controlled for the structure of the labor force, the presence of multinational corporations, another dimension of the periphery trade syndrome, predicts to a lower PQLI ($-.17$), in part because of its similar impact on the large rightist state ($+.26$) and social insurance program experience ($-.22$).[3] As noted in Chapter 8, these reinforcing effects are sufficiently small individually that they are best represented collectively by the peripheral status dummy in interaction with trade size.

In short, the picture of development suggested by this analysis challenges the stylized facts depiction of a single universal development path. Instead, development may occur along any of several paths, beginning from a number of diverse starting points. These findings also suggest that paths of development defined by economic form correspond to trajectories of social change and political development. For the most part, the complexity of these dynamics together with limitations in data availability and the scope of this study prohibit a rigorous effort to capture them statistically in any more elaborate form. The structural roots identified here constitute only a small portion of the explanation for most of these developments. This limitation is hardly surprising since the focus of the book on basic needs performance dictates that the variables included in the analysis are those most relevant to those issues. A more explicit emphasis on democracy or spending priorities, for example, would surely reveal other major determinants, but it appears that such political dimensions, though hardly autonomous of economic ones, are far from completely determined by them either.

Political Economy Perspectives on the State

Still, I would not want to leave this topic without acknowledging that the political economy perspective reminds us that the state must be considered both an independent and a dependent variable. It is certainly a key institution with limited, though real, autonomy to affect social outcomes and alter its own face. Yet the state also has deep structural roots that make it a visible manifestation of more elusive and perhaps ultimately more powerful forces. While we cannot pursue this

---

3. Multinational corporations also predict to slightly greater democracy ($+.19$) and lower levels of both military spending ($-.27$) and troop levels ($-.25$).

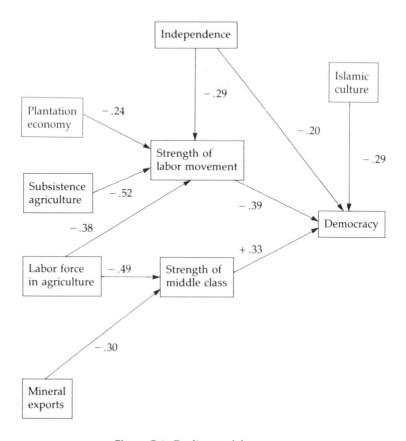

Figure C-1. Predictors of democracy

subject in great depth, a partial analysis should serve to illustrate the point.

Figure C-1 offers one representation of this complexity in the form of a path analysis with the determination of levels of democracy as the dependent variable. The independent variables are organized into three blocks: economic structures, social structures, and political and social origins. The first—which includes mineral exports, the share of the labor force in agriculture, and the presence of plantation and sub-sistence agriculture sectors—affects levels of democracy principally through its impact on the social structures of the second block. The factors represented in this second block—the strength of the middle class and the labor movement—are intervening variables that are shaped by the other two blocks and, in turn, affect the degree of democracy. The third block—composed of dummy variables for Islamic culture and independence from colonial rule—affects levels of democracy both directly and indirectly. Although the system is far from closed, and data limitations shrink the sample to seventy-one cases, the status of democracy as a partial consequence of structural roots is established by an r^2 indicating that 56 percent of the variance in democracy is explained by these variables.

Thus, proponents of democracy cannot ignore the impediments suggested by these relationships nor democracy's relatively low frequency in societies lacking the traditional preconditions. Democracy is not routinely possible—or at least not likely—in all structural settings. The findings of this analysis concerning the role of democracy and the political system must always be seen in this light. Advocates of political designing to help the poor through indirect means must understand this limitation. Though democracy helps basic needs levels, the extent to which democracy is historically associated with certain economic and social preconditions limits the ability to wield this tool as effectively as our earlier regression equation might seem to suggest. Not only can democracy not be created by force of will alone—most especially from the outside—but it also cannot deliver on the basis of institutional structure only. When the effort is made, most often the democratic structure is exposed as more fragile than the resistant constellation of societal forces. The consequences for the advent of domestic political conflict, military interventions, and rightist backlashes make the analysis difficult to net out; suffice it to say that the democratic option is promising, but the road is long and hard.

Thus, there are sharp limits to what can be done by government policy. Conditions of basic needs attainment are heavily bound by inertia and enormously resistant to rapid change. Further, the constraints on government are especially severe in areas involving redistribution of social wealth, power, and well-being. Vested interests are successful in resisting fundamental change, not least because they are strongly represented by the state itself.

Moreover, the effect of state policy must be relatively small because basic needs levels are relatively slowly changing phenomena. As our earlier analysis indicated, PQLI levels of 1960 and 1980, for example, are correlated above +.95. Even with the effect of GNP removed, the relative basic needs performance of a nation in 1980 is correlated above +.85 with the parallel measure of twenty years previously.[4] Thus,

---

4. "Relative" basic needs performance is computed as the residual from a regression of

when the final model is applied in a panel design, the political effects are small, though they do conform in general to the cross-sectional findings.

The relatively small apparent effect of these political variables on short-term change suggests that the causal consequences of state policy are too small to be easily measured unless "aggregated across time." Impacts are aggregated across time by the cross-sectional research design, which permits long-term adjustment, while the panel design partitions basic needs levels into that increment produced after 1960, which is retained in the dependent variable, and that achieved prior to 1960, which is lumped into the lagged dependent variable. Worse yet, panel designs attribute to this serial term variance it can predict without being able to causally explain—the PQLI improvements proportional to prior performance. With a focus on PQLI levels within a cross-sectional design, the accumulated effects of the political system on basic needs provision prior to 1960 remain visible rather than being stripped from the analysis.

Though we must concede that major barriers to basic needs improvements are structural, there is still an area in which state policy can matter. Within this realm, theoretical understandings are no doubt key in shaping the perceptions of trade-offs, which have always cast a long shadow on efforts to improve the welfare of the poor. Trade-offs do exist—that much is confirmed by this analysis—but they are not necessarily the ones identified by orthodox liberal theory and they do not necessarily dominate the complementarities that also clearly exist. Most explicitly, Chapter 3 showed that basic needs improvements do not slow economic growth; indeed, nations with relatively good basic needs attainments grow more rapidly than underachievers. It is to be hoped that policy planners will apply this finding to their judgments about appropriate developmental directions.

But our analysis of the effects of individual programs suggests that limitations in technical know-how or mistaken calculations concerning the welfare impacts of programs are not the chief barriers to effective state action to raise basic needs levels. Instead, the choice of a political economy rather than a policy analysis approach has been vindicated by these analyses, which yield two conclusions. First, the effect of individual programs is too small to be discerned amid the noise of internation

---

PQLI upon GNP in that same year. The cited correlation is between the residual from the 1960 regression and the residual from the 1980 regression. This method removes both GNP level and GNP growth as the source of serial correlation, leaving an enduring propensity of a nation to better or poorer basic needs provision than found in the sample as a whole.

Table C-1. Determinants of social insurance program experience

Variables	Simple r	Economic variables			All variables		
		Beta	St. beta	t	Beta	St. beta	t
% labor agriculture	− .74	− .42	− .25	− 1.9	− .32	− .19	− 1.5
Logged GNP/cap	.67	20.78	.59	4.6***	17.81	.50	4.1***
Trade percentage	− .12	− .34	− .21	− 3.3***	− .31	− .19	− 3.2***
Multinational corps.	− .13	− .05	− .12	− 1.8	− .04	− .09	− 1.5
Socialist	.28				35.16	.22	3.3***
Democracy	.39				.37	.22	3.1***

Model	N	r	r^2	adj. r^2	SEE	F
Economic variables	109	.82	.67	.65	27.96	51.6***
All variables	109	.84	.70	.69	26.55	40.4***

*Significant (p < .05)
**Significant (p < .01)
***Significant (p < .001)

variation and measurement error. Only by characterizing the state in terms of its basic structural form and ideological orientation can we "aggregate across programs" sufficiently to show the impact of policy on welfare outcomes. Second, this very step demonstrates that the commitment of the state to such programs is predictable from more general characteristics of both the state and the political economy in which it is embedded.

In this respect, the effect of social insurance program experience (SIPE) is instructive. Its zero-order correlation with PQLI (.76) and its partial correlation after controlling for GNP (.38) suggest it is a major influence on basic needs levels, though its effect is visible only in the absence of a fully specified model. As other political effects are added—democracy, ideology, and so on—the parameter estimate for the SIPE variable recedes into insignificance. The obvious conclusion is that SIPE is one of the many mechanisms—each exerting individually small impact—whereby the form of the political system translates into social welfare outcomes.

Indeed, SIPE is nearly as predictable from economic and political structures as is the PQLI itself. The models estimated in Table C-1 represent the major linkages. The left side shows that economic structures (labor force structure, trade levels, GNP, and the presence of multinational corporations) combine to explain more than 65 percent of the variance. The model presented on the right side adds aspects of the political system (democracy and a dummy variable for state socialism) as a further determinant. Finally, in an analysis not shown, the addition of regional and colonial effects completes a prediction equation yielding an r^2 of more than .78.[5] It is quite evident that social insurance programs, no doubt like many other aspects of state policy, should not be seen as an autonomous path to welfare outcomes. Instead, they constitute a mechanism by which the distributional imperatives of social and political structures are expressed.

Validating Methodological Premises

At this juncture, it would be well to revisit the methodological premises that constitute the framework of the study and the context within which the conclusions must be understood. In particular, several of these theoretical observations relate to methodological issues that can be thoroughly evaluated now that the study is complete. First, both the cross-sectional design of our model and the sequential way it was built are adequate for representing the main lines of basic human needs determination. In particular, the design can represent histories without encountering the problems of time-series or panel designs. Second, a universal sample of nations is an appropriate choice because the processes that shape basic needs can be represented by a single equation even though they vary somewhat in relative weight at different levels of development. Third, data problems are not disabling.

The premise that a cross-sectional model rather than a time-series model of basic needs processes would be more enlightening can be fully evaluated only at this point in the analysis. As noted in Chapter 2, the choice between these two approaches hinges on both technical questions concerning the measures themselves and theoretical questions concerning the processes being modeled. A time-series or panel design, which analyzes change rather than levels, is preferable if the change rate is more important theoretically or substantively than the level of the variable. Such a design also avoids simultaneity bias in the model estimation if the causal direction of the relationships among the variables can be easily mistaken. Where there is clear temporal priority between the predictor variables and the outcome variables, this approach is not required for technical purposes. Moreover, long causal lags and slow-moving outcomes are contraindications of a time-centric model. The former inhibit accurate model specification and the latter minimize the relevance of change relative to level.

The theoretical specification of basic needs causes and the statistical model of PQLI predictors now make it clear that the process conforms

5. The alternative representation of a path diagram would also illustrate the degree to which the economic structures affect these characteristics of the state, but the relatively modest strength of the interrelationships does not warrant the additional complexity.

quite closely to the ideal type of one for which cross-sectional analysis is adequate whereas time-series designs are unnecessary and relatively ineffectual. PQLI changes relatively slowly over time, limiting the relevance of conclusions derived from panel designs. Moreover, other findings confirm that the determination of basic needs levels involves quite long causal lags. It appears, for example, that colonial effects are not yet exhausted even after several decades. Thus, it is more appropriate to examine long-term adjustment processes through a cross-sectional design than to focus on relatively slow change. Fortunately, my examination of colonial effects indicates that we are able to capture the historical dimension within a cross-sectional design. We have also been able to make at least an initial inquiry into the dynamics that produce these cross-sectional results. Although the design limits our capacity to penetrate these dynamics, we are reassured that panel and time-series designs would do little better in the context of this kind of causal structure.

Nor has the organization of this volume produced any major impediment. Because the model as identified early in the analysis has remained largely intact with the sequential additions, it retains tractability and coherence without sacrificing an accurate vision of the overall causal structure. The central findings concerning economic structure and political influences have withstood the addition of other factors without major change in the direction or size of the initial parameter estimates. This chapter further clarifies the causal structure by examining some of the interactions among the independent variables.

The success of the sequential approach to model building is gratifying in another sense as well. The results have been shown to be highly robust across the different samples of nations produced by the deletion of cases having missing data for some of the variables. Such sample changes are helpful for diagnosing relationships that may not be universal or that result from the large influence of a small number of cases. No evidence for the existence of these flaws was found; the model estimates have remained stable even though various analyses systematically omitted, for example, the poorest countries, the most recently independent, the state socialist countries, and OPEC members in analyses ranging from an N of 63 (using Adelman and Morris data) to an N of 109 (using Bornschier and Heintz data). Moreover, as we see below, the conclusions embodied in the parameter estimates of the final model apply to nations at all levels of income. This robustness contrasts with the known propensity of many similar cross-national models to behave unstably over different population samples and of parameter estimates to fluctuate with the inclusion of additional variables. From this stability we may conclude that the model does not contain artifactual effects or misspecifications resulting from either sample bias or the omission of relevant variables.

Moreover, we are now in a position to investigate more thoroughly a theme that first arose in Chapter 3. The apparent shift in the strength and shape of the relationship between GNP and the PQLI at different points on the curve raises more general questions. When citizen welfare rises with aggregate economic growth, is that rise more rapid, more regular, or more predictable at some ranges than others? Is the rise driven by different processes at different levels?

In this respect, we observed originally that the greatest differentiation among nations in welfare performance occurs in the middle income range. Above incomes of about $2,300, welfare performance improves relatively more slowly, more proportionally to income, and with smaller deviations among nations. Below incomes of about $300, national performance is also more uniform across nations than among the middle income group, though it does not approach the predictability of the high-income nations. These conclusions were based on the bivariate relationship between GNP and PQLI, however; revisiting this question in light of the completed model suggests a somewhat different pattern.

Among the poorest nations in the sample (the thirty-six below $300 per capita in 1970 U.S. dollars), basic needs performances fall within a rather narrow range. The standard deviation of the PQLI among this group (14.7), for example, is barely half that of the nations in the middle income range, inviting the interpretation that the very low level of societal resources available to nations at this stage is incapable of supporting welfare levels much above the mean PQLI level of 31—regardless of how carefully those resources may be targeted. Moreover, even this small variance is inflated by three cases: Sri Lanka (82), China (69), and Burma (51). The existence of such deviant cases may be seen as either a challenge to the above interpretation or indicative of some idiosyncrasy of process, outcome, or data quality. An analysis possible only now that the final model is complete suggests the former.

In fact, the evidence of the final model suggests that basic needs performance is no more predictable among the poorest nations than among the middle income group. For example, the mean size of the error term is actually fractionally higher among the poorest nations. Furthermore, in the final analysis the three nations noted above are not even deviant cases—in fact, based on the final model of Table 9-5, only Sri Lanka has a positive residual (less than three PQLI points), while the other two actually underperform relative to expectations.

The implication is that the relatively uniform performance occurs because nations at this level of development seldom display the social and political features that are capable of targeting resources toward basic needs outcomes. Such features are not ineffective at this stage nor even impossible to develop; they are only improbable and infrequent. When present, however, they function as effectively as they do in other circumstances. Democracy, for example, with a *t* value of 3.8 when the model is estimated separately over these thirty-six cases, is a more powerful basic needs predictor over this range than over any other.

To be sure, the model as a whole does not predict quite as well for these nations as over the larger sample, but this difference appears to be due to two factors. First, the full range of most of these variables is not displayed over these cases. Military effects, for example, do not significantly predict to basic needs levels among this group. The coefficients are all in the same direction as found among other samples, but military resources are seldom great enough to have statistically significant leverage on basic needs. Consider that mean military spending is about 3 percent of GNP, with a standard deviation of about 3, and military personnel comprise on average a similar percentage of the population with a similar variance. By contrast, among middle- and upper-income countries both the average and the standard deviation are much greater. As a result, none of the military effects is substantial enough in magnitude to stand out against the noise of internation variation.

Second, among these countries there are very substantial differences in forms of economic, social, and political organization which probably affect basic needs levels but which are not adequately measured in the model. For example, the importance of the subsistence sector and the alternative forms found in the agricultural sector is not easily captured by cross-national studies. As noted in Chapter 4, the extent of the subsistence sector is the single best predictor of basic needs levels in countries at this income level, though data limitations prevent us from including it in the comprehensive model.

Among more developed countries, a quite different pattern emerges. Excluding two oil-exporting countries, among the twenty-six nations with per capita GNP greater than $2,300 the variation in basic needs performance is less than two PQLI points. Further, nearly half of that variation is accounted for by per capita GNP. Among the other forces known to affect basic needs outcomes, only the negative impact of rightist ideology and military spending appears to operate in this range. Together these factors reduce the standard error to about one PQLI point.

Interestingly, neither the presence of democracy nor that of state socialism is among the variables required to achieve this level of predictability. Two interpretations are possible. First, it may be that at such income levels basic human needs will be met by virtually any economic, political, and social system. Simply put, such wealth overwhelms the problem even if large quantities of resources are wasted or maldistributed. A second interpretation stems from the observation that each of these nations falls into one of two basic patterns—either state socialist or an advanced industrial democracy—both of which are known to induce very effective targeting of resources on basic needs. Thus, the presence of such distributional mechanisms remains important, but their effect is invisible because their universality makes them a constant and not a variable among these nations.

The latter interpretation receives support from both of the sets of cases in which income and political systems are not so collinear. The two oil-exporting countries are neither democratic nor state socialist; despite similar GNPs, their PQLIs are 29 and 45 while the others range from 89 to 97. Among all other income groups, these two political-economic systems yield distinctive welfare orientations and significantly enhanced basic needs levels; there is no reason to suppose that their distributional propensities change or become less effective at higher welfare levels, though the diminishing returns principle or other ceiling effects may reduce somewhat the incremental outcome.

In either case, it is apparent that this narrowing of forms at higher levels of development stands in sharp contrast to the great diversity in forms present at lower levels. Between the great, though unpatterned, diversity of the poorest countries and the convergence observed in the richest lie fifty-seven middle-income countries. Here all of the factors identified in the full model are at work so that the estimation is nearly identical to that derived from the sample as a whole.

The reason is not hard to find. In this middle income range the diversity of social, political, and economic forms is very great. Further, the level of resources available permits a far more extensive expression of these alternative paths than can occur among the poorest nations. The difference in the capacity of the state, for example, makes the orientation of the state more consequential in the middle-income countries than in the poorer group. As a result, not only is a wider range of paths possible, a wider range is also capable of yielding decent basic needs performance. Thus the situation is unlike that of the poorest nations, in which limited resources reduce the margin of error and permit basic needs success only when everything is done right.

Note, for example, that Sri Lanka is a plantation economy superimposed on a Buddhist culture; it is also a former British colony whose legacy includes a large democratic state with leftist political leanings and a welfare orientation, no significant military spending, and a rather long period of political independence. Simply put, basic needs levels in Sri Lanka have been supported by every major mechanism identified by this analysis, but have not suffered from any of the various leakages or impediments. Thus, though Sri Lanka's PQLI of 82 is remarkable for its income level, such a performance is matched quite easily by middle-income nations that have relied on a more singular mechanism of basic needs achievment. Cuba's 84 presumably reflects its state socialist economic structure and the leftist commitments of its state. Jamaica's 84 is a consequence of a combination of a democratic political system and a social dynamic rooted in the plantation past. Taiwan's 86 and South Korea's 82 result from unique historical (colonial) factors and the development of human capital stemming from labor-intensive industrialization and widespread military service.

What, then, does this say about the adequacy of a "stylized facts" characterization of the economic development process? At least three comments are in order. First, there is considerable evidence that a single, universal development path does not exist. Of course, it is quite evident that the diversity of forms does diminish progressively during development. Although relatively isolated systems manifest great variety, the convergence of forms which begins to narrow the range of development paths is starkly evident around $1,300 and essentially complete by about $2,300. Prior to this level, a stylized facts approach is misleading in that it ignores the existing variety of trajectories.

Second, the patterned differences between welfare levels among poor nations and those among richer ones should not be seen as some automatic consequence of increasing income levels. Rather, income is a proxy for a series of nonlinear processes that include social and political developments. Indeed, as this analysis has proceeded, the direct effects of income have been seen to lessen as other dimensions have been added. Thus, a fully satisfying explanation of basic needs provision must simultaneously trace the consequences of economic development for the various other social and political features that are relevant. That is, as noted above, the study of basic needs is especially interesting because it offers a window on development processes that are also key for a variety of outcomes besides basic needs.

Third, per capita income is not even the best proxy for development because we know that there are other summaries of these changes which are more highly correlated with basic needs. These other processes—the shift of the labor force from the agricultural to the industrial sector in particular—are also better predictors of the mechanisms partially responsible for these basic needs improvements (state characteristics, for example). It is instructive that per capita GNP is a superior predictor of PQLI only at income levels above $2,300, essentially the point at which the labor force transition is already complete.

Finally, we are now in a position to reevaluate our assumptions about the quality of the data. Though the validity of the conceptualizations represented by key variables was discussed at some length in Chapter 1, questions of data reliability have been addressed in a more scattered fashion. The first-cut attempt to establish the validity of the dependent variables and to uncover measurement error is summarized in Chapter 2 and reported more fully in Appendix 1. Despite discrepancies in a few individual data points, the analysis reveals that the overall reliability of the data is quite high. The examination of cross-sectional correlates, alternative measures, and composite indices revealed relatively small differences. Further, the time-series analysis reported in Chapter 3 and Appendix 2 provides evidence of data reliability in the form of the relative stability of measures reported at half-decade intervals.

The seriousness of data problems must ultimately be judged in relation to their impact on findings, however; all social scientists are aware that cross-national data contain random errors that can be largely ignored until their magnitude or their distribution affect the conclusions of the analysis. Of course, that diagnosis can be made only by testing the robustness of the final results. If the structure of the final model appears similar when the effect of questionable cases is removed, we may conclude that the data error is both too small and too random to affect substantive conclusions. Indeed, the results shown in Appendix 3 demonstrate that the substantive conclusions do not shift when the final model is estimated over smaller, more reliable, samples of nations.

The decision to utilize the PQLI rather than its components is also supported by tests of robustness. Appendix 4 repeats the final analysis with each of the components and finds no significant difference among the results. The verdict is as unequivocal as any quantitative study can hope for: there is considerable evidence that the substantive conclusions are not a consequence of any decisions concerning data sources or index construction. The lessons derived from this study of basic human needs would have been no different had alternative constructions been used.

Conclusion

By now, the conclusions derived from this study are evident. Plainly we must note that that which maximizes growth need not maximize welfare. Univariate and unitheoretical perspectives that fail to recognize the multiple and complex causal paths emanating from government policy cannot possibly give reliable policy advice. Consider liberal economic theory's prescription that nations should pursue comparative advantage and rely on trade for development. Within its own domain and set of assumptions, the theory is convincing, but this analysis shows that the consequences are far broader and longer-term than usually recognized by liberal arguments. High commodity concentrations bring not only direct and indirect economic effects (including, but not limited to, higher short-term growth and maximized output), but also all of the social, political, and cultural consequences of a monoculture. For welfare purposes, the latter frequently appear to outweigh the former. In any case, they certainly cannot be ignored.

Yet the preponderance of growth-centric theories has tended to distort development by focusing on one alleged trade-off to the exclusion of another. It now appears from the evidence of Chapter 3 that, on the one hand, nations experiencing rapid economic growth tend to achieve a significantly slower than proportional growth in basic needs levels. But in another sense it appears that growth and equity are more a value bundle than alternative goals: we have also seen that nations that provide unusually high levels of basic needs also achieve markedly higher levels of subsequent growth. Thus, while it remains difficult to aid the poor, it is at least apparent that such efforts need not require major compromises of growth goals.

Unhappily, some value trade-offs are all too real. Choices between capitalism and state socialism—which are obviously too fundamental to be addressed here—must confront the evidence concerning the *physical* quality of life propensities of both systems. Of course, the bundling of democracy with basic needs also suggests complementarity among some goals. Still, the complexity of the political economy processes involved with basic needs provision can lead to counterintuitive outcomes, most evidently in the case of plantations. The book must close with the hope that the first-cut attempt to answer the questions concerning the sources of differential basic needs performance will train attention on this most key aspect of political and economic development.

APPENDIXES

Methodological Premises

Appendix 1. Initial Tests of Data Reliability

The basic PQLI data used in this study are taken from Morris (1979), who, in turn, compiled the data from two basic sources. Literacy rates were taken from the 1973 and 1976 editions of the *Statistical Yearbook* published by the United Nations Educational, Social, and Cultural Organization (UNESCO). Both the original infant mortality and life expectancy data were derived from the *1977 World Population Data Sheet* of the Population Reference Bureau, Inc., Washington, D.C. The latter were transformed according to a formula reported by Morris (1979: 126) which estimates life expectancy at age one from life expectancy at birth and infant mortality rates. Because the original data sometimes refer to slightly different years, all data points—including the comparable GNP data also used in this study—were adjusted to represent "the early 1970s" by averaging and/or regression procedures.

Many other international agencies gather and report similar health and education data. Although many of these compilations originate from the same basic national surveys, reports, and estimates, there are certainly differences in both the original source material and the subsequent processing of it. In fact, several alternative sources exist for each of the three components of the PQLI. As the first step in assessing the reliability of Morris's data, two of these sources—both well known and frequently used by cross-national analysts—are examined for consistency with the Morris data. This limited survey should be sufficient to verify the general comparability of these alternative sources and to identify particular cases with unusually divergent estimates. Of course, a full examination would constitute a study in itself and is well beyond the bounds of this analysis.

The first source is the World Bank's 1983 edition of *World Tables*, perhaps the single most used reference source for cross-national aggregate data. It reports data on all three components of the PQLI at half-decade intervals for 108 nations. Most of the twelve missing nations are either small and poor (e.g., Guinea), independent only circa 1970 or later (e.g., Mozambique), nonmembers of the United Nations (e.g., Taiwan), or countries generally not reported by the World Bank (such as some state socialist nations). *World Tables* reports data taken from World Bank files, some of which are gathered by other organizations. Infant mortality rates, for example, originate from the United Nations *Demographic Yearbook* and estimates of the United Nations Population Division; they are augmented by the World Bank files. Life expectancy data are from these same World Bank files. Literacy rates are taken from the same UNESCO source used by Morris and for that reason have not been separately analyzed here.

The second source is Sheehan and Hopkins's 1979 compilation of all three PQLI components, drawn largely from the United Nations Research Institute for Social Development's comprehensive collection (UNRISD, 1976) and additional World Bank sources. The UNRISD collection is itself derived from several sources, some of which are also used in the data sets described above. However, UNRISD also consults sources not tapped in the others (such as the World Health Organization). Moreover, the use of elaborate error recognition and correction procedures makes this the most heavily processed data set of social indicators available (McGranahan et al., 1985). Where possible, verification and correction routines have been employed to yield more reliable data estimates than found elsewhere. Where this has not been possible, data are not reported. This conservative approach pays for greater reliability with a much smaller sample, which is also reduced by the inclusion of data on less developed countries only.

The first step in assessing the reliability of Morris's data involves the simple correlation between the measures originating from the three sources. Comparing the Morris data with those of Sheehan and Hopkins offers sixty-nine common cases. The correlation between the two PQLIs constructed from each of the two data sets is .976. The correlation of the three components is .973, .951, and .860, the latter figure for infant mortality. Differences between the data sets do not necessarily indicate error in either since they represent slightly different years (1970 for Sheehan and Hopkins, an average of the early 1970s for Morris). This factor has the largest impact on infant mortality figures because temporal fluctuations make this the most volatile element of the index.

Similar comparisons involving the World Bank source offer 108 common data points for infant mortality, life expectancy, and the two-item "semi-PQLI." (Literacy rates are not compared because the basic sources of the two are identical). The respective correlations are .975 for the index, .969 for life expectancy, and .932 for infant mortality.

These correlations document a test-retest reliability in the estimates of quality of life indices which is quite high by the usual standards of social science. It is certainly far higher than usually found in intercoder reliability of "soft" data and even greater than data such as exchange rate corrected national account statistics, which are ordinarily regarded as "hard" data. In general, then, the Morris data set should be quite adequate for representing cross-national variance in basic human needs.

More broadly, however, I want to use this analysis as a first cut in identifying particular data points that are somewhat suspect. Given the high correlation between the variables as a whole, any particular data point in the Morris collection out of line with comparable estimates in the other sources must be viewed with a certain suspicion. Of course, though significant differences call into question the accuracy of the data, it cannot be known which of the estimates—if any—are correct. The primary purpose is not to choose the best estimate, however. Rather, we seek only to identify cases in which highly discrepant estimates exist and to prevent these data points from distorting the results of the analysis.

Discrepancies were identified by regressing the PQLI reported by Morris on the indices constructed from the data of the other two

Table A-1. Nations with source-divergent PQLI estimates

Compared to Sheehan and Hopkins, Morris estimates are:

High (positive residuals)		Low (negative residuals)	
Lebanon	2.4	Jordan	−3.4
Ghana	2.4	Mali	−2.4
Nepal	2.2	Kenya	−2.1
Dominican Rep.	1.6	Burma	−2.1
		Mauritania	−1.3
		Algeria	−1.2

Compared to World Bank, Morris estimates are:

High (positive residuals)		Low (negative residuals)	
Brazil	4.3	Congo	−2.9
Sierra Leone	3.1	Gabon	−2.1
Sudan	2.2	Tanzania	−1.9
P.R. China	1.8	Niger	−1.8
Ecuador	1.7	Mauritania	−1.7

Table A-2. Nations with suspect estimates of literacy

World Bank estimate high	World Bank estimate low
Somalia	Burundi
Tanzania	Cameroon
Tunisia	Ghana
Iran	Rwanda
	Zaire

Source: McGranahan et al., 1985: 92

sources. Positive residuals indicate nations whose Morris PQLI is markedly higher than would be expected on the basis of the other estimate; negative residuals, on the other hand, signify cases in which the Morris value is suspected as being too low. Table A-1 contains the nations found to have the nine highest residuals in each of the two analyses. The residual is expressed in Z scores with a standard error of estimate of 5.2 in the Sheehan-Hopkins regression and 5.8 in the *World Tables* regression. Thus, for example, the Morris-computed PQLI of Lebanon was 14.48 points higher than expected from the UNRISD data (2.4 × 5.2). While there are certainly some widely divergent estimates, it is noteworthy that only one nation—Mauritania—is found suspicious by both analyses. The implication is that among the other nations, any error is as likely to lie in the alternative sources as in Morris.

This study is not the first to inquire about source differences in these data. For example, McGranahan et al. (1985: 92) identify ten nations for which widely different estimates of literacy in 1970 have been offered by UNESCO, United Nations, and World Bank sources. Although the list was not compiled systematically, these nations—listed in Table A-2 above—should be added to the inventory of initially suspect data points. Comparison of Tables A-1 and A-2 again reveals few nations that appear on both lists—only Ghana and Tanzania, in fact.

A second approach to the identification of inaccurate data points takes advantage of the known correlation between components of the PQLI and various other international indicators. In particular, health care researchers have identified and estimated models of a so-called technical production function, which expresses health outcomes—especially life expectancy—as a function of both socioeconomic "development" factors and the availability of various health care facilities and personnel. In the search for potentially inaccurate data, nations reporting health outcomes seemingly out of line with health inputs are to be regarded with suspicion. The most comprehensive of such studies is that of Fulop and Reinke (1983), whose regression equation using data from the World Bank and World Health Organization yields an r^2 above .90 in predicting life expectancy in 1975. The ten nations they

Table A-3. Nations with suspect
estimates of life expectancy

Positive residuals	Negative residuals
Gabon	Jamaica
Bolivia	Albania
South Africa	Guyana
Congo	El Salvador
Cameroon	Sri Lanka

Source: Fulop and Reinke, 1983: 347

identify with the largest positive and the largest negative residuals are
listed in Table A-3.

This table contains only two cases familiar from previous tables,
Gabon and the Congo. It is most interesting that World Bank data
credit these two with higher life expectancy than predicted. Both these
cases were also found in Table A-1 as examples in which World Bank
estimates were higher than comparable Morris estimates. On the basis
of this information alone, of course, it cannot be determined whether
these large residuals result from measurement error or simply reflect
nations whose development patterns include a relatively unusual level
of life expectancy. By comparing these lists with those of data points
suspect on other grounds, however, we may be able to choose the
correct interpretation. It may sometimes even be possible—as in these
two cases—to speculate as to which of the diverging estimates is most
likely to be in error.

These lists of data points called into question by cross-sectional correlates are augmented by similar analyses in Chapter 3 and Appendix 2
which consider cross-time correlates. Since we must be especially alert
to cases identified as suspect by more than one piece of evidence, special mention must be made of one type of analysis which some have
suggested as an option. Russett et al. (1981) use health status statistics
as a means of estimating income inequality, but the reverse predictive
procedure would not be adequate for our purposes for several reasons.
First, income inequality data are available for far fewer cases than
would be necessary. Second, it is widely acknowledged that the quality
of the income data is insufficient. Third, no doubt in part for that reason, the correlation between inequality and health is not especially
high (Russett et al., 1981; Ram, 1985; Leipziger and Lewis, 1980; Sheehan and Hopkins, 1979).

Appendix 2. Cross-Time Tests of Data Reliability

The availability of World Bank data on the components of PQLI at half-
decade intervals, together with the predictable pace of change in these

Table A-4. Nations with temporal discontinuities in PQLI estimates

Compared to 1960 levels, 1970 estimates are:

High (positive residuals)		Low (negative residuals)	
Venezuela	2.4	Congo	−3.3
South Korea	2.1	Zambia	−2.3
Peru	1.9	Niger	−2.2
El Salvador	1.9	South Africa	−1.9
Turkey	1.7	Zaire	−1.9

Compared to 1980 levels, 1970 estimates are:

High (positive residuals)		Low (negative residuals)	
Afghanistan	2.3	Congo	−3.8
Upper Volta	2.1	Tanzania	−2.9
Sudan	1.9	Somalia	−2.5
Sierra Leone	1.8	Jordan	−2.5
Malawi	1.8	Zambia	−1.6

variables, provides an opportunity to predict/postdict PQLI values in 1970. When these predictions are compared with the actual values reported by Morris (1979) and used in this study, the residuals can be used to identify data points that may be in error. This approach is particularly valuable in detecting deliberate government manipulation or other large errors, which may show up more vividly as a blip in a time series than as an anomaly in a cross-sectional analysis.

This approach requires an accurate model of PQLI change; the simple two-variable specification discussed Chapter 3 is adequate for our purposes. The first independent variable is a lagged dependent variable, while the second is a GDP growth rate over the lag. In addition to using 1960 PQLI data to estimate 1970 data, we may also use 1980 PQLI data to postdict 1970 levels. While the latter, of course, does not represent a causal model, we can take full advantage of the three data points in order to identify 1970 values that are out of line with those of both the earlier and the later period.

These two predictive models of 1970 PQLI levels yielded adjusted r^2 values of .980 and .956 for 104 nations. The respective standard errors were 4.1 and 5.9. Table A-4 lists the ten largest residuals from each analysis. These should not, of course, be taken as cases involving unreliable or manipulated figures. Most of the positive residuals from the 1960 analysis and the negative residuals from the 1980 analysis simply identify nations with greater than average improvement in basic needs provision over one or both periods. Nations having slower than average improvement occupy the other two columns. The only really suspicious cases are the Congo and Zambia, both of which have 1970 values far below expectations based on both 1960 and 1980 projections. It seems unlikely that both experienced dramatic dips after 1960 and then remarkable accelerations prior to 1980, all net of changes in GNP levels.

ble A-5. Final model estimated with various samples

Cases omitted	N	F	r	adj. r^2	SEE
one (Table 9-5)	120	144.1	.975	.944	6.69
NRISD residuals	111	131.1	.975	.943	6.75
orld Tables residuals	110	128.7	.975	.942	6.71
orld Tables missing data	108	130.6	.976	.944	6.71
cGranahan literacy	111	129.8	.976	.946	6.51
lop/Reinke residuals	110	149.8	.976	.947	6.61
60 → 1970 residuals	110	140.9	.977	.947	6.56
80 → 1970 residuals	110	122.8	.975	.944	6.56
onsensus problems	105	125.3	.975	.944	6.54

	t values of parameter estimates						
Cases omitted	State socialism	LGNP/ capita	Agric. labor	Military expend.	Right × expend.	Democ- racy	Troops/ capita
one (Table 9-5)	6.9	5.4	−6.4	−4.4	−3.6	2.6	3.6
NRISD residuals	6.5	5.0	−5.9	−4.2	−3.2	2.3	3.4
orld Tables residuals	6.6	5.2	−5.9	−3.5	−2.9	2.8	2.7
orld Tables missing data	5.4	4.1	−5.3	−3.7	−2.9	2.0	3.2
cGranahan literacy	6.5	5.9	−6.1	−4.6	−3.9	2.1	3.7
lop/Reinke residuals	5.8	5.4	−5.5	−3.6	−3.4	3.2	3.3
60 → 1970 residuals	6.8	5.3	−6.0	−4.3	−3.9	2.7	3.7
80 → 1970 residuals	6.7	4.5	−6.6	−4.4	−3.2	2.5	3.8
onsensus problems	6.8	5.2	−5.5	−4.2	−3.2	2.6	3.7

Cases omitted	Plan- tation	Periphery trade	Mineral export	Inde- pendence	U.K. colony	Budd- hist	Islamic	Africa
one (Table 9-5)	3.9	−3.0	−2.8	1.6	2.2	3.2	−4.3	−6.7
NRISD residuals	3.4	−2.9	−2.6	1.6	2.2	3.1	−4.4	−6.6
orld Tables residuals	3.8	−2.2	−3.0	1.6	1.9	3.4	−4.2	−6.0
orld Tables missing data	3.8	−2.6	−2.2	1.0	2.1	3.3	−4.0	−6.5
cGranahan literacy	3.5	−2.3	−3.4	1.8	3.2	3.7	−3.6	−5.0
lop/Reinke residuals	3.7	−2.6	−2.6	.4	1.4	3.0	−4.4	−5.2
60 → 1970 residuals	3.0	−1.6	−4.2	2.2	3.2	3.5	−2.9	−5.1
80 → 1970 residuals	3.6	−1.7	−2.8	1.8	2.4	3.3	−3.3	−5.1
onsensus problems	2.9	−1.4	−3.8	2.2	3.2	3.8	−3.3	−4.2

Appendix 3. The Robustness of the Final Model

The analyses reported in Appendixes 1 and 2 identify cases in which substantial measurement error may be present in the Morris PQLI data used to estimate the model. The seriousness of this problem, however, must ultimately be judged against the central goal of the statistical portion of this study—to identify and estimate an unbiased model of basic needs provision. Thus, the final test of the adequacy of the data concerns the robustness of the final results. If the general structure of the final model remains similar when the effect of questionable cases is removed, we may conclude that the data error is not responsible for the substantive conclusions. At this juncture, then, we must identify especially suspect data points, remove them from the analysis, reestimate the model, and compare the results.

Of course, we cannot be certain that these data are, in fact, inaccurate. Moreover, we have alternative lists of somewhat suspicious cases. Beginning with Table A-1, I omit each list from the analysis and rerun the analysis first reported in Table 9-5. The last list ("Consensus problems") is comprised of the fifteen nations found in more than one of the above lists. The results found when the model was estimated over these various samples are represented in Table A-5.

As can be seen, there is little impact on either the overall predictive power of the model or the parameter estimates of individual variables. The overall structure of the model remains intact. From this outcome I conclude that while the data matrix certainly contains errors, they are neither so large nor so systematic as to meaningfully affect our substantive results. In particular, we can rule out the interpretation that this pattern of error is responsible for the results.

Appendix 4. Final Model with Alternative Dependent Variables

As a check on the robustness of the final model, the specification of Table 9-5 is reestimated with five different dependent variables. In addition to the PQLI, the three individual components are employed as dependent variables as well as an index that omits literacy (the "semi-PQLI" reported in Chapter 3). Finally, the logit transformation of PQLI discussed in Chapter 3 is tested. The results are displayed in Table A-6. Not surprisingly, the PQLI and, to a lesser extent, the "semi-PQLI" are more predictable than any of the individual components. Still, the summary statistics make clear that the determinants of the three components are very similar. Moreover, the t values for the individual de-

ble A-6. Final model estimated with various dependent variables

ependent variable	N	F	r	adj. r^2	SEE
LI (Table 9-5)	120	144.1	.975	.944	6.69
ant mortality index	120	79.0	.956	.902	8.65
e expectancy index	120	120.6	.965	.923	6.78
eracy rate	120	100.1	.958	.909	10.48
LI minus literacy	120	129.6	.974	.942	6.16
LI (logit transform)	120	160.5	.977	.955	(.344)

	t values of parameter estimates						
ependent variable	State socialism	LGNP/ capita	Agric. labor	Military expend.	Right × expend.	Democ- racy	Troops/ capita
LI (Table 9-5)	6.9	5.4	−6.4	−4.4	−3.6	2.6	3.6
ant mortality index	3.9	4.6	−4.0	−2.0	−3.8	2.0	2.5
e expectancy index	7.6	5.5	−4.9	−5.3	−1.1	2.3	4.4
eracy rate	5.4	2.8	−6.1	−3.6	−3.5	2.2	2.1
LI minus literacy	6.5	6.2	−5.4	−4.3	−3.2	2.5	4.2
LI (logit transform)	5.6	8.2	−5.8	−3.5	−5.0	2.6	2.3

Dependent variable	Plan- tation	Periphery trade	Mineral export	Inde- pendence	U.K. colony	Budd- hist	Islamic	Africa
LI (Table 9-5)	3.9	−3.0	−2.8	1.6	2.2	3.2	−4.3	−6.7
ant mortality index	2.9	−2.8	−1.9	.9	2.4	2.4	−4.0	−4.8
e expectancy index	3.0	−.6	−4.7	2.4	4.5	1.9	.8	−6.2
eracy rate	3.0	−3.4	−1.1	1.1	−.5	3.2	−5.5	−4.2
LI minus literacy	3.8	−1.9	−3.6	1.8	4.2	2.8	−2.2	−5.8
LI (logit transform)	3.1	−3.8	−3.2	.8	1.8	3.9	−4.6	−4.8

pendent variables confirm that none of the significant findings depends for its validity on a particular definition of the dependent variable. To be sure, the parameter estimates do differ marginally, but there is no hint of a different model estimation for alternative dependent measures. Thus, the substantive results of this analysis of basic needs provision are not limited to the PQLI. Furthermore, alternative specifications such as the logit transformation of the PQLI serve only to improve the fit of the model while not changing any substantive conclusions. In short, the model is extremely robust over different definitions of the dependent variable, just as it is shown to be extremely robust over different samples in Appendix 3.

References

Abrahamsson, Bengt (1972). *Military Professionalization and Political Power*. Beverly Hills: Sage.

Abramovitz, Moses (1959). "The Welfare Interpretation of Secular Trends in National Income and Product." In *The Allocation of Economic Resources: Essays in Honor of Bernard Francis Haley*. Stanford: Stanford University Press, pp. 1–22.

Abu-Lughod, Janet, and Richard Hay, eds. (1977). *Third World Urbanization*. Chicago: Maaroufa Press.

Adekson, J. Bayo (1978). "On the Theory of the Modernising Soldier: A Critique." *Current Research on Peace and Violence* 1:28–31.

Adelman, Irma, and Cynthia Morris (1967). *Society, Politics, and Economic Development: A Quantitative Approach*. Baltimore: Johns Hopkins University Press.

—— (1973). *Economic Growth and Social Equity in Developing Countries*. Stanford: Stanford University Press.

Ahluwalia, Montek (1974). "Income Inequality: Some Dimensions of the Problem." In Hollis Chenery et al., *Redistribution with Growth*. London: Oxford University Press, pp. 3–37.

—— (1977). "Inequality, Poverty, and Development." *Journal of Development Economics* 3,4:307–42.

Ahluwalia, Montek, N. G. Carter, and Hollis Chenery (1979). "Growth and Poverty in Developing Countries." *Journal of Development Economics* 6,3:229–341.

Ahluwalia, Montek, and Hollis Chenery (1974). "The Economic Framework." In Hollis Chenery et al., *Redistribution with Growth*. London: Oxford University Press, pp. 38–51.

Ake, Claude (1981). *A Political Economy of Africa*. New York: Longman.

Alford, Robert (1975). "Paradigms of Relations between State and Society." In Leon Lindberg et al., eds., *Stress and Contradiction in Modern Capitalism*. Lexington, Mass.: D. C. Heath.

Alleyne, Mervyn C. (1985). "A Linguistic Perspective on the Caribbean." In Sidney Mintz and Sally Price, eds., *Caribbean Contours*. Baltimore: Johns Hopkins University Press, pp. 155–79.

Alt, James E., and K. Alec Chrystal (1983). *Political Economics*. Berkeley: University of California Press.

Amin, Samir (1972). "Underdevelopment and Dependence in Black Africa—Origins and Contemporary Forms." *Journal of Modern African Studies* 10,4:503–24.

—— (1974a). "Accumulation and Development: A Theoretical Model." *Review of African Political Economy*, no. 1:9–26.

—— (1974b). *Accumulation on a World Scale*. New York: Monthly Review Press.

—— (1976). *Unequal Development: An Essay on the Social Formations of Peripheral Capitalism*. New York: Monthly Review Press.

—— (1977). *Imperialism and Unequal Development*. New York: Monthly Review Press.

Andreski, S. (1954). *Military Organization and Society*. London: Routledge and Kegan Paul.

Anstey, Roger (1970). "Belgian Rule in the Congo and the Aspirations of the Evolé Class." In L. H. Gann and Peter Duignan, eds., *Colonialism in Africa, 1870–1960*. London: Cambridge University Press, 2:286–319.

Anton, Thomas (1984). "Intergovernmental Change in the United States: An Assessment of the Literature." In Trudi Miller, ed., *Public Sector Performance: A Conceptual Turning Point*. Baltimore: Johns Hopkins University Press, pp. 15–64.

Aranson, Peter H., and Peter C. Ordeshook (1985). "Public Interest, Private Interest, and the Democratic Polity." In Roger Benjamin and Stephen Elkin, eds., *The Democratic State*. Lawrence: University of Kansas Press, pp. 87–99.

Arriaga, E. E., and Kingsley Davis (1969). "The Pattern of Mortality Change in Latin America." *Demography* 6,3:223–42.

Ayers, Robert (1983). *Banking on the Poor: The World Bank and World Poverty*. Cambridge: MIT Press.

Baeta, C. G. (1970). "Missionary and Humanitarian Interests, 1914 to 1960." In L. H. Gann and Peter Duignan, eds., *Colonialism in Africa, 1870–1960*. London: Cambridge University Press, 2:422–49.

Ball, Nicole (1982). "Military Expenditure in the Development Process: An Overview." Paper presented at the annual meetings of the International Studies Association.

—— (1983). "Defense and Development: A Critique of the Benoit Study." *Economic Development and Cultural Change* 31,3:507–24.

Banks, Arthur (1971). *Cross-Polity Time-Series Data*. Cambridge: MIT Press.

Baran, Paul (1957). *The Political Economy of Growth*. New York: Monthly Review Press.

Baran, Paul, and Paul M. Sweezey (1966). *Monopoly Capital: An Essay on the American Economic and Social Order*. New York: Monthly Review Press.

Bardhan, Pranab K. (1974). "India." In Hollis Chenery et al., *Redistribution with Growth*. London: Oxford University Press, pp. 255–62.

Barlow, Robin (1977). "A Test of Alternative Methods of Making GNP Comparisons." *The Economic Journal* 87 (September): 450–59.

Bauer, Peter (1972). *Dissent on Development: Studies and Debates on Development Economics.* Cambridge: Harvard University Press.

Bebler, Anton (1972). *Military Rule in Africa: Dahomey, Ghana, Sierra Leone, and Mali.* New York: Praeger.

Beckerman, P., and D. Coes (1980). "Who Benefits from Economic Development." *American Economic Review* 70:246–49.

Beckerman, Wilfred (1966). *International Comparisons of Real Incomes.* Paris: Organisation for Economic Co-operation and Development.

——, ed. (1979). *Slow Growth in Britain: Causes and Consequences.* Oxford: Clarendon Press.

Beckford, George L. (1972). *Persistent Poverty: Underdevelopment in Plantation Economies of the Third World.* New York: Oxford University Press.

Beer, Samuel (1977). "Political Overload and Freedom." *Polity* 10,1:5–17.

Belsley, D. A., E. Kuh, and R. E. Welsch (1980). *Regression Diagnostics.* New York: Wiley.

Bell, C. L. G. (1974). "The Political Framework." In Hollis Chenery et al., *Redistribution with Growth.* London: Oxford University Press, pp. 52–72.

Bell, C. L. G., and John H. Duloy (1974). "Formulating a Strategy." In Hollis Chenery et al., *Redistribution with Growth.* London: Oxford University Press, pp. 91–112.

Benjamin, Roger, and Raymond Duvall (1985). "The Capitalist State in Context." In Roger Benjamin and Stephen Elkin, eds., *The Democratic State.* Lawrence: University of Kansas Press, pp. 19–57.

Benoit, Emile (1973). *Defense and Economic Growth in Developing Countries.* Lexington, Mass.: Lexington Books.

—— (1978). "Growth and Defense in Developing Countries." *Economic Development and Cultural Change* 26 (January): 271–80.

Berg, Alan, et al., eds. (1973). *Nutrition, National Development, and Planning.* Cambridge and London: MIT Press.

Bergesen, Albert, and Ronald Schoenberg (1980). "Long Waves of Colonial Expansion and Contraction, 1415–1969." In Albert Bergesen, ed., *Studies of the Modern World System.* New York: Academic Press, pp. 231–78.

Berg-Schlosser, Dirk (1984). "African Political Systems: Typology and Performance." *Comparative Political Studies* 17,1 (April): 121–51.

Berry, Albert (1984). "Income Distribution Trends in Labor Surplus Economies." In Gustav Ranis et al., *Comparative Development Perspectives.* Boulder, Colo.: Westview, pp. 182–200.

Berry, R. Albert, and William R. Cline (1979). *Agrarian Structure and Productivity in Developing Countries.* Baltimore and London: Johns Hopkins University Press.

Best, Lloyd (1968). "Outlines of a Model of Pure Plantation Economy." *Social and Economic Studies* (September): 283–326.

Best, Michael, and William Connolly (1982). *The Politicized Economy.* 2d ed. Lexington, Mass: D. C. Heath.

Bienen, Henry, ed. (1971). *The Military and Modernization.* Chicago: Aldine.

Biersteker, Thomas J. (1978). *Distortion or Development? Contending Perspectives on the Multinational Corporation.* Cambridge: MIT Press.

Bigsten, Arne (1983). *Income Distribution and Development.* London: Heinemann Educational Books.

Birnbaum, Pierre (1985). "States, Ideologies, and Collective Action in Western Europe." In Ali Kazancigil, ed., *The State in Global Perspective*. Shaftsbury, Dorset: Blackmore Press, pp. 232–49.

Bliss, Christopher, and Nicholas Stern (1978). "Productivity, Wages, and Nutrition." *Journal of Development Economics* 5,4 (December): 331–98.

Block, Fred (1977). "The Ruling Class Does Not Rule: Notes on the Marxist Theory of the State." *Socialist Revolution* 7,3:6–28.

Blondel, Jean (1969). *An Introduction to Comparative Government*. New York: Praeger.

Boardman, Anthony E., and Robert P. Inman (1983). "Early Life Environments and Adult Health: A Policy Perspective." In David Salkever et al., *Research in Human Capital and Development*. Greenwich, Conn.: JAI Press, pp. 183–207.

Bollen, Kenneth A. (1979). "Political Democracy and the Timing of Development." *American Sociological Review* 44,4:572–87.

—— (1980). "Issues in the Comparative Measurement of Political Democracy." *American Sociological Review* 45:370–90.

—— (1983). "World System Position, Dependency, and Democracy: The Cross-National Evidence." *American Sociological Review* 48 (August): 468–79.

Bollen, Kenneth A., and Burke Grandjean (1981). "The Dimension(s) of Democracy: Further Issues in the Measurement and Effects of Political Democracy." *American Sociological Review* 46:651–59.

Bollen, Kenneth A., and Robert W. Jackman (1985a). "Economic and Noneconomic Determinants of Political Democracy in the 1960s," in *Research in Political Sociology*. Greenwich, Conn.: JAI Press.

—— (1985b). "Regression Diagnostics: An Expository Treatment of Outliers and Influential Cases." *Sociological Methods and Research* 13:510–42.

Bornschier, Volker (1981). "World Economy, Level of Development, and Income Distribution: An Integration of Different Approaches to the Explanation of Income Inequality." Paper prepared for the European Association of Development Research and Training Institutes, April 8–10, Paderborn, FRG.

—— (1985). "World Social Structure in the Long Economic Wave." Paper presented to the International Studies Association, Washington, D.C.

Bornschier, Volker, and Christopher Chase-Dunn (1985). *Transnational Corporations and Underdevelopment*. New York: Praeger.

Bornschier, Volker, Christopher Chase-Dunn, and Richard Rubinson (1978). "Cross-National Evidence of the Effects of Foreign Investment and Aid on Economic Growth and Inequality: A Survey of Findings and a Reanalysis." *American Journal of Sociology* 84,3:651–83.

Bornschier, Volker, and Peter Heintz (1979). *Compendium of Data for World Systems Analyses*. Special Issue, *Bulletin of the Sociological Institute of the University of Zurich* (March).

Brett, E. A. (1973). *Colonialism and Underdevelopment in East Africa: The Politics of Economic Change 1919–1939*. New York: Nok.

Brooks, Ezriel, and Enzo Grilli (1979). "Commodity Price Stabilization and the Developing World." In John Adams, ed., *The Contemporary International Economy*. New York: St. Martin's, pp. 440–48.

Brooks, Joel E. (1983). "Left-Wing Mobilization and Socioeconomic Equality: A Cross-National Analysis of the Developed Democracies." *Comparative Political Studies* 16,3:393–416.

Bulatao, Rodolfo, and Ronald Lee (1983). *Determinants of Fertility in Developing Countries*. Vol. 1. New York: Academic Press.

Bunce, Valerie (1983). "The Political Economy of the Brezhnev Era: The Rise and Fall of Corporatism." *British Journal of Political Science* 13 (January): 129–57.

—— (1985). "The Empire Strikes Back: The Evolution of the Eastern Bloc from a Soviet Asset to a Soviet Liability." *International Organization* 39,1:1–46.

Bunce, Valerie, and Alexander Hicks (1987). "Capitalisms, Socialisms, and Democracy." In Maurice Zeitlin, ed., *Political Power and Social Theory*, vol. 6. Beverly Hills: Sage.

Bunker, Stephen (1985). *Underdeveloping the Amazon.* Urbana: University of Illinois Press.

Calvin, Melvin (1974). "Solar Energy by Photosynthesis." *Science* 184, 4134:375–81.

Cameron, David (1978). "The Expansion of the Public Economy: A Comparative Analysis." *American Political Science Review* 72:1243–61.

Caporaso, James, ed. (1978). *Dependence and Dependency in the Global System.* Madison: University of Wisconsin Press.

Caporaso, James A. (1982). "The State's Role in Third World Economic Growth." *Annals of the American Academy* (January): 103–11.

Caparaso, James, ed. (1987). *A Changing International Division of Labor.* Boulder, Colo.: Lynne Rienner.

Cardoso, Fernando (1973). "Associated-dependent Development: Theoretical and Practical Implications." In Alfred Stepan, ed., *Authoritarian Brazil: Origins, Policies, and Future.* New Haven: Yale University Press, pp. 142–76.

—— (1977). "The Consumption of Dependency Theory in the United States." *Latin American Research Review* 12,3:7–24.

Cardoso, Fernando, and Enzo Faletto (1979). *Dependency and Development in Latin America.* Berkeley: University of California Press.

Castles, Francis (1982). *The Impact of Parties.* Beverly Hills: Sage.

Caves, Richard E., and Ronald W. Jones (1973). *World Trade and Payments: An Introduction.* Boston: Little, Brown.

Chase-Dunn, Christopher (1975). "The Effects of International Economic Dependence on Development and Inequality: A Cross-national Study." *American Sociological Review* 40 (December): 720–38.

—— (1980). "Socialist States in the Capitalist World-Economy." *Social Problems* 27:505–26.

—— (1981). "Interstate System and Capitalist World-Economy: One Logic or Two?" *International Studies Quarterly* 25 (March): 19–42.

—— (1983). "Inequality, Structural Mobility, and Dependency Reversal in the Capitalist World Economy." In Charles F. Doran, George Modelski, and Cal Clark, eds., *North/South Relations: Studies of Dependency Reversal.* New York: Praeger, pp. 73–95.

Chenery, Hollis, et al. (1974). *Redistribution with Growth.* London: Oxford University Press.

Chenery, Hollis, and Moises Syrquin (1975). *Patterns of Development, 1950–1970.* London: Oxford University Press.

Chilcote, Ronald (1984). *Theories of Development and Underdevelopment.* Boulder, Colo.: Westview.

Chilcote, Ronald, and Dale Johnson, eds. (1983). *Theories of Development: Mode of Production or Dependency?* Beverly Hills: Sage.

Chirot, Daniel (1977). *Social Change in the Twentieth Century.* New York: Harcourt Brace Jovanovich.

Chorley, Katherine (1943). *Armies and the Art of Revolution.* Boston: Beacon.

Clark, Colin (1951). *Conditions of Economic Progress.* 3d ed. London: Macmillan.

Cochrane, Susan H., Donald J. O'Hara, and Joanne Leslie (1980). *The Effects of Education on Health.* Washington D.C.: World Bank.

Colella, Cynthia Cates (1979). "The Creation, Care, and Feeding of Leviathan: Who and What Makes Government Grow." *Intergovernmental Perspective* 5,4:6–11.

Crouch, Harold (1978). *The Army and Politics in Indonesia*. Ithaca: Cornell University Press.

Crowder, Michael (1964). "Indirect Rule, French and British Style." *Africa* 34,3.

—— (1968). *West Africa under Colonial Rule*. London: Hutchinson.

—— (1970). "The White Chiefs of Tropical Africa." In L. H. Gann and Peter Duignan, eds., *Colonialism in Africa, 1870–1960*. London: Cambridge University Press, 2:320–50.

Cutright, Phillip (1967). "Inequality: A Cross-National Study." *American Sociological Review* 32:562–78.

Davis, Kingsley, and Wilbert E. Moore (1945). "Some Principles of Stratification." *American Sociological Review* 11:242–49.

Dealy, Glen (1977). *The Public Man*. Amherst: University of Massachusetts Press.

Deger, S., and S. Sen (1983). "Military Expenditures, Spin-off, and Economic Development." *Journal of Development Economics* 13:67–83.

Deger, Saadet, and Ron Smith (1983). "Military Expenditure and Growth in Less Developed Countries." *Journal of Conflict Resolution* 27 (June): 335–53.

de Janvry, Alain (1981). *The Agrarian Question and Reformism in Latin America*. Baltimore: Johns Hopkins University Press.

de Janvry, Alain, and Carlos Garramon (1977). "Laws of Motion of Capital in the Center-Periphery Structure." *Review of Radical Political Economics* 9 (Summer): 29–38.

Delacroix, Jacques (1977). "Export of Raw Materials and Economic Growth." *American Sociological Review* 42:795–808.

Delacroix, Jacques, and Charles Ragin (1978). "Modernizing Institutions, Mobilization, and Third World Development: A Cross-National Study." *American Journal of Sociology* 84:123–50.

—— (1981). "Structural Blockage: A Cross-National Study of Economic Dependency, State Efficacy, and Underdevelopment." *American Journal of Sociology* 86: 1311–47.

Delavignette, Robert L. (1970). "French Colonial Policy in Black Africa, 1945 to 1960." In L. H. Gann and Peter Duignan, eds., *Colonialism in Africa, 1870–1960*. London: Cambridge University Press, 2:251–85.

Denison, Edward F. (1971). "Welfare Measurement and the GNP." *Survey of Current Business* 51 (January): 13–16.

Deschamps, Hubert (1970). "France in Black Africa and Madagascar between 1920 and 1945." In L. H. Gann and Peter Duignan, eds., *Colonialism in Africa, 1870–1960*. London: Cambridge University Press, 2:226–50.

de Silva, S. B. D. (1982). *The Political Economy of Underdevelopment*. Boston: Routledge and Kegan Paul.

Dixon, William (1983). "Trade Dependence and the Provision of Basic Human Needs." Paper prepared for the Annual Meetings of the International Studies Association, Mexico City.

Dixon, William J., and Bruce E. Moon (1985). "Military Effects on the Provision of Basic Human Needs." Paper prepared for the annual meeting of the International Studies Association, Washington, D.C., March.

—— (1986). "The Military Burden and Basic Human Needs: An Analysis of Military Effects on Individual Well-being." *Journal of Conflict Resolution* 30 (December): 660–84.

—— (1989). "Domestic Political Conflict and Basic Needs Outcomes: An Empirical Assessment." *Comparative Political Studies* 22,2:178–98.

Dolan, Michael, and Brian Tomlin (1980). "First World–Third World Linkages: External Relations and Economic Development." *International Organization* 34:41–63.

Domhoff, G. William (1967). *Who Rules America?* Englewood Cliffs, N.J.: Prentice-Hall.

—— (1969). "Who Made American Foreign Policy 1945–1963?" In David Horowitz, ed., *Corporations and the Cold War*. New York: Monthly Review Press, pp. 25–69.

—— (1978). *Who Really Rules? New Haven and Community Power Reexamined*. New Brunswick, N.J.: Transaction.

dos Santos, Theotonio (1970). "The Structure of Dependence." *American Economic Review* 60,2:231–36.

Drewnowski, Jan, and Wolf Scott (1966). "The Level of Living Index." Report no. 4 Geneva: United Nations Research Institute for Social Development.

Drucker, Peter (1969). "The Sickness of Government." *Public Interest* 14:3–23.

Duchin, Faye (1982). "How Much Development Can Disarmament Buy?" Paper presented at the Annual Meetings of the International Studies Association, Cincinnati, March 24.

Duffy, James Edward (1962). *Portugal in Africa*. Cambridge: Harvard University Press.

—— (1970). "Portuguese Africa, 1930 to 1960." In L. H. Gann and Peter Duignan, eds., *Colonialism in Africa, 1870–1960*. London: Cambridge University Press, 2:171–93.

Duncan, W. Raymond (1978). "Development Roles of the Military in Cuba: Modal Personality and Nation Building." In Sheldon Simon, ed., *The Military and Security in the Third World: Domestic and International Impacts*. Boulder, Colo.: Westview, pp. 77–121.

Duvall, Raymond (1978). "Dependence and Dependencia Theory: Notes toward Precision of Concept and Measurement." *International Organization* 32 (Winter): 51–78.

Duvall, Raymond, and John Freeman (1983). "The Technocratic Elite and the Entrepreneurial State in Dependent Industrialization." *American Political Science Review* 77:569–87.

Dye, Thomas R. (1976). *Who's Running America?* Englewood Cliffs, N.J.: Prentice-Hall.

Eberstadt, Nick (1980). "Recent Declines in Fertility in Less Developed Countries." *World Development* 8 (January): 37–60.

Echols, John (1980). "Does Communism Mean More Equality?" *American Journal of Political Science* 25 (February): 1–31.

Edwards, D. T. (1961). "An Economic View of Agricultural Research in Jamaica." *Social and Economic Studies* (September):306–39.

Edwards, Linda N., and Michael Grossman (1983). "Adolescent Health, Family Background, and Preventive Medical Care." In David Salkever et al., *Research in Human Capital and Development*. Greenwich, Conn.: JAI Press, pp. 77–109.

Elkin, Stephen (1985). "Between Liberalism and Capitalism: An Introduction to the Democratic State." In Roger Benjamin and Stephen Elkin, eds., *The Democratic State*. Lawrence: University of Kansas Press, pp. 1–17.

Emmanuel, Arghiri (1972). *Unequal Exchange: A Study of the Imperialism of Free Trade*. New York: Monthly Review Press.

Engels, Friedrich (1969). "Introduction to the Civil War in France." In *Marx and Engels: Selected Works*, vol.2. Moscow: Progress.

Etchinson, Don L. (1975). *The United States and Militarism in Central America*. New York: Praeger.

Evans, Peter (1979). *Dependent Development: The Alliance of Multi-national, State, and Local Capital in Brazil*. Princeton: Princeton University Press.

Evans, Peter, and Michael Timberlake (1980). "Dependence, Inequality, and the Growth of the Tertiary: A Comparative Analysis of Less-developed Countries." *American Sociological Review* 45:531–52.

Faini, R., P. Arnez, and L. Taylor (1984). "Defense Spending, Economic Structure, and Growth: Evidence among Countries and over Time." *Economic Development and Cultural Change* 32:487–98.

Fainstein, Susan, and Norman Fainstein (1978). "National Policy and Urban Development." *Social Problems* 26:125–46.

Fanon, F. (1963). *The Wretched of the Earth*. New York: Grove.

Fei, J. C. H., and G. Ranis (1961). "A Theory of Economic Development." *American Economic Review* 51,4:533–65.

Feld, M. D. (1971). "Professionalism and Politicalization: Notes on the Military and Civilian Control." In M. R. Van Gils, ed., *The Perceived Role of the Military*. Rotterdam: Rotterdam Finer.

Fernandes, Castro (1960). "The Presence of Portugal in Africa." *Portugal: An Informative Review* 4,4:262.

Fields, Gary S. (1977). "Who Benefits from Economic Development? A Reexamination of Brazilian Growth in the 1960's." *American Economic Review* 67:570–82.

—— (1980). *Poverty, Inequality, and Development*. London: Cambridge University Press.

Finer, S. E. (1962). *The Man on Horseback*. New York: Praeger.

—— (1975). *The Man on Horseback*. Englewood Cliffs, N.J.: Prentice-Hall.

Firebaugh, Glenn (1985). "Core-Periphery Patterns of Urbanization." In Michael Timberlake, ed., *Urbanization in the World-Economy*. London: Academic, pp. 293–304.

Fishlow, Albert (1972). "Brazilian Size Distribution of Income." *American Economic Review* 62:391–402.

—— (1973). "Some Reflections on Post 1964 Brazilian Economic Policy." In Alfred Stepan, ed., *Authoritarian Brazil*. New Haven: Yale University Press, pp. 69–113.

—— (1980). "Who Benefits from Economic Development? Comment." *American Economic Review* 70:250–56.

Flammang, Robert A. (1979). "Economic Growth and Economic Development: Counterparts or Competitors." *Economic Development and Cultural Change* 28 (October): 47–61.

Forrester, Jay W. (1971). *World Dynamics*. Cambridge, Mass.: Wright-Allen.

Foster-Carter, Aidan (1978). "The Modes of Production Controversy." *New Left Review* 107:47–77.

Frank, Andre Gunder (1966). "The Development of Underdevelopment." *Monthly Review* 18 (September): 17–31.

—— (1969). *Latin America: Underdevelopment or Revolution*. New York: Monthly Review Press.

Friedman, Milton (1962). *Capitalism and Freedom*. Chicago: University of Chicago Press.

Fulop, T., and W. A. Reinke (1983). "Health Manpower in Relation to Socio-economic Development and Health Status." In David Salkever et al., *Research in Human Capital and Development*. Greenwich, Conn.: JAI Press, pp. 329–52.

Furtado, Celso (1970). *Economic Development of Latin America*. Cambridge: Cambridge University Press.

—— (1979). "An Age of Global Reconstruction." In Kenneth Jameson and Charles Wilber, eds., *Directions in Economic Development*. Notre Dame, Ind.: University of Notre Dame Press, pp. 130–82.

Galenson, Walter, and Harvey Liebenstein (1955). "Investment Criteria, Productivity and Economic Development." *Quarterly Journal of Economics* (August): 343–70.

Galtung, Johan (1971). "A Structural Theory of Imperialism." *Journal of Peace Research* 13:81–117.

Garnier, M. A., and Lawrence E. Hazelrigg (1977). "Military Organization and Distributional Inequality: An Examination of Andreski's Thesis." *Journal of Political and Military Sociology* 5 (Spring): 17–33.

Gerth, Hans H., and C. Wright Mills, eds. (1946). *From Max Weber: Essays in Sociology*. New York: Oxford University Press.

Gidengil, Elisabeth L. (1978). "Centers and Peripheries: An Empirical Test of Galtung's Theory of Imperialism." In *Journal of Peace Research* 15:51–66.

Gilder, George (1981). *Wealth and Poverty*. New York: Bantam.

Godelier, Maurice (1986). "Processes of State Formation." In Ali Kazancigil, ed., *The State in Global Persepctive*. Shaftbury, Dorset: Blackmore Press, pp. 3–19.

Goffman, Erving (1961). *Encounters: Two Studies in the Sociology of Interaction*. Indianapolis: Bobbs-Merrill.

Gold, David, C. Lo, and Erik Olin Wright (1975). "Recent Developments in Marxist Theories of the State." *Monthly Review* 27, 5/6:29–43, 36–51.

Goldstein, Joshua S. (1985). "Basic Human Needs: The Plateau Curve." *World Development* 13,5:595–609.

Grand Pre, Don R. (1970). "A Window on America—The Department of Defense Information Program." *International Education and Cultural Exchange* 6:86–93.

Gregory, Paul (1970). *Socialist and Nonsocialist Industrialization Patterns: A Comparative Appraisal*. New York: Praeger.

Griffin, Keith (1977). "Increasing Poverty and Changing Ideas about Development Strategies." *Development and Change* 8 (October): 491–508.

—— (1978). *International Inequality and National Poverty*. New York: Holmes and Meier.

—— (1981). *Land Concentration and Rural Poverty*. 2d ed. New York: Homes and Meier.

Griffin, Keith, and Jeffrey James (1981). *The Transition to Egalitarian Development: Economic Policies for Structural Change in the Third World*. New York: St. Martin's.

Grosse, Robert N., and Barbara H. Perry (1983). "Correlates of Life Expectancy in Less Developed Countries." In David Salkever et al., *Research in Human Capital and Development*. Greenwich, Conn.: JAI Press, pp. 217–53.

Groves, Charles Pelham (1969). "Missionary and Humanitarian Aspects of Imperialism from 1870 to 1914." In L. H. Gann and Peter Duignan, eds., *Colonialism in Africa, 1870–1960*. London: Cambridge University Press, 1:462–96.

Gurley, John (1979). "Economic Development: A Marxist View." In Kenneth Jameson and Charles Wilber, eds., *Directions in Economic Development*. Notre Dame, Ind.: University of Notre Dame Press, pp. 183–251.

Gurr, Ted Robert (1970). *Why Men Rebel*. New York: Free Press.

Gutteridge, William F. (1970). "Military and Police Forces in Colonial Africa." In L. H. Gann and Peter Duignan, eds., *Colonialism in Africa, 1870–1960*. London: Cambridge University Press, 2:286–319.

Habermas, Jürgen (1975). *Legitimation Crisis*. Boston: Beacon.

Hagelberg, G. B. (1985). "Sugar in the Caribbean: Turning Sunshine into Money." In Sidney Mintz and Sally Price, eds., *Caribbean Contours*. Baltimore: Johns Hopkins University Press, pp. 85–126.

Hailey, William (1941). *Native Administration and Political Development in British Tropical Africa*. London: H.M. Stationery Office.

Halliday, Fred. (1988). "State and Society in International Relations: A Second Age." *Millennium: Journal of International Studies* 16,2:215–29.

Halperin, Morton H. (1974). *Bureaucratic Politics and Foreign Policy*. Washington, D.C.: Brookings Institution.

Halpern, Manfred (1963). *The Politics of Social Change in the Middle East and North Africa*. Princeton: Princeton University Press.

ul Haq, Mahbub (1971). "Employment and Income Distribution in the 1970's: A New Perspective." *Development Digest* 9,4:3–8.

Hargreaves, John D. (1969). "West African States and the European Conquest." In L. H. Gann and Peter Duignan, eds., *Colonialism in Africa, 1870–1960*. London: Cambridge University Press, 1: 199–219.

Heise, David R. (1970). "Causal Inference from Panel Data." In Edgar F. Borgatta and George W. Bohrnstedt, eds., *Sociological Methodology 1970*. San Francisco: Jossey-Bass, pp. 3–27.

Heller, Peter S., and Alan Tait (1982). "Comparing Government Expenditures Internationally." *Finance and Development* 19, 1:26–29.

Hermann, Charles F., et al. (1987). *New Directions in the Study of Foreign Policy*. Boston: Allen and Unwin.

Herring, Ronald (1983). *Land to the Tiller: The Politics of Agrarian Reform in South Asia*. New Haven: Yale University Press.

—— (1985). "The Meaning of Development." Presentation, Evanston, Ill.: Northwestern University.

Hewitt, Christopher (1977). "The Effect of Political Democracy and Social Democracy on Equality in Industrial Societies." *American Sociological Review* 42:450–64.

Hibbs, Douglas A., Jr. (1973). *Mass Political Violence: A Cross-National Causal Analysis*. New York: Wiley.

Hicks, Alexander, and Duane Swank (1984). "On the Political Economy of Welfare Expansion: A Comparative Analysis of 18 Advanced Capitalist Democracies, 1960–1971." *Comparative Political Studies* 17 (April): 81–119.

Hicks, Norman (1980). "Is There a Trade-off between Growth and Basic Needs?" *Finance and Development* 17 (June): 17–20.

Hicks, Norman, and Paul Streeten (1979). "Indicators of Development: The Search for a Basic Needs Yardstick." *World Development* 7:567–80.

Hirschman, Albert (1958). *The Strategy of Economic Development*. New Haven: Yale University Press.

Hoadley, J. Steven (1981). "The Rise and Fall of the Basic Needs Approach." *Cooperation and Conflict* 16:149–64.

Hobsbawm, E. J. (1973). *Revolutionaries: Contemporary Essays*. New York: Pantheon.

Hoetink, H. (1985). "'Race' and Color in the Caribbean." In Sidney Mintz and Sally Price, eds., *Caribbean Contours*. Baltimore: Johns Hopkins University Press, pp. 55–84.

Hofferbert, Richard (1985). "Policy Analysis Priorities in the Third World: Basic Needs and the Barefoot Evaluator." Paper prepared for the Annual Meetings of the Midwest Political Science Association, Chicago, April.

Horowitz, David (1969). *Empire and Revolution*. New York: Random House.

Horowitz, Irving Louis (1967). "The Military Elites." In Seymour Lipset and Aldo Solari, eds., *Elites in Latin America*. New York: Oxford University Press.

Hout, Michael (1980). "Trade Dependence and Fertility in Hispanic America 1900–1975." In Albert Bergesen, ed., *Studies of the Modern World System*. New York: Academic, pp. 159–88.

Huntington, Samuel (1968). *Political Order in Changing Societies*. New Haven: Yale University Press.

Hymer, Stephen (1972). "The Internationalization of Capital." *Journal of Economic Issues* 6,1:91–110.

Inkeles, Alex, and David Smith (1974). *Becoming Modern: Industrial Change in Six Developing Countries*. Cambridge: Harvard University Press.

International Labour Organization (1966). *Plantation Workers—Conditions of Work and Standards of Living*. Geneva: ILO.

—— (1977), *Employment, Growth, and Basic Needs: A One-World Problem*. New York: Praeger.

Intrilligator, Michael (1978). *Econometric Models, Techniques, and Applications*. Englewood Cliffs, N.J.: Prentice-Hall.

Isenman, Paul (1980). "Basic Needs: The Case of Sri Lanka." *World Development* 8 (March): 237–58.

Jackman, Robert W. (1974). "Political Democracy and Social Equality: A Comparative Analysis." *American Sociological Review* 39:29–45.

—— (1975). *Politics and Social Equality: A Comparative Analysis*. New York: Wiley.

—— (1976). "Politicians in Uniform: Military Governments and Social Change in the Third World." *American Political Science Review* 70 (December): 1078–97.

—— (1982). "Dependence on Foreign Investment and Economic Growth in the Third World." *World Politics* 34:175–96.

Jackson, Robert H., and Carl G. Rosberg (1982). "Why Africa's Weak States Persist: The Empirical and the Juridical in Statehood." *World Politics* 35 (October): 1–24.

Jackson, Steven, Bruce Russett, Duncan Snidal, and David Sylvan (1978). "Conflict and Coercion in Dependent States." *Journal of Conflict Resolution* 22:627–57.

Jalee, Pierre (1968). *The Pillage of the Third World*. New York: Modern Reader.

Janda, Kenneth (1980). *Political Parties: A Cross-National Survey*. New York: Free Press.

Janowitz, Morris (1964). *The Military in the Political Development of New States*. Chicago: University of Chicago Press.

Johnson, Dale L. (1983). "Class Analysis and Dependency." In Ronald Chilcote and Dale Johnson, eds., *Theories of Development: Mode of Production or Dependency?* Beverly Hills: Sage, pp. 231–55.

Johnson, Harry G. (1967). *Economic Policies toward Less-Developed Countries*. New York: Praeger.

Johnson, J. J., ed. (1962). *The Role of the Military in Underdeveloped Countries*. Princeton: Princeton University Press.

—— (1964). *The Military and Society in Latin America*. Stanford: Stanford University Press.

Jolly, Richard, ed. (1978). *Disarmament and World Development*. Oxford: Pergamon.

Kaldor, Mary (1978). "The Military in Third World Development." In Richard Jolly, ed., *Disarmament and World Development*. Oxford: Pergamon, pp. 57–82.

Kasarda, John D., John Billy, and Kirsten West (1968). *Status Enhancement and Fertility: Reproductive Responses to Social Mobility and Educational Opportunity*. Orlando, Fla: Academic Press.

Katzenellenbogon, Simon (1975). "The Miner's Frontier, Transport and General Economic Development." In Peter Duignan and L. H. Gann, eds., *Colonialism in Africa, 1870–1960*. Cambridge: Cambridge University Press, 4:360–426.

Katzenstein, Peter, ed. (1978). *Between Power and Plenty: Foreign Economic Policies of Advanced Industrial States*. Madison: University of Wisconsin Press.

Kaufman, Robert R., et al. (1975). "A Preliminary Test of the Theory of Dependency." *Comparative Politics* 7:303–30.

Kaunda, Kenneth D. (1968). *Zambia's Guideline for the Next Decade*. Lusaka, Zambia: Government Printer.

Kay, Geoffrey (1975). *Development and Underdevelopment: A Marxist Analysis*. New York: St. Martin's.

Kazancigil, Ali (1986). *The State in Global Perspective*. Shaftbury, Dorset: Blackmore Press.

Keller, Albert Galloway (1931). *Societal Evolution: A Study of the Evolutionary Basis of the Science of Society*. New York: Macmillan.

Kennedy, Gavin (1974). *The Military in the Third World*. London: Duckworth.

Kentor, Jeffrey (1985). "Economic Development and the World Division of Labor." In Michael Timberlake, ed., *Urbanization in the World-Economy*. London: Academic, pp. 25–40.

Kilson, Martin (1970). "The Emergent Elites of Black Africa, 1900 to 1960." In L. H. Gann and Peter Duignan, eds., *Colonialism in Africa, 1870–1960*. London: Cambridge University Press, 2:351–98.

Kling, Merle (1956). "Toward a Theory of Power and Political Instability in Latin America." *Western Political Quarterly* 9 (March): 21–35.

Kocher, J. E. (1973). *Rural Development, Income Distribution, and Fertility Decline*. New York: Population Council.

Krasner, Stephen (1978). *Defending the National Interest: Raw Materials Investments and U.S. Foreign Policy*. Princeton: Princeton University Press.

—— (1984). "Approaches to the State: Alternative Conceptions and Historical Dynamics." *Comparative Politics* (January): 223–46.

Kravis, Irving, et al. (1975). *A System of International Comparisons of Gross Product and Purchasing Power*. Baltimore: Johns Hopkins University Press.

Kravis, Irving, Alan Heston, and Robert Summers (1978a). "Real GDP Per Capita for More than One Hundred Nations." *Economic Journal* 88 (June): 215–42.

—— (1978b). *International Comparisons of Real Product and Purchasing Power*. Baltimore: Johns Hopkins University Press for the World Bank.

Kugler, Jacek, et al. (1983). "Political Determinants of Population Dynamics," *Comparative Political Studies* 16,1:3–36.

Kuznets, Simon (1953). *Economic Change*. New York: Norton.

—— (1963). "Quantitative Aspects of the Economic Growth of Nations: VIII. Distribution of Income by Size." *Economic Development and Cultural Change* 11,2 (Part II): 1–80.

—— (1972). "Problems in Comparing Recent Growth Rates for Developed and Less Developed Areas." *Economic Development and Cultural Change* 10 (January): 185–209.

Laclau, Ernesto (1971). "Feudalism and Capitalism in Latin America." *New Left Review* 67:13–38.

Lall, Sanjaya (1975). "Is 'Dependence' a Useful Concept in Analysing Underdevelopment?" *World Development* 3,11–12:799–810.

Lane, David (1976). *The Socialist Industrial State: Towards a Political Sociology of State Socialism*. Boulder, Colo.: Westview.

Lang, Kurt (1972). *Military Institutions and the Sociology of War: A Review of the Literature with Annotated Bibliography*. Beverly Hills: Sage.

Lappé, Frances Moore, and Joseph Collins (1977). *Food First*. Boston: Houghton Mifflin.

Larkey, Patrick, Chandler Stolp, and Mark Winer (1984). "Why Does Government Grow?" In Trudi Miller, ed., *Public Sector Performance: A Conceptual Turning Point*. Baltimore: Johns Hopkins University Press, pp. 65–101.

Larson, David A., and Wilford T. Walton (1979). "The Physical Quality of Life Index: A Useful Social Indicator?" *World Development* 7 (June): 581–84.

Lasker, Judith (1977). "The Role of Health Services in Colonial Rule: The Case of the Ivory Coast." *Culture, Medicine, and Psychiatry* 1:277–97.

Lee, John M. (1969). *African Armies and Civil Order*. New York: Praeger.

Leipziger, Danny M., and Maureen A. Lewis (1980). "Social Indicators, Growth, and Distribution." *World Development* 8:299–302.

Lenin, Vladimir (1965). *Imperialism: The Highest Stage of Capitalism*. Peking: Foreign Languages Press.

Lenski, Gerhard (1966). *Power and Privilege: A Theory of Social Stratification*. New York: McGraw-Hill.

Lenski, Gerhard, and Jean Lenski (1974). *Human Societies: An Introduction to Macrosociology*. 2d ed. New York: McGraw-Hill.

Lentner, Howard H. (1984). "The Concept of the State: A Response to Stephen Krasner." *Comparative Politics* (April): 367–77.

Levy, Marion (1966). *Modernization and the Structure of Societies*. Princeton: Princeton University Press.

Levy, Marion J., Jr. (1971). "Armed Force Organizations." In Henry Bienen, ed., *The Military and Modernization*. Chicago: Aldine, pp. 41–73.

Lewis, W. Arthur (1954). "Economic Development with Unlimited Supplies of Labor." *Manchester School of Economic and Social Studies* 22 (May): 139–91.

——— (1955). *The Theory of Economic Growth*. London: Allen and Unwin.

——— (1976). "Development and Distribution." In Alec Cairncross and Mohinder Puri, eds., *Employment, Income Distribution, and Development Strategy: Problems of the Developing Countries*. London: Macmillan, pp. 26–42.

Lieuwen, Edwin (1960). *Arms and Politics in Latin America*. New York: Praeger.

Lim, D. (1983). "Another Look at Growth and Defense in Less Developed Countries." *Economic Development and Cultural Change* 31:377–84.

Lindblom, Charles (1977). *Politics and Markets: The World's Political-Economic Systems*. New York: Basic.

Lipton, Michael (1968). *Assessing Economic Performance*. London: Staples.

——— (1977). *Why Poor People Stay Poor: A Study of Urban Bias in World Development*. London: Temple Smith.

——— (1988). "The Poor and the Poorest: Some Interim Findings." World Bank Discussion Papers 25. Washington, D.C.: World Bank.

Little, Ian Malcolm David (1957). *A Critique of Welfare Economics*. 2d ed. Oxford: Clarendon.

Loup, Jacques (1983). *Can the Third World Survive?* Baltimore: Johns Hopkins University Press.

Lovell, John, ed. (1970). *The Military and Politics in Five Developing Nations*. Kensington, Md.: American Institutes for Research.

Luckham, Robin (1971). *The Nigerian Military*. Cambridge: Cambridge University Press.

——— (1978). "Militarism and International Dependence." In Richard Jolly, ed., *Disarmament and World Development*. Oxford: Pergamon, pp. 35–56.

MacBean, Alasdair I. (1966). *Export Instability and Economic Development*. London: Allen and Unwin.

MacEwan, Arthur (1981). *Revolution and Economic Development in Cuba*. New York: St. Martin's.

MacPherson, Crawford B. (1973). *Democratic Theory: Essays in Retrieval*. Oxford: Clarendon.

Magdoff, Harry (1969). *The Age of Imperialism*. New York: Monthly Review Press.

Magubane, Bernard (1985). "The Evolution of the Class Structure in Africa." In Peter C. W. Gutkind and Immanuel Wallerstein, eds., *Political Economy of Contemporary Africa*. 2d ed. Beverly Hills: Sage, pp. 198–227.

Mahler, Vincent (1980). *Dependency Approaches to International Political Economy*. New York: Columbia University Press.

Martin, Andrew (1975). "Is Democratic Control of Capitalist Economies Possible?" In Leon Lindberg et al., eds., *Stress and Contradiction in Modern Capitalism*. Lexington, Mass.: D. C. Heath, pp. 13–56.

Martin, John Bartlow (1966). *Overtaken by Events: The Dominican Crisis from the Fall of Trujillo to the Civil War*. Garden City, N.Y.: Doubleday.

Marx, Karl (1943). *Articles on India*. Bombay: People's Publishing House.

Marx, Karl, and Friedrich Engels (1969). "The Manifesto of the Communist Party." In *Marx and Engels: Selected Works*, vol. 1. Moscow: Progress.

Massell, Benton F. (1964). "Export Concentration and Fluctuations in Export Earnings: A Cross-Section Analysis." *American Economic Review* 54:47–63.

Maynard, Harold W. (1978). "Views of the Indonesian and Philippine Military Elites." In Sheldon W. Simon, ed., *The Military and Security in the Third World: Domestic and International Impacts*. Boulder, Colo.: Westview, pp. 123–53.

McAlister, Lyle (1966). "Recent Research and Writings on the Role of the Military in Latin America." *Latin America Research Review* 2 (Fall): 5–36.

McGowan, Patrick, and Dale Smith (1978). "Economic Dependence in Black Africa: A Causal Analysis of Competing Theories." *International Organization* 32 (Winter): 179–235.

McGowan, Pat, and Stephen Walker (1981). "Radical and Conventional Models of U.S. Foreign Economic Policy Making." *World Politics* 33 (April): 347–82.

McGranahan, Donald V. (1979). *International Comparability of Statistics on Income Distribution*. Geneva: UNRISD.

McGranahan, Donald, Eduardo Pizarro, and Claude Richard (1985). *Measurement and Analysis of Socioeconomic Development*. Geneva: UNRISD.

McGranahan, Donald V., Claude Richard-Proust, N. V. Sovani, and Muthu Subramanian (1972). *Contents and Measurement of Socio-Economic Development*. New York: Praeger.

McHale, John, and Magda Cordell McHale (1978). *Basic Human Needs*. New Brunswick, N.J.: Transaction.

McKinlay, Robert, and A. S. Cohen (1976). "Performance and Instability in Military and Non-military Regime Systems." *American Political Science Review* 70 (September): 850–64.

Meade, James E. (1964). *Efficiency, Equality, and the Ownership of Property*. London: Allen and Unwin.

Meegama, S. A. (1986). "The Mortality Transition in Sri Lanka." In *Determinants of Mortality Change and Differentials in Developing Countries*. U.N. Department of International Economic and Social Affairs, Population Studies no. 94. New York: United Nations.

Meyer, John W., and Michael T. Hannan (1979). *National Development and the World*

System: Educational, Economic, and Political Change, 1950–1970. Chicago: University of Chicago Press.

Michaely, Michael (1967). *Concentration in International Trade.* Amsterdam: North-Holland.

Milliband, Ralph (1969). *The State in Capitalist Society.* New York: Basic.

Mills, C. Wright (1956). *The Power Elite.* New York: Oxford University Press.

Mintz, Sidney W. (1985). "From Plantations to Peasantries in the Caribbean." In Sidney Mintz and Sally Price, eds., *Caribbean Contours.* Baltimore: Johns Hopkins University Press, pp. 127–53.

Mintz, Sidney W., and Sally Price, eds. (1985). *Caribbean Contours.* Baltimore: Johns Hopkins University Press.

Moon, Bruce E. (1982). "Exchange Rate System, Policy Distortions, and the Maintenance of Trade Dependence." *International Organization* 36,4:715–39.

—— (1983). "The Rise of Interdependence and the Fall of Conceptual Clarity." Mimeo, Northwestern University.

—— (1987a). "Structural Position and Welfare Outcomes: World System Explanations of the Provision of Basic Human Needs." Paper presented to the International Studies Association Annual Meeting, Washington, April 14–18.

—— (1987b). "Political Economy Approaches to the Comparative Study of Foreign Policy." In Charles F. Hermann, Charles W. Kegley Jr., and James N. Rosenau, eds., *New Directions in the Study of Foreign Policy.* Boston: Allen and Unwin, pp. 33–52.

Moon, Bruce, and William Dixon (1985). "Politics, the State, and Basic Human Needs: A Cross-National Study." *American Journal of Political Science* 29,4:661–94.

—— (1988). "The Growth-Welfare Trade-Off: A Basic Needs Perspective." Paper presented to the Annual Meetings of the International Studies Association, St. Louis.

Moore, Barrington (1966). *Social Origins of Dictatorship and Democracy.* Boston: Beacon Press.

Morawetz, David (1977). *Twenty-five Years of Economic Development: 1950 to 1975.* Baltimore: Johns Hopkins University Press.

—— (1978). "Basic Needs Policies and Population Growth." *World Development* 6 (November/December): 1251–59.

Morgenstern, Oskar (1963). *On the Accuracy of Economic Observations.* 2d ed. Princeton: Princeton University Press.

Morgenthau, Hans J. (1967). *Politics among Nations: The Struggle for Power and Peace.* 4th ed. New York: Knopf.

Morgenthau, Ruth Schachter (1964). *Political Parties in French-Speaking West Africa.* Oxford: Clarendon.

Morris, Cynthia Taft (1984). "The Measurement of Economic Development: Quo Vadis?" In Gustav Ranis et al., *Comparative Development Perspectives.* Boulder, Colo.: Westview, pp. 145–81.

Morris, Morris David (1979). *Measuring the Condition of the World's Poor: The Physical Quality of Life Index.* New York: Pergamon.

Most, Benjamin (1980). "Authoritarianism and the Growth of the State in Latin America: An Assessment of Their Impacts on Argentine Public Policy, 1930–1970." *Comparative Political Studies* 13 (July): 173–204.

Myrdal, Gunnar (1957). *Rich Lands and Poor.* New York: Harper and Row.

—— (1968). *Asian Drama: An Inquiry into the Poverty of Nations.* New York: Twentieth Century Fund.

—— (1973). "Equity and Growth." *World Development* 1,11:43–47.

Needler, Martin (1963). *Anatomy of a Coup d'Etat: Ecuador, 1963.* Washington, D.C.: Institute for the Comparative Study of Political Systems.

—— (1966). "Political Development and Military Intervention in Latin America." *American Political Science Review* 60 (September): 616–26.

Nehru, Jawaharlal (1961). "Strategy of the Third Plan." In *Problems in the Third Plan: A Critical Miscellany.* New Delhi: Ministry of Information and Broadcasting, Government of India.

Nemeth, Roger J., and David A. Smith (1985). "International Trade and World System Structure: A Multiple Network Analysis." *Review* 8,4:517–60.

Nettl, J. P. (1968). "The State as a Conceptual Variable." In Wolfram F. Hanrieder, ed., *Comparative Foreign Policy: Theoretical Essays.* New York: David McKay, pp. 51–89.

Newman, Peter (1983). "Conceptual Framework for the Planning of Medicine in Developing Countries." In David Salkever et al., *Research in Human Capital and Development.* Greenwich, Conn.: JAI Press, pp. 29–56.

Nkrumah, Kwame (1969). *Dark Days in Ghana.* New York: International.

Nolan, Patrick (1983). "Status in the World Economy and National Structure Development: An Examination of Developmentalist and Dependency Theories." *International Journal of Comparative Sociology* 24:109–20.

Nolan, Patrick, and Ralph White (1983). "Demographic Differentials in the World System: A Research Note." *Social Forces* 62:1–8.

—— (1985). "Macrosociological Theories of Demographic Change: A Critical Examination of the Evidence." Paper presented at the International Studies Association, Washington, D.C., March 9.

Nordhaus, William, and James Tobin (1973). "Is Growth Obsolete?" In Milton Moss, ed., *The Measurement of Economic and Social Performance.* Studies in Income and Wealth no. 38. New York: National Bureau of Economic Research, pp. 509–64.

Nordlinger, Eric (1970). "Soldiers in Mufti: The Impact of Military Rule upon Economic and Social Change in the Non-Western States." *American Political Science Review* 64 (December): 1131–48.

North, Douglas (1979). "A Framework for Analyzing the State in Economic History." *Explorations in Economic History* 16:249–59.

Northedge, F. S. (1976). *The International Political System.* London: Faber and Faber.

Nun, Jose (1969). *Latin America: The Hegemonic Crisis and the Military Coup.* Institute of International Studies, Politics of Modernization no. 7. Berkeley: University of California Press.

O'Connor, James (1973). *The Fiscal Crisis of the State.* New York: St. Martin's.

O'Donnell, Guillermo (1973). *Modernization and Bureacratic-Authoritarianism: Studies in South American Politics.* Institute of International Studies, Politics of Modernization no. 9. Berkeley: University of California Press.

—— (1980). "Comparative Historical Formations of the State Apparatus and Socio-Economic Change in the Third World." *International Social Science Journal* 32,4:717–29.

Okun, Arthur (1971). "Should GNP Measure Social Welfare?" *The Brookings Bulletin* 8:4–7.

—— (1975). *Equality and Efficiency: The Big Trade-off.* Washington, D.C.: Brookings Institution.

Oliver, Roland (1965). *The Missionary Factor in East Africa.* 2d ed. London: Longmans.

Olson, Mancur (1982). *The Rise and Decline of Nations: Economic Growth, Stagflation, and Social Rigidities.* New Haven: Yale University Press.

—— (1985). "Ideology and Economic Growth." Mimeo.

Organisation for Economic Co-operation and Development (OECD) (1973). "Performance Compendium: Consolidated Results of Analytical Work on Economic and Social Performance of Developing Countries." Paris: OECD.

Otley, C. B. (1978). "Militarism and Militarization in the Public Schools, 1900–1972." *British Journal of Sociology* 29 (September): 321–39.

Paige, Jeffery M. (1975). *Agrarian Revolution*. New York: Free Press.

—— (1985). "Cotton and Revolution in Nicaragua." In Peter Evans, Dietrich Rueschemeyer, and Evelyn Huber Stephens, eds., *States versus Markets in the World-System*. Beverly Hills: Sage, pp. 91–114.

Pant, Pitambar (1974). "Perspective of Development, India 1960–61 to 1975–76: Implications of Planning for a Minimum Level of Living." In T. N. Srinivasan and P. K. Bardhan, *Poverty and Income Distribution in India*. Calcutta: Statistical Publishing Society.

Peemans, Jean-Philippe (1975). "Capital Accumulation in the Congo under Colonialism: The Role of the State." In Peter Duignan and L. H. Gann, eds., *Colonialism in Africa, 1870–1960*. Cambridge: Cambridge University Press, 4:165–212.

Pelz, Donald C., and Frank M. Andrews (1964). "Detecting Causal Priorities in Panel Study Data." *American Sociological Review* 29 (December): 836–48.

Pelz, Donald C., and Robert A. Lew (1970). "Heise's Causal Model Applied." In Edgar F. Borgatta and George W. Bohrnstedt, eds., *Sociological Methodology 1970*, San Francisco: Jossey-Bass, pp. 28–37.

Perlmutter, Amos (1977). *The Military and Politics in Modern Times: On Professionals, Praetorians, and Revolutionary Soldiers*. New Haven: Yale University Press.

Petras, James (1978). *Critical Pespectives on Imperialism and Social Class in the Third World*. New York: Monthly Review Press.

Piven, Frances Fox, and Richard A. Cloward (1971). *Regulating the Poor*. New York: Pantheon.

—— (1977). *Poor People's Movements*. New York: Pantheon.

Polanyi, Karl (1944). *The Great Transformation*. New York: Rinehart.

Porch, Douglas (1977). *The Portuguese Armed Forces and the Revolution*. Stanford, Calif.: Hoover Institution Press.

Portes, Alejandro (1976). "On the Sociology of National Development: Theories and Issues." *American Journal of Sociology* 82 (July): 55–85.

—— (1985). "The Informal Sector and the World-Economy: Notes on the Structure of Subsidized Labor." In Michael Timberlake, ed., *Urbanization in the World-Economy*. Orlando, Fla.: Academic Press, pp. 53–62.

Portes, Alejandro, and John Walton (1976). *Urban Latin America: The Political Condition from Above and Below*. Austin: University of Texas Press.

—— (1981). *Labor, Class, and the International System*. New York: Academic.

Post, K. W. J. (1970). "British Policy and Representative Government in West Africa, 1920 to 1951." In L. H. Gann and Peter Duignan, eds., *Colonialism in Africa, 1870–1960*. London: Cambridge University Press, 2:31–57.

Poulantzas, Nicos (1973). *Political Power and Social Classes*. London: New Left.

Powell, G. Bingham (1982). *Contemporary Democracies: Participation, Stability, and Violence*. Cambridge: Harvard University Press.

Prebisch, Raul (1959). "Commercial Policy in the Underdeveloped Countries." *American Economic Review* 49 (May): 251–73.

—— (1962). "The Economic Development of Latin America and Its Principal Problems." *Economic Bulletin for Latin America* 7 (February): 1–22.

Preston, Samuel H. (1976). "Causes and Consequences of Mortality: Declines in

Less Developed Countries during the 20th Century." In R. A. Easterlin, ed., *Population and Economic Change in Developing Countries*. Chicago: University of Chicago Press.

Price, Robert M. (1971). "A Theoretical Approach to Military Rule in New States: Reference-Group Theory and the Ghanian Case." *World Politics* 23:399–430.

Pyatt, Graham, and Jeffrey Round (1977). "Social Accounting Matrices for Development Planning." *Review of Income and Wealth* 23 (December): 339–64.

Pye, Lucian (1959). *Armies in the Process of Political Modernization*. Cambridge: MIT Center for International Studies.

—— (1962). "Armies in the Process of Political Modernization." In John J. Johnson, ed., *The Role of the Military in Underdeveloped Countries*. Princeton: Princeton University Press, pp. 69–89.

Ragin, Charles, and York Bradshaw (1985). "International Economic Dependence and Human Misery, 1938–1980: A Global Perspective." Mimeo, Northwestern University.

Ragin, Charles, and Jacques Delacroix (1979). "Comparative Advantage, the World Division of Labor, and Underdevelopment." *Comparative Social Research* 2:181–214.

Ram, Rati (1982). "Composite Indices of Physical Quality of Life, Basic Needs Fulfillment, and Income." *Journal of Developing Economies* 11:227–47.

—— (1985). "The Role of Real Income Level and Income Distribution in Fulfillment of Basic Needs." *World Development* 13,5:589–609.

Rao, D. C. (1974). "Urban Target Groups." In Hollis Chenery et al., *Redistribution with Growth*. London: Oxford University Press, pp. 136–57.

Rao, Potluri, and Roger LeRoy Miller (1971). *Applied Econometrics*. Belmont, Calif.: Wadsworth.

Rawls, John (1971). *The Theory of Justice*. Cambridge: Harvard University Press.

Resnick, Phillip (1986). "The Functions of the Modern State: In Search of a Theory." In Ali Kazancigil, ed., *The State in Global Perspective*. Shaftbury, Dorset: Blackmore Press, pp. 155–82.

Robinson, Sherman (1976). "A Note on the U-Hypothesis Relating Income Inequality and Economic Development." *American Economic Review* 66:437–40.

Ronfeldt, David (1974). "Patterns of Civil-Military Rule." In Luigi Einaudi, ed., *Beyond Cuba: Latin America Takes Charge of Its Future*. New York: Crane, Russak Co., pp. 107–26.

Rosenau, James N. (1976). *In Search of Global Patterns*. New York: Free Press.

—— (1988). "The State in an Era of Cascading Politics: Wavering Concept, Widening Competence, Withering Colossus, or Weathering Change?" *Comparative Political Studies* 21 (April): 13–44.

Rostow, Eugene (1960). *The Stages of Economic Growth*. Cambridge: Cambridge University Press.

Rubinson, Richard (1976). "The World Economy and the Distribution of Income within States." *American Sociological Review* 41:638–59.

—— (1977). "Dependence, Government Revenue, and Economic Growth, 1955–1970." *Studies in Comparative International Development* 12:3–28.

Rubinson, Richard, and Deborah Holtzman (1981). "Comparative Dependence and Economic Development." *International Journal of Comparative Sociology* 22:86–101.

Rubinson, Richard, and Dan Quinlan (1977). "Democracy and Social Inequality: A Reanalysis." *American Sociological Review* 42 (August): 611–23.

Ruccio, David, and Lawrence Simon (1988). "Radical Theories of Development: Frank, the Modes of Production School, and Amin." In Charles Wilber, ed., *The*

Political Economy of Development and Underdevelopment. 4th ed. New York: Random House, pp. 121–73.

Rueschemeyer, Dietrich, and Peter Evans (1985). "The State and Economic Transformation: Toward an Analysis of the Conditions Underlying Effective Intervention." In Peter Evans, Dietrich Rueschemeyer, and Theda Skocpol, eds., *Bringing the State Back In.* Cambridge: Cambridge University Press, pp. 44–77.

Russett, Bruce (1983). *The Prisoners of Insecurity: Nuclear Deterrence, the Arms Race, and Arms Control.* New York: W. H. Freeman.

Russett, Bruce, Steven Jackson, Duncan Snidal, and David Sylvan (1981). "Health and Population Patterns as Indicators of Income Inequality." *Economic Development and Cultural Change* 29,4:759–79.

Salkever, David, Ismail Sirageldin, and Alan Sarkin, eds. (1983). *Research in Human Capital and Development,* vol. 3. Greenwich, Conn.: JAI Press.

Sarkesian, Sam (1978). "A Political Perspective on Military Power in Developing Areas." In Sheldon Simon, ed., *The Military and Security in the Third World: Domestic and International Impacts.* Boulder, Colo.: Westview, pp. 3–14.

Schmitter, Phillippe (1971). "Military Intervention, Political Competitiveness, and Public Policy in Latin America, 1950–1967." In Morris Janowitz and Jacques van Doorn, eds., *On Military Intervention.* Rotterdam: Rotterdam University Press, pp. 425–506.

——, ed. (1973). *Military Rule in Latin America: Functions, Consequences, and Perspectives.* Beverly Hills: Sage.

Schumpeter, Joseph (1954). *Capitalism, Socialism, and Democracy.* London: Allen and Unwin.

Seers, Dudley (1973). "The Meaning of Development." In Charles Wilber, ed., *The Political Economy of Development and Underdevelopment.* New York: Random House, pp. 6–14.

—— (1974). "Cuba." In Hollis Chenery et al., *Redistribution with Growth.* London: Oxford University Press, pp. 262–68.

—— (1976). "The Political Economy of National Accounting." In Alec Cairncross and Mohinder Puri, eds., *Employment, Income Distribution, and Development Strategy: Problems of the Developing Countries.* New York: Holmes and Meier, pp. 193–209.

—— (1977). "Life Expectancy as an Integrating Concept in Social and Demographic Analysis and Planning." *Review of Income and Wealth* series 23 (September): 195–203.

Sen, Amartya K. (1976). "Poverty: An Ordinal Approach to Measurement." *Econometrica* 44 (March): 219–31.

—— (1981). *Poverty and Famines: An Essay on Entitlement and Deprivation.* New York: Oxford University Press.

Sheehan, Glen, and Mike Hopkins (1979). *Basic Needs Performance: An Analysis of Some International Data.* Geneva: International Labour Office.

Shils, Edward (1962). "The Military in the Political Development of the New States." In John J. Johnson, ed., *The Role of the Military in Underdeveloped Countries.* Princeton: Princeton University Press, pp. 7–67.

Shin, Don C., and Wayne Snyder (1983). "Economic Growth, Quality of Life, and Development Policy: A Case Study of South Korea." *Comparative Political Studies* 16,2:195–213.

Shin, Eui Hang (1975). "Economic and Social Correlates of Infant Mortality: A Cross Sectional and Longitudinal Analysis of 63 Selected Countries." *Social Biology* 2,4:315–25.

Silber, Jacques (1983). "ELL (The Equivalent Length of Life) or Another Attempt at Measuring Development." *World Development* 11,1:21–29.

Singer, Hans (1950). "The Distribution of Gains between Interest and Borrowing Countries." In G. Dalton, ed., *Economic Development and Social Change*. New York: Natural History Press, pp. 336–50.

—— (1979). "Poverty, Income Distribution, and Levels of Living: Thirty Years of Changing Thought on Development Problems." In C. H. Hanumantha Rao and P. C. Joshi, eds., *Reflections on Economic Development and Social Change: Essays in Honour of Professor V. K. R. V. Rao*. Delhi: Institute of Economic Growth; and Bombay: Allied Publishers, pp. 29–40.

Singer, Marshall (1972). *Weak States in a World of Powers*. New York: Free Press.

Sivard, Ruth (1979). "World Military and Social Expenditures, 1979." Leesburg, Va.: World Priorities.

Skocpol, Theda (1979). *States and Social Revolutions*. Cambridge: Cambridge University Press.

—— (1985). "Bringing the State Back In: Strategies of Analysis in Current Research." In Peter Evans, Dietrich Rueschemeyer, and Theda Skocpol, eds., *Bringing the State Back In*. Cambridge: Cambridge University Press, pp. 3–37.

Smith, Adam (1976). *An Inquiry into the Nature and Causes of the Wealth of Nations*. Ed. R. H. Campbell and A. S. Skinner. Oxford: Clarendon Press.

Smith, Dan, and Ron Smith (1979). "Reflections on Neuman." *Orbis* 23,2:471–77.

—— (1980). "Military Expenditures, Resources, and Development." Mimeo (April), Birkbeck College, University of London, Department of Economics.

Smith, David M. (1979). *Where the Grass Is Greener: Living in an Unequal World*. New York: Penguin.

Smith, Raymond T. (1967). "Social Stratification, Cultural Pluralism, and Integration in West Indian Societies." In S. Lewis and T. G. Mathews, eds., *Caribbean Integration*. Rio Piedras, Puerto Rico: Institute of Caribbean Studies, University of Puerto Rico, pp. 226–58.

Snyder, David, and Edward Kick (1979). "Structural Position in the World System and Economic Growth, 1955–1970: A Multiple Network Analysis of Transnational Interactions." *American Journal of Sociology* 84,5:1096–1126.

Sokolovsky, Joan (1985). "Logic, Space, and Time: The Boundaries of the Capitalist World-Economy." In Michael Timberlake, ed., *Urbanization in the World-Economy*. London: Academic, pp. 41–52.

Solaun, Mauricio, and Michael Quinn (1973). *Sinners and Heretics: The Politics of Military Intervention in Latin America*. Urbana: University of Illinois Press.

Sraffa, Piero (1972). *Production of Commodities by Means of Commodities*. Cambridge: University Press.

Stack, Steven (1978). "The Effects of Political Participation and Socialist Party Strength on the Degree of Income Inequality." *American Sociological Review* 44:168–71.

Stepan, Alfred (1971). *The Military in Politics: Changing Patterns in Brazil*. Princeton: Princeton University Press.

—— (1978). *The State and Society: Peru in Comparative Perspective*. Princeton: Princeton University Press.

—— (1985). "State Power and the Strength of Civil Society in the Southern Cone of Latin America." In Peter Evans, Dietrich Rueschemeyer, and Theda Skocpol, eds., *Bringing the State Back In*. Cambridge: Cambridge University Press, pp. 317–43.

Stewart, Frances (1985). *Basic Needs in Developing Countries*. Baltimore: Johns Hopkins University Press.

Stone, Richard (1975). *Toward a System of Social and Demographic Statistics*. New York: United Nations.

Streeten, Paul (1976). "Industrialisation in a Unified Development Strategy." In Alec Cairncross and Mohinder Puri, eds., *Employment, Income Distribution, and Development Strategy: Problems of the Developing Countries*. London: Macmillan, pp. 90–105.

—— (1979). "A Basic Needs Approach to Economic Development." In Kenneth Jameson and Charles Wilber, eds., *Directions in Economic Development*. Notre Dame and London: University of Notre Dame Press, pp. 73–219.

—— (1981) (with Shahid Javed Burki, Mahbub ul Haq, Norman Hicks, and Frances Stewart). *First Things First: Meeting Basic Human Needs in Developing Countries*. New York: Oxford University Press.

Sunkel, Osvaldo (1973). "Transnational Capitalism and National Disintegration in Latin America." *Social and Economic Studies* 22:132–76.

Swamy, Subramanian (1967). "Structural Changes and the Distribution of Income by Size: The Case of India." *Review of Income and Wealth* 13,2:155–74.

Sylvan, David, Duncan Snidal, Bruce Russett, and Steven Jackson (1979). "A Formal Model of 'Dependencia Theory': Some Empirical Results." Paper prepared for the annual meeting of the American Political Science Association, Washington, D.C.

Szcepanik, E. F. (1970). "Agricultural Capital Formation in Selected Developing Countries." Agricultural Planning Studies no. 11. Rome: Food and Agriculture Organization of the United Nations.

Szentes, Tamas (1985). "Socioeconomic Effects of Two Patterns of Foreign Capital Investments." In Peter Gutkind and Immanuel Wallerstein, eds., *Political Economy of Contemporary Africa*. Beverly Hills: Sage, pp. 279–316.

Tannahill, R. Neal (1976). "The Performance of Military Governments in South America." *Journal of Political and Military Sociology* 4 (Fall): 233–44.

Taylor, Charles, and David Jodice (1982). *World Handbook of Political and Social Indicators III: 1948–1982*. Ann Arbor, Mich.: Inter-university Consortium for Political and Social Research.

Terhal, P. (1981). "Guns or Grain: Macro-economic Costs of Indian Defence, 1960–1970." *Economic and Political Weekly* 16,49:1995–2004.

Therborn, Goran (1986). "Neo-Marxist, Pluralist, Corporatist, Statist Theories and the Welfare State." In Ali Kazancigil, ed., *The State in Global Perspective*. Shaftbury, Dorset: Blackmore Press, pp. 204–31.

Thompson, Edgar T. (1957). "The Plantation Cycle and Problems of Typology." In Vera Rubin, ed., *Caribbean Studies—A Symposium*. Kingston, Jamaica: Institute of Social and Economic Research, University of West Indies, pp. 29–33.

Thompson, William (1973). *The Grievances of Military Coup-Makers*. Sage Professional Papers in Comparative Politics 01–047. Beverly Hills: Sage.

—— (1975). "Systematic Change and the Latin American Military Coup." *Comparative Political Studies* 7:441–59.

—— (1980). "Corporate Coup-Maker Grievances and Types of Regime Targets." *Comparative Political Studies* 12,4:485–96.

Timberlake, Michael (1985). "The World-System Perspective and Urbanization." In Timberlake, ed., *Urbanization in the World-Economy*. London: Academic, pp. 3–22.

Timberlake, Michael, and James Lundy (1985). "Labor Force Structure in the Zones of the World-Economy, 1950–1970." In Michael Timberlake, ed., *Urbanization in the World-Economy*. London: Academic, pp. 325–49.

Titmuss, Richard M. (1958). *Essays on the Welfare State*. London: Allen and Unwin.

Todaro, Michael (1976). *Internal Migration in Developing Countries: A Review of Theory,*

Evidence, Methodology, and Research Priorities. Geneva: International Labour Organization.

—— (1981). *Economic Development in the Third World.* 2d ed., New York: Longman.

Tullis, F. LaMond (1983). "The New View on Rural Development." Paper presented at the annual meeting of the American Political Science Association, Chicago.

Tyler, William G., and J. Peter Wogart (1973). "Economic Dependence and Marginalization: Some Empirical Evidence." *Journal of Interamerican Studies and World Affairs* 15:36–45.

United Nations Economic and Social Council (ECOSOC) (1975). "Developing Countries and Levels of Development." New York.

United Nations Educational, Scientific and Cultural Organization (UNESCO) (1976). *The Use of Socio-Economic Indicators in Development Planning.* Paris.

United Nations Research Institute for Social Development (UNRISD) (1976). *Research Data Bank of Development Indicators,* vol. 1: *Compilation of Indicators for 1970.* Report no. 76.1/Rev. 1. Geneva: UNRISD.

—— (1977). *Notes on the Indicators.* Report no. 77.2. Geneva: UNRISD.

United States Agency for International Development (USAID) (1977). "Socioeconomic Performance Criteria for Development." Washington, D.C.

United States Arms Control and Disarmament Agency (1980). *World Military Expenditures and Arms Transfers, 1969–1978.* Washington, D.C.

United States Department of State (1974). Bureau of Public Affairs, *The Planetary Product in 1973.* Washington, D.C.

Vagts, Alfred (1959). *A History of Militarism.* New York: Free Press.

Valenzuela, J. Samuel, and Arturo Valenzuela (1978). "Modernization and Dependency." *Comparative Politics* 10 (July): 535–57.

Van Gils, M. R., ed. (1971). *The Perceived Role of the Military.* Rotterdam: Rotterdam University Press.

Veltmeyer, Henry (1983). "Surplus Labor and Class Formation on the Latin American Periphery." In Ronald Chilcote and Dale Johnson, eds., *Theories of Development.* Beverly Hills: Sage, pp. 201–30.

Vernon, Raymond (1971). *Sovereignty at Bay: The Multinational Spread of U.S. Enterprises.* New York: Basic.

—— (1979). "The Product Cycle Model." In John Adams, ed., *The Contemporary International Economy: A Reader.* New York: St. Martin's.

Von der Mehden, Fred (1970). "Politics and the Military in Burma." In John Lovell, ed., *The Military and Politics in Five Developing Nations.* Kensington, Md.: Center for Research in Social Systems.

Von der Mehden, Fred, and Kim Quaile Hill (1980). "Area Experts' Images of African Nations: A Test of a Reputational Measurement Approach." *Comparative Political Studies* 12,4:497–510.

Walleri, R. Dan (1978). "Trade Dependence and Underdevelopment: A Causal-Chain Analysis." *Comparative Political Studies* 11:94–127.

Wallerstein, Immanuel (1974a). *The Modern World System.* New York: Academic.

—— (1974b). "Dependence in an Interdependent World: The Limited Possibilities of Transformation within the Capitalist World Economy." *African Studies Review* 18 (April): 1–26.

—— (1974c). "The Rise and Future Demise of the World Capitalist System: Concepts for Comparative Analysis." *Comparative Studies in Society and History* 16:387–415.

—— (1979). *The Capitalist World Economy.* Cambridge: Cambridge University Press.

—— (1985). "The Three Stages of African Involvement in the World-Economy." In Peter Gutkind and Immanuel Wallerstein, eds., *Political Economy of Contemporary Africa*. Beverly Hills: Sage, pp. 35–63.

Ward, Michael Don (1978). *The Political Economy of Distribution: Equality versus Inequality*. New York: Elsevier North Holland.

Warren, Bill (1980). *Imperialism: Pioneer of Capitalism*. London: New Left.

Weaver, James, and Kenneth Jameson (1981). *Economic Development: Competing Paradigms*. Lanham, Md.: University Press of America.

Weaver, Jerry (1973). "Assessing the Impact of Military Rule." In Phillippe Schmitter, ed., *Alternative Approaches to Military Rule in Latin America: Functions, Consequences, and Perspectives*. Beverly Hills: Sage, pp. 58–116.

Weede, Erich (1980). "Beyond Misspecification in Sociological Analyses of Income Inequality." *American Sociological Review* 45 (June): 497–501.

—— (1982). "The Effects of Democracy and Socialist Strength on the Size Distribution of Income." *International Journal of Sociology* 25:255–82.

—— (1983). "Political Democracy, State Strength, and Economic Growth in LDC's: A Cross-National Analysis." Paper delivered to the Annual Meetings of the American Political Science Association.

Weede, Erich, and Horst Tiefenbach (1981a). "Some Recent Explanations of Income Inequality." *International Studies Quarterly* 25,2:255–82.

—— (1981b). "Three Dependency Explanations of Economic Growth." *European Journal of Political Research* 9:391–406.

Welch, Claude (1970). *Soldier and State in Africa*. Evanston, Ill.: Northwestern University Press.

—— (1978). "Long-term Consequences of Military Rule: Breakdowns and Extrication." *Journal of Strategic Studies* 1 (September): 139–53.

Whynes, David (1979). *The Economics of Third World Military Expenditure*. London: Macmillan.

Wilber, Charles, ed. (1979). *The Political Economy of Development and Underdevelopment*. 2d ed. New York: Random House.

Wilber, Charles, and Kenneth Jameson (1979). "Paradigms of Economic Development and Beyond." In Kenneth Jameson and Charles Wilber, eds., *Directions in Economic Development*. Notre Dame: University of Notre Dame Press, pp. 1–41.

——, eds. (1981). *Socialist Models of Development*. Special issue, *World Development* 9 (August/September).

Wiles, Peter (1974). *Distribution of Income East and West*. Amsterdam: North Holland.

Wilkinson, Paul (1977). *Terrorism and the Liberal State*. London: Macmillan.

Woddis, Jack (1977). *Armies and Politics*. London: Lawrence and Wishart.

Wolf, Charles (1967). *United States Policy in the Third World*. Boston: Little, Brown.

Wolf, Eric R., and Sidney W. Mintz (1957). "Haciendas and Plantations in Middle America and the Antilles." *Social and Economic Studies* 6 (September): 380–412.

Wolpe, Harold (1975). "The Theory of Internal Colonialism: The South African Case." In Ivar Oxaal, Tony Barnett, and David Booth, eds., *Beyond the Sociology of Development: Economy and Society in Latin America and Africa*. London: Routledge and Kegan Paul, pp. 229–52.

Wolpin, Miles (1981). *Militarism and Social Revolution in the Third World*. Totowa, N.J.: Allanheld, Osmun.

World Bank (1980a). *The Effects of Education on Health*. Washington, D.C.: World Bank.

World Bank (1980b). *Health Sector Policy Paper*. Washington, D.C.: World Bank.

World Bank (1980c). *World Development Report, 1980*. New York: Oxford University Press.

World Bank (1980d). *World Tables*. Baltimore: Johns Hopkins University Press.

World Bank (1981). *Education and Basic Human Needs*. Washington, D.C.: World Bank.

Wriggins, W. Howard (1969). *The Ruler's Imperative*. New York: Columbia University Press.

Wright, Eric Olin (1978). *Class, Crisis, and the State*. London: New Left.

Young, Crawford (1970). "Decolonization in Africa." In L. H. Gann and Peter Duignan, eds., *Colonialism in Africa 1870–1960*. London: Cambridge University Press, 2: 450–502.

Yudelman, Montague (1975). "Imperialism and the Transfer of Agricultural Techniques." In Peter Duignan and L. H. Gann, eds., *Colonialism in Africa, 1870–1960*, Cambridge: Cambridge University Press, 4:329–59.

Zolberg, A. R. (1969). "Military Rule and Political Development in Tropical Africa." In J. Van Doorn, ed., *Military Profession and Military Regimes*. The Hague: Mouton.

Zuk, Gary, and William Thompson (1982). "The Post-Coup Military Spending Question: A Pooled Cross-Sectional Time Series Analysis." *American Political Science Review* 76 (March): 60–74.

Index

Library of Congress Cataloging-in-Publication Data

Moon, Bruce Edward. 1950–
    The political economy of basic human needs / Bruce E. Moon. 91-14912
      p. cm.
    Includes bibliographical references and index.
    ISBN 0-8014-2448-8 (cloth : alk. paper). — 0-8014-9982-8 (pbk. : alk. paper)
    1. Basic needs   I. Title.
   HC79.B38M66   1991
   338.9—dc20